Eduardo Chibás

Eduardo Chibás

The Incorrigible Man of Cuban Politics

Ilan Ehrlich

ROWMAN & LITTLEFIELD
Lanham • Boulder • New York • London

Published by Rowman & Littlefield
A wholly owned subsidiary of
The Rowman & Littlefield Publishing Group, Inc.
4501 Forbes Boulevard, Suite 200, Lanham, Maryland 20706
www.rowman.com

Unit A, Whitacre Mews, 26-34 Stannary Street, London SE11 4AB,
United Kingdom

Copyright © 2015 by Rowman & Littlefield

All rights reserved. No part of this book may be reproduced in any form or by any electronic or mechanical means, including information storage and retrieval systems, without written permission from the publisher, except by a reviewer who may quote passages in a review.

British Library Cataloguing in Publication Information Available

Library of Congress Cataloging-in-Publication Data

Ehrlich, Ilan, 1971–
 Eduardo Chibás : the incorrigible man of Cuban politics / Ilan Ehrlich.
    pages cm
 Includes bibliographical references and index.
 ISBN 978-1-4422-4117-6 (cloth : alk. paper) — ISBN 978-1-4422-4118-3 (electronic)
 1. Chibás, Eduardo, 1907–1951. 2. Politicians—Cuba—Biography. 3. Cuba—Politics and government—1933–1959. I. Title.
 F1787.5.C515E47 2015
 972.9106'3092—dc23
 [B]
 2014042273

∞ ™ The paper used in this publication meets the minimum requirements of American National Standard for Information Sciences Permanence of Paper for Printed Library Materials, ANSI/NISO Z39.48-1992.

Contents

Acknowledgments	vii
Introduction	1
1 "As Long As Any Cuban Suffers, I Will Fight for Him"	7
2 "Shoot Me in the Heart—the Ortodoxos Need a Martyr"	19
3 "No One Respects the Constitution"	37
4 "We Are Alone with the People"	57
5 "The Miracle of Chibás"	73
6 "I Would Proudly Go to Prison to Defend the Cuban People"	93
7 "The Cave of Ali Baba and His 40,000 Thieves"	119
8 "I'm Not One of Those Generals Who Die in Bed"	151
9 "Time Will Prove Me Right Once Again"	187
10 "I Am Going to Open My Briefcase"	207
Epilogue	237
Notes	255
Bibliography	301
Index	307

Acknowledgments

I began this book in September of 2007 infused with giddiness and caution. Only later did the coincidences become clear. Sixty years earlier, my mother had been born in Havana, and this coincided nearly perfectly with the Ortodoxo party's inauguration on September 8, 1947. My maternal grandfather cut his teeth in Santiago de Cuba, as did Eddy Chibás. On the other hand, I grew up in Scotch Plains, New Jersey, learning Spanish from textbooks and knowing Cuba only through the odd record my mother had brought from the island. I had never heard of Chibás until graduate school but was initially intrigued by his portrait in Hugh Thomas's *Cuba: The Pursuit of Freedom*. Later on, José Luis Rénique suggested I study his case further as way of exploring political suicide in Latin America. Finally, to my surprise, I found there was very little written about one of the most curious and influential figures in twentieth-century Cuban politics. Above all, I was giddy at the prospect of narrating this story and cautious because I was wary of ruining it.

In terms of thanks, I am grateful to my parents, Dov and Fran Ehrlich, especially their boundless faith in education. My wife, Patricia Ruiz Navarro, generously agreed to marry me in 2009 despite my constant seclusion with old documents. Alfonso Quiroz, my late and dearly missed advisor, allowed me the space to err and find my own way. As an historian, I owe him everything. Samuel Farber explained countless things about Cuba that only someone born and raised on the island could understand. His suggestions improved the final draft beyond measure. Meg Crahan shared many important contacts from her travels to the island. Marissa Chibás Preston graciously agreed to speak to me about her father and uncle while visiting New York City in 2007. Much later, she was kind enough to share many of the photos of Chibás that appear in this book. The National Archives and Records Administration staff in College Park, Maryland, provided me with an excellent introduction to archival research. My constant visits to the New York Public Library's microform reading room were enhanced by dependably polite and efficient service. In addition, a Leon Levy Center for Biography fellowship afforded me the time and resources to complete much of this work.

At the Archivo Nacional de Cuba everyone was accommodating, pleasant, and quick with a smile. In particular, Julio López Valdés fulfilled my requests with unfailing good humor and meticulous care. Staff members of the Universidad de la Habana's Sección de Libros Raros were also tremendously supportive. Plenty of Cuban historians were kind to a fault and enormously obliging. Marial Iglesias Utset pointed out several essential sources, provided others herself, and offered context for some archival documents. Dina Martínez Díaz and Ana Cairo shared valuable knowledge about Chibás and the Ortodoxos. Gloria León Rojas arranged a host of useful interviews, including one with the late Pastorita Núñez. Olga Portuondo Zúñiga invited me to her home to photograph the unpublished manuscript of Gloria Cuadras, an Ortodoxo leader in Santiago de Cuba. Ambrosio and Pablo Fornet's anecdotes about Ortodoxo family members from Bayamo helped me construct a more three-dimensional portrait of the party's appeal. Pablo's knowledge of Havana's neighborhoods during the late 1940s and early 1950s was a godsend as well. Lela Sánchez Echeverría took time out from a family visit in Miami to speak to me at length about her father, Aureliano Sánchez Arango, and his quarrel with Chibás. She also presented me with a copy of her perceptive book, *La pólemica infinita: Aureliano vs. Chibás y viceversa*. María Eugenia Fornés answered my questions about Havana's architecture, including the Chibás family residence and Edificio Chibás, with alacrity. All manner of conversations about Cuban history with Marco Taché, Marilola Sala, José Fornés, and the late Sonia Varona yielded insights without which this book would have been incomparably poorer.

Finally, I would like to thank Susan McEachern for taking a chance on this book along with her light editing touch. I am also indebted to Jehanne Schweitzer, who answered my ceaseless copyediting questions with celerity and aplomb.

Introduction

When Eduardo Chibás shot himself three weeks before his forty-fourth birthday, he supposed history would treat him kindly. After all, many Cubans considered him a savior who would rid Cuba of corruption. The family of novelist Reinaldo Arenas, which hailed from the pro-Chibás town of Holguín, was typical of his supporters in many ways. On one occasion, Arenas's grandfather brought such an enormous poster of Chibás to a family Christmas photo shoot that it turned out to be the only thing visible in the picture. Years later, when Chibás's death coincided with that of Arenas's great-grandmother, he observed his relatives "crying seas" of tears.[1] Arenas's mother soon confessed that "I'm not crying for my grandmother, I'm crying for Chibás." Arenas added, "I believe the rest of my family was crying for the same reason."[2] In time, though, Chibás was reduced to caricature. During Cuba's long alliance with the Soviet Union, Chibás was largely ignored due to his ardent anti-Communism. In the 1990s, he was dusted off but grossly miscast as the "seed" that flowered into Fidel Castro's revolution.[3] Among Cuban exiles, Chibás often fared even worse. One of his political contemporaries, Eduardo Suárez Rivas, slandered him as an intellectual lightweight and deadbeat legislator who was obsessed with becoming president.[4] In fact, Chibás was the most innovative politician of his day. Backed by a bare-bones party organization and fantastically popular radio show, he led Cuba's presidential polls throughout 1951. He threatened to upend Cuba's crooked system by luring voters through the airwaves rather than sleazy operatives. In an age when ballots were commonly bought, Chibás forged close emotional ties with supporters—sometimes by hurling himself into their adoring arms after campaign speeches. Above all, he sought to end politics as a money-making ruse and fill Cuba's Capitolio with honest legislators who would honor the island's 1940 constitution.

Eddy, as he was commonly known, first gained public notice in the late 1920s and early 1930s. During that time, he emerged as a leading figure in Cuba's radical student movement. He and like-minded classmates protested President Gerardo Machado's attempt to extend his term via a special constitutional amendment. They were also disgusted by political corruption that turned Cuban presidents into millionaires. Radical students deplored the privileged position of foreign firms, such as the US-owned Cuban Electric Company, which routinely received tax breaks and free access to public lands. Another frustration was the tendency of Cuban governments to cover budget shortfalls with loans from US banks—invariably on onerous terms. Worst of all was the despicable Platt Amendment. This coda to Cuba's constitution, forced upon the island at gunpoint in 1901, legalized periodic interventions by the United States. Even after Machado resigned, on August 12, 1933, and the Platt Amendment was abrogated ten months afterward, Eddy's concerns as a radical student would always loom large in his thinking.

Chibás also began to appreciate the growing power of radio during spells as a political refugee in New York City and Washington, DC, during the late 1920s and early 1930s. To his horror, he saw how effectively the commentator Edwin C. Hill had disseminated falsehoods about Cuba's revolutionaries and turned US public opinion against them.[5] Eddy began hosting his own program in October of 1933 during the provisional presidency of Ramón Grau San Martín. His charisma translated easily, and many listeners were instantly riveted. In the late 1940s, his command of the airwaves proved vital in an era when radio ownership was nearing a rate of one per family.[6] By then, most Cuban politicos availed themselves of the medium, but none derived more advantage than Chibás. Already, by 1947, Chibás had garnered the highest rating for a single broadcast in Cuban history—surpassing even the island's wildly popular radio soap operas.

At 8:00 p.m. on Sunday evenings, upward of 550,000 Cubans dropped whatever they were doing to hear Chibás. This estimate, courtesy of the Cuban Advertisers' Association, almost certainly undercounted his audience. After all, many villagers without radios walked for miles to reach one. Others congregated by the hundreds in neighbors' houses to cheer their idol together. In Havana, crowds descended on downtown hotels, such as the Inglaterra, where his show was broadcast. Another throng waited for Chibás to emerge from his penthouse apartment in the López Serrano building so they could accompany him to CMQ studios. On the air, he comforted listeners with vows to defend them against powerful figures or crooked officials. When necessary, he titillated them with scandalous revelations or ruinous gossip about political opponents. Of course, he religiously roused their ire with investigations into shady deals and sleazy public servants. On some nights, he might offer a civics lesson by reading aloud sections of Cuba's 1940 constitution, which he had a hand in crafting. More often, he would remind Cubans that former Machado supporters remained in politics, which was a national disgrace, or that Fulgencio Batista, who had ruled by force in the mid and late 1930s, savored stolen riches and liberty despite his murderous past as the island's military chief.

Even before Chibás had become Cuba's premier radio host, he demonstrated an all-important proficiency in garnering votes for himself and the Auténtico party—which served as a vehicle for many onetime student revolutionaries. During the 1939 election for Cuba's constituent assembly, Eddy outpolled every politician on the island except ex-president Ramón Grau San Martín. Chibás was just thirty-two years old at the time and had never before sought public office. Given his obvious star power, the Auténtico party subsequently nominated him for congressional and senate seats, both of which he easily captured. In 1944, Eddy's radio diatribes, tireless stump speeches, and considerable fortune inherited from his father helped the Auténtico candidate, Ramón Grau San Martín, win Cuba's presidency. In a fit of euphoria, he deemed Grau's election "the glorious journey." Along with many of his countrymen, he possessed absolute faith in Grau and celebrated the fact that Cuba's presidential palace would house a revolutionary for the first time in ten years. His confidence was shaken by Grau's campaign to change Cuba's constitution so he could run for reelection. Chibás was further dismayed by Grau's tolerance for shady ex-revolutionaries like Alberto Inocente Álvarez and the serial embezzler José Manuel Alemán.

By mid-1946, Chibás was the popular choice among rank-and-file Auténticos to succeed Grau. However, their wishes were trumped by Grau's control of the party and a bitter falling out between former mentor and protégé. In the past, Chibás had happily submitted to Grau when he believed the party's interests were at stake. As recently as 1945, Eddy had dropped his bid for mayor of Havana at Grau's urging. Two years later, as funds for Cuban schoolchildren were being stolen and commerce ministry hacks profited from a pervasive black market, Chibás realized he no longer belonged to a revolutionary outfit. In May of 1947, he launched the Ortodoxo party and served as its presidential nominee eleven months afterward. Eddy's campaign was a quixotic affair that flouted every convention of Cuban politics. Since the republic's earliest days, parties of all stripes had traded jobs, favors, and cash for votes. Chibás claimed the moral high ground instead with his slogan of "Shame versus Money" and vows to jail government thieves. From 1936 onward, electoral coalitions had been essential as no party commanded an outright majority. Eddy nonetheless preferred a solo operation to prevent "understandings" with parties tainted by corruption or ties to Machado. Lastly, opposition candidates typically relied on affluent backers to finance their campaigns. Eddy duly counted a handful of such figures but covered most expenses by selling the Havana manse built by his father in 1924. He therefore became one of the few men in Cuba who lost money by practicing politics. Above all, Chibás aimed to forge a relationship of intense personal feeling and loyalty with voters that would preclude them from selling their ballots.

When the election results were announced, Chibás defied all expectations by securing 16.42 percent of the vote. By contrast, the victorious Carlos Prío boasted a mere 45.83 percent despite flooding Cuba with largesse. Ricardo Núñez Portuondo, the lavishly backed runner-up, garnered 30.42 percent. Eddy's showing was even more striking because his nascent party had been too short of time and treasure to open offices in rural areas. Ortodoxos were so hobbled by money woes that pro-Chibás rallies often featured homespun posters and banners. The popular weekly magazine *Bohemia* gushed that Chibás had performed a "miracle" and proved Cuba was ready for a fresh brand of politics.[7] Eddy's appeal was further bolstered by two spectacular scandals shortly after the poll. On October 10, 1948, the infamous ex-education minister José Manuel Alemán nabbed roughly $20 million from Cuba's treasury in broad daylight. In one fell swoop, 10 percent of the island's national budget disappeared. Less than three months later, a meticulously detailed lawsuit accused Ramón Grau San Martín of looking the other way while his ministers embezzled more than 174 million pesos. Carlos Prío, who oversaw Cuba's government on a day-to-day basis during much of Grau's term, was now president himself and undoubtedly liable. At the same time, Chibás received letters from all corners of Cuba describing schools without desks or textbooks, where children were deprived of state-sponsored free breakfasts. Other missives mentioned hospitals where vital medicines were missing. For Chibás, the link between government thieves and Cuba's jilted poor was unmistakable.

Eddy's momentum carried over into the 1950 midterm poll, where he edged his millionaire Auténtico rival for a Havana senate seat. Chibás boasted support from Cubans of all stripes, but was especially adored by the island's youth. This augured well for the Ortodoxos and provided an immediate jolt from twenty-four-year-old José Pardo Llada. A popular radio host and muckraker extraordinaire, Pardo Llada won a record seventy-two thousand votes in his Havana congressional race. Pardo Llada's success demonstrated that Eddy's style and methods could be realistic as well as romantic. In fact, national opinion polls conducted between December of 1950 and May of 1951 consistently showed Chibás to be Cuba's most popular politician. While he longed to be president, Eddy's abiding obsessions were his place in Cuba's annals and stirring "the sleeping conscience of the Cuban people."[8] He trusted that his struggle against Machado as a student had already gained him favorable standing in the former. On the other hand, Chibás occasionally despaired that his countrymen were too deeply mired in moral slumber. He was haunted by the erstwhile comrades-in-arms who had "assassinated themselves" by cashing in when they gained political power.[9] Further, substantial portions of the population remained indifferent to his message. After one of Eddy's habitual exposés fell flat in July of 1951, he sought to "wake up" fellow Cubans by firing a bullet into his stomach.[10]

Cuba's presidential contest of 1952 was in many respects a tribute to Chibás. The two leading candidates were Carlos Hevia for the Auténticos and Eddy's cousin, Roberto Agramonte, of the Ortodoxos. Both were honest, capable men with genuine revolutionary credentials. When Hevia was tapped to head Cuba's foreign ministry in 1948, Eddy had conceded that he possessed "undoubted prestige."[11] Regardless of the outcome, Cuba was poised to benefit from a clean administration. Meanwhile, yet another magnetic and media-savvy Ortodoxo who dabbled in scandal mongering was running for congress. This was twenty-five-year-old Fidel Castro. However, the poll was canceled after a military coup led by Fulgencio Batista on March 10, 1952. Many of Eddy's contributions thus were buried under a layer of martial rule. Nonetheless, his obsession with honesty and intensely personal political style became a hallmark for the so-called generation of 1950 that reached maturity during the mid-twentieth century and has ruled Cuba since 1959. Billboards in contemporary Cuba declaring that "revolution means never lying or violating ethical principles" are one of many testaments to this ongoing influence. Of course, Eddy may have been the first Cuban politico whose surname seemed incidental, but he would hardly be the last.

Chapter One

"As Long As Any Cuban Suffers, I Will Fight for Him"

By spring of 1947, Havana's mayor was perturbed, perplexed, and pondering drastic measures. Having been elected on a platform of bringing water to the parched capital, Manuel Fernández Supervielle had failed, and his constituents were irate. Upon being recognized in public, he was relentlessly trailed by chants of "*agua*." During trips to the cinema, he sat apart from the crowd so as not to be seen. If his image appeared on a newsreel, it was greeted with derisive whistles. Even Havana's merchants, whom Supervielle had saved from a series of onerous taxes in his former post as treasury minister, turned their backs on him. Presiding over the celebration of Retailer's Day, in the lush gardens of the Tropical Brewery, the mayor was greeted by angry demands that he fulfill his pledge to build a new aqueduct.[1]

Supervielle was a proud man who took these slights to heart. His campaign, marked by the slogan, "Havana will have water!" had aroused a genuine fervor—especially as the city, with a population of 600,000, counted a water supply suitable for 150,000.[2] Now, a short while later, and despite his lengthy career as an honest and conscientious politician, Havana's denizens assumed he was a fraud and a liar. Even so, he was not the sort to complain or wallow in pity. At times, Supervielle attempted to explain his predicament but always did so privately. On Sunday, April 20, he accompanied some municipal employees to a hospital where the city's education department chief was convalescing. Finding himself among a sympathetic crowd and responding to gentle prodding, he began recounting the details of his ordeal.[3] He confessed that his friend Ramón Grau San Martín, Cuba's president, had persuaded him to leave his post as treasury minister and run for mayor. After taking office in September of 1946, everything initially proceeded smoothly and with the president's full support. Grau's enthusiasm was such that he once kept Clinton P. Anderson, the US secretary of agriculture, waiting for two hours while he and Supervielle examined plans for the aqueduct.

Once the blueprints were finalized, Supervielle estimated the cost to be 6 million pesos.[4] He then contacted José Morell Romero, president of the Sugar Workers' Retirement Fund, who had offered to finance the aqueduct.[5] Morell Romero not only considered lending to the city a good investment, he confessed to unhappily presiding over 21 million "unproductive" pesos.[6] The two quickly reached a verbal agreement and then considered the legality of their proposed transaction. Supervielle, who was a lawyer, devised a formula by which the loan would agree with the city's legal code. The following day, Supervielle arranged a meeting with Grau, Morell Romero, and Jesús Menéndez, president of the National Federation of Sugar Workers. Menéndez expressed approval, saying that water was always a good business and the aqueduct would represent "another triumph for the working class."[7] As everyone prepared to leave, Grau, who had been silent until then, warned in his smiling, affable manner that the loan presently being negotiated did not fulfill "specific requirements" of the constitution and urged them to be careful. According to Morell Romero and Menéndez, the mayor turned "intensely pallid" upon hearing these words, and for good reason.[8] Instantly, the project was thrust into quicksand. First, a commission of legal experts was convened to examine the issue. After they assented, Grau convoked a committee of engineers to inspect the aqueduct's blueprint for design flaws. When none were encountered, the president contracted a panel of financiers to analyze the cost. Finding no irregularities, Supervielle once again approached Morell Romero. In the intervening two months, however, the president of the Sugar Workers' Retirement Fund had developed a case of cold feet. Claiming the loan was now "a very big responsibility," Morell Romero deferred to the assemblies of workers, tenants, and landowners that governed the fund.[9] When two of these delegations attached unreasonable conditions to their consent, Supervielle was forced to abandon this avenue.[10]

At various points during Supervielle's monologue, his listeners suggested he make a declaration that would clarify the facts. The mayor replied that he preferred not to harm anyone nor did he wish to hinder the country's progress. As treasury minister, he had witnessed the negative effect of scandals on Cuba's economy. At the same time, Supervielle repeatedly wondered why he had been made mayor if he was only going to be thwarted. He also groped for an explanation as to why Grau, whom he had believed to be a close friend, had changed his mind suddenly and so completely. While the president's behavior was surely vexing, both the mayor and his sympathizers were wrong to imply his harassment in the street was the result of an ignorant citizenry. For example, *Bohemia*, the nation's most popular magazine, reported on every stage of the negotiations.[11] A piece appearing on January 26, 1947, informed readers not only of Grau's reservation regarding the Sugar

Workers' Retirement Fund but also of shady dealings in the municipal council, where opposition aldermen demanded a "slice" of the 6 million pesos earmarked for the project in exchange for their support.[12] The public was even aware that the "municipal first lady" had suggested her husband visit a blood bank as a way of drumming up positive publicity. Cubans were later notified that Supervielle had deceived them even in this small endeavor. After being photographed by the Havana newspapers with his shirtsleeve rolled up, the mayor refused to have any blood drawn on account of his fragile health.[13]

As Supervielle wrestled with mounting disappointment, he was acutely aware of the looming first anniversary of his election. With the Sugar Workers' Retirement Fund off-limits, the mayor had no choice but to seek foreign investors. At the same time, they would almost certainly not pass muster with a president who had sloganeered to the tune of "An aqueduct without concessions and with Cuban money." Nevertheless, Supervielle courted a series of overseas firms, including Frederick Snare Corporation of the United States, but each time he balked before a deal could be reached. On a different occasion, the mayor apparently considered a loan from the owner of the building where he lived—perhaps believing the man, who was Cuban, would be preferable to a foreigner. The feverish, semi-distracted state of Supervielle's dealings led a *Bohemia* correspondent to write that "In municipal circles, there is speculation as to the identity of the next fortunate mortal who, within a week's time, will enter into negotiations with the mayor, with the objective of beginning the eagerly awaited aqueduct, although it's suspected the mayor will accommodate whomever crosses his path next."[14]

Two weeks after that Sunday in April, when Supervielle had unburdened himself before some of the few people who still sympathized with him, he awoke early and appeared bathed and clean-shaven in his garage at around 7:40 a.m. There, as usual, he encountered Sergio Álvarez—the policeman assigned to protect him since his days as treasury secretary. "Sergio," said the mayor in a playful tone, "you carry a revolver I don't like. It's old and ugly. Show it to me. One day, I'm going to give you a new one."[15] Álvarez disarmed the pistol, a .38 caliber, and handed it over. Supervielle briefly examined the weapon, insisted again it was not to his taste, and told Álvarez to call for a police car as he had an errand that required attention. Álvarez, who was seated next to the mayor, asked for his gun, saying he felt uncomfortable going out into the street unarmed. Supervielle returned the weapon, watched Álvarez insert the magazine, and then snatched it from him. Before Álvarez could respond, Supervielle quickly shot himself in the chest. Later on, as the mayor's corpse was laid out on a city hospital's operating table, two letters escaped from his jacket pocket: one addressed to the judge of instruction, the other to his wife of eighteen years. The former was dated May 2, two days before his suicide. "I deprive myself of life," it read, "because in spite of my efforts to resolve the problem of water in Havana, multiple inconveniences and obstacles have been placed in my way, making it impossible, and this represents a political failure and leaves unfulfilled the promise I made to the people."[16]

Among the first to arrive at Supervielle's residence in the plush suburb of Miramar was Eddy Chibás, accompanied by his friend and political confidant, Luis Orlando Rodríguez. They, along with two reporters who had preceded them, listened as Aurelia Palacios, the mayor's grief-stricken widow, screamed, "Grau is responsible! He's the only one responsible for Manuel's death!" She then looked at Chibás and said, "You know everything. You have to awaken the people. You have to open their eyes."[17]

The thirty-nine-year-old Auténtico senator was by now a bona fide radio celebrity and budding messianic figure whose followers often compared him to Jesus Christ.[18] His Sunday evening broadcasts regularly topped the popularity charts, often surpassing the island's famed *radionovelas*.[19] Richard Pack, a *New York Times* correspondent, characterized Chibás as a "reporter, crusader, gossip and muckraker" who treated listeners to a weekly half-hour dose of "verbal fireworks."[20] The show offered more than mere entertainment, however. Chibás urged his audience to expose examples of injustice or corruption, and every week letters poured in from all corners of the island. "As long as any Cuban suffers," he reminded listeners, "I will fight for him." Supervielle's widow pinned her hopes on Chibás for this reason, adding that some city council members had demanded $5,000 in exchange for supporting the aqueduct.[21]

More to the point, Chibás had lately suffered troubles of his own with Grau. On January 19, 1947, Chibás addressed a twelve-page letter to his friend.[22] He urged Grau to end the reelection campaign being waged on his behalf by government functionaries, to fire corrupt ministers and send them to the courts for trial, and crush the black market that raised the cost of living and enriched dishonest officials.[23] The reelection effort was particularly galling for Chibás on two accounts. First, Cuba's 1940 constitution, which both men had a hand in crafting as members of the constituent assembly, strictly forbade the practice and Grau's own Auténtico party had proposed the measure, which had been approved unanimously.[24] Second, Chibás harbored presidential hopes of his own and longed to correct his erstwhile master's mistakes. In any case, Grau ignored the missive even as many of his policies sowed anger and distrust among Cubans, who had expected great things from him. Thus, an editorial in the weekly magazine *Carteles* declared, "Never has a government defrauded the faith of Cubans so rapidly and radically as that of Dr. Ramón Grau San Martín."[25]

THE GRUPO ORTODOXO

On March 1, 1947, a bloc of pro-Chibás Auténticos, known as the grupo ortodoxo, met in Senator Pelayo Cuervo Navarro's home to discuss the formation of a new political party. By this time, Grau had renounced reelection, but those present were certain he would take revenge. In their view, remaining within the fold would be "political suicide."[26] Nevertheless, Chibás promptly shocked everyone by asserting that the right "historical juncture" had not yet presented itself.[27]

Cuba's political sphere was fragmented, with no party attracting more than half the island's votes in presidential polls. As head of a new entity, Chibás reasoned, he would require pacts in order to win the presidency. This would entail diluting the prospective party's platform just as the Auténticos had done in 1944 when they allied with the Republicans.[28] Chibás thus told the group, in what would become one of his political hallmarks, that he was interested more in "ideology without pacts than pacts without ideology."[29] Aside from an attachment to the organization he had helped build, Chibás also believed the Auténticos were capable of winning the presidency without coalitions if they chose the right candidate, namely himself, and jettisoned the party's crooked elements.[30] Eight days later, on his radio show, Chibás likened the Auténtico party to a warship lashed by a tempest, leaking water and infiltrated by enemies. What, he asked, must loyal crew members do under such circumstances? They should denounce traitors and struggle to save the boat along with the ideals it represents regardless of the consequences. Amused by this allegory, *Bohemia*'s correspondent noted that Chibás had "turned himself into a mariner, whose love of the sea rivaled Sinbad."[31] In a less metaphorical moment, Chibás announced that forming a new "political instrument" and heading a coalition of the island's other parties would almost surely guarantee him the nation's highest office in 1948. Even so, he declared, "I am unwilling to exchange my historic position in Cuba's revolutionary movement for the presidency of the republic."[32] All the same, Chibás continued associating with the grupo ortodoxo—whose leaders set a date for leaving the party. One of Eddy's closest friends, Manuel Bisbé, assured them he would join after resolving his "emotional conflict."[33]

While Auténtico bigwigs viewed the man known as El Loco (the crazy one) with mistrust, the grupo ortodoxo wondered when Chibás would realize, as Bisbé had said, "the impossibility of continuing in the party."[34] Hence, each new development became a test of Eddy's loyalties and intentions. On March 17, grupo ortodoxo senators drew up a motion to interpellate Grau's sleaziest cabinet members: Education Minister José Manuel Alemán and Commerce Minister César Casas. Asked whether he would add his name, Chibás agreed on two conditions. First, the motion must not attack the Auténticos as a party, and second, no politicians from other parties would be asked to sign. If the grupo ortodoxo hoped Chibás would see the futility of his situation, this was indeed a shrewd tactic. In 1945, when Alberto Inocente Álvarez submitted to a seven-hour interpellation and Cuba's chamber of representatives subsequently voted "no confidence," Grau was indignant and resisted removing him. When Álvarez did finally bow to calls for his resignation, Grau flouted the island's semi-parliamentary system by making him foreign minister shortly thereafter. Zeroing in on Alemán and Casas would almost certainly lead to similar contempt—especially as the president considered Alemán his "best minister."[35] Though the grupo ortodoxo did not intend the motion as a ruse to lure Chibás, its members surely realized the potential symbolism. After all, Chibás and Alemán were nearly perfect foils.

GRAU'S CORRUPT MINISTERS

Eddy joined the Auténticos in 1938, before the party was allowed to function legally in Cuba and when it could offer members little aside from persecution. Alemán, on the other hand, had been a Democrat and career civil servant in the ministry of education who supported Grau's opponent in 1944. Elevated to education minister in 1946, the erstwhile chief of budgets and accounts quickly padded his briefcase. When that was full, he employed a suitcase. With his ill-gotten gains, he acquired a *finca* twelve miles south of Havana and prime Miami real estate, for starters.[36] Alemán was no garden-variety grafter, however. Besides lining his pockets, he used the ministry's funds to become a major power broker within the Auténtico party.[37] In this respect, the ministry of education proved an ideal plaything. Its budget was swollen beyond that of other ministries by a nine-centavo tax on each bag of sugar produced, the result of a law passed on April 5, 1943. Known as *inciso K* (clause K) for the section of the law's first article that mandated the tax, it was designed to finance the hiring of new professors, teachers, and other necessary personnel. Alemán diverted a substantial portion of this money toward Auténtico candidates in 1946, helping the party gain a majority in congress and, fatefully, the mayoralty of Havana. With an eye toward the presidential poll in 1948, Alemán launched an all-purpose political fund known as BAGA (Bloque Alemán-Grau Alsina) in conjunction with Grau's favorite nephew, Francisco Grau Alsina. Chibás, who had taken note of these activities, taunted Alemán over the airwaves—accusing him on December 12, 1946, of stealing schoolchildren's breakfasts. Being dressed down in this manner before a nationwide audience was undoubtedly embarrassing for Alemán, but he inoculated himself against such attacks by charming the president.

As a lifelong bureaucrat, Alemán was adept at cultivating vastly different masters. During Fulgencio Batista's presidency, he served Education Minister Anselmo Alliegro—helping him pillage inciso K from its inception. After Grau was elected, Alemán radically changed course. References to Batista's civic-military schools were scrapped. He demolished the Cangrejeras military barracks on the western edge of Havana and replaced them with a polytechnic school named for Paulina Alsina, Grau's widowed sister-in-law, who was Cuba's "First Lady." Alemán also encouraged Grau's reelection hopes. This endeared him to the austere ex-physiology professor, who eschewed cigarettes, alcohol, and even snacks between meals but devoured flattery. Alemán consolidated his position in the party by taking indirect control of the armed action group known as Movimiento Socialista Revolucionario (MSR). This outfit was one of numerous self-styled *grupos de acción* with ties to the Auténticos. After Grau won the presidency, these violent organizations sought government positions and pursued deadly rivalries among themselves. They also engaged in lucrative rackets, such as monopolizing the sale of textbooks at the University of Havana.[38] Alemán utilized the MSR as a private army to bully detractors and forcibly shut down schools, especially out-of-the-way rural institutions. In this manner, he increased the available resources for his own purposes.[39]

On April 8, 1947, the senate voted to interpellate Alemán and Casas. Chibás had prepared for this eventuality by asking listeners to send examples of government corruption. One letter, signed by thirty-one parents and neighbors of two nearby rural schools in Las Villas province, declaimed their children's lack of paper, pencils, books, desks, and blackboards. The authors begged Chibás, as "one of the purest men of our republic," to tell the education minister to "SPEND MONEY ON SCHOOL MATERIALS" because local children "HUNGER FOR TEACHING."[40] Rolando Roque of Guara in Havana province claimed the right to an education in his town was a "sarcasm" given the absence of textbooks, seats, desks, and water filters in the school.[41] Manuel Barruecos of Bayamo informed Chibás that the education minister was closing the Rural Normal School in order to rob the money designated for its upkeep. Further, he described the recent visit of a group of MSR gangsters "pantomiming" the role of school inspectors.[42] In Calabazar de la Habana, the locale of Alemán's recently acquired finca, residents noticed that construction workers and supplies were diverted from a nearby school to the education minister's property. Chibás was thus urged to "fall with zeal upon the thieves."[43]

César Casas, the minister of commerce, was a less sinister figure than Alemán, but his toleration of Cuba's black market profoundly angered many citizens. The intermittent scarcity of goods such as rice, lard, flour, meat, and milk had originally begun in 1942, when the United States entered World War II. Now, more than a year after the fight had ended, Cubans continued to endure shortages and black market prices. Responding to complaints, ministry officials denied the existence of a black market and, rather indelicately, grumbled that Cubans were "eating too much."[44] Casas qualified these assertions, saying no "organized" black market was in force.[45] Everyday Cubans knew otherwise. One letter described how a treasury ministry employee bought 350 sacks of cement at the officially controlled price of ninety-eight centavos and subsequently sold them for three pesos each on the black market.[46] The man, named Andrés Plumas, was a recent hire and confessed to a pal that his longer-serving colleagues were entitled to far more. Esther Pérez, a fervid Chibás supporter, lamented the scarcity of rice in the town of Carlos Rojas because of a common trick employed by wholesalers. This involved billing shopkeepers for one quantity while delivering a much smaller amount. As a result, local stores faced a dilemma: break the law and sell items for more than the official price so as not to lose money or avoid vending them altogether. For good measure, Pérez added that the town's children did not receive their school breakfasts nor did they have sufficient educational materials.[47] Another missive reported that the chief of Santa Clara's office of commerce and his second in command controlled supplies of the city's basic items and sold them for exorbitant rates on the black market. As a result, rice and soap were unavailable at official prices. Noting that the Grau administration had "turned out worse than we thought," the author deemed himself a "Chibás Auténtico" and praised the grupo ortodoxo.[48]

Worst of all, the sordidness of Cuba's black market underbelly, teeming as it was with dodgy functionaries and wholesalers, was only half the story. The government's official policy of price controls for foodstuffs such as rice, lard, and flour, all of which were largely imported, amounted to subsidies for US producers. A wiser tactic would have been to stimulate domestic markets—particularly for rice, a Cuban staple suitable to the island's terrain. This was especially imperative now, while sugar prices were high, so that Cuba would have other options when profits inevitably dropped. After all, sugar-growing rivals such as the Philippines, whose capacity had been largely destroyed during World War II, would not stay down indefinitely. Many of these points were outlined in a memo drawn up for Chibás on April 12, four days after the interpellations were approved. The document also censured Alemán for sporadic distribution of school breakfasts and the building of showcase schools next to Cuba's Central Highway while rural inhabitants languished in want. Taking into account the gravity of these offenses and the vast resources at Alemán's disposal, it warned that the senate's obligation to examine and analyze the education ministry was "not to be delegated."[49] Chibás had no intention of shirking this responsibility, nor did many of his fellow legislators, especially those from other parties who were placed at a disadvantage by Alemán's campaign contributions.

At the same time, both ministers were determined to resist appearing before the senate. Prior to the vote, Alemán and Casas informed the president they suffered from stage fright. Upon learning of the motion's approval, Grau refused to honor it but seemed far less concerned with protecting his ministers than ridding himself of congress altogether. Notified by senate president Miguel "Miguelito" Suárez Fernández that the upper chamber was exercising a constitutional prerogative, Grau, wearing his characteristic smile, responded with the following anecdote:

> Truly amigos, the constitution is charging me for more than the amount on the bill. At this moment, I'm remembering something very suggestive. A short while after assuming the presidency of the republic, I passed through Luyanó [a working-class Havana neighborhood] on the way to Varadero [a beach resort eighty-five miles east of the capital] and noted a horrible smell emanating from a tallow factory. The next day, I called the minister of health and asked him to close it but he told me he couldn't do that because the factory was functioning in accordance with the constitution and the laws. A short time afterward, I again passed through Luyanó and the horrible odor still bothered me. This time, I called Lieutenant Colonel Hernández Nardo and instructed him to take some men along and close the factory immediately without any further explanation. Acting with great efficiency, he shut down the factory and said only that he was acting on orders from above. Right now, the congress is bothering me a great deal because it too smells horribly. It's a center of foul smells.[50]

The following Sunday, Chibás repeated this story on his radio show, spreading the "tallow factory of Luyanó" to an even wider audience than those who read about it in *Bohemia*. The island's cartoonists happily joined the fray as well. For example, a sketch by Juan David portrayed Grau and the Republican senator Guillermo Alonso Pujol speaking to each other behind gas masks.[51]

Tensions were exacerbated on April 21, when MSR gunmen loyal to Alemán fired shots into the Capitolio during an evening senate session dedicated to resolving the crisis. Two days later, as the senate awaited him, Casas sent word that he would not attend his interpellation. In response, Chibás submitted a motion of no confidence against Grau's entire cabinet, which was duly approved, as the only way to defend the senate's "legislative sovereignty."[52] Even as this was humiliating, Grau was favored by a provision in the constitution excusing his new cabinet from interpellation for one year. Once again flouting the document he helped draft, Grau elevated deputies in each ministry and made no secret of his intent to restore the original cabinet when the senate recessed. On May 2, when the no-confidence vote became official, Prime Minister Carlos Prío Socarrás termed Casas's refusal to appear before the senate "legal and legitimate."[53] For Prío, a lawyer, senator, and former delegate to the constituent assembly, this statement was understandable only in the context of his own presidential aspirations. Even as Grau had relinquished his reelection campaign, it was clear he, and not the party assembly, would choose the next Auténtico presidential nominee. Thus, the prospect of Chibás rescuing the party from the likes of Grau and Alemán seemed increasingly remote.

On the other hand, the president's high-handedness was unpopular. As Chibás had attempted to collect signatures for his no-confidence motion, Eduardo Suárez Rivas, a Liberal senator, exclaimed that those who refused would "look like idiots" before the public.[54] Grau, who once averred that his government represented "the combat of virtue against vice,"[55] now preferred to defy the constitution rather than surrender two widely disliked and corrupt ministers.[56] Two days after this crisis had been resolved, essentially by sidestepping the legislative branch, Havana's mayor shot himself. Supervielle, who had been derided in the press and on the streets up to the moment of his demise, instantly achieved martyrdom. During his broadcast that evening, Chibás characterized the mayor's death as a "desperate cry of alarm in the midst of political confusion."[57] He also reminded listeners of the Auténtico congressman (and unconditional Grau supporter) Segundo Curti's attempt to pass a law that would place the aqueduct under central government control because the mayor was a "failed, inept and incapable public servant."[58] The next day a crowd of four thousand, composed of all social classes, squeezed into Havana's Colón Cemetery to attend Supervielle's burial. A reporter from *Diario de la Marina* called the ceremony "one of the most well attended in recent memory."[59] A *Bohemia* correspondent noted that Supervielle's suicide was "taken by the people as an act of protest in favor of honest politics against the habit, too frequent among elected figures, of scorning the needs and necessities of the community."[60] Although Grau delivered a glowing eulogy, Supervielle lacked the president's full support even in death. The national government, unlike that of the city, did not declare an official day of mourning nor were the flags of the presidential palace, the prime minister's office, or the foreign ministry flown at half-mast.[61] The administration's most pressing concern was to keep the multitude's palpable anger from bubbling over. Thus, a police cordon restricted access to the mausoleum and the cemetery was lined with uniformed and plainclothes officers. The government also canceled eulogies slated to be given by figures representing the mayor's family and Havana's city hall, alleging a shortage of time.

Chibás, who had zealously campaigned for Supervielle in 1946 and dubbed him "Super-votes," was ideally placed to understand the frayed relationship between mayor and president. After all, Chibás had once coveted the mayoralty for himself but yielded to Grau's preference for Supervielle. Grau purportedly favored Supervielle because the post required an administrator rather than a politician. Most likely, Supervielle's middling popularity caught Grau's eye more than his efficiency or managerial skill as treasury minister. In terms of power, Havana's mayoralty paled only before the presidency, and

Grau, who cherished the idea of reelection, desired a weak candidate. Supervielle, who had twice run unsuccessfully for a congressional seat, was ideal. Even so, the prospect of bringing water to Havana aroused such passion that Supervielle became a sensation. He defeated his two opponents in a landslide and immediately set to work on the promised aqueduct. Supervielle also began mentioning himself as a presidential candidate. If he succeeded in supplying the water *Habaneros* so desperately yearned for, his popularity would have soared and turned him into a natural contender for Cuba's highest office. Hence, Grau effectively squashed the financing for Supervielle's aqueduct in late January 1947 for this reason and refused to reverse himself even after the mayor publicly supported the president's reelection campaign. Nor was this the first time Grau had played politics with the city's water supply. In August 1944, as president-elect, he rejected a scheme by then Mayor Raúl García Menocal because the proposed aqueduct called for the use of foreign capital.[62] Supervielle was also not the only Auténtico to have his career derailed for becoming too popular. Grau's first education minister, Luis Pérez Espinós, was forced to resign in 1945 because his success in adding new classrooms and expanding the school breakfast program was considered threatening.[63]

A NEW PARTY

When Chibás took to the microphones on Sunday evening of May 11, he was ready to cast off what his young friend Luis Conte Agüero called "the psychological conflict."[64] He began his address by revisiting Supervielle's death. The mayor's suicide note, he mused, was reminiscent of a "patrician from the legendary age of Roman greatness."[65] He contrasted this document, which avoided accusation or recrimination, with the "sordid meanness" of those responsible for his demise.[66] Chibás also reminded his audience that the flag adorning the presidential palace fluttered at the top of its mast, "challenging public opinion" and smirking at the man whose poignant fate "destroyed thousands and thousands of hearts."[67] Following this prelude, Chibás devoted the remainder of his twenty-five-minute show to yet another unfolding tragedy. The same underhanded characters, led by Grau, who had driven Supervielle to end his life had also irreparably harmed the Auténtico party. This damage could not be reversed because the party's national, provincial, and municipal assemblies, which represented rank-and-file delegates, no longer possessed any influence over the current government. Chibás pointed out that the national assembly had not been convoked a single time since Grau had taken office in October of 1944. Declaring that "the crisis of the government produces a crisis in the party, which in turn gives rise to a crisis in the Cuban revolution," Chibás signaled his readiness to found a new party based on the original Auténtico ideals of economic independence, political liberty, and social justice.[68]

The following Thursday, grupo ortodoxo members and their sympathizers met in the Auténtico youth headquarters on the corner of Neptuno and Amistad. They included 6 of the nation's 54 senators, 9 of its 127 congressmen, the governor of Matanzas province, and the mayors of Bayamo, Holguín, and Victoria de las Tunas. Among younger notables were nineteen-year-old Natasha Mella, daughter of Julio Antonio Mella, the magnetic student leader and founder of Cuba's Communist party.[69] Also present was twenty-year-old Fidel Castro, then a University of Havana law student. Chibás opened the proceedings saying, "We can't rebuild the party from within but don't want to be accused of being impulsive or acting out of personal ambitions."[70] He thus proposed that Grau be given seventy-two hours to convene the Auténtico national assembly, in front of which the grupo ortodoxo would accuse him of betraying the party's founding principles. This proposal was uniformly approved. Later on, Senator Emilio "Millo" Ochoa submitted a motion, which also received unanimous consent, to form a committee charged with establishing a "new political force."[71] On May 18, two hours after the deadline for a response from Grau had passed, Chibás ascended his radio pulpit and launched the organization. He described this entity, so freshly born it lacked a name, as a refuge for Cuba's honorable politicians. "In a party," Chibás proclaimed, "fundamental ideas are very important but also essential are the men charged with putting them into practice. The world's most beautiful program, backed by empty speakers or a group of delinquents will never be able to win over public opinion or the people's enthusiastic support."[72]

Asked by a reporter for his opinion, Grau dismissed the new party as *ortofónicos*, or noisemakers. However, there was no denying this represented yet another black eye for the man viewed as a messiah less than three years earlier. Grau had subverted his party's rank and file by ignoring Auténtico assemblies. Well-meaning Auténticos who were horrified by the depredations of José Manuel Alemán and César Casas thus had no recourse for reforming the party. In addition, rather than allowing an open competition for his successor, Grau first tried an illegal reelection campaign and subsequently decided to handpick the party's next presidential candidate. Such calculations had condemned Supervielle to suicide and Chibás to exile in a new outfit. This set the stage for something different in the island's political sphere. Chibás, whose new organization would not have the time to place deep roots before the 1948 elections, would attempt to win office with a novel brand of politics based on his fantastically popular radio show and intense emotional bond with Cuba's workaday citizens.

Chapter Two

"Shoot Me in the Heart—the Ortodoxos Need a Martyr"

By the late 1940s, Chibás regularly began receiving missives from the likes of América González de Martínez, a Havana resident who asserted that "you are the only salvation of our fatherland and all the evils we suffer."[1] Julián Padrón, also of Havana, wrote, "I consider you the only pure one among all our politicians."[2] Twenty-two-year-old Armando Hernández of Banes in Oriente province revealed that "I am ready to defend you under any circumstances because you are the only defender of us Cubans."[3] In a sense, he represented the hopes of Cubans frustrated by Grau. However, Chibás was a unique politician who distinguished himself from contemporaries in two important respects. First, he developed an easy and genuine rapport with the needy. As the eldest child of an affluent family, this did not come naturally. However, Chibás began visiting poor neighborhoods and sounded out *maniceros* (peanut sellers), fruit vendors, and others he met on the street. Pastorita Núñez, who grew up in the humble Pocitos section of Marianao and later joined the new party's Women's Wing, watched him course through the area on numerous occasions. "While other politicians stopped by to purchase votes," she said, "Chibás penetrated the masses and practiced the truth."[4] At the same time, practicing "the truth" was not always initially appreciated and occasionally met with incredulous disbelief. Eddy's secretary, Conchita Fernández, recalled that

> As many people were accustomed to appearing before politicians with their identity cards in their hand, when they came to see Eddy they asked for scholarships for their children, a hospital bed for a sick relative, things like that, and they offered their identity cards in exchange. When he said he

wouldn't accept them—and he did the same thing when money was offered—people didn't understand and it was necessary to explain himself many times.[5]

Of course, Chibás tried to help whenever possible, often referring cases to his personal physician and friend, Pedro Iglesias Betancourt, or buying textbooks for impoverished secondary school students. However, he did so without asking for identity cards—which could later be converted into votes. This approach sought to peck away at the edges of an ingrained and corrupt political culture. Just as important, Chibás could not possibly assist every worthy petitioner, but he offered the defrauded and downtrodden a voice over the airwaves each Sunday. This gave rise to the commonly repeated refrain, "I'm going to tell Chibás."[6]

Hearing their hero denounce venal officials or injustice not only provided a measure of solace but also raised hopes that better times lay ahead. This was the second respect in which Chibás surpassed fellow politicians. His weekly broadcast consistently garnered an audience several times greater than any other political offering. A survey conducted by the Cuban Advertisers' Association measuring listeners in Havana and its outskirts recorded a 45 percent share for Eddy's show in June of 1947, the highest rating for any program in the island's history, with an estimated 550,000 listeners.[7] This was more than double the usual number, which Chibás took as a sign that "the people are with the opposition."[8] However, the show soon returned to its previous levels, which were still among the highest in Cuba. Between January 11 and January 31, 1948, Eddy's show had a 22.22 percent share. The second-most popular commentator was Salvador García Agüero of the Communist station Mil Diez, with 9.75 percent. The third-place Auténtico program mustered only a 3.41 percent share. A subsequent survey, taken between March 5 and March 18, 1948, favored Chibás by an even wider margin. This time, his 21.35 percent rating was slightly lower but far outpaced García Agüero's 6.77 percent and the Auténticos' 5.65 percent. Moreover, Eddy's show was one of only three in Cuba that topped 20 percent during this period—the other two were radio soap operas.[9]

Well before his 8:00 p.m. broadcasts, throngs gathered to wait for Chibás at his apartment in Havana's Vedado district. When he appeared, the multitude would accompany him on foot to the studios of radio station CMQ. Invariably dressed in a suit and with a cigarette tucked between his fingers, he would chat with the crowd, which included friends, fellow politicos, and admirers. At the end of the six-block journey, a cadre of close associates or party members followed him inside and surrounded him as he addressed the country. In cities across Cuba, those without radios packed hotels or the homes of friends so they could listen. Those who inhabited rural areas sometimes walked several miles to the nearest radio. Filiberto Porven of Cortés, a village in Pinar del Río province, wrote Chibás to say that eight hundred people arrived at his house every Sunday to hear him and confessed that those present would applaud, "as if you were there in person."[10] After the twenty-five-minute broadcast, Chibás would exit and once again encounter a group lingering, eager to speak with him about the broadcast on the way back to his flat. Throughout Cuba, adherents addressed letters to Chibás later that evening or the next day. Some opted for telegrams. Many of these reflected the inchoate grammar of Cuba's humblest citizens. For instance, José Zamora of Manzanillo in Oriente province wrote, "*estamos escuchando su oracion todos los domingo donde nosotro i todo el pueblo cubano conose que es uste la unica esperanza de esta nación,*" (we listen to your speech every Sunday and we and the entire Cuban people know that you are the only hope of this nation).[11]

ORTODOXOS

Dedicated Chibás supporters, who expected him to one day save Cuba as its president, now had a new political home. On May 19, 1947, the fledgling party's national committee elected Chibás its president and twenty-three-year-old Luis Conte Agüero as secretary. The next order of business involved a name. Chibás sought the advice of Fernando Ortiz, Cuba's most renowned scholar and a friend of his late father. He had also hoped the sixty-six-year-old Ortiz would join the party, adding a patina of experience and wisdom to a group drenched in youth. Ortiz respectfully declined to sign up, claiming he was too elderly, but gladly offered his opinion. He counseled that the words *ortodoxo* and *revolución* should be avoided as the former lacked "emotional resonance" and the latter had been so abused by current politicians as to sound like a "synonym for criminality and impudence" to most Cubans.[12] In the end, these words were heeded but only partially. Leonardo Fernández Sánchez, a former student leader, proposed the new organization's name—Partido del Pueblo Cubano (Ortodoxos) or PPC (O). The freshly minted Cuban People's Party also required an insignia. This was resolved through a nationwide contest launched by Chibás during his radio show, which promised one hundred pesos to the winner. Eventually, the party opted for a convoluted design incorporating a palm tree, a peasant's hat, and a wheel with twenty gears on the outside (one for each year of revolutionary struggle, beginning in 1927) and six spokes on the inside (for each province in Cuba). However, the Ortodoxos quickly became known for an unofficial emblem, a broom, symbolizing their determination to sweep away graft.

Aside from Ortiz, Chibás courted other influential figures that could help swell PPC ranks. These included the popular Afro-Cuban pugilist Eligio Sardiñas, known as Kid Chocolate. A former junior lightweight, Sardiñas gained acclaim as the first Cuban to win a world boxing championship, in

1931. In a shrewd public relations gesture, the Ortodoxos renovated his old gym and utilized it as their headquarters. Sardiñas demonstrated his approval by attending the inaugural ceremony on June 2. Eddy noted that the venue would be used to train "our revolutionary muscles to knock out corruption and sleazy politicking."[13] In addition, Chibás enlisted Jorge Mañach, a founder of the anti-Machado ABC party and Batista's foreign minister in 1944. A Harvard graduate, philosophy professor, and literary critic, Mañach was Cuba's second leading public intellectual after Ortiz. In an open letter to Chibás, Mañach argued for unified opposition to the Auténticos along with a specific program, writing, "Denouncing the present is not sufficient; what's needed is a vision of the future."[14] He then listed the aspirations of Cubans in minute detail and urged Chibás to devise a plan to satisfy them.

> They want an end to incompetence and greedy public servants; they want the rule of law, that courts are respected and respectable, that someday a dishonest "big fish" goes to jail; they want indispensable public services which they've been asking for since the republic was founded: buses, schools, houses, land, hospitals, water; they want the education and health ministries to be administered transparently; they want a national bank and if possible a merchant marine; that our diplomats serve well and are well paid; that the state uses modern technology; they want true social justice rendered by the courts and commissions interested in equality and not a bribed oligarchy on one side and demagogic class warriors on the other; they want the political bureaucracy and useless army reduced to a minimum as both eat up too much of the national budget and decrease the State's ability to invest and each individual Cuban's ability to work for his own financial independence; they want the salaries of some public servants reduced so that such work is no longer an avenue to riches and that other state employees, conversely, be paid more as their services are essential and their earnings an embarrassment; they want a revision of the tax system; they want an honest police force that can put an end to gangsters and drugs; they want to modify the electoral system so that those who represent the people in office are effective rather than mercenary.[15]

"All this and a bit more," concluded Mañach "is what you need to clearly say."[16] Despite the difficult task at hand, he was optimistic.

Chibás also lured Federico Fernández Casas, a Republican senator and sugar magnate. He represented a sensible but potentially risky catch. For a party starting from scratch with limited funds, Fernández Casas offered credibility and deep pockets. In addition, his defection dealt a blow to the Auténticos, given their alliance with the Republicans. On the other hand, Fernández Casas possessed a reputation, like many landowners, for using shady means to evict peasants from their property and acquire it for themselves. Specifically, Fernández Casas had ousted Eusebio Maceo, a descendant of Cuba's most revered independence war general. Chibás himself had exploded with indignation over this fact during his broadcast of May 21,

1946. Adding Fernández Casas to the party could potentially damage its image among small farmers or rural dwellers. At the same time, Fernández Casas had committed himself to agrarian reform—advocating small landownership. Chibás allowed that while he and Fernández Casas had strongly disagreed in the past, the Republican senator's political behavior had always been "transparent and honest."[17] More importantly, Fernández Casas conducted a straw poll among the workers at his sugar mill and 868 out of 991 expressed a preference for Chibás. Sensing the Republicans would reap a popular backlash for supporting their coalition partners, Fernández Casas followed the prevailing winds.

Ortodoxo prospects were further enhanced on July 12, 1947, when the ABC party voted to dissolve itself and join Chibás. The ABC would not deliver a mother lode of votes—having gained a mere 66,607 in the 1944 elections.[18] Still, the group possessed bona fide revolutionary credentials from its days as a clandestine, anti-Machado terrorist society. Its incorporation was very much a feather in Eddy's cap. Then again, the persistent roll call of individuals, committees, and now parties that switched to the PPC, which by now had become a staple of Eddy's weekly broadcasts, created its own dilemma. The growing and ever more varied Ortodoxo constituency was a testament to his popularity but also a potential stumbling block. Shortly after the ABC party was brought on board, Chibás received a call from his longtime friend Ramón "Mongo" Miyar.[19] Miyar, who was secretary general of the University of Havana and a member of the Ortodoxo National Directorate, expressed alarm at the influence of the ABC's ex-president, Joaquín Martínez Sáenz. Chibás quickly reassured him, but this was by no means an isolated incident. In fact, the deepest fissure existed within the original grupo ortodoxo. Many of its leading figures, including Pelayo Cuervo Navarro, Agustín Cruz, and Millo Ochoa, favored political pacts. Chibás, along with Leonardo Fernández Sánchez, Luis Orlando Rodríguez, and Manuel Bisbé among others, adamantly opposed them.[20] He believed the Auténtico program had been watered down by its alliance with the Republicans. Further, Chibás held Cuba's "traditional" parties, the Liberals and Democrats, in contempt. Machado, after all, had been a Liberal, and the Democrats, heirs to the pre-1933 Conservative party, had collaborated with him.[21]

Regardless of the aversion felt by Chibás, pacts were a basic element of Cuban politics.[22] Had Grau's tenure been less disappointing, the Auténticos could reasonably have stood alone in the elections of 1948. However, Chibás had been the only high-ranking party member to advocate this option. For the grupo ortodoxo, shunning pacts would essentially mean renouncing legislative power. According to a 1943 electoral law, the nine senate seats allotted to each Cuban province were apportioned by coalition—with the winner gaining six and the second-place finisher taking three. Between March and May of 1947, while Chibás stood apart from the grupo ortodoxo, Cuervo

Navarro plotted a pragmatic course for the renegades. On March 23, 1947, *Bohemia* reported that he hoped to capture the grupo ortodoxo's leadership, formalize it as a new party, and "immediately" negotiate an alliance.[23] The benefit of this strategy was indisputable. Without Chibás, the grupo ortodoxo would lose substantial popularity. However, it could still attract sufficient voters to be relevant in 1948. Ochoa controlled the Auténtico party machinery in Oriente province and his brother, Eduardo "Guarro" Ochoa, was mayor of Holguín—a midsize town in the region. Cuervo Navarro was widely admired in his native Havana and would win plenty of votes there.[24] Given these circumstances, the new party could strike a deal guaranteeing spots on the opposition ticket for many of its prominent figures. Indeed, maintaining a senatorial contingent was a practical way to ensure the grupo ortodoxo could continue promoting a more ethical and constitutional brand of Cuban politics.[25]

When Chibás decided to leave the Auténtico fold in May of 1947, this boosted both the new party's prospects and its isolationist faction. The doubling of Eddy's radio show rating and seemingly limitless possibilities of the Ortodoxos as they added prestigious figures from all walks of Cuban society soothed but did not eliminate friction between the two camps. Chibás himself maintained cordial relations with Cuervo Navarro, who regularly spoke as a guest during his broadcasts, and other like-minded Ortodoxos, such as Agustín Cruz. The same did not always hold among the party faithful, especially those ardently devoted to Chibás. Hence, Pastorita Núñez remembered Millo Ochoa with contempt as belonging to the PPC's "political portion" and Cruz as someone who "was mainly interested in winning."[26] In the same vein, during a meeting of the Ortodoxo organizing committee, Pelayo Cuervo Navarro chastised an overzealous young devotee, saying, "We are building a political party, not a Jacobin sect." Another of the youthful attendees replied that if they were interested in "moderate language," they could join the Democrats or Liberals.[27] Nevertheless, Ortodoxo unity was buoyed by the party's momentum along with continued Auténtico mismanagement and scandals.

AN IDOL OF MUD

On May 18, 1947, the archbishop of Havana, Cardinal Manuel Arteaga, condemned Cuba's black market during his homily and deemed those who monopolized or speculated in basic goods to be "doubly criminal."[28] In doing so, he served as an unwitting warm-up act to Chibás, who inaugurated the Ortodoxo party later that evening and proclaimed it a bulwark against this sort of tawdry profiteering. The cardinal's rebuke also stung administration officials who continued to deny the black market's existence and dismissed protests against price gouging organized by leftists as Marxist funny business. Another embarrassment arrived in early June, when the so-called Capitolio diamond mysteriously appeared on President Grau's desk more than fourteen months after having been stolen. The jewel had originally been set in the floor of the Capitol's Salon de Pasos Perdidos (Hall of Lost Steps) and marked point zero for determining distances to all parts of Cuba. Since vanishing on March 25, 1946, it had simultaneously caused a sensation and vexed Havana's notoriously incompetent police. The diamond's sudden resurfacing, without apparent explanation, incubated all manner of conspiracy theories. A persistent rumor was that José Manuel Alemán paid 5,000 pesos for the gem and stealthily placed it in Grau's office.[29] Conversely, the cartoonist José Roseñada forsook hearsay in favor of outright mockery. His drawing showed a man reading the headline "Capitolio Diamond Returned to Grau" and laughing uncontrollably.[30]

During his June 8 radio show, Chibás noted that "other stolen objects . . . may appear on Grau's desk but what will not return is the faith of the Cuban people."[31] He also accused César Casas of "clandestinely" running the commerce ministry despite the senate's no-confidence vote.[32] Eddy's foremost concern, however, was the increasingly acrimonious relationship between himself and his former mentor. "Never," he told his audience, "has any political leader in our country had such a loyal and disinterested supporter as I was for Dr. Grau San Martín. All Cuba has been a witness to this."[33] Even so, continued Chibás,

> Little by little, day by day, he who for 20 years was the living symbol of our ideals was becoming converted before my very eyes into an idol of mud. What a profound tragedy I've had to live through during the past few months! Long sleepless nights assaulted by doubts in which my conscience struggled with the factual evidence! Nevertheless, faced with illegal dealings of all kinds perpetrated by the government, faced with the reelection campaign, faced with the gigantic fraud that Grau has represented both for the revolution and the Cuban people, I felt an enormous disappointment that easily overshadowed my original devotion.[34]

Certainly, none of this was news. The wrinkle was that Grau had decided to retaliate against Eddy's accusations by resorting to dirty tricks. Specifically, a man appeared who claimed to possess a letter in Eddy's handwriting inciting him and others to throw stones during a session of Cuba's chamber of representatives in 1945. This story, which appeared in many Havana dailies, represented an attempt to remind Cubans why Chibás was unfit for high office. He was El Loco, an impulsive firebrand who could not be trusted. Chibás assured his listeners he had never corresponded with the man and dared the president to make the letter public. He also deemed the campaign against him "the vilest ever waged against someone in our country in its forty years as a republic."[35] Rhetoric of this sort energized Eddy's unconditional supporters, who allowed their leader was crazy but only as an honest politician among thieves and a truth teller among slanderers.

In mid-June, Grau reappointed José Manuel Alemán as education minister. Writing for *Bohemia*, Enrique de la Osa noted the "all powerful" Alemán was also sure to emerge as a top Auténtico leader during party reorganizations in October and might even snatch the presidential nomination.[36] In any event, Grau's decision surprised no one, least of all Chibás, who opined during his June 22 broadcast that such "arbitrary conduct" was now typical.[37] For instance, Grau's preference for presidential decrees over congressional laws debilitated the very institutions he had helped create seven years earlier. Moving on, Chibás warned, "the most gigantic 'affaire' ever realized in Cuba's 45 years as a republic" was afoot and must be stopped.[38] This involved a reputed price manipulation on the three hundred thousand tons of sugar Cuba was annually authorized to sell outside the United States market. Theoretically, the difference between the price paid by the Cuban government for homegrown sugar and the amount it earned on the open market was allotted for socially useful projects such as roads or rural schools. In an echo of the barter deal scandal of 1945, Chibás charged that Carlos Prío, Alberto Inocente Álvarez, and José Manuel Casanova were planning to inflate the price of refining one hundred thousand tons of sugar destined for Latin America and pocket a hefty profit. The remaining two hundred thousand tons would be sold to a firm in New York with ties to the government. This company intended to sell its sugar on the black market at a fabulous gain. In all, Chibás estimated the Cuban people would be cheated out of 22 million pesos. The basis for this accusation was a piece in the June 22 edition of *Bohemia* outlining the scheme and how it could be prevented. However, the article made no mention of specific ringleaders. This was Eddy's doing. Álvarez and Casanova were logical suspects as both had been implicated in the 1945 brouhaha involving overseas sugar sales. His judgment was also skewed by personal dislike for Casanova, a Liberal senator and sugar tycoon who headed the Cuban Sugar Stabilization Institute.

Conversely, Carlos Prío had once been a friend and fellow revolutionary, lending a particular bitterness to their falling out. Chibás knew Prío had become enormously wealthy since entering politics. Skimming cash off the sugar differential was one of many lucrative avenues open to him.[39] The day after Eddy's broadcast, Prío accused him of slander and demanded a duel to satisfy his honor. Casanova also chimed in, calling him "the clown of scandal."[40] Chibás responded to the former in a four-page letter typed on senate stationery. He pronounced himself satisfied at having "rendered a service to my country" and asked Prío why he had "systematically opposed" efforts in the senate to investigate "irregularities" in the government's overseas sugar sales.[41] Chibás found it "strange" that every time the matter was raised in the upper chamber, Prío withdrew Auténtico senators loyal to the administration—thereby ensuring the lack of a quorum.[42] He further challenged Prío to demand an inquiry into their respective finances. Chibás claimed it would prove "very interesting," especially as Prío had neglected to declare the extent of his wealth upon accepting a position in Grau's cabinet as all Auténticos had promised.[43] In any event, this was no mere political disagreement, but rather a very personal and rancorous quarrel. Moreover, the feud was part of a wider battle encompassing Prío's older brother Paco as well, who was also a senator from Pinar del Río province. On April 19, Paco Prío had snuck up behind Chibás in the Capitolio and punched him in the neck. This led to a brawl shortly thereafter in the senate and a saber duel on April 27 in the Capitolio. Chibás, who prepared for the encounter by practicing with a swordsman at the University of Havana, wounded his foe twice before an audience of Cuban legislators, after which a doctor stopped the duel.[44] As with Carlos Prío, the crux of their dispute involved venality. Among other things, Chibás had accused Paco Prío of links to the Italian American mobster Lucky Luciano. In fact, when Paco had hit Chibás, he shouted, "Lucky Luciano sends you this!"[45] As for Carlos Prío, he and Chibás dueled in the Sala de Armas on July 13. The minister of labor avenged his brother by wounding Chibás on the right elbow and cheekbone, perhaps because Eddy could not find the time to train beforehand.

As Chibás persisted with his strategy of needling Auténtico leaders, the PPC welcomed two more high-profile defections. Roberto Agramonte, Eddy's cousin and Cuba's ambassador to Mexico, resigned his post in late July and enrolled the following month. He was joined by Aurelio Álvarez de la Vega, a senator from Camagüey province, veteran of the island's independence war and erstwhile member of the grupo ortodoxo. Meanwhile, Chibás and Pelayo Cuervo Navarro supervised the final stages of the party's legal certification process with the Superior Electoral Tribunal.[46] With official status looming, Chibás planned a grand ceremony in Havana's Parque Central to formally inaugurate the party. Eddy, who possessed a keen eye for symbolism, initially chose August 12—the anniversary of Machado's resignation. However, a torrential downpour foiled this design. August 30 was then agreed upon until the Ortodoxos realized this was the feast day of Saint Raymond, the president's namesake. To celebrate the event then would obviously bode poorly. Thus, the occasion was slated for Sunday, September 7—the eve of the feast day of the Virgen de la Caridad, Cuba's patron saint. When the date arrived, Chibás telephoned the National Observatory and inquired whether rain was in the forecast. He was informed that a squall could never be ruled out during the island's rainy season. Chibás, who saw the handiwork of Grau or inciso K in every crack and crevice, wondered if they were trying to addle him with a phony weather advisory. In the end, there was no thunderstorm but rather a constant drizzle that desisted just before the gathering started at 9:00 p.m. Chibás told the crowd he always knew the Virgen de la Caridad would clear the skies on behalf of the Cuban People's Party. The meeting, which lasted five hours, featured a parade of speakers—including the party's newest catch, Aurelio Álvarez. He quickly established his Ortodoxo bona fides, saying he hoped the nation's gangsters would not be offended by his references to "government gangsters" because even among the former a few "decent people" could be found.[47] Not to be outdone, Chibás, speaking in the wee hours of the morning, offered to renounce his aspiration for the presidency if Grau would accuse his "delinquent functionaries" before Cuba's courts.[48]

ORFILA

Eight days later, serendipity bestowed a timely and unexpected bounty. At 3:00 p.m. on September 15, a massive gunfight broke out in the Havana suburb of Marianao. The point of contention was an arrest warrant served by Mario Salabarría, head of the Bureau of Special Investigations, to Emilio Tro, director of the National Police Academy. Tro was wanted for the murder three days earlier of Raúl Ávila, the health ministry chief of police. Even more so than Cuban politics, the island's myriad police forces were a repository of enmities and violent rivalries. This was because Grau had filled their ranks with members of the island's thuggish action groups as a reward for their help during his election campaign. Salabarría and Ávila, for example, were members of the Movimiento Socialista Revolucionario (MSR), which doubled as the personal army of Grau's pal Alemán. Tro, on the other hand, founded the Unión Insurreccional Revolucionaria (UIR) in 1946 after serving in the United States military during World War II—where he earned a Purple Heart. While Salabarría and Tro were friends of the president, they detested each other. Tro accused Salabarría of profiting from the black market. Salabarría viewed Tro as an upstart. On September 5, assailants had fired sixty bullets into Tro's automobile. The UIR leader was unhurt, as he had not been inside. Shortly thereafter, Ávila was shot to death in a Vedado bodega. Afterward, Ávila's widow testified that Tro and Luis Padierne, another UIR member, had appeared armed on her doorstep in search of her husband. As a result, an arrest warrant for Tro was issued on September 13.

Two days later, Salabarría crammed a pair of cars with his men and headed toward the home of Antonio Morín Dopico, the Marianao police chief—who lived in a prosperous district known as Orfila. Tro, Padierne, and a few other UIR deputies had arrived there earlier for lunch. As Salabarría's group approached, one of the cars crossed in front of the house and began firing. Thus began a pitched battle in which Salabarría's men sprayed Dopico's residence with machine-gun fire and those inside responded with their own weapons, hoping to buy time until help could be located. The Cuban public was aware of this ghastly incident from the beginning thanks to Germán Pinelli, a well-known reporter and radio announcer, who provided listeners with a live account from the scene. In addition, the cameraman Eduardo "Guayo" Hernández of Cuba's Noticiero Nacional recorded everything on film. Two hours into the clash, a UIR contingent secured an audience with Paulina Alsina, Grau's influential sister-in-law, who told them the president had ordered the army to intervene. Grau himself was not receiving visitors owing to an illness that had left him feverish and twenty pounds lighter than usual. Tro also telephoned another UIR lieutenant, instructing him to visit the Columbia military barracks on Havana's outskirts and request assistance. This led to the dispatch of a mechanized troop unit to the area. General Ruperto Cabrera promptly gave those inside ten minutes to hand themselves over and pledged to safeguard their lives. Tro and his comrades rejected the offer, probably because Salabarría and his men remained present. After the house was bombarded with tear gas, figures appeared in the windows waving white cloths and shouting for the police to hold fire, as women and children would be exiting. Morín Dopico was the first to emerge, carrying his injured ten-month-old daughter. They were immediately whisked away to the military hospital. It was now approaching 6:00 p.m. and Cubans were riveted by this spectacle as they returned home from work or milled about their living rooms. The next to appear was Morín Dopico's pregnant wife, Aurora Soler Amor, accompanied by Tro. As hundreds of thousands listened intently, expecting a reasonable finale to an unreasonable situation, they were shocked to find the police had murdered first Mrs. Morín and then Tro, whose body was riddled with eighteen bullets. By day's end, Salabarría was under arrest, the military was in control of the police, and the Auténtico party's reputation was in tatters.

The following week, Grau was universally berated. Every major publication denounced the government and graphic photos of the dead were splashed across Cuba's newspapers and magazines. *El Mundo*,[49] one of Havana's most respected dailies, wrote:

> What has the president of the republic reaped with his ineffective behavior? Three years ago he was the popular idol, the smiling hope of a nation anxious for administrative honesty, a civilian government and the realization of the incomplete program genuinely drawn up in (the constitution of) 1940. Today, he contemplates unpopularity, he looks on as his powerful party has split, he must ponder the vibrant, admonitory voices raised against him in congress without a single member coming to his defense, he must confront how badly people react when they see his image during newsreels at the cinema and (ever since the events at Orfila) he should perceive how other forces are gaining popularity, ones in which the Cuban people previously never would have placed their faith.[50]

In the senate, Auténticos attempted to avoid a session devoted to Orfila by staying away en masse and hoping a quorum would not be reached. This strategy was thwarted by the party's coalition partner, the Republicans, who appeared in deference to public opinion. The first to speak was Pelayo Cuervo Navarro, the Ortodoxo senate delegation's recently designated leader. He claimed the previous day's events had "filled our society with panic" and underlined that Morín Dopico's wife, Tro, and the other four who lost their lives had been killed after handing themselves over.[51] At this point Chibás interrupted, waving a copy of *Información* with its pictures of the slain Mrs. Morín and her injured ten-month-old daughter, Miriam. He reiterated that the government was incapable of guaranteeing the safety of women and young children—both of whom had been respected "even during the worst epochs of terror in Cuba."[52] Eddy also accused Grau of fomenting chaos as a pretext for a coup that would perpetuate him in power. The Liberal senator Eduardo Suárez Rivas drew a round of applause among his peers and also in the visitor's gallery after declaring his party would never enter a pact promoted by the erstwhile doctor of physiology. In the chamber of representatives, Auténticos were dismayed to learn that one of their own was preparing to embarrass the party. Guillermo Ara, an Auténtico congressman from Manzanillo with links to UIR, told all who would listen that "I was there and saw everything. Those people were massacred after surrendering. They left with their hands in the air and were shot repeatedly."[53] In this case, however, the Auténticos achieved the dubious victory of preventing a quorum even as Ara's words were reprinted in the press.

On September 17, General Genovevo Pérez Dámera invited Havana's newspaper directors to view footage taken by Guayo Hernández. In doing so, the army chief known as El Gordo (Fatso) was making some calculated mischief. The day before, Interior Minister Alejo Cossío del Pino had issued a decree banning the film, which he deemed "a not very edifying spectacle."[54] Nonetheless, two Havana cinemas had briefly shown the movie before it was suppressed. With an eye toward his Sunday broadcast, Chibás had wangled a screening in the Columbia military barracks as a guest of Colonel Oscar Díaz, the military official investigating the affair. By the time Pérez Dámera convoked his audience of journalistic honchos, the film had ostensibly been prohibited. Nonetheless, he explained that he wanted them to see for themselves that Orfila had been an "assassination."[55] He judged Salabarría the prime culprit and revealed the purportedly honest police chief was hiding $14,000 in his shoes when he was arrested. Unlike the press or opposition politicians, Pérez Dámera did not believe the ordeal reflected poorly on the president. The thirty-seven-year-old general owed his spectacular rise to Grau and bore him no grudges.[56] Rather, he abhorred José Manuel Alemán, and Orfila provided an exquisite pretext to move against him. The education minister's links to MSR rendered his country estate fair game, and on September 20, troops arrived for a surprise inspection. Later on, Pérez Dámera invited reporters to examine the colossal stockpile of arms found there, which included enough bombs, machine guns, and .50-caliber bullets to fill thirteen trucks. Viewing this stash, an irreverent correspondent wondered whether "a single book or modest coloring pencil" had turned up.[57] In fact, Alemán had been collecting weapons for a clandestine expedition against the Dominican dictator Rafael Trujillo. Entrusted by Grau with planning and financing the venture, this represented yet another repository of the funds meant for Cuba's schoolchildren. In response to this newest outrage, the senate voted no confidence against Alemán on October 1—after which Grau named him minister without portfolio.

By then, Chibás had publicized the most gruesome portions of the proscribed Orfila tapes. He related that Tro had been murdered while trying to carry a wounded and very pregnant Mrs. Morín back into her house. Eddy then described how one of Salabarría's "jackals" approached the injured Mrs. Morín, placed his machine gun against her swollen belly, and pulled the trigger.[58] Chibás also seized upon the money hidden in Salabarría's footwear and asked, "How many pairs of shoes are needed to hide the millions of pesos robbed by functionaries of the present government, beginning with the president of the republic himself?"[59]

GROWING PAINS

Two days after the broadcast, Eddy's friend Ignacio Mendoza typed him a letter. Mendoza had been a bomb-making student revolutionary during the early 1930s, like Chibás and Carlos Prío. In 1932, he devised a parcel bomb that killed the police chief of Artemisa—a town thirty-three miles southwest of Havana.[60] Mendoza planned to blow up Machado as well, but the plot was foiled and he landed in jail. Currently, he was a broker specializing in the Cuban stock market and the New York Coffee and Sugar Exchange. He was also an Ortodoxo. As Chibás and the party reveled in its largest public relations victory to date, Mendoza warned against relying too heavily on scandal mongering. "You were perhaps the one who contributed most to clarifying the facts (regarding Orfila)," he wrote, "but that won't be enough in the future as your principal theme." He reminded Chibás that "sympathy for you is incalculable and the people consider you honorable, valiant and civic-minded but there are many doubts about your ability to govern and many point out that you have never occupied an executive post either in private business or public office." He thus urged Chibás to "demonstrate that you can organize a government."[61]

Eddy's most immediate challenge, however, would be the upcoming party reorganizations, scheduled between October 5 and October 19. By law,

Cuba's political entities were required to hold a registration drive every two years and enlist a minimum of fifty thousand members. In practice, the ritual represented a zealous competition to induct the largest possible number of supporters. Incumbency allowed the Auténticos to buy affiliations with government largesse or to enforce them among federal employees, who could be laid off for placing their lot with rivals. For this reason, they were expected to lead the field. At the same time, hopes were high among Ortodoxos for a strong showing. Many were encouraged by *Bohemia*'s projection that they would dispute second place with the Liberals. Nevertheless, the PPC's rudimentary political network suggested impending disappointment. The Ortodoxos had little or no presence in many parts of the island—especially rural areas. They were also periodically short of campaign materials. Thus, an Ortodoxo from Cienfuegos who wanted to publish Eddy's photo in a local magazine was informed that none were available. An adherent from Punta Alegre in Oriente province who requested party propaganda was similarly denied. Chibás could hardly have been shocked when a town councilman from Camagüey province conveyed that the local Ortodoxo effort was "in a state of disorganization" and that "our adversaries are taking advantage of the situation."[62] He added that Miguelito Suárez Fernández, the Auténtico senate president, had paid Ortodoxos in Santa Cruz del Sur to switch sides. In the town of Florida, the Auténtico mayor and congressmen were spending "immense quantities" of money and offering "hundreds" of education ministry jobs as inducements to join them. Chibás received similar reports from other areas. Two Ortodoxos from the sugar mill town of Coliseo in Matanzas province related that Chibás boasted "an extraordinary majority of sympathizers" in the area, but the party lacked a "natural organizer."[63] Blanca and María Rodríguez of Paradero Lugareño in Camagüey province wrote, "Many here in our town who sympathize with you and your candidacy have signed up with the Auténticos only because they are government employees and otherwise they would be fired."[64] In a similar vein, an Ortodoxo from the town of Manaquitas in Las Villas province disclosed that workers seeking jobs on a local highway construction project had to first hand over their identity cards.

As the affiliation period drew to a close, the Ortodoxos finished fifth among Cuba's political parties, with 164,705 members. Only the Communists signed up fewer members. Chibás was not at fault for the party's rudimentary organization or Auténtico chicanery, but his nonchalance about the process raised eyebrows. In a letter of October 6, Federico Fernández Casas expressed surprise that Chibás did not mention the registration drive during the previous day's broadcast. "I don't know how much importance you concede to the event," he stated, "but undoubtedly this is our first great test and we should render a supreme effort to prove before public opinion, even those who doubt us, our enormous popular backing."[65] Three weeks later, Chibás told listeners the registration drive was a "mere formality."[66] The goal had not been to compete for the most adherents but to engage the minimum fifty thousand as the rules demanded. An all-out attempt would have diverted the party's energies from other objectives. He had insisted that Ortodoxo legislators remain in Havana and attend congressional sessions, thereby demonstrating their commitment to constituents, unlike the chronically absent politicians of other parties.[67] Chibás also believed the PPC's internal structures required further refinement and attention, which could not be accomplished if its leading figures were scattered throughout the island in pursuit of memberships.

The registration drive galvanized the opposing Ortodoxo camps as never before. Rumors swirled about possible defections—including Pelayo Cuervo Navarro. Millo Ochoa informed the press that prospective coalition partners must back Chibás for president. However, this was impractical given the party's unimpressive numbers. Factional tempers flared during a conference of the PPC National Directorate on October 29 when Aurelio Álvarez urged the party to join a unified opposition and Rafael García Bárcena, the philosopher and University of Havana professor, pushed for autonomy. Chibás attempted to soothe the party's divisions. During his broadcast of November 9, references to Ortodoxo independence were conspicuously absent. In their stead, Chibás repeatedly stressed "unity."[68] However, anti-pact zealots quickly ignited another furor. Believing a commission of PPC lawmakers charged with resolving internal disagreements was a vehicle for deal making, they sent a letter to Chibás accusing him (and them) of behaving like traditional politicians and violating the party's constitution. Shortly thereafter, the commission directed a letter to Chibás signaling its intent to resign in the face of what they considered unfair attacks. Yet again, an effort was devised to bring the two sides together. Represented by Cuervo Navarro, Ochoa, and Agustín Cruz, among others, the pact-friendly group met with so-called activists, including Leonardo Fernández Sánchez, Luis Orlando Rodríguez, and Rafael García Bárcena, on November 21. They were set to gather the next day, but Chibás asked them to cancel, as he was busy composing his radio address.[69] This turned out to be an appeal for independence, in which Chibás argued that necessary "reforms" would be diluted by pact-inspired "transactions." He deemed the PPC's internal squabbles "very natural" for a party that was democratic by nature and counted a wide base of support. These words had barely left his lips when he undermined them with a strident rallying call. "Let the sellouts and weak spirits go!" he shouted. "The strong will stay and continue to fight!"[70] Understandably, the Ortodoxo lawmakers were rankled by the name-calling and irked by their leader's failure to consult with them beforehand. Some also wondered whether he was fit to be party president.

On December 4, Chibás convened the Ortodoxo legislators and pleaded his case behind closed doors. If the party stood apart, he claimed, it could "capitalize on the neutral masses" frustrated by the Auténticos and pessimistic regarding the opposition. In a three-way race, those who were most deserving of public confidence would be victorious.[71] This reasoning convinced no one. Chibás was reminded that on other occasions he had agreed to discuss deals with certain opposition parties. He allowed this was true but said he had done so only to please party members whom he respected and considered friends. "At bottom," he confessed, "I never agreed with it."[72] Two days later, Cuervo Navarro and Joaquín Martínez Sáenz published a public response on behalf of the PPC's senators and congressmen. One section advanced their view that independence played into the government's hands. "Without an integrated national force capable of defeating Grauism at the ballot box," they wrote, "all the eagerness for renewal demanded by public opinion would be frustrated and the present chaotic situation accentuated with tragic consequences for the country."[73] As for Chibás, they opined that "we oppose all personalist or dogmatic postures and maintain, with a profoundly democratic spirit, that only the party's national assemblies, elected with the votes of its members, can determine the political line in accordance with majority opinion."[74]

The atmosphere was further poisoned as delegates to the municipal assemblies weighed competing party platforms. In Havana, the epicenter of Ortodoxo popularity and home turf to Cuervo Navarro and Chibás, allegations of dirty tricks and bribery were bandied about on both sides. The final vote, taken on December 14, favored independence, but Cuervo Navarro vowed to contest the outcome in court. He also offered an exceedingly bitter statement to the press saying, "If Chibás were a statesman, it would be worthwhile to defend the idea of political independence to the end. But he is nothing more than a rabble-rouser, a demagogue incapable of realizing anything constructive. I would never dare propose him as the opposition candidate for president."[75] The following week, Cuervo Navarro accused Chibás of hypocrisy. Speaking to a *Bohemia* reporter, he divulged that the Ortodoxo leader's stubbornness on the issue of pacts was of recent vintage. When the first party documents were drafted, the original PPC position called for "no pacts of any type." According to Cuervo Navarro, he brought this to Eddy's attention, and they discussed its potential ramifications. He then claimed Chibás and his ally Manuel Bisbé agreed to modify the statement to "pacts lacking in ideology."[76] In reality, this was hardly a smoking gun. Eddy had always spoken of "pacts lacking in ideology" to denigrate electoral "understandings" rather than to leave the door open for them. Cuervo Navarro's interview had less to do with the charges leveled than the very public and highly spiteful manner in which he and Chibás had fallen out. A month earlier, Cuervo Navarro had signed a letter to Chibás, "your affectionate companion and friend."[77] Now, Chibás hurled barbs at him on the radio, and Cuervo Navarro replied with insults in the press.

While this carried on, Chibás attended the provincial assembly in Camagüey province on December 28. The event took place in the home of Ramón Pereda Pulgares, the popular doctor and Chibás ally who had died in a tragic automobile accident seven months earlier.[78] Almost immediately, Eddy clashed with the pact-friendly Aurelio Álvarez. Early on, Chibás asked permission to speak about the party's "internal situation."[79] Álvarez, whose stentorian voice was amplified by a megaphone, interrupted him, saying, "I would like to remind Senator Chibás that the purpose of this meeting is only to elect the local executive committee and designate delegates to the National Assembly."

"Don't forget," responded Chibás, "that I'm president of the party and you are my delegate."

"Right now, I'm not your delegate," snapped Álvarez. "I'm the master of ceremonies."[80]

Chibás relented after this exchange but only temporarily. He asked a sympathetic delegate to request a one-hour recess, which was eventually granted. As the proceedings paused, Chibás attempted to address the assembly. Once again, Álvarez objected. Ignoring him, Chibás stood on a chair and began pontificating. This ignited a fistfight among the opposing factions. During the ensuing melee, gunshots were fired—one of which nearly hit Chibás in the head. The Ortodoxo leader promptly jumped on a nearby table, pointed to his chest, and exclaimed, "Shoot me in the heart—the Ortodoxos need a martyr!"[81] Having shocked the crowd into silence, Chibás finished speaking even as the smell of gunpowder wafted through the air. Afterward, the Camagüey senator José Enrique Bringuier addressed the crowd. Asserting that "the Ortodoxos without Chibás are a fortress without a flag," he offered his ten delegates in favor of the independent line.[82] These votes would have ensured victory for the pro-Chibás side, but the Ortodoxo leader rejected them, much to the astonishment of Aurelio Álvarez and his supporters. Admitting to "moral scruples," Chibás claimed he preferred to lose the province to deal makers within the PPC rather than relying on a deal himself. The *Bohemia* reporter present noted that Chibás had repudiated a "pact lacking in ideology" even within his own party.[83]

Chibás was now in the awkward position of being marginalized within the party he had recently founded. Nearly every Ortodoxo who held elective office opposed him and his momentum, which had crested following the Orfila massacre, had all but dissipated. Unable to sidestep Cuba's established political rules, Chibás had instead endangered his position as Ortodoxo president. In the coming months, he would continue to gain popularity by capitalizing on Auténtico missteps and inciting his supporters over the radio.

Chapter Three

"No One Respects the Constitution"

On January 4, 1948, *Bohemia* published an opinion poll on the attitudes of Cubans toward past and present leaders. One query asked residents of Las Villas province to name the best and worst president in the island's history. Ramón Grau San Martín topped the list as Cuba's greatest chief executive, with 36 percent. However, many factors tempered this seeming endorsement of the ex-physiology professor. For one thing, 17 percent fingered him as the nation's poorest president, more than Fulgencio Batista and second only to Gerardo Machado. In addition, among Cubans in their twenties and thirties, Grau was the only president they had known who never ruled as a dictator, strongman, or figurehead. Another possible indictment of Grau was the fact that Tomás Estrada Palma, elected as Cuba's first president in 1902, was deemed the best ever by 13 percent of respondents. Obviously, few Cubans remembered Estrada Palma's term, but his reputation for probity was apparently very appealing. Grau's tenure was also impugned by a question asked in four of the island's six provinces, namely whether Cubans intended to vote for the Auténtico coalition or an opposition candidate in the June elections. Respondents chose the latter in Havana, Oriente, and Las Villas—the country's three most populous provinces. Furthermore, in Havana, 36 percent said they would vote for the opposition, against only 19 percent who would vote for the government. At the same time, between 18 and 20 percent of the respondents confessed to being undecided.[1]

Bohemia was owned by Eddy's former schoolmate, Miguel Ángel Quevedo.[2] He received an advance copy every Thursday, a day before the magazine reached subscribers or newsstands. Chibás assuredly perused these figures with interest as they suggested a united opposition could defeat the government. They may have inspired his self-described "master stroke" three days later in which he proposed to back a candidate without links to traditional parties (i.e., the Liberals or Democrats) if that person counted the support of Cuba's "neutral masses."[3] The man Chibás had in mind was Miguel Coyula, a respected veteran of Cuba's independence war who was free of party ties and served as editor of the Havana daily *El Mundo*. Eddy's timing was also influenced by knowledge of a looming agreement between the Liberals and Ortodoxo legislators. Now that Chibás lacked the delegates for independence at the upcoming PPC national assembly, his primary goal was to ensure no bargains were struck with Liberals or Democrats. Regardless, PPC lawmakers pursued contacts with members of the opposition. Prior to the national assembly, Millo Ochoa, José Manuel Gutiérrez, and Emeterio Santovenia met traditional party representatives in the home of Liberal senator Eduardo Suárez Rivas. As they gathered, Gutiérrez (an ex-Liberal himself) argued that any alliance must offer a detailed plan, including guarantees that Cuba's legislature be allowed to function as envisioned under the 1940 constitution. Later on, Gutiérrez mused before a group of friends from his home province of Matanzas that the PPC's "great tragedy" involved having a leader capable of uniting the opposition but who resolutely eschewed "reasonable conduct." "It's almost as if [Chibás] were under the influence of a pernicious being!" he exclaimed.[4] Jorge Mañach, in his weekly *Bohemia* column, offered a more nuanced critique. "The grace and difficulty of politics," he counseled, "consists in knowing how to use impure elements of reality for the purest ends possible." He also asked acerbically if Chibás meant to "irradiate" his politics, whether all those who followed him would be "angels."[5]

On January 22, the Ortodoxo national assembly was convoked in the old ABC party headquarters in Havana.[6] Chibás entered the event serenely despite being outnumbered. Two days earlier, he had been given a powerful trump card when the PPC assembly from Havana ratified the independent line. This limited the possibilities of deal makers because, according to the Electoral Code of 1943, alliances required unanimous assent among a party's provincial assemblies. The pact-friendly faction nonetheless asserted itself, choosing Millo Ochoa to supplant Chibás as party president. During his address, Chibás urged followers not to be resentful. He also cautioned against interfering with the assembly, especially as nothing of substance had been decided yet. On the other hand, Chibás warned that if the PPC attempted to reach an understanding with traditional parties, he and his adherents would "denounce the traitors."[7] Predictably, news of Eddy's diminished position was the subject of much speculation. Alejo Cossío del Pino, the Auténtico legislator and former interior minister, deemed him "alone" and "defeated."[8] His Communist colleague, Blas Roca, thought otherwise. He replied:

Chibás will always win. You will see why. 'Eddy' is popular for two reasons: his invariable attack against administrative immorality and his disgust, no less constant, with political crimes. He can never resort to old politics in order to retain his senate seat, something he doesn't really need anyway. Were he to do such a thing, he would lose his place in history. Whether the government or the opposition triumphs in the next elections, Chibás's position remains the same. Regardless of which Auténtico candidate claims the legacy of shady deals and errors of the present regime, he will have 'Eddy' as an incorruptible critic. If Núñez Portuondo (the Liberal party candidate) is elected at the head of a coalition, the same thing will happen because they are parties based on money and compromises directed not by the men who lead them but by the system that keeps them in line. Embezzlement will continue and Chibás will fight it. He is, definitively, the inheritor of the mystique the people created for Grau and he will keep growing politically even though he won't return to the senate for its next term. Grau was never a senator and his popularity increased every year because he remained the living reserve of his opponents' errors.[9]

Cossío and Roca were speaking in the Capitolio's marble-encrusted Hall of Lost Steps. Aside from being congressmen, they knew each other from the time when their parties were coalition partners. The Communists formed part of the Auténtico-Republican congressional alliance between November 1945 and September 1947.[10] This had been a quintessential "pact lacking in ideology" meant to build a legislative majority. When the deal no longer served Grau's interests, he authorized a campaign to purge the Communists from positions of influence.[11] Thus, Carlos Prío, his red-baiting labor secretary, helped the Auténticos seize control of the Confederación de Trabajadores Cubanos (Confederation of Cuban Workers). This umbrella organization of the island's unions had been Communist led since its inception in 1939.[12] The loss was compounded when Prío briefly shut down the Communist newspaper *Hoy* and its radio station Mil Diez in response to the party's calls for strikes and protests. Arguably, the worst was yet to come. On the same afternoon Chibás was dethroned in Havana, the Communist legislator Jesús Menéndez was shot to death by an army captain in Manzanillo. This incident had been the initial focus of Cossío and Roca's conversation in the Capitolio—where the deceased's coffin was publicly displayed on January 25.

In addition to being a congressman, the thirty-six-year-old Menéndez had also directed the National Federation of Sugar Workers. This union competed for membership and prestige with Auténtico sugar worker unions run by Emilio Surí Castillo. Before being killed, Menéndez had been coursing through Oriente province and negotiating on behalf of laborers at various sugar mills—a task of particular importance as January was the month when harvesting began. Menéndez had been joined in this effort by two companions, Paquito Rosales, a Communist member of Cuba's lower house, and Manuel Quesada, a union organizer. According to these two, they had been headed toward Bayamo where they hoped to convince a mill administrator to accept collective bargaining. The first leg of their journey involved an excursion to Manzanillo, during which they were approached by Captain Joaquín Casillas Dupuy. As the train neared the station, Casillas informed Menéndez and Quesada of his intent to detain them pending an investigation over whether they had broken the law. When Menéndez reminded him that he enjoyed parliamentary immunity as guaranteed by the constitution, the captain shouted, "Let the chamber protest if I violate your parliamentary immunity and if I violate the constitution, I do so under my responsibility! Regardless, I'm taking you in dead or alive!"[13] Shortly thereafter, the train halted. Before exiting, Menéndez reiterated that he was not subject to arrest and would thus not accompany Casillas to the military barracks. When Menéndez reached the platform, Casillas withdrew his pistol and shot him in the back. This version was strenuously denied by Army Chief Genovevo Pérez Dámera. Appearing before the press, he declared that Captain Casillas had been assaulted and opened fire in self-defense.[14] The general added that

> Mr. Menéndez, taking advantage of his congressional immunity and abusing it, both as a legislator and as a communist, was not only inciting sugar workers to strike in order to paralyze the harvest but was also encouraging the army and the police to rebel, arguing that they too were poorly paid.[15]

Despite such protestations, the weekly magazine *Carteles* reported that nearly every media outlet and political leader viewed Menéndez's death as an "assassination."[16] In his January 25 broadcast, Chibás denounced the killing as "an outrageous crime" and "a brutal and deliberate attack by the government against the working class, parliamentary immunity, the congress and constitutional order."[17]

At a minimum, the Menéndez killing represented yet another affront against Cuba's beleaguered rule of law, especially as Grau refused to discipline his army chief and Captain Casillas remained an officer in good standing.[18] Nor was this an isolated incident of the military overstepping its authority. Five days before Menéndez was shot, General Pérez Dámera issued a statement criticizing two recent rulings of the island's Superior Electoral Tribunal. These allowed the results of a political party's provincial and municipal assemblies to be appealed. Pérez Dámera claimed the process could result in public disorder and warned the military would remain alert against anyone who "tries to mock the people's free expression."[19] To this, the Havana daily *El Siglo* issued a wry response in keeping with the views of many journalists.

> In our judgment, we believe the army chief has addressed something that is none of his business. It is said that General Pérez Dámera has given himself the airs of a referee and savior. He has built himself up as the supreme judge of the electoral process and has romantically taken on his shoulders the generous

task of saving us in case someone plots our political ruin. To this we reply, "Dear Lord, save us from the saviors."[20]

Sergio Carbó, director of the newspaper *Prensa Libre*, asserted that Pérez Dámera's remarks were aimed at Miguelito Suárez Fernández—the Auténtico presidential aspirant who was disputing the party's provincial assembly result in Camagüey.[21] Although Suárez Fernández had won the delegations in his native province of Las Villas and in Matanzas, Grau resented his periodic insubordination and opposed his efforts to win the party's nomination. Unlike Carlos Prío, who supported Grau's refusal to present his education and commerce ministers for interpellation in April of 1947, Suárez Fernández had resigned as senate president in protest. Grau had scant tolerance for defiance, preferring instead the sycophancy of Prío and José Manuel Alemán. Given Grau's opposition and control of the party, Suárez Fernández hoped to rely, as Chibás once had, on his popularity among the Auténtico rank and file. This was a remote prospect, as the Auténticos were no more respectful of their own party's constitutional structures than those of the nation. On January 25, the political comic strip, *El Reyecito Criollo* (The Little Cuban King) deftly lampooned the rivalry between Grau and Suárez Fernández. This serial appeared every week in *Bohemia* and satirized the president, who always appeared in regal garb. In the first frame, Suárez Fernández sneaks up behind Grau and yells "Uh!" startling him. However, the president responds by brandishing a pole topped by a life-size head of General Pérez Dámera and shouting "Uh!" back at Suárez Fernández, causing him to flee in fear.[22]

ANGLING FOR THE NOMINATION

Celebrated in late January, the Auténtico national assembly was a tightly scripted affair. Representatives from the pro–Suárez Fernández provinces of Las Villas and Matanzas were excluded. As the outcome was foreordained, delegates sipped liquor or soft drinks in a bodega across the street instead of showing their faces inside party headquarters—located on Fifth Street and Avenue A in Havana's district Vedado. When their presence was required, they appeared briefly, signed any necessary documents, and returned. After the proceedings concluded, a group was sent to the presidential palace to inform Grau he had been reelected as party president. While this result had no immediate consequences for Auténtico hopefuls, Carlos Prío and Pepe San Martín were the obvious beneficiaries. San Martín, the minister of public works, was widely considered the star of Grau's cabinet. Known affectionately as "Pepe Plazoleta" (Pepe Town Square) for the construction projects he had distributed evenly throughout Cuba, he also was lauded for being an honest public servant. Even Chibás considered him a "good functionary."[23]

San Martín also happened to be the president's cousin. This was a potentially decisive advantage in a country whose politics oozed with nepotism.

José Manuel Alemán lacked the glittering record of San Martín, the revolutionary credentials of Prío, and charisma of Suárez Fernández but was nonetheless convinced he could maneuver himself into Cuba's presidency. The Auténtico slush fund maven and current minister without portfolio was hardly an ideal candidate due to his fear of public speaking and scandalous management of Cuba's school system. On the other hand, within the last two years he had risen from obscurity to become a dominant figure in Cuba's largest political party. The distance between his present situation and the presidency must have seemed far shorter than the one he had already traveled. He thus summoned Republican senator Guillermo Alonso Pujol to one of his country estates for advice. Alemán confessed to his closest political ally a desire to "win the elections in any way possible, including with military backing."[24] However, army assistance was doubtful given the hostility of General Pérez Dámera. Further, the "monarch of inciso K" was hampered by an opinion poll that appeared on January 18 in which he finished a distant third as the hypothetical Auténtico candidate—trailing Núñez Portuondo by nearly twenty-two points and Chibás by six.[25] The same query showed San Martín, Prío, and Suárez Fernández to be far more competitive against the opposition. Alonso Pujol thus listened politely but without encouragement. Following a three-hour talk with Grau, Alemán withdrew his bid and declared himself for Prío.

While this development appeared to indicate a preference on Grau's part, the president continued to withhold his endorsement. Even as his term wound down, Grau seemed loath to step aside and reluctant to anoint a successor until the last possible moment. While the president's attitude vexed his party, Chibás was convinced something sinister was afoot. In a conversation with Raúl Menocal on February 9, he said, "It seems to me there won't be any elections. All the running around and discussions about pacts are a waste of time as Grau seems more inclined each day to remain in power through a *golpe de Estado*. I've been convinced of this for a year now."

"No!" gasped the Democratic leader. "Interrupting the constitutional rhythm would be terrible for the country!"

"Raúl, this doesn't alarm me," responded Chibás, his voice rising. "Not very long ago there was no constitutional rhythm in Cuba. No one respects the constitution. Grau violates it at every opportunity. I don't see why we fear such a false rhythm being broken. Let's not forget that our current government is merely disguised as a constitutional regime. The preferable thing would be for Grau to unmask himself finally."[26]

Menocal had originally called on Chibás to enlist his help in rallying the PPC behind Ricardo Núñez Portuondo. Ortodoxo *pactistas* had expressed doubts about the Liberal nominee, a noted surgeon and man of probity whose dour personality inspired scant popular enthusiasm. As a compromise, Millo Ochoa proposed a so-called equidistant candidate from outside the major opposition parties. The Liberals, however, were adamant in their backing of Núñez Portuondo. They had garnered 357,469 supporters during the party registration drive, first among all opposition parties, and claimed the right to lead any coalition. Menocal repeated this argument, adding that Núñez Portuondo was "a good person."[27] Chibás, who always possessed an exquisite sense of the national mood, said, "I believe the Cuban people are discontented, but if forced to choose between Núñez Portuondo and the government's candidate they will elect the latter, whomever it ends up being, because voters want to overcome the present rather than returning to the past."[28] Menocal chided Eddy for continuing to associate the Liberals with Machado's bygone era. However, Núñez Portuondo had been the tyrant's personal physician and represented an indisputable link to that epoch. Although he had never been implicated in any wrongdoing, his personal ties to Machado and the party's retention of some *machadista* elements would undoubtedly be an issue if he remained a candidate.[29]

The opposition's inability to settle on a contender gratified Miguelito Suárez Fernández, who founded the semi-independent Auténtico Reaffirmation Movement and offered to lead a so-called third front against the government. Despite fears that Suárez Fernández intended only to gain leverage within his own party, the Democrats and Ortodoxos were willing to listen.[30] Conversely, the Liberals held fast behind Núñez Portuondo and threatened to face Cuba's voters alone rather than abandon their leader.[31] This posture was almost certainly a bluff, as the Liberals were consummate pragmatists. They could gain nothing and would lose much by entering the election solo. With his enhanced bargaining power, Suárez Fernández visited Guillermo Alonso Pujol and José Manuel Alemán at the latter's residence in Alturas de Miramar—one of Havana's plushest neighborhoods. In a show of confident informality, the Republican leader and former education minister received their guest clad in pajamas. The portly Alonso Pujol went a step further, displaying his massive belly. Alemán informed the senate president he would soon issue a statement reiterating his support for Carlos Prío.[32] He would also urge Auténtico candidates aside from Prío and Suárez Fernández to withdraw, as these were the only two with delegates in the party's national assembly. Alemán was especially anxious to eliminate Pepe San Martín, whom he detested.[33] Suárez Fernández was fond of San Martín but disliked Prío and saw no reason why anyone should be "vetoed."[34] Further, Suárez Fernández boasted more delegates than any other Auténtico and concluded that such a strategy would only ensure his nomination. After an uncomfortable silence, Pujol asked the senate president to recommend a solution. "[T]here are many solutions you two can try," he said. "For example, a military coup."[35]

Alemán and Pujol objected, saying they had no such plans. Suárez Fernández speculated they might conspire to suspend the elections. Failing that, he dared them to run Prío on the Republican ticket and announced, "I would then look for another organization to nominate me and we would see who triumphs."[36] Before either could reply, Suárez Fernández pointed out yet another option. The Superior Electoral Tribunal was due to rule shortly on the Auténtico provincial assembly's disputed result in Camagüey. The senate president was confident he would win this appeal unless, of course, Alemán and Pujol exerted "very strong and very violent" pressure on the judges.[37] Once again, his hosts denied thinking anything of the sort. As the nearly five-hour meeting drew to a close, Suárez Fernández asked how Alemán planned to avoid prosecution for embezzlement in the event of a third front victory. "I have a million pesos to spend on a senate campaign," he said.

"José Manuel," quipped his guest. "A flight to Miami would be much cheaper."[38]

While Auténticos threatened each other in private, Ortodoxo factions feuded before Cuba's judges. On February 14, the Superior Electoral Tribunal annulled the PPC provincial assembly result in Havana. Pelayo Cuervo Navarro had brought this case before the court to dispute the victory of PPC isolationists in December. Citing a legal technicality, Cuervo Navarro argued the assembly was illegal because eight delegates had not been convoked.[39] However, as PPC party chief in Havana, Cuervo Navarro himself had been responsible for summoning them. Enrique de la Osa noted dryly that "Pelayo had appealed a result tampered with by Pelayo."[40] Seizing on this contradiction, Chibás subsequently filed a motion to remove Cuervo Navarro from his post for "negligence."[41] This request was unanimously approved, allowing Chibás to replace him with Manuel Bisbé. He thus gained a trusted friend and ideological ally in the party's upper reaches. Chibás, who was restless in both victory and defeat, did not savor this development for long. His attention was diverted forthwith by a column in *Prensa Libre* criticizing his juridical good fortune. Chibás spent hours every day combing through newspapers and magazines in search of material for his radio show. As one of Cuba's thinnest-skinned politicians, Chibás was also on the lookout for attacks so that he might reproach the director or retort with a letter to the editor. *Prensa Libre* was an unlikely source of disappointment as it was run by his friend Sergio Carbó and usually provided the most favorable coverage of any Havana daily. On February 20, Chibás composed a missive to Carbó conveying his dismay but also stating he was certain the article had appeared "without your consent."[42] Chibás defended his dismissal of Cuervo Navarro, claiming he acted to "fulfill my responsibility" and ensure the assembly functioned properly.[43] Given his well-known grudge against Cuervo Navarro, many were likely to view the move as tit for tat, although by the standards of Cuban politics this was gentle indeed.

Chibás also revealed his latest thinking and offered a preview of his Sunday broadcast. Lately, Chibás had become intrigued by the third-party candidacy of Henry Wallace in the United States.[44] He saw a parallel between the Progressives and Ortodoxos, both of which stood against "traditional and decrepit" parties in their respective countries.[45] Chibás was particularly encouraged by the recent triumph of a candidate supported by Wallace in a special election for a Bronx congressional seat. This event confounded US political pundits and delighted Chibás. He also noted that Wallace was being accused of dividing the Democrats much as he had been reproved for splitting the Auténticos.[46] Chibás drew two seemingly contradictory conclusions from this state of affairs. First, he asserted that "Wallace's victory" confirmed the need for a third front against Cuba's "old and corrupt politics."[47] Next, he pointed out that

> Wallace's party is the smallest in the United States and scarcely has any members but has won the election carrying more than 50 percent of the vote. The candidate of this party has obtained, by himself, more votes than all the others combined. The same will occur, in Cuba, with the PPC candidate.[48]

Chibás was clearly extrapolating a great deal from a single congressional race in a foreign country.[49] During his February 22 broadcast, he repeated this argument—leading the jilted Pelayo Cuervo Navarro to brand him a hypocrite. Luis Conte Agüero held that Chibás stood "at the most difficult crossroads of his life" after being supplanted as PPC president and realizing his faction was a minority within the party.[50] These were unwelcome setbacks, but neither was particularly devastating. Although Chibás no longer ruled the Ortodoxos, he remained the party's most prominent figure. As for his pact-shunning followers, their ranks would swell when frustration with the usual politics mounted. This pointed to the real dilemma facing Chibás. Nothing would boost his popularity more than another mistake-ridden, scandal-prone, or sleazy administration. At forty years old, Chibás was already a budding superstar. His greatest weakness was the lack of a political machine, but this could be remedied with time. On the other hand, he rued Cuba's likely presidential contenders. Similar to Grau, Carlos Prío had not respected the constitution. He was also corrupt and maintained links with gangsters. Ricardo Núñez Portuondo represented an even more distasteful Liberal restoration. Chibás, who was constantly aware of his "duty before history" to advance Cuba's revolution, felt the electorate deserved better.[51] He was also hedging his bets. If a third front were agreed upon and headed by a candidate without links to Grau or traditional parties, it would potentially be very popular. Chibás, who closely tracked his own poll ratings, was almost certainly loath to oppose such a venture. He could brush off the inevitable charges of flip-flopping from fellow politicos, as he knew the public would applaud.

Later that evening, the familiar sounds of Havana's three-week carnival were supplemented by more ominous but equally recognizable noises. Just after 11:00 p.m. as the last echoes of floats and merrymaking faded from the streets, UIR militants gunned down Manolo Castro and two companions. The thirty-seven-year-old Castro was Cuba's national sports director and an MSR member who was close to the now-infamous Mario Salabarría.[52] Castro had infuriated UIR leaders for allegedly investigating whether his friend might be freed from prison. Informed that he had been targeted for assassination, Castro visited the presidential palace and appealed to Grau's sister-in-law Paulina Alsina and Police Chief Enrique Hernández Nardo, who was a fellow MSR man. However, the latter was reluctant to become involved—perhaps due to the Orfila fiasco. Ironically, the one assailant captured by the authorities turned out to be Grau's godson, a twenty-year-old agronomy student named Gustavo Ortiz Fáez. He belonged to a UIR "tendency" at the University of Havana led by Fidel Castro and Justo Fuentes whose fierce rivals were devotees of Manolo Castro.[53] At the burial, the Auténtico politician René Moreno poignantly summed up the killing, saying, "We ourselves are responsible for this deed. We haven't learned how to unite in order to overcome, as good revolutionaries should. We are responsible for Manolo's death."[54]

Gang violence was a reminder of Auténtico foibles but offered no guarantee of an opposition victory. Millo Ochoa, the new PPC president, thus remained in pursuit of his elusive quarry—someone who could unite Cuba's so-called progressive forces. Among those he considered was Carlos Hevia, an Auténtico founder, respected engineer, and the first Cuban graduate of the United States Naval Academy. An industrious man and able administrator, Hevia also possessed first-rate revolutionary credentials. In 1931, he was among forty volunteers who stormed the city of Gibara in an ill-fated attempt to overthrow Machado. Hevia told Ochoa he would accept the third front nomination but urged him to speak first with Miguelito Suárez Fernández, whom he called the "operative factor" in Cuban politics.[55] Ochoa then revealed his plan to isolate the Liberals until they dropped Ricardo Núñez Portuondo. If their intransigence persisted, he claimed many Liberal senators would "peel away" toward the third front in order to save their seats.[56]

Hovering above these negotiations was yet another appeal pending before the Superior Electoral Tribunal. By a 4–1 vote the court had recently overturned a ruling from 1944 requiring a party's provincial assemblies to approve national coalition deals. On February 23, politicians of every stripe packed the Tribunal's O'Reilly Street headquarters in Old Havana.[57] Much to their disappointment, nothing was decided and a further delay was incurred when one of the judges fell ill for three days. Although the verdict promised consequences for all of Cuba's political parties, the Auténticos and Ortodoxos were especially on edge. A free hand for national assemblies would greatly benefit Grau and his chosen successor, Carlos Prío. With the provincial assemblies of Matanzas and Las Villas backing him, Suárez Fernández had been able to hold up the Auténtico-Republican alliance. Deprived of this trump card, he would lose leverage within the party. Speculation was rampant that a pro-government ruling was forthcoming. On February 26, a pessimistic Suárez Fernández met with Chibás and broached the possibility of another mass exodus toward the Ortodoxos. Contemplating an unfavorable outcome, the senate president's chief lieutenant in Matanzas, Diego Vicente Tejera, believed the *miguelistas* would bolt, saying, "We have no choice but to scorch the earth behind us."[58] Even as Chibás contemplated adding Suárez Fernández and his legion of supporters, he too was preoccupied by the court's impending decision. His control of the Havana assembly had until now assured him a veto against any pact he considered unacceptable. Conversely, Pelayo Cuervo Navarro and Joaquín Martínez Sáenz were eager to free themselves from their adversary's oversight. On February 27, the judges rendered a verdict that confounded expectations. The new "instruction" pertaining to unresolved pacts stated that if a coalition were stalled due to objections from a party's provincial assembly, the alliance's presidential and vice-presidential candidates would have to be substituted. Noting the revulsion of Carlos Prío when the verdict was read aloud, a *Bohemia* correspondent wrote that "a jar of cold water poured down the neck of ex–Prime Minister Prío Socarrás and his friends present with him wouldn't have caused as much disgust on their part."[59]

On February 29, Suárez Fernández met Chibás once again and confirmed his group's readiness to "consider" integrating a third front.[60] That evening, Chibás imbued the new project with his characteristic showmanship. After coining a catchy slogan ("third front against third floor"), he told listeners the alliance also required a "Cuban salute of victory."[61] This, he suggested, should feature an arm raised with three fingers pointing toward the sky. Despite such enthusiasm, the third front faced innumerable pitfalls. Foremost among these was the ambivalence of all parties involved. On March 7, Chibás and the Ortodoxo party chiefs of each province signed a declaration of "total identification" with the third front.[62] Nevertheless, many who argued for independence were poised to bolt if the party entered an alliance. Among the Democrats, a heated debate ensued over whether to join Suárez Fernández and the Ortodoxos. Although a majority approved, many top figures expressed reservations. Carlos Saladrigas, the party's presidential nominee in 1944, described Chibás and Suárez Fernández as demagogues who were "utterly crazy."[63] Antonio Martínez Fraga, a party chief from Las Villas, also objected to Suárez Fernández—citing his failure to officially abandon the Auténticos and past praise for Grau, which he called "an immorality."[64] These leaders and others, including ex–treasury secretary Jorge García Montes, advocated a pact with the Liberals. As for Suárez Fernández, his self-assured pose before Ortodoxo and Democrat delegations was a façade. As senate president, he was all too familiar with the potpourri of personalities that would need reconciling, and perhaps this was the basis for his qualms. Regardless of the reason, his discreet albeit noticeable contacts with Auténtico bosses were a sign of wavering commitment. Needless to say, the Democrats' pro-Liberal rumblings and Suárez Fernández's political philandering were embarrassing and potentially damaging to Chibás. His public endorsement of the third front now appeared either naïve or expedient. Hence, he and Manuel Bisbé issued a statement intended to bolster their reputations and serve warning to their unscrupulous potential allies.

> We absolutely disagree with any steps that will transform the original idea of the third front into a horrible caricature of the beautiful portrait we painted for the Cuban people in our previous radio broadcasts. The third front is (and cannot be other than) the political solution capable of liberating the Cuban people from robberies, crimes and other shameless acts of the present without backsliding toward the Machado era. For this reason we have passionately defended the third front with an uplifted spirit, declining all personal aspirations, but under no circumstances are we ready to renounce our long-standing principles and revolutionary convictions.[65]

While Chibás fulminated, his pact-friendly colleagues negotiated. On March 9, the Democratic railroad magnate José Miguel Tarafa invited leaders from his own party along with Ortodoxo and Liberal contingents to his country estate in Matanzas province. Addressing the Liberals, Senator Tarafa noted that Miguelito Suárez Fernández had offered to withdraw his candidacy in the name of third front unity and proposed Ricardo Núñez Portuondo follow suit. The Liberal chief responded with indignant disbelief. "Everyone here agrees I am a decent person; nevertheless, all of you want to veto my candidacy. I have spent 54 years in Cuban society and no one can accuse me of anything . . . I can't understand this attitude."[66] Núñez Portuondo, who did nothing during the meeting to debunk his reputation for petulance, proceeded to threaten those present that he would not tolerate being portrayed as intransigent in newspapers sympathetic to the Ortodoxos or Democrats. He then declared himself willing to stand down if everyone agreed that was best but warned "not a single Liberal" would vote for the third front without him heading the ticket.[67] Núñez Portuondo then moderated his position slightly, saying his replacement might be acceptable but only if the substitute were one of the provincial Liberal party bosses. This idea was quickly dismissed by Millo Ochoa, who said everyone had been gathered to discuss a "unified opposition" rather than "party questions."[68] To everyone's surprise, the Liberal congressman Prisciliano Piedra then suggested they nominate a figure without ties to any of the three parties. This plan so agitated Núñez Portuondo that other members of the Liberal delegation whisked their leader to Tarafa's office, where he could calm down in private. Shortly thereafter, the Liberals abandoned their host's sumptuous finca despite pleas to stay and smooth out a deal.

The political spotlight now shifted toward the Auténticos. On March 10, Education Minister Carlos de Arazoza met with José Manuel Alemán at his home in Miami Beach. The scourge of Cuba's schoolchildren whose sudden exile had inspired much speculation, he ordered his surrogate to lend Carlos Prío "whatever help he needs" for the imminent national assembly meeting.[69] This arrived around noon the next day in the form of trucks and busloads full of armed men. Another group that descended on Auténtico headquarters was Havana's pickpockets, who took advantage of the crowded conditions and constant jostling to relieve many delegates of their wallets. Among the victims was Arazoza himself, who shouted in displeasure after discovering his billfold, containing more than 800 pesos, had been filched. The assembly officially commenced at 3:00 p.m. with a so-called functional quorum of seventy-nine delegates. This number reflected the absence of representatives from Matanzas and Las Villas, provinces controlled by Miguelito Suárez Fernández. Even some of those nominally present were elsewhere. Alemán, the new Havana party boss, was in Florida. Grau, the Auténtico chief, preferred the presidential palace. Apart from petty thieves, no one had any reason to attend the convention, for everything had been decided in advance. Grau had not only chosen the nominee, he had leaked word of his decision to the crowds waiting outside the presidential palace before a vote had been taken across town.[70] Remarking on the farcical nature of the process, an Auténtico lawyer from Camagüey ruefully predicted that "whatever Miguelito loses here he'll gain back later before the Superior Electoral Tribunal."[71]

In reaction to Prío's nomination, third front negotiations were redoubled. On March 12, Democratic provincial bosses exchanged views at the home of Raúl Menocal and provisionally agreed to join the Ortodoxos and Suárez Fernández. That evening, the national assembly was convened and a rancorous debate ensued between third front partisans and those aiming for a Liberal-Democratic pact. When Antonio Martínez Fraga, the Democratic boss of Las Villas, told the convention he had tirelessly campaigned in his province for "this great Cuban" Ricardo Núñez Portuondo, a delegate from Havana rejoined, "It's true then what they say, that you have been promoting Liberal politics in Las Villas instead of doing so for your own party!"[72] Martínez Fraga was undeterred, and continued to defend his position for three and a half hours until his exasperated opponents submitted a motion limiting the amount of time for speeches to twenty minutes. A vote was finally taken at around 4:00 a.m., and those favoring the third front prevailed 71–31. That afternoon, the Ortodoxo national assembly voted 90–22 for the alliance—although Chibás and nearly all the Havana representatives dissented. Explaining this stance during subsequent negotiations with Democratic and miguelista representatives, Manuel Bisbé assured them the Havana delegation "with all due respect for the Democrats" was signaling its loyalty to the independent line and Chibás himself had been "enthusiastic" when the Democrats elected to join the third front.[73] Unfortunately, this latest round of talks was stalled over the issue of senate candidacies. Principally, the four Ortodoxo senators who were former ABC members demanded places on the third front ticket. Their insolence shocked all involved, but especially fellow Ortodoxos. Manuel Bisbé, the professor of Greek who admired Plato, wistfully told Chibás that "here in Cuba no one respects hierarchies." He then confessed, "I never imagined they would behave with such a lack of ethics."[74] Far less surprising but equally devastating was news that the implacable Martínez Fraga formally vetoed the alliance after promising not to do so.[75]

After these hiccups, Suárez Fernández dispatched four acolytes to meet with envoys of Carlos Prío. They promised a return to the Auténtico mainstream in exchange for four senate seats in Matanzas and Las Villas and one each in the island's other four provinces. Prío was initially amenable, although Grau expressed disapproval and warned him that Miguelito was "playing dirty."[76] Indeed, during a meeting on March 15, the senate president upped the ante. Besides the senate candidacies, he now requested assurances from Prío that key Auténtico figures would support his presidential candidacy in 1952.[77] While Prío mulled these new terms, Suárez Fernández abruptly changed course toward the third front once again. By now, Miguelito's flip-flopping had inspired near universal exasperation. "Let it be said," lamented *Bohemia*, "that politics in Cuba has ceased to be a public service and a patriotic duty and has converted itself into the most cynical game imaginable of ambition and greed."[78] The magazine added that a "decided, heroic gesture" was required on his part to maintain popular enthusiasm for the third front.[79] *Carteles* added that "in Cuba, politics is a veritable swamp and the majority of politicians are vermin splashing around in their element."[80] "Where," asked the editor, "are the sincere revolutionaries who struggled and risked their lives to overthrow the decadent regime of President Machado even as his innumerable successors have behaved even worse than he ever did?"[81]

Chibás, of course, was very much a revolutionary but he proved that sincerity in politics was a complicated matter. After all, he truly felt pacts were harmful, and yet for the past month he had vigorously promoted the third front. Because of the former belief, he voted against the Ortodoxo-Democratic alliance and refused all entreaties to run for a senate seat on the coalition ticket or participate in any third front commissions. At the same time, despite occasional hints to the contrary, Chibás never seriously threatened to undermine an agreement—at least while an acceptable figure like Suárez Fernández was the probable leader. When a reporter asked Miguelito about Chibás, he replied, "Eddy is a perfect gentleman!"[82] This was because Eddy, like his Ortodoxo colleague Roberto García Ibáñez, was convinced the third front was "a solution to the dilemma facing the people over whether to vote for Machado in the person of Núñez Portuondo or Grau in the person of Prío."[83] Even so, Chibás was beset by serious qualms. On March 16, he attended third front proceedings for the first time, and Suárez Fernández promptly begged his help in resolving "the Ortodoxo problem of Camagüey," a euphemism for Aurelio Álvarez. The tenacious veteran of Cuba's independence war had been pushing hard for the third front nomination of late. Álvarez had also not been shy about attacking Suárez Fernández for his dalliances with the Auténticos. Rather than refusing this appeal outright, Chibás fobbed it off onto Millo Ochoa. Later on, as a group of Ortodoxos discussed the distribution of senate candidacies, Chibás remarked to a friend that "no one here is thinking of the revolution."[84]

Nor was Chibás alone in this thought. Rafael García Bárcena, María Teresa Freyre de Andrade, Regla Peraza, and Pastorita Núñez had recently abandoned the PPC to protest its dealings with Suárez Fernández and the Democrats. All were close to Chibás and considered the possibility of returning if the Ortodoxos adopted an independent line. Like Chibás, García Bárcena had been a member of the 1927 Student Directorate and a militant Auténtico. He was also one of Cuba's most acclaimed public intellectuals. Aside from occasional contributions to *Bohemia*, he founded the *Revista Cubana de Filosofía* (Cuban Philosophical Review) and was an original member of the Cuban Philosophical Society. Along with Leonardo Fernández Sánchez, García Bárcena had been among the party's most outspoken critics of pacts. Freyre de Andrade and Peraza carried the surnames of well-known martyrs, which imbued their opposition to coalitions with great moral standing. Agents of Machado had murdered Freyre de Andrade's three brothers in 1932, while Peraza's father was a general in Cuba's independence war who was accidentally shot by one of his own men during an ambush. Pastorita, now twenty-seven years old, had known Chibás since she was fourteen and viewed him as a mentor much as he had once been Grau's protégé. Ironically, their decision to forsake the Ortodoxos coincided with a stream of defections by the sort of pact-friendly, office-seeking types they despised. Federico Fernández Casas jumped to the Liberals and secured a place on their party list in Oriente. Senator José Enrique Briguier, the ex-Democrat from Camagüey, followed suit after learning he would be left off the provincial ticket. Adriano Galano, a former grupo ortodoxo member, also renounced the PPC.

Certainly, party-hopping politicians were nothing new in Cuba. Around this time, in fact, the Liberals were also suffering losses. First, the senator and political journalist Ramón Vasconcelos joined the Auténticos.[85] In an interview with *Bohemia* reporters, he blamed his switch on Alfredo Hornedo—a party bigwig and director of the pro-Liberal daily *El País*—who had continually undermined him. Shortly thereafter, the Liberals were tempted with a bold offer courtesy of Carlos Prío. Although he was confident of winning the presidency, Prío worried a contentious congress would tie his hands. He thus proposed an "understanding" between the two parties that would ensure him a comfortable majority. In exchange, he was willing to concede three senate candidacies per province, three provincial governments, half his cabinet appointments, and a million pesos to pay for the electoral campaign. Emilio Núñez Portuondo, the Liberal nominee's brother and a senator from Las Villas, could barely contain his glee as he listened to Prío. However, Ricardo Núñez Portuondo still refused to retire his candidacy, adding sarcastically, "So what if they give us a million pesos? What am I going to do with that much money? I'd be so worried about losing it I wouldn't be able to sleep."[86] When Prío was informed, he and Guillermo Alonso Pujol attempted to force Núñez Portuondo to resign as party president by poaching Liberal lawmakers. They succeeded in peeling away Representative Prisciliano Piedra and Senator Ricardo Campanería, both of Matanzas province, but Núñez Portuondo retained control.

BULLYING THE JUDGES

Auténtico leaders remained supremely confident despite their failure to turn the Liberals. Earlier that month, Grau's former interior minister Alejo Cossío del Pino had reprised the party's thinking, saying, "We'll win the elections even though we'll have to inundate the island with millions of pesos."[87] Only a single fear nagged Auténtico self-assuredness, and this was the prospect of an unfavorable ruling by the Superior Electoral Tribunal.[88] Accordingly, Grau summoned the court's president, Francisco Llaca Argudín, for an interview on March 16. Reluctant to face the erstwhile physiology professor alone, Llaca Argudín brought along his four colleagues for what he presumed would be an intimidating session. He was not mistaken, as shortly after arriving at the presidential palace Grau's obese justice minister, Evelio Álvarez del Real, read aloud a long and menacing document. Specifically, the government charged that appeals before the court regarding provincial assemblies were causing delays and leading toward a "dangerous crisis" that threatened electoral guarantees.[89] More ominously, Álvarez alluded to the dissenting opinion of Judge Delio Silva that would have removed the veto of provincial assemblies and claimed, "today's difficulties could have been overcome" had it been approved.⁹⁰ Unexpectedly, Grau then reminded the judges of Decree 2665 issued in 1940 by Batista's front man, President Federico Laredo Brú, which effectively allowed him to nullify appeals before the court. At the time, this decree had been aimed against the opposition Auténticos—who had styled themselves as a party of virtue and legality before they lacked access to power. In any event, the implication was unmistakable, although Grau assured the judges that "of course, the situation nowadays is quite different."⁹¹ On March 19, the court received a letter from Carlos Prío and Guillermo Alonso Pujol. As luck would have it, these two lawyers preferred not to dwell on actual laws but on the "chaos" that would result from an "erroneous interpretation" by the Tribunal.⁹² This last bit of hectoring came to naught, however. Later that day, Llaca Argudín upheld the integrity of Cuba's judicial branch—declaring the Tribunal would not limit the "legitimate right" to appeal assembly results.⁹³

Obviously, there would be no need for lawsuits if the Auténticos could coax Miguelito Suárez Fernández and his followers back into the fold. At first, this seemed improbable when the PPC and Democratic national assemblies approved Suárez Fernández and Raúl Menocal as their presidential and vice-presidential candidates on March 17. Four days later, however, Menocal was in Las Villas attempting to stave off a veto from the Democratic provincial assembly. During a brief speech in which he implored delegates not to sink the coalition, many vacated their seats and left. Bodyguards were sent to retrieve them, but too many escaped to reach a quorum. This ploy was attributed to the Liberal-leaning Polo Figueroa, who feared Menocal would unduly influence the assembly. When the assembly convened again, the Las Villas party bosses Antonio Martínez Fraga and Jorge García Montes ensured the Ortodoxo-Democratic alliance was nixed. Meanwhile, the Auténticos courted wavering miguelista legislators with bribes of $20,000. Their first taker was Salvador Acosta Casares, a congressman from Camagüey. During his March 28 broadcast, Chibás incited the outrage of workaday Cubans, whose average yearly income was $341, asking, "Government or opposition? Whoever gives the most money!"⁹⁴ Chibás told listeners that decent men were being "deliberately irradiated" from Cuba's politics.⁹⁵ Nevertheless, he said, the third front offered a chance to vote against the "ignominious present" and would persevere even if the Ortodoxos were its sole support.⁹⁶ By every indication, this scenario now seemed likely. On April 1, Suárez Fernández was publicly mourning the third front—reserving his harshest words for the Democratic provincial chiefs of Las Villas, saying they had "put their small-minded interests above the nation's greater good."⁹⁷ The next day, he and Raúl Menocal officially withdrew their candidacies. Confronted with limited options, a return to the Auténticos now seemed logical for Suárez Fernández. Grau's former prime minister, Félix

Lancís, established preliminary contacts precisely for this reason. Nonetheless, the senate president was too bitter to capitulate just yet.

THE INDEPENDENT LINE

Actually, there was plenty of animosity to go around. Chibás lambasted "false Ortodoxos" who ditched the party and sought to maintain their positions elsewhere. Among these were Pelayo Cuervo Navarro and Joaquín Martínez Sáenz, who obtained senate candidacies on the Liberal ticket. Also, Pedro López Dorticós accepted a congressional bid with the Auténtico-Republican alliance. Chibás did not specify names, but when he reviled those who had "stabbed me in the back" and deserted upon "seeing their petty personal aspirations in danger" there could be no doubt as to whom he was referring.[98] On the other hand, Chibás effusively praised María Teresa Freyre de Andrade and Regla Peraza, who had rejoined the party now that the specter of pacts had receded. Indeed, the tables had turned a great deal for independence-minded Ortodoxos. As the third front's collapse loomed, PPC leaders had convened a series of meetings to decide their next step. Chibás argued they should enter the elections alone. Manuel Bisbé, Agustín Cruz, and José Manuel Gutiérrez concurred. Millo Ochoa initially claimed this would be "suicide" and pushed for a deal with Prío.[99] The future turncoat Pedro López Dorticós deemed independence a "utopia," as the party lacked both money and a political machine.[100] Eventually, Ochoa agreed to support Chibás and promised his delegates would support him. The Pinar del Río boss, Dominador Pérez, followed suit. With the provincial chiefs behind him, Chibás was assured of the PPC nomination.[101] He subsequently recruited his cousin, Roberto Agramonte, to run as vice president.

During his April 4 broadcast, Chibás attempted to enhance this bit of momentum for the independent line by providing a revisionist account of the previous six weeks. Chibás told listeners he and Suárez Fernández had envisioned a third front composed solely of the latter's Auténtico Reaffirmation Movement integrated within the PPC. The Democrats, he claimed, were invited to form a pact at the behest of Suárez Fernández adherents in Camagüey. Chibás reminded everyone he had spoken and voted against their participation in the Ortodoxo national assembly. However, this was a largely symbolic gesture. If Chibás had verily abhorred the Ortodoxo-Democratic coalition, he could have sought a veto in the Havana provincial assembly. Instead, he conducted a series of pro-third front radio appeals while conveniently ignoring that a traditional party was involved. In fact, Chibás had met privately (albeit informally) with Raúl Menocal on multiple occasions to discuss third front business. Exactly why Chibás suddenly wanted to portray himself as a hard-liner is unclear. Having recently been stung by the resignations of fickle deal makers, perhaps he felt independence oriented Ortodoxos would prove more steadfast. Chibás emphasized that his support for the third front had been "absolutely disinterested," but in some respects he had been merely uninterested.[102] He had refused any official role in negotiations, avoided most meetings, and rejected entreaties to accept a senate candidacy. Although he had vigorously promoted the third front, Chibás seemed almost relieved by its demise.

While the third front's disintegration had cured Chibás of his vacillating, plenty of Ortodoxos were alarmed. The party's nominating convention was pegged for April 5, and Chibás spent most of that afternoon receiving delegates in his apartment. Many revealed their support would not extend beyond that evening. "Just show up tonight," Chibás told them, smiling, "After they nominate me you can do what you want."[103] The proceedings began at 11:30 p.m. Accompanied by Millo Ochoa, Chibás drove to PPC headquarters on the corner of Industria and Dragones in central Havana. A teeming crowd greeted them in the street, obligating the two men to wade slowly toward the former boxing gym now known as "The People's Lyceum." Once inside, Ochoa addressed the delegates. He openly acknowledged the divisions between Ortodoxos, saying the party had engaged in a "sterile debate" between isolationists and those like him who felt electoral coalitions were the surest way to "triumph."[104] Undoubtedly, as the assembly followed its protocols, the PPC's mess of contradictions was on full display. When the roll call of delegates reached Joaquín Martínez Sáenz, the traitor's name was greeted with chants of "Out!" and "Guerrilla!"[105] Subsequently, Agustín Cruz told Ochoa that the Las Villas delegation poised to vote for Chibás was composed entirely of *pactistas*. The isolationists from that province, who had lustily berated Cruz during the past months, followed the example of their leader Joaquín Escribiano and joined the Auténtico-Republican alliance. Finally, Chibás and Agramonte were proclaimed the nominees. While the building shook with applause, José Manuel Gutiérrez commented that "this is the end of the adventure."[106] The Matanzas party chief was correct, at least with respect to himself, as he would soon return to the Liberals.

As the clapping ebbed, Chibás prepared to close the ceremony with a speech. He commenced on a conciliatory note, urging followers not to direct "bitter words" at those unwilling to join them.[107] Chibás recognized that numerous Ortodoxos believed he was embarking on a "crazy mission."[108] He swiftly confirmed their fears by describing the quixotic campaign he intended to wage. Chibás concluded that

> Campaign posters are masks that disguise a candidate's intentions. We won't need them. In the public square we will raise our modest soap box without requiring a grand stage. And we will carry it from person to person. To get from here to there, my automobile, which is very old but very good, shall

suffice. All we have to do is lower the top in order to convert it into a platform! I'm running for president to set an example of sacrifice and disinterest. That's why I'm accepting this nomination even though many would prefer otherwise.[109]

This was the sort of homespun morality tale that had long ago established Chibás as an idol of Cuba's masses. That same day, a parish priest and Chibás aficionado named Jaime Genescá y Rovira typed a letter to his hero using similar rhetoric. "Take inspiration and accept the idea that some journalists have labeled you a ROMANTIC," he wrote. "All of us citizens will be romantics when we give you our votes in the elections."[110] He then illuminated why Eddy's quest might be less dreamy than many supposed.

In my continual travels I hear many workers and employees commenting on national politics and it's always the same story—they don't know who to vote for because they consider all politicians *horrible* and for this reason everyone is hoping to sell their vote and make a little money. This is why I believe your party can offer a dignified option for the citizenry of good conscience. The party you direct only has to be slightly better or a little less bad than those we are already familiar with and you will surely obtain the votes of the good citizens who are thinking about Cuba rather than their pockets.[111]

Previously, no serious presidential contender in Cuba had attempted to win office without the backing of a strong party network. Chibás would now have the opportunity to test whether his overwhelming radio popularity and impassioned followers could, largely by themselves, carry him to victory.

Chapter Four

"We Are Alone with the People"

After his presidential term concluded in October of 1944, Fulgencio Batista had settled in Daytona Beach, Florida. This was scarcely the "hard bread of exile" often rued by Cubans, especially as Batista had accumulated an estimated $50 million during his years in power.[1] As a private citizen, Batista tended to the delicate matter of divorcing his wife of eighteen years and marrying his mistress for the past seven.[2] The former general also oversaw his extensive real estate holdings, including several Miami Beach hotels, and stayed fit by rowing in the nearby Halifax River. In April of 1948, a new crinkle was added to his routine when he agreed to run for senate on the Liberal ticket. This was an unexpected development, not least of all for Batista himself—who had rejected the offer at first glance, claiming the government would respond by "unleashing a wave of unspeakable aggression against my friends."[3] The idea had initially been floated by Salvador García Ramos, a Liberal representative from Las Villas, who believed Batista's name would draw substantial votes in that province. Batista relented after personal appeals from Ricardo Núñez Portuondo and the Las Villas party chief Eduardo Suárez Rivas. Shortly thereafter, the columnist Francisco Ichaso reported that Batista was receiving daily visits from American and Cuban journalists. He was also in "almost permanent" contact with Havana via telephone.[4]

Batista ruled out any campaign trips to Las Villas, however, as he feared his lack of immunity left him at the mercy of a hostile government. In fact, there was a corruption case pending against him in the courts. Lawsuit 30 dated back to October 20, 1942, when Batista's public works minister, Evelio Govantes, announced he was laying off a number of ghost workers, or *botelleros*, who had been assigned to dredge two of Cuba's harbors and clean Varadero beach. Govantes declared that the money allocated for these tasks was being devoted entirely to salaries with "not a single centavo" invested in actually improving the ports or the beach.[5] In the senate, José Manuel Gutiérrez, then an Auténtico senator, submitted a motion to interpellate Govantes. The public works minister subsequently revealed that a total of $1,877,632 had been allotted for the three projects but only $1,623 was spent on materials necessary to complete them. Govantes ended his testimony with a flourish, saying, "In Cuba, we confront the horrific and disconcerting reality whereby someone who steals a stale piece of bread for his hungry children is sent to prison but he who robs public funds is elevated to the rank of social and political leader."[6] A tremendous public outcry followed, and a special judge was designated to oversee the prosecution of all those involved. In 1946, Cuba's attorney general, Rafael Trejo Loredo, requested Batista's extradition to face criminal charges.[7] To be sure, an element of politics was also driving the process—particularly as Trejo was a fanatical Grau devotee. In addition, Trejo actively pressured Cuba's Supreme Court to bring a formal indictment against Batista. That the case seemed to be moving forward just as the ex-general had been nominated was an unlikely coincidence.

One reason Liberal higher-ups may have tabbed Batista was that the Democrats looked poised to join the third front until late March. Accordingly, the Liberals required a contingency plan to fill their senatorial tickets. After the Democratic assembly of Las Villas vetoed the third front, the party's national convention opted for a pact with the Liberals in exchange for fourteen senate seats and three provincial governments. Although these parties had also been coalition partners in 1940 and 1944, Raúl Menocal averred there was no "ideological affinity" between them aside from a shared hostility toward Grau.[8] He added that Genovevo Pérez Dámera would have a greater impact on the elections than any party or candidate, as he alone would decide whether to ensure a fair vote. Cuba's army chief was also pivotal in restoring a semblance of unity to the Auténticos. On April 3, Pérez Dámera brokered a meeting between Miguelito Suárez Fernández and Carlos Prío. The senate president offered to bury the hatchet in exchange for seven senators along with the provincial governments of Las Villas and Matanzas. He also demanded that César Casas be removed from the Matanzas ticket despite Grau's dogged insistence that he remain. Prío was amenable but lacked the authority to extract Cuba's widely despised ex–commerce minister or grant any other concessions without consulting Grau, Guillermo Alonso Pujol, or José Manuel Alemán. Suárez Fernández had no chance of being received by the president and preferred to avoid the rotund Republican boss, so he flew to Miami to speak with Alemán.[9]

The former education minister was living rather well in the "Magic City," having installed himself in swanky beachfront headquarters.[10] Nonetheless, Alemán was eager to avoid any scenario that would complicate his return to Cuba. He especially feared the prospect of a coup backed by his foe Pérez

Dámera or an opposition president who would be tempted to levy corruption charges against him. Alemán agreed with Suárez Fernández that a divided Auténtico party enhanced both these possibilities and therefore accepted his conditions. Later that day, Alemán telephoned his friend Alonso Pujol—who arrived on the next plane. Without the slightest fuss, the Republican leader agreed to cede his party's senate candidacies in Las Villas and Matanzas to Suárez Fernández. In an even greater show of muscle, Alemán subsequently permitted Prío to nix César Casas. Suárez Fernández was thus placated, although his resentment at being mangled by the Auténtico party machinery continued to fester. Speaking to some associates about the upcoming polls, the senate president confessed his unwillingness to campaign for Prío or Alonso Pujol—adding that he would not share a stage with them "even for 10 million."[11]

CHIBÁS THE INSURGENT

The consolidation of the Auténtico-Republican alliance on one side and the Liberal-Democratic coalition on the other underlined the formidable challenge facing Chibás. On April 2, a Chibás supporter named Gonzalo Fernández penned a letter to his idol. Fernández, who was from the working class Havana neighborhood of Luyanó, invoked a famous anecdote from 1871, a low point in Cuba's first independence war. At that time, an official in the rebel army asked Major General Ignacio Agramonte with what resources they would carry on the fight since there appeared to be none left. According to legend, Agramonte fiercely replied, "With the shame of the Cuban people!" Fernández proposed this phrase as the Ortodoxo "combat motto" in the face of politicians "who lose their heads chasing after senate seats and think neither of decorum nor the people."[12] After reading it, Chibás scribbled the words "kind letter" in the upper left-hand corner. However, he was clearly intrigued. Agramonte, who was killed by a stray bullet two years after his famous utterance, was one of Cuba's most revered martyrs and a quintessential exemplar of self-sacrifice. He also happened to be a distant blood relative. When he was a boy, Eddy's maternal grandmother, Luisa Agramonte, had plied him with tales of the family's exploits during the independence struggle. These invariably ended in tragedy but were also a source of tremendous pride.[13] Although Eddy's fight was of a different nature, he delighted in the allegory.

Always a believer in the value of symbolism, Chibás appeared on the air with Roberto Agramonte on April 11, thereby adding yet another descendant of the man who would feature prominently in his broadcast. He told his audience that

> Some people ask me: With what resources are you counting on for the electoral campaign in order to rescue Cuba from the hands of so many bandits and frauds who have imprisoned her? Before this question, I cannot but remember the response of Ignacio Agramonte to the skeptics who also asked of him: With what resources are you counting on for the campaign to rescue Julio Sanguily (a rebel general) from the hands of the guerrillas that have captured him? My answer is the same.... [W]e are alone, alone with the people but aim to win with the most powerful of resources, the resource of Agramonte: The shame of the Cuban people!
>
> Thirty five horsemen armed only with machetes were enough for Agramonte to rescue Sanguily, who was guarded by a thick column of guerrillas and Spanish soldiers armed with bayonets, rifles and artillery. A handful of Ortodoxos of shame, like those thirty-five horsemen, will be sufficient to save the republic from the ignoble spectacle offered by the present political corruption.[14]

Chibás expected this message to hearten Ortodoxo partisans but was overjoyed to learn that it had also stirred some of the island's "neutral masses." Manuel Anca, a Havana medical surgeon, confessed somewhat brusquely that "I don't belong to your political party or any other and I don't know you personally nor am I interested in getting to know you." Just the same, he praised Chibás and the Ortodoxos for "being able to renew the confidence and faith in the future of our beloved and hardworking Cuban people."[15]

Although Chibás did not say so on the radio, his presidential campaign was, in fact, counting on a resource besides the shame of the Cuban people. Specifically, this was the luxurious family residence built by his father in 1924. Situated on Seventeenth Street and Avenue H in Havana's Vedado district, the edifice was an architectural jewel with custom-designed doors and windows. Since his father's death in 1941, Chibás had lived there intermittently, and in 1946 he and his brother Raúl rented the building to the Peruvian government—which used it as its embassy. By April of 1948, Chibás decided to sell the place and invested much of the 25,000 pesos he received in his campaign. In doing so, Chibás burnished his credibility even further in a nation where politicians typically acquired houses.[16] Chibás also resorted to the timeworn method of accepting donations from individuals and businesses. For example, his friend Ignacio Mendoza, an erstwhile revolutionary and current stockbroker, contributed the substantial sum of 10,000 pesos. Alfredo Fernández Supervielle, brother of Havana's deceased mayor, and the banker Jacobo Lobo chipped in 200 pesos apiece. Chibás also received financial support from the posh El Encanto department store (1,000 pesos), the Tropical Brewery (1,000 pesos), and National Concrete (1,000 pesos), among others.[17]

Even as Chibás cultivated a high-profile insurgent persona, he remained pragmatic behind closed doors. On April 9, for example, he authorized an Ortodoxo delegation to discuss a senatorial pact with the Communists.[18]

Both parties saw an opportunity to gain second place in Havana and Oriente provinces if they joined forces. Such a result would have netted three senators for each. Millo Ochoa, the Ortodoxo nominee for governor of Oriente, was another potential beneficiary, and he strongly advocated the deal. Initially, the proceedings showed promise. However, when Manuel Bisbé insisted the Communists support Eddy's presidential candidacy as well, they demurred and suggested a nominee who would be acceptable to all. Chibás, predictably, vetoed the idea. While this was a setback for the party's senatorial hopes, he felt there was still much to be gained in Oriente—Cuba's largest, poorest, and most neglected province. On May 17, Chibás and an Ortodoxo retinue set out on a nine-day tour of the region to drum up support for his presidential candidacy.[19] In Santiago de Cuba, Chibás addressed an enthusiastic gathering of sixty thousand, many of whom brandished the party's signature brooms. Among those who warmed up the audience beforehand was Fidel Castro. Given his well-known involvement in gangster politics at the University of Havana, the twenty-one-year-old Oriente native was an anomalous presence among the straitlaced Ortodoxos. His rhetorical talent, however, was already an asset to the party. Referring to Chibás, he declared,

> This lunatic, out of sublime craziness for the sublime ideal of an improved Cuba, values the recognition of his own people above all else. He would be incapable of disappointing the devotion professed by the masses, as that would deprive him of the very oxygen he breathes. The day Chibás senses a reduction in citizens' affection he would put a bullet through his heart, not out of cowardice in the face of failure, but so that his self-sacrifice ensures the victory of his disciples. No uncertainties! We are in the presence of a great man![20]

Shortly thereafter, Chibás mounted a truck top and from those modest heights proceeded to whip the throng into frothy exuberance. Gloria Cuadras, a member of the Ortodoxo Women's Wing from the city, recalled that his speech was met with "delirious acclaim and applause."[21] After Chibás finished, with the multitude's roar still echoing in the background, a group of supporters clamored for him to leap into their arms. Without hesitation, Chibás dived headfirst into the giddy mass of hats and limbs as a local photographer snapped pictures for the next day's newspapers.[22]

In short order, Chibás roused the province to such an extent that Enrique de la Osa claimed he had "destroyed all previous political calculations."[23] Before Eddy's arrival in Santiago de Cuba, a collection box had been placed on the city's main commercial thoroughfare, in order to raise funds for his reception. In three days, nearly 4,000 pesos were contributed in small donations. Nor did Chibás limit his excursion to Oriente's urban centers. His itinerary included stops in the midsize towns of Victoria de las Tunas, Campechuela, Bayamo, Niquero, Puerto Padre, Gibara, Holguín, and Manzanillo—where he evoked tears of anger over the murder of native son Jesús Menéndez. Chibás also stopped in the villages of Bocas, Delicias, Jobabo, Media Luna, and San Manuel—all of which counted fewer than eight thousand inhabitants. Rather than speaking in an ample square, as he had in Santiago de Cuba, he held forth from cane fields or under banana trees. Often, these remote areas were accessible only by horse. In one instance, he traveled by motorboat in a torrential downpour. As Chibás improvised modes of transportation, his adherents did the same to spread the candidate's message, especially as funds were always in short supply. Ortodoxo aficionados lent their trucks, cars, and buses to the party in an effort to chauffeur fellow *chibasistas* to rallies, meetings, or receptions organized in his honor. The PPC's publicity effort followed a similar fashion. De la Osa explained that "the banners of Chibás's sympathizers were not constructed from colorful or elegant materials but rather were modest leaflets or home-made posters, usually of brooms and raised flag-like to signal that 'they were going to sweep the way clear for Chibás to enter the presidential palace.'"[24]

On the evening of May 30, Chibás devised a final parallel between his candidacy and Cuba's independence struggle. In 1895, the rebel plan had involved an initial incursion in Oriente and gradual advances toward Havana. Having just won many hearts in Cuba's easternmost province, Chibás planned "The invasion of Shame," a motorized Ortodoxo caravan that would symbolically banish criminality from the capital. Unfortunately, the PPC horde was stalled at the village of Arroyo Arenas on Havana's outskirts by a group of squad cars from the National Police. The officers explained that Cuban law forbade formal campaigning after May 25. Instead of arguing, Chibás avoided a potentially violent confrontation by requesting they wait a few minutes while he called General Pérez Dámera. The army chief agreed with Chibás, suggesting only a change of route into the city to avoid disturbing traffic. Hence, even as the danger of a coup seemed to be receding, the army remained the final arbiter of Cuba's statutes.

EXODUS

Several days before Chibás had been nominated for president, *Bohemia* reported the Ortodoxos were in such disarray that "nobody knew anything."[25] This was because they were increasingly unsure of who was in the party from one day to the next. During a meeting prior to the PPC convention, Aurelio Álvarez spoke of Pelayo Cuervo Navarro and Joaquín Martínez Sáenz as if they were still Ortodoxos before Chibás informed him they had joined the Liberals. The Camagüey party chief, who had stridently denounced "opportunists," became one himself by joining the Liberal-Democratic ticket a few days later. Shortly thereafter, José Manuel Gutiérrez, the Matanzas boss, followed suit. Pablo Carrera Jústiz, an ex-revolutionary and wealthy University of Havana professor, also abandoned the party in favor of the Liberals. On April 12, Natasha Mella addressed a letter to Chibás renouncing her candidacy for a seat in the chamber of representatives. Mella, who was only twenty-one years old, expressed a willingness to remain a party member but preferred to reduce her commitment. She had also been romantically involved with Chibás, and this perhaps influenced the situation as did the jealousy of older Ortodoxos who resented her exalted status in the party.[26]

On April 25, Agustín Cruz, the party boss of Las Villas, published his resignation in *Bohemia*. Cruz had been offered a spot on the Liberal-Democratic ticket in that province but opted to withdraw from public life rather than appear alongside Fulgencio Batista. A keen proponent of pacts, Cruz decried "dogmatic isolationism" as both "antidemocratic" and "lacking political sense" under Cuba's current electoral law.[27] In facing the elections alone, Cruz claimed the PPC "now finds it impossible to offer citizens congressional candidates with a chance of winning" and thereby deprived the Cuban people of a realistic option for change.[28] Cruz thus became the third Ortodoxo provincial head to quit within the space of one month. In early May, Pastor Torres Sánchez relinquished his candidacy for governor of Las Villas and Eduardo Díaz Ortega forsook his campaign for representative from Pinar del Río. Both men joined the Auténtico-Republican alliance. Lower-level defections were common as well. In Camagüey province, the entire municipal assemblies of Guimaro and Esmeralda switched to the Auténticos. The Ortodoxo network, which had always been rudimentary, was devastated by an exodus of local directors, councilmen, and organizers. On a daily basis during this period, Chibás received missives like that of Alberto Madrigal Valdés—who related that the president of his neighborhood's Ortodoxo organizing committee had jumped to the Liberal-Democratic coalition. Madrigal described this development as lamentable but affirmed, "the man who writes to you, who loves his *patria*, will know how to rescue the flag and direction of our party just as Ignacio Agramonte with 35 men rescued General Sanguily from enemy forces."[29] Undoubtedly, many of the new Ortodoxo officers were devoted and competent. However, this was not always the case. Hence, Chibás was informed by a supporter in the town of La Maya in Oriente province that "no one here is campaigning for your candidacy or even mentioning you."[30] The party was also damaged by Ortodoxos who devoted themselves elsewhere while nominally remaining in the fold. Thus, an adherent from Placetas in Las Villas province notified Chibás about "members of the executive committee in this city, some of whom sold themselves to the Liberal-Democratic coalition and others to BAGA, but all of whom are using your clean name to benefit their shady political campaigns and confusing public opinion in this way."[31]

Needless to say, loyal Ortodoxos were outraged by such duplicity and responded with defiance. Hugo Mir, a director of the PPC Youth Section, confronted the issue of defections in an article published in *La Correspondencia*, a newspaper based in the city of Cienfuegos. He wrote that

> It's extremely painful when such things happen, especially when we are talking about *compañeros* with the best references and in whose integrity of character we trusted. We don't know what induced them to desert the Ortodoxo cause and cross over to the government. The public justification they have offered . . . is that for money, jobs or the promise of one thing or another they have put themselves at the service of Prío Socarrás and Alonso Pujol in their labor of defamation against our maximum leader, Senator Eduardo Chibás and those by his side who defend the continuity of the revolutionary movement, or better said, hope to save it. In any case, these acts, this opportunism doesn't dishearten us; on the contrary it stimulates us to struggle with more enthusiasm, certain that we have taken the correct political stance, assisted by the truth, defending the noble ideology of the Cuban revolution, for which many of our compañeros sacrificed their young lives.[32]

During his May 2 broadcast, Chibás himself allowed that "some known Ortodoxo revolutionaries" had "sold themselves like pigs to Carlos Prío Socarrás," but he dwelled on more comforting news as well.[33] Chibás explained that one month earlier Ricardo Núñez Portuondo had commissioned an expensive national survey paid for by Federico Fernández Casas and administered by Raúl Gutiérrez Serrano, Cuba's most respected pollster.[34] According to the results, leaked to Chibás by a "credible source," he had placed first, with Núñez Portuondo a close second and Prío trailing well behind them both.[35] Núñez Portuondo and Fernández Casas were so shocked by Eddy's unexpected popularity that they opted to keep their research private, ostensibly to hide the truth from ordinary citizens. Chibás also cheered his followers by citing a host of smaller more informal polls that yielded similar outcomes. For example, employees of the public relations firm Guastella, the Sinclair Oil Company, and the La Corona Cigar Factory all favored Chibás in elections by secret ballot.[36] Throughout the month, the Ortodoxos bought advertisements in *Diario de la Marina* publicizing victories by Chibás in straw poll elections at Cuba's engineering school, Havana's dock, the United States Rubber Company, Cubana Airlines, Bank of Nova Scotia, Insular Underwriters, the Sarrá pharmacy, and the department stores El Encanto and Fin del Siglo. They also boasted that

> We have hundreds of surveys ratified by the signatures of thousands of workers but it is impossible to publish every one. The details we have cited are rigorously exact. Anyone who doubts them can question the employees and workers of the factories and businesses above. The result is the same everywhere. This is a reflection of public opinion.[37]

Given his superior position, Chibás claimed he rather than Prío was the best hope of averting a machadista restoration led by Núñez Portuondo. Further, he reminded listeners that the Ortodoxos were an official party in all six provinces and every Cuban who wanted to would have the chance to vote for him. He thus urged them to heed his new slogan, "Shame vs. Money."

THE PARTY OF MACHADO

Setting his own aspirations aside for a moment, Chibás opined that "it would be disastrous if the government thieves won the elections, but it would be even more terrible if the bandits of the Liberal-Democratic coalition triumphed because the latter, in addition to robbing as much as those currently in power, would inundate the country in blood."[38]

Chibás bore two intractable grudges against the Liberals. First, they were tainted as the party of Gerardo Machado, Cuba's all-purpose villain and bogeyman par excellence. Second, they were one of two "traditional" parties that had mismanaged Cuba during the republic's first three decades. On April 4, Chibás dismissed Ricardo Núñez Portuondo as a "fervent sympathizer" of Machado who remained "deaf and mute" while the tyrant assassinated workers, journalists, professors, students, and veterans of Cuba's independence war. In addition, Chibás charged Núñez Portuondo with maintaining a similar silence during the mass strikes of 1935 against Batista's military regime.[39] Two weeks later, he revealed a new and damaging piece of information. After offering a public roll call of Machado's early victims, Chibás disclosed that Núñez Portuondo had traduced their memories during a two-hour speech on February 24, 1930, in which he lauded the dictator for "putting into practice the revolutionary program of Martí."[40] Núñez Portuondo, who had delivered the address on behalf of the Cuban Medical Federation, had further deemed Machado "an example of austerity and virtue" and "deserving of the eternal gratitude of his people" even as he suspended the activity of opposition parties and illegally had himself elected to a second presidential term.[41] Moreover, Chibás pointed out that Núñez Portuondo maintained a close friendship with the *porrista* Clemente Carreras, a known assassin and torturer.[42] Chibás also reminded his audience that Núñez Portuondo remained "surrounded by the flower of Machado-ism."[43]

Indeed, the Liberal party was top-heavy with Machado-era figures, including Carlos Miguel de Céspedes, the tyrant's erstwhile public works minister; Viriato Gutiérrez, Machado's ex-secretary of the presidency; Rafael Guas Inclán, president of the chamber of representatives during Machado's rule; Juan Antonio Vázquez Bello, the dictator's erstwhile boss in Las Villas province; Núñez Portuondo's younger brother Emilito, president of the Machado-era Civil Service Commission; and Salvador García Ramos, who, on

August 7, 1933, had stood on the Capitolio steps and fired into a crowd that had assembled after an underground radio station falsely reported that Machado had resigned.[44] Chibás predicted that if the Liberal-Democratic coalition won the elections, even more infamous characters from the 1930s would return to public life. He estimated that the notorious Arsenio Ortiz would retake control of the National Police and have prisoners murdered under the catchall excuse "shot while trying to escape," and Captain Manuel Crespo would return to his post as chief of the Atarés fortress and resume his role as tormentor and executioner. Chibás also claimed a reinstatement of machadista personnel would be followed by reverses of gains won by the revolution, including the right to strike for urban workers and freedom from "semi-slavery" for their rural counterparts—who would be exploited without mercy by the many large landowners in the Liberal party running for senate.[45] Alluding to recent newspaper advertisements promising that Núñez Portuondo would effect a "revolution of honor" if elected, Chibás accused the Liberals of treating Cuba's citizens like "idiots."[46] In a voice saturated with irony and indignation, Chibás wondered how Núñez Portuondo would implement his planned revolution with such a compromised cast of characters.

Batista's decision to join the Liberal ticket afforded Chibás yet another inviting target. Chibás noted that the ex-general, whose senate candidacy had been supported "with great fanfare" by Ricardo Núñez Portuondo, currently owned eleven buildings in Havana alone.[47] Of course, he also counted choice properties in Venezuela, Mexico, and the United States as well, including a fifteen-story apartment building in Miami. "It would seem," concluded Chibás, "that just as little boys delight in collecting stamps, Batista takes pleasure in acquiring real estate."[48] Later on, Chibás characterized the six years between 1934 and 1940, when Batista wielded behind-the-scenes power, as a "reign of terror" and warned Cubans if they united pro-Machado and pro-Batista tendencies on their ballots, "God will hold us responsible."[49]

On May 31, Chibás issued a final appeal over the airwaves. He bid his audience to respect the memories of Cuba's fallen revolutionaries by denying public office to machadistas. Doing otherwise, he asserted, would represent a "betrayal of our highest principles."[50] At the same time, he was convinced that support for the Liberal-Democratic coalition had crumbled of late and his chief rival would be Carlos Prío. Chibás thus attempted to court Liberals and Democrats by asserting their votes for Núñez Portuondo would be "wasted" and he represented the only "practical and efficient way" to defeat the government.[51]

THE CASE AGAINST PRIO

Although his nominal opponent was Carlos Prío, Chibás fixed a suspicious eye on Grau throughout the campaign season. He remained certain his former mentor was planning something and saw plots behind every corner. For instance, Chibás claimed Grau had sought to "provoke public disorder" during the annual May Day parade at the presidential palace as a pretext for suspending the elections.[52] This belief may also partly explain Eddy's pains to portray himself as a latter day *mambí* (who better to lead Cuba in the event of a coup?) and the weekly declarations that he was leading the polls (who better than the people's choice to lead the opposition until democracy is restored?). Then again, these tactics served just as well for his conventional presidential run. On balance, Cubans held members of the liberation army in high esteem. Comparing his quest and their exploits was a shrewd strategy. As for the public surveys, Chibás was anxious to peel the Auténtico rank and file from its leaders and hoped evidence of his popularity would sway them. At the same time, Chibás also hoped to elicit their disgust by asking, "What type of government can we expect from Prío and Pujol?"

For starters, the venality that characterized Grau's administration would continue unabated. Prío had already "dirtied his hands" in murky deals involving the island's sugar differential, the US-owned Cuban Electric Company, and "other foreign monopolies."[53] Chibás further pointed out that Guillermo Alonso Pujol, while senate president in 1938, had fled to Europe having stolen millions of pesos in public works bonds, an act constituting "the republic's greatest scandal to date."[54] Just as revolting was the fact that the Auténtico-Republican alliance had allotted prominent roles for José Manuel Alemán and César Casas. The former was now Auténtico party chief of Havana and a senate candidate from that province. More importantly, BAGA, his political vehicle, was largely financing Prío's campaign. In characteristic fashion, Chibás averred that Alemán and his minions were capable of selling anything and everything on the island, including its principal emblem—Havana's sixteenth-century Morro fortress. Regarding César Casas, Chibás procured a letter to the widely despised "black market boss" from Carlos Prío and read it over the air on May 2. The missive essentially offered Casas a congressional candidacy on the Republican ticket as a sop for his "service" to the Auténticos.[55] Prío also assured the ex–commerce minister that he would "fully retain" his "legitimately acquired rights," which Chibás interpreted as a promise to restore him to the cabinet after the elections.[56] Recalling yet another Auténtico scandal, he noted that the party had nominated Luis Caíñas Milanés, a former senator, known murderer, and fugitive from justice, for the assembly seat of the man he killed, in Oriente province.

Aside from shamelessness and sleaze, four years of Prío and Pujol would be disastrous for urban workers, who could expect interference with their unions and a government-imposed leadership. Even worse, such an administration would also subjugate workers' interests to the whims of foreigners. As proof, Chibás alleged that Prío, as Grau's former labor secretary, had ousted the Communist Lázaro Peña as president of the Cuban Workers Confederation in accordance with "international pressures."[57] Chibás charged that Prío's anti-Communism was more a matter of convenience than conviction and suggested his rival was actually "anti-worker."[58] By contrast, Chibás promised never to meddle in "union matters" and supported the right of workers to elect their chosen representatives regardless of whether they were Communist or not.[59]

Chibás contended the outlook for rural laborers would be equally dreary under Prío. He recalled that a group of *guajiros* from Oriente province had organized a march in Havana the year before, demanding that Grau fulfill his promises of cement floors for their huts, sanitary latrines, and new wells.[60] Rather than receiving or addressing the protesters, the government violently dispersed the crowd. "During those moments," said Chibás, "now and forever, I was and always will be on the side of the *campesinos*."[61] Chibás asserted that Prío would make no effort to improve their lives but aimed merely to pacify them with sympathetic folk tunes broadcast on the radio. He urged country dwellers to reject this "opium."[62] Chibás also assured them that the "fundamental motive" for his separation from the Auténticos had been Grau's "betrayal" of the campesinos.[63]

The Auténticos, in turn, considered Eddy's run for the presidency an act of perfidy against the revolution and were fond of using Ortodoxo recreants to deliver this message—which often concluded with an appeal for Chibás to abandon his campaign and support Prío. During his May 9 broadcast, Chibás declared that Grau and Prío had requested an audience with him, ostensibly to discuss an agreement.[64] Emissaries of the latter had already offered Chibás the prime ministry along with the education, commerce, and treasury portfolios if he agreed to join them. Chibás responded that he would much prefer to see criminals like José Manuel Alemán, César Casas, Alberto Inocente Álvarez, and Emilio Núñez Portuondo brought before a judge. "When all these men are in jail," said Chibás, "then and only then will I receive President Grau or Carlos Prío in my house."[65]

THE ORTODOXO PROGRAM

Journalists who interviewed Chibás often remarked upon the difference between his rambunctious radio demeanor and the measured comportment he demonstrated away from the studio. Arturo Alfonso Roselló, the editor-in-chief of *Carteles*, represented one such case. After a four-hour conversation with him, he confessed that in "intimate settings" Chibás "speaks slowly, taking the time to sift through ideas without hurrying and reiterates his points without gesticulation or undue emphasis."[66] Gastón Baquero, the editor-in chief of *Diario de la Marina*, concurred, stating that "silence and a conversation full of pauses, rather than screams, marked the interview's rhythm."[67] In this sense, such encounters provided an ideal forum in which to debunk the notion, spread by detractors, that he was a demagogue. They were also an excellent venue for disseminating the Ortodoxo platform, especially as Chibás devoted his broadcasts to spectacle and revelation rather than the intricacies of party doctrine. Thus, in the last month before the election, Chibás sat down with *Bohemia*, which usually offered flattering coverage; *Carteles*, which viewed him with suspicion; *Diario de la Marina*, which was mildly sympathetic; and *El Crisol*, which considered Eddy's broadcasts to be of such importance that it published complete transcripts every Monday.[68]

In all these sessions, Chibás evinced a great concern for Cuba's peasants. This was logical in two respects. First, he regularly received correspondence from the island's rural dwellers detailing the heartbreaking circumstances of their lives. Second, he was aware that his party had scant presence in Cuba's villages and small towns. If the inhabitants of these areas were going to resist the urge to sell their votes, they required a compelling program. Hence, Chibás told *Bohemia*'s Antonio Ortega that Cuba's "fundamental" problem was in its countryside and campesinos deserved the same "social benefits" enjoyed by industrial workers.[69] At a minimum, rural Cubans were entitled to cement floors in their huts, sanitary latrines, and potable drinking water. Once these basic requirements were satisfied, Chibás proposed a second stage of improvements, including farming cooperatives, an agricultural development bank, crop diversification, and the creation of a scientific institute to develop species and breeds best suited to Cuba's climate. Asked about land distribution, Chibás recommended the establishment of a national registry to catalog vacant land and uncultivated private holdings. In addition to disbursing the former, he planned to impose a tax on the latter, which would stimulate the sale of disused acreage. Chibás emphasized his respect for property rights but stated that land also had a "social function" and Cuba's priority was to help farmers own the plots they worked.[70] "The current administration," said Chibás, "turns Cubans into state employees. The Communists make them proletarians. The Cuban People's Party would like them to be proprietors."[71]

During the *Carteles* interview, Chibás argued that rural rehabilitation was central to the Ortodoxo slogan of "economic independence, political liberty and social justice." He proclaimed that "the rural population suffers the prejudice of a shameful stagnation, lives in the most primitive conditions, endures horrible neglect and has lost all faith and enthusiasm, not only in the fatherland's destiny but in its own as well."[72] Chibás planned to use the "millions" in revenues from Cuba's sugar differential to improve rural health and acquire land, tools, seeds, livestock, and technical advice for peasants.[73] Freed from maladies such as typhus, malaria, and intestinal parasites, campesinos could increase their productivity. Putting the *land* in *fatherland* would also imbue them with a real and defined sense of patriotism. Hence, Chibás imagined economic opportunity would extend beyond Cuba's cities into its interior. This, in turn, would herald changes in the island's political culture. Chibás explained that rural desolation essentially transformed many runs for public office into financial transactions. After all, he said, "it is easy to seduce the guajiro into selling his vote for a few pesos so at least he can feed his children."[74] As a result,

> the governor or legislator who arrives at his position in this way does not feel obligated to the voter. He purchased his office or executive position; he didn't obtain it on merit or because of an effective campaign. He owes his office to money rather than a program. His interest and his end can be none other than recuperating his investment. In this way, public opinion, which is inherent to democracy and political liberty, disappears. In other words, free expression of the will of the citizens becomes prostituted.[75]

Nor were peasants the only ones deprived of the right to vote their conscience. Government employees had an irresistible incentive to choose the ruling party as otherwise their jobs would be given to members of the opposition. For this reason, Chibás proposed a professional bureaucracy chosen by competitive examinations rather than party affiliation. Adopting this practice would also eliminate the *botella*, or government employee who collects a salary but performs no service.

Reminded by Roselló that political liberty was an "ambitious" term that could not be reduced to "purity of the vote," Chibás mentioned the importance of equality before the law.[76] "There will be political liberty," he said, "when an anonymous worker has the same guarantees in the courts of justice as a millionaire or politician. Just the same," he continued, "there can be no political liberty when the pickpocket goes to jail while the corrupt functionary who robs millions gets to spend his money abroad."[77] In this vein, Chibás expressed a need for the long-delayed Tribunal of Accounts that would audit government expenditures and passage of the General Accounting Law for the State, Provinces, and Municipalities to ensure public funds were monitored at every level.[78]

Chibás described the third aspect of Ortodoxo doctrine, social justice, in roughly the same vague terms as Cuba's 1940 constitution—a document he knew intimately. For instance, the "principle of social justice" is lionized in Title VI, Article 86. Further, he spoke of "betterment of the working classes" with the goal of "conciliation between Capital and Labor."[79] Such conciliation is provided for in Title VI, Article 84—albeit more formally through special commissions of workers and management. In a nod to the red-hating subscribers of *Carteles*, Chibás claimed harmonious relations between the classes would eliminate the risk of "communist penetration."[80] Chibás also sought the approval of *Diario de la Marina*'s conservative readership by declaring, "I am the only national leader who has never allied with the Communist party," and added, "My opposition to them is neither electoral nor political but comes from the bottom of my heart."[81] In fact, Chibás presented his most thorough and highly detailed program during the conversation with Baquero. His top priorities entailed agricultural diversification, a national bank, nationalized public utilities, subsidized fuel and electricity, reduced foreign concessions, lowered prices for basic goods, prosecution of black market speculators, an ambitious public works program, an increased budget for the ministry of agriculture, and, of course, his package of reforms to revitalize Cuba's countryside.

Above all, the Ortodoxo agenda depended on Eddy's personal trustworthiness because most of its policy recommendations could also be found in the Auténtico-Republican and Liberal-Democratic platforms. The rural poor could take comfort in Carlos Prío's announcement that agricultural reform deserved his "deepest and most sincere interest."[82] Moreover, Prío promised to oversee creation of the Agricultural and Industrial Development Bank and Tribunal of Accounts. He even called for a merit system in the civil service. Ricardo Núñez Portuondo favored land distribution, touting the social and economic benefits of ownership for a peasantry that was "practically nomadic."[83] For those outraged by illegality and graft, he trumpeted his so-called two revolutions of constitutionality and honor. In advertisements, he and his running mate, Gustavo Cuervo Rubio, both of whom were physicians, sold themselves as "University of Havana professors," "notable professionals," and men of "moral integrity." As such, they would confront the "upsetting and demoralizing" political climate and impose "administrative honesty."[84] A *Carteles* editorial corroborated this image, noting that Núñez Portuondo enjoyed "recognized prestige, a firm will and good judgment."[85] Without jobs to distribute, money for votes, or an organized political machine, Chibás could only rely on his charisma and the conviction that "the Cuban people know that if I am elected, these robberies will be punished."[86]

Chapter Five

"The Miracle of Chibás"

On the morning of Tuesday, June 1, shortly before voting was to commence, Chibás was fast asleep. He had maintained his usual busy schedule the previous evening, appearing before the Havana Bar Association, the Commercial Street Business Owners Group, and, of course, on the radio. Eddy had arrived home at 2:30 a.m., and when a *Bohemia* reporter stopped by the next day, he was mired in slumber. With some difficulty, the journalist succeeded in stirring Chibás. He banished the remnants of his grogginess by playing a recording, composed for him in Santiago de Cuba, which was a parody of the famous tune "Quizás, Quizás." After hearing a few notes of the refitted jingle, entitled "Chibás, Chibás," which described him "sweeping" to victory in June, he was once again his loquacious, energetic self.[1] Before setting out to cast his ballot, Chibás gilded his cheerfulness with a layer of romanticism—hanging the following proverb in front of his desk. It read:

> Let the world think of us what it may. That's its own affair. If it doesn't put everything in its rightful place by the time we die, or even ever, that's its own prerogative. Ours is to work as if the nation were grateful, as if the world were righteous, as if public opinion were shrewd, as if life were just and as if men were superior beings.[2]

That evening, after the polls closed, Chibás dined with Roberto Agramonte. Eddy told his cousin that "during the course of our travels, I have observed a certain collective craziness that could potentially result in a surprise. I'm convinced we will receive a great quantity of votes. The people have internalized our slogan of 'Shame vs. Money.' And our campaign only began a few months ago. If only we had more time!"[3] Later on, Chibás visited the Columbia military barracks at the invitation of Genovevo Pérez Dámera. The Cuban army, which supervised the elections, was also the surest source of information regarding their result. There, Chibás listened to the returns from all corners of the island and learned that Carlos Prío would be Cuba's next president.[4]

The Auténtico candidate, who had emphasized his smiling, cordial nature throughout the campaign, won all six of Cuba's provinces. However, he collected only 45.83 percent of the popular vote even with nearly unlimited resources at his disposal. Moreover, the Auténtico-Republican alliance obtained 145,823 fewer votes than in 1944—a worrying sign given the tremendous advantages of incumbency. In a similar vein, the government parties captured majorities in the senate and chamber of representatives, but these results were less encouraging than would appear at first glance. This is because many nominally Auténtico senators and representatives were followers of Miguelito Suárez Fernández, who felt little or no loyalty to the new president.[5] On the other hand, José Manuel Alemán's senate victory proved lucre could still buy plenty of goodwill. With his immunity from prosecution assured, he immediately returned to Havana. While there were scattered indications that Auténtico attempts to buy votes had backfired, in general, the tactic was highly successful. A notable exception was Enrique Rousseau, an Auténtico candidate for the chamber of representatives who was heard lamenting the fact that he had paid 8,000 pesos to so-called political sergeants in Havana's Cayo Hueso neighborhood without receiving the votes promised to him.[6] Given his obvious advantages, Prío's victory seemed inevitable even before the polls had closed. Sensing as much, foreign correspondents gravitated to his residence during the afternoon of June 1. These included representatives from *Hollywood Reporter*, Twentieth Century Fox, and the French magazine *INS*.

Ricardo Núñez Portuondo finished second with 30.42 percent of the vote, and was hardly a picture of grace in defeat. He chalked up the results to "betrayals by many elements of the party."[7] When an advisor suggested a congratulatory phone call to Prío was in order, Núñez Portuondo responded that he would do so the next day and shortly thereafter abandoned party headquarters in a huff. Rather than condemning traitors within the coalition, Raúl Menocal fingered Chibás as the "maximum cause" of their defeat, saying the Ortodoxo leader preferred Prío over Núñez Portuondo.[8] Conveniently ignoring the fact that members of his own Democratic party had undermined the third front, Menocal told Enrique de la Osa, "You see? My thesis has been proved correct. Without a united opposition, it was always going to be difficult to beat the government." He added, "We are like the children of a millionaire who believe we will inherit a fortune when in reality there were fewer riches than we had imagined."[9] Across the Florida Straits, Fulgencio Batista had awaited the elections with barely contained brio. Claiming Núñez Portuondo would win by 150,000 votes, the ex-general rented a luxury suite at the Hotel Martinique in Miami Beach and summoned his expatriate military buddies to share in the expected merrymaking. Although Batista ultimately won his senate race, once news of Núñez Portuondo's defeat spread, those gathered were in no mood to celebrate.

Such was not the case for Chibás, who placed third with 16.42 percent of the electorate. Even as the surveys and straw polls he cited on the hustings proved mistaken, Chibás collected 320,929 votes—nearly double his party's total from the registration period. Unfortunately, the PPC did not win a single provincial governorship or senate race and placed just six party members in the chamber of representatives—the most prominent being Manuel Bisbé. Nevertheless, William Stokes, a political scientist from the United States who chronicled the campaign, claimed Chibás "won a great moral victory at the expense of the Auténtico-Republican alliance."[10] This was because most of those who chose Chibás, apart from registered Ortodoxos, appeared to have been members of the government parties.[11] Eddy's friends in the media saw his performance in far more effusive terms. *Bohemia* ran an editorial entitled "The Miracle of Chibás," extolling the Ortodoxo chief's "beautiful and exemplary" campaign, adding that

> It can, without hyperbole, be affirmed that the disinterested pyramid of votes bestowed upon Eduardo R. Chibás—whose combativeness and immaculate conduct already anoint him as leader of the future political opposition—has cemented the undeniable reality that the Cuban people have left behind, forevermore, the slimy electoral customs that have stunted its progress.[12]

Enrique de la Osa, writing in the magazine's *en Cuba* section, stated that

> Neutral and enemy observers alike consider the votes obtained by the Ortodoxo candidate to be an indicator of his political talents, especially as he struggled against the current against powerful parties, assisted only by his personal prestige and independence from the mercenary figures used by other politicians. The votes earned by the PPC chief, who didn't offer jobs, bribes or anything else of that sort, can be utilized as a lever by which he can raise a great party, one that would be the undisputed leader of the opposition in the coming years.[13]

Sergio Carbó, writing in *Prensa Libre*, added that "there is not the least bit of popular enthusiasm for Prío's victory."[14] Of course, not all journalists were so accommodating. Francisco Ichaso, in his June 3 column for *Diario de la Marina*, could not resist a jab when the opportunity presented itself. Noting that a survey just before the elections had predicted Chibás would win more votes in Havana than he actually garnered, Ichaso explained this was a consequence of the "frothy" yet "ephemeral" emotions inspired by the Ortodoxo leader.[15] He estimated that if the elections had been held immediately after his Sunday evening broadcast, the vote totals and survey would have corresponded with more exactitude.

CRIES OF FRAUD

Chibás was fond of saying that his twenty years in public life were largely free of contradictions. However, his take on the election was a zigzag writ large. Initially, Chibás appeared satisfied with his performance and expressed both optimism and magnanimity in a public statement released on June 2. He allowed that the government's "enormous financial resources" had ensured victory but claimed its triumph would be fleeting.[16] "Four years represents very little time in the life of a people," he said, and recalling how quickly the tide had changed during World War II, offered, "It's the time between the Battle of Dunkerque and the Battle of Berlin."[17] Chibás duly mentioned the "betrayal" of PPC bosses who "deserted to the enemy" but emphasized the efforts of ordinary Cubans who replenished the party's ranks with "astonishing speed."[18] He also lauded Cuba's military men for their impartiality and the citizenry for voting in an orderly fashion. Eddy even promised to be the "first to recognize it" if Carlos Prío presided over a good government.[19]

During his June 6 radio show, however, Chibás spewed pure bile. He asserted that Prío owed his victory to a "giant fraud" and "the most corrupt electoral process in the history of our republic."[20] This was an astonishing and reckless charge, not least because of Cuba's substantial record of ballot box manipulation in years past. Even as the 1948 poll was flawed, especially in terms of vote buying, there was no evidence of military intervention as in 1940.[21] Moreover, the present irregularities, contemptible as they were, could hardly compare to the election of 1916 when Mario García Menocal (Raúl Menocal's father) maintained himself in office with the assistance of three hundred thousand ghost voters and the not-so-mysterious disappearance of masses of opposition ballots.[22] Nor were they a match for the tightly managed 1936 contest, in which the Auténticos, Communists, and ABC party refused to participate because their leaders were exiled or imprisoned for the most part. Chibás, of course, knew better but his hatred of Prío overwhelmed any logical considerations. Aside from paying cash for votes, Eddy accused the communications ministry of retaining at least fifty thousand registration cards, which were converted to pro-government tallies on election day. He also mentioned that the Auténtico-Republican alliance distributed more than twenty thousand government jobs in exchange for votes. Some were obvious botellas. For example, two thousand Havana residents were named coffee plantation inspectors although their closest connection to plant life was the capital's tree-lined sidewalks.

Nor was Chibás alone in questioning the election results. Juan Marinello, the Communist candidate who finished a distant fourth, also impugned Prío's victory.[23] During the second week of June, Ricardo Núñez Portuondo piled on as well. Speaking to reporters, he announced that the "apparently legal" Auténtico-Republican triumph was in fact "spurious."[24] Núñez Portuondo recognized that the Superior Electoral Tribunal and military, provincial, and municipal authorities had performed their duties transparently. Nevertheless, the Liberal chief asserted that "the government of President Grau San Martín shamelessly unleashed every facet of the state's machinery in order to falsify the results of the elections, which have brought dishonor and ignominy to our democracy."[25] In a monologue reminiscent of his Ortodoxo opponent, Núñez Portuondo mused that a new, more subtle sort of tyranny had taken shape and was compromising the soul of his compatriots.

> When the armed forces use violence to impede the exercise of voting rights, it produces a reaction of indignation, of anger culminating in gestures of gallant rebellion that, in the end, result in vindication and reform. Such rebellions have, since independence, achieved all the political and social advancements of the Cuban people. However, when part of the citizenry yields to bribes of the most varied forms, ranging from party assemblies that offer their services for dozens or hundreds of thousands of pesos to people in high positions who accept botellas or "protection" or those who are complicit with the black market, embezzlement, speculation, illegal dealings, unpunished crimes and the exploitation of social evils; or purchasing votes freely and openly without intervention from the authorities or its agents because it is precisely they who have organized the entire corrupt system, then one feels deep inside his spirit the immense pain of the great moral tragedy shaking the Cuban people.[26]

This statement caused a predictable uproar and, despite its poignancy, earned him contempt as well as sympathy. For instance, a *Bohemia* correspondent remarked that the tactics Núñez Portuondo railed against had also been employed by Liberal and Democratic bigwigs and were less successful only because they no longer controlled the levers of government power. Left unsaid but clear to all was the Liberal head's greatest failing, a defect cited by sympathizers as well as foes, that he could never claim to represent a "revolution of honor" while he presided over a party swollen with Machado-era speculators and murderers.

BUILDING THE PARTY

In many respects, the 1948 elections were a coming-out party for Chibás. Although he had long been one of Cuba's most charismatic orators, and his gifts as a showman were evident every Sunday evening, the presidential campaign marked him as a rising star in the island's political firmament—

one that had exclusively belonged, since 1933, to Grau and Batista. His unique style of politics, one that demolished all formal barriers between candidate and voter, was clearly popular. Flinging himself off truck beds and into the arms of admirers was merely the newest and most sensational in a series of similar gestures. Chibás also liked to fill his Packard with close friends every few weeks, drive to a barbershop, and invite people to discuss politics with them while his locks were trimmed. Of course, his walks to CMQ studios on Sunday evenings always attracted substantial crowds.

Given his undeniable acclaim among Cuba's masses, the challenge now was for Chibás to build a party capable of securing the presidency in 1952. This involved two immediate tasks. First, it was imperative to enroll most or all of the 156,054 citizens who had voted for him but did not belong to the PPC. Second, the party required a bloodletting of traitors and the establishment of a loyal, competent hierarchy. Before Chibás could ponder these tasks, he needed to regain the PPC presidency, currently held by Millo Ochoa. He did so formally on June 5, during a meeting at Ortodoxo headquarters. Ochoa himself was under suspicion by party hard-liners, particularly as he had appeared in the Liberal-Democratic column during the race for provincial governor of Oriente—which he lost. In late May, an Ortodoxo official had written to Ochoa's brother Guarro, the mayor of Holguín, requesting an explanation. The scarcely believable reply was that Millo "had not agreed to a pact" but rather had been "recommended" for the post in "disinterested" fashion by the other parties because he had the best chance of winning.[27] Chibás was aware of the situation but turned a blind eye, having always shown more nuance and tolerance than fanatical isolationists within the PPC.[28] Hence, after Ochoa was replaced as party president, he remained the Ortodoxo boss in Oriente with Eddy's wholehearted support.

By contrast, Chibás was less sanguine about other deviators—especially in the party's lower rungs. During and after the campaign, letters detailing every sort of duplicity arrived on his desk courtesy of livid Ortodoxo loyalists. In response, Chibás published an article in *El Crisol* on June 10 outlining his plan to cleanse the party of double-dealers. This gesture was received enthusiastically by the PPC rank and file, including Manuel Mozo Toledo of Havana, who stated that "one needs to come to our party willing to give everything for the good of Cuba without expecting personal rewards; those who want something more can go to the other parties that offer inciso K and sinecures or to the Liberal millionaires club; we offer only shame and honor for the people of Cuba."[29] Ofilia Khouray, a PPC leader in Camagüey, put the matter more succinctly, informing Chibás that "just as you wish, all the traitors will be eliminated."[30] During his August 1 broadcast, Chibás thundered, "To those traitors who haven't resigned already, we are warning you to do so immediately. In this way, you will save us the trouble of expelling you."[31] He added, "We desire a pure party, composed of men and women of proven honor, without opportunists or sleazy politicians."[32] To drive his point home once and for all, Chibás referred to an article in *Bohemia* regarding a meeting of Batista and other Cuban politicos in Miami who were contemplating the formation of a new party. Among other things, the ex-general told his guests that "when I was president, many politicians who today occupy elevated positions alongside Grau and now refer to me with rancor, used to approach me in order to ask favors or for money. Chibás, on the other hand, never asked me for anything."[33] Eddy retorted that "Batista is right to say that I never asked him for anything. But now, since he's no longer president of the republic, I would indeed like to request something: don't ever think of joining the Cuban People's Party."[34]

Running parallel to the fury directed toward renegade Ortodoxos was pride at having contributed to a worthwhile endeavor. On June 2, a party member named Carmen Hernández wrote Chibás a letter expressing her "profound sense of spiritual satisfaction" with his campaign.[35] She added that

> For me and the many others who surely think the same way, we recognize that you have triumphed over thievery and pillage. The eloquence of those votes toward your candidacy shows us that we can still have faith in a people who know how to choose what's best and will be ready to do so in future opportunities. As a soldier in the ranks, I am ready to receive your orders![36]

Similarly, a supporter from the city of Cárdenas with a literary bent declared, "The election result has reaffirmed our belief that 'not everything is rotten in the state of Denmark.'"[37] An Ortodoxo couple from Bauta, a town twenty-five miles southwest of Havana, confirmed that *chibasista* fervor extended beyond Cuba's adult population. They recounted an anecdote involving their four-year-old son, Nivaldo, who was accustomed to spending weekend afternoons in a nearby park. On June 16, while his parents were lost in conversation, the boy wandered across the playground toward the local Auténtico party office, whereupon he opened the door and shouted, "Long live Chibás!" to the surprise of those assembled. This was hardly surprising as Nivaldo apparently had acquired the habit of yelling "Vote for Chibás!" at anyone who visited the family home.[38] Chibás drew strength from these and other confessions of unconditional support. On his radio show, he reinforced the enthusiasm of his followers by announcing that

> Our party, which is the party of the great masses, the Cuban People's Party, the only real opposition party, must demonstrate, both in its platform and in actual practice to be against the vices of traditional politics: *personalismo*, sleaze, squabbling factions, clans, elitism, cabinet intrigues, etc. This is not the party of no one but rather the people's party.[39]

As the Ortodoxos proceeded to rebuild, Chibás ruled out any possibility of joining the government. This was a statement of principle but also indicated that Chibás was now firmly in charge of the party and would remain so for the foreseeable future. After all, most of the pact-friendly faction had deserted or been expelled, and those who remained were in no position to challenge him. Nonetheless, this tactic flew in the face of conventional Cuban politics and would be tested early and often. Shortly after the election, rumors began circulating that Carlos Prío would offer Chibás the commerce ministry. Speculation heightened on June 17, when Sergio Carbó endorsed his friend for the position in a *Prensa Libre* editorial entitled "Chibás Could Be the Man of the Hour." Four days later, however, Chibás sent an extensive private letter to Carbó explaining why he could never accept such an offer. Chibás claimed, "In moments of great crisis, be they social or economic, true leaders, in order to be useful to their countries, must not compromise their moral authority by accommodating themselves to shady politics."[40] Chibás cited Georges Clemenceau in 1914 and Charles de Gaulle in 1940 as examples of men who refused to join their nation's government during difficult times because it would have involved damaging ethical concessions. Instead, both jealously guarded their prestige and waited until their moral authority could effect a greater impact. Of course, Chibás also employed these parables to defend himself against two oft-repeated charges. Namely, Ortodoxo deal makers had accused him of forsaking attainable albeit incremental improvements in the name of an unrealistic ideal. The Auténticos, for their part, continually reprimanded him for dividing the country's revolutionaries. In any case, Chibás emphasized that Carlos Prío could create much goodwill even without Ortodoxo assistance. For example, if the president-elect appointed a universally respected figure like Miguel Coyula as prime minister, Chibás pledged his party would support the government without asking for anything in return. In this way, Chibás revealed his second objective as Ortodoxo party chief. Besides constructing an organization capable of reaching power, he would, in the meantime, pressure Cuba's leaders into behaving more honorably.

THE NEW ADMINISTRATION

On September 26, two weeks before his inauguration, Carlos Prío announced the composition of his cabinet. Prío's appointments were a mélange of good intentions and backroom lobbying by his three patrons: Ramón Guillermo Grau, Alonso Pujol, and José Manuel Alemán. For example, Prío knew the treasury had been sacked during Grau's term and wished to place an honest man in charge of Cuba's finances. His first choice for the post was the universally respected Carlos Hevia. In short order, Hevia proposed a thorough audit and aimed to publish the results as a means of restoring public confidence. Horrified, Grau summoned Prío to the presidential palace and told him, "this cannot be."⁴¹ He explained that

> This is just too dangerous! You know we have a small deficit and, in addition, I've just been informed that Alemán asked Isauro (the present treasury secretary Isauro Valdés) for certain sums of money, at your request, in order to pay for your electoral campaign . . . I ignored that such things were going on in the treasury and I'm not ready for these errors to be publicly pinned on my administration. It seems to me that the best thing would be to leave Isauro in his place. This way we can all rest easy.⁴²

Prío left the palace without contradicting Grau, but he was obviously troubled by the president's suggestion. Valdés was a devotee of Alemán and much as Prío had welcomed the support of BAGA during the electoral season, he was now anxious to free himself of the ex–education minister's hirelings. Forced to surrender Hevia, he decided to name someone who would agree to cover up the treasury's shortfall but whose loyalty would not be in doubt. Hence, Prío tapped his younger brother Antonio.

The foreign ministry presented a different dilemma. As Prío had no specific candidate in mind, he was besieged by solicitations. Diego Vicente Tejera, the Auténtico boss of Matanzas and chief lieutenant of Miguelito Suárez Fernández, applied for the job but was vetoed by Grau. Ramón Corona, a protégé of Alonso Pujol, also threw his hat in the ring.⁴³ Alonso Pujol, who was presently in Brussels and always on the lookout for mammon, had recently hatched a scheme requiring a sympathetic figure in the foreign ministry. This involved hawking Cuban visas to an estimated twenty-five thousand Jews in war-torn Europe for 500 pesos apiece. Prío was less than enamored by this prospect and decided to place Corona in charge of the justice ministry instead. At the same time, he remained eager to find a position for Hevia and thus settled the contest for the foreign ministry by selecting him.

Expectations ran particularly high for education and commerce, given how brazenly they had been abused under Grau. Prío evinced his concern for Cuba's schoolchildren by entrusting them to Aureliano Sánchez Arango, one of his closest political confidants. Sánchez Arango boasted outstanding revolutionary credentials, having been a member of the 1927 Student Directorate and later on joining the violent, anti-Batista outfit Joven Cuba. More importantly, he was competent and honest. Sánchez Arango also possessed a brash temperament that reveled in controversy, which seemed ideal for the task of eradicating the assortment of grafters and gangsters inhabiting Cuba's education ministry. As for the black market, long a source of ill feelings, Prío designated José Andreu to tame the island's hodgepodge of scarce items. Andreu was a Republican and medical doctor who had served in Grau's cabinet as health minister. Although he was an able man, his appointment mainly requited a campaign debt to the Auténticos' electoral partner. In fact, this trend was evident in most of Prío's choices. To placate Grau and Alemán, he chose Francisco Grau Alsina as agriculture minister. Aside from being one of the president's favorite nephews, "Pancho" was so closely linked with the former education minister that his surname's initials formed the "GA" in BAGA. Prío further appeased Grau by naming Primitivo Rodríguez to his cabinet as minister without portfolio. Rodríguez was an Auténtico congressman whose exaggerated sycophancy toward the president was the subject of many a political cartoon.[44]

Chibás, who touted himself as the leader of Cuba's "real" opposition, scoffed that Prío had "announced the birth of a giant but a dwarf emerged instead."[45] Eddy acknowledged that some future ministers, principally Hevia, were "figures of undoubted prestige," but on the whole, he dubbed Prío's appointees "the council of mockery."[46] With an unrivaled memory for political foibles, Chibás recounted a host of embarrassing anecdotes about the cabinet members to be. For example, he reminded his radio audience that Interior Minister Rubén de León and minister-without-portfolio Ramón Vasconcelos had both served together before, under Batista, but with less than stellar results. In fact, León had been tried for misconduct because Vasconcelos had accused him of removing a marble staircase from the education ministry and installing it in his home. Chibás recalled that Virgilio Pérez, the communications minister, had been a member of the judicial police during Machado's regime and was director of the National Institute of Coffee under Grau, where he had engaged in various "scandalous dealings."[47] Edgardo Buttari, the labor minister, had been commerce minister under Batista, where he had allegedly used scarce supplies of condensed milk to buy the support of Liberal party delegates. Chibás reserved his harshest words for Francisco Grau Alsina, whom he accused of stealing 2 million pesos destined for Cuba's peasants while serving his uncle as assistant agriculture minister. Following the cue of his BAGA coconspirator, "Pancho" invested the embezzled funds in two country estates and commandeered agriculture ministry equipment to work the lands. Lastly, Chibás pointed out that the cabinet violated Article 126 of Cuba's constitution, which stated that half the ministers must be non-legislators. A week later, he proudly announced that Prío had recognized the error and rectified it.

October 10 was Cuba's most sacred national holiday. On that date in 1868, Carlos Manuel de Céspedes had declared the country's independence and initiated the struggle for liberation from Spain with a modest army of 147 men, 30 of whom were freed slaves from his plantation—the "Demajagua." In choosing October 10 as inauguration day, the framers of Cuba's 1940 constitution laid a symbolic burden on the presidency that both Batista and Grau had shirked: namely, to honor the example of Cuba's founding father.[48]

During his address, the handsome and congenial Prío said all the right things. He spoke of a national renewal headlined by land reform, an anti-gangster law, and creation of a national bank. However, even as Prío attempted to set a new tone, José Manuel Alemán struck a devastating final blow on behalf of the previous regime. While Cubans sized up their new president, Alemán, now a senator from Havana, matter-of-factly looted the island's currency reserves.

Accompanied by a group of suitcase-bearing sidekicks, Alemán headed a convoy of four education ministry trucks destined for the treasury building. Walking breezily past the guards, they scooped up millions of US dollars, Italian lire, British pounds, French francs, Portuguese escudos, Soviet rubles, and, of course, Cuban pesos. Their baggage swollen with booty, they proceeded to Havana's airfield, where a chartered DC-3 awaited. Alemán and three cronies lugged the US cash aboard and took off for Florida. This portion of the stash, estimated at $19 million, was transferred to Alemán's business headquarters in Miami Beach. An employee later confessed that "bundles of $1000 dollar bills were tossed around like wrapped packages of pennies."[49] As for the remaining treasure, Alemán's henchmen were instructed to exchange it in local banks. Two weeks later, details of the heist began trickling out. On October 25, Raoul Alfonso Gonsé, director of *Alerta*, censured the previous regime's "last raid" against the treasury and lamented that the new administration had no alternative but to "tighten its belt" in order to meet its financial obligations.[50] Urging Prío not to be an "accomplice" to this crime, he concluded with a favorite phrase of Chibás, namely, "jail the thieves."[51]

Instead of focusing on this issue, Chibás had become obsessed with the "fascist penetration" of Argentine president Juan Domingo Perón into Latin America generally and Cuba specifically.[52] In fact, he spent a considerable amount of time collecting documents on Argentine agents in Cuba, their code names and supposed objectives. During his October 24 broadcast, Chibás noted that the Havana radio station RHC Cadena Azul, one of the capital's largest and most prominent, had recently begun spouting pro-Perón propaganda. Chibás stated that a secret deal was in place between the station's Cuban owner, Amado Trinidad, and Argentina's government-controlled Radio Belgrano. In exchange for favorable coverage, the latter had agreed to pay a million pesos over a four-year period. "It is grave," said Chibás, "when a Cuban broadcaster with the public influence of RHC Cadena Azul, which has listeners throughout Central America, is controlled by a foreign dictator with the fascist characteristics of Perón."[53] Chibás pointed out that Perón had already purchased the allegiance of radio stations in Peru, Bolivia, Chile, and Paraguay. He also maintained cozy relations with authoritarian regimes in the Dominican Republic, Nicaragua, and Honduras. Just as damaging, "General Perón" suppressed free speech in his native land and employed his surrogates to do the same abroad.

The following week, Chibás devoted nearly his entire show to Perón's overarching shadow. He was spurred partly by a military coup in Peru that toppled the elected president, José Luis Bustamante, on October 29. Chibás believed it was no coincidence the plot originated in southern Peru, which was suspiciously close to Argentina's border. Styling himself something of a prophet, Chibás declared, "What do they say now, those who last Sunday called me crazy for my accusations against Perón?"[54] Within Cuba, the Ortodoxo chief accused Perón of co-opting labor leaders such as Ángel Cofiño, president of the Cuban Federation of Labor, and Vicente Rubiera, who headed the Union of Cuban Telephone Workers. Both men, he claimed, were regular guests at the Argentine embassy. Chibás also revisited the presumed deal between RHC Cadena Azul and Radio Belgrano, which he considered the most pressing threat. He cited a statement by Manuel Fernández, president of the Cuban Radio Broadcasters Federation, who expressed "serious worry" that Amado Trinidad "has converted himself into a propagandist for Perón, who is an opponent of free speech in Argentina."[55] Given Trinidad's sudden affinity for all things Argentine, Chibás mused that he should refer to himself as a *gaucho* rather a guajiro.[56] More ominously, this affair confirmed Eddy's view that constitutionalism remained fragile in Cuba and was under siege from both external and internal sources.

In this sense, RHC Cadena Azul represented an ideal bogeyman because the station also towed a pro-government line.[57] Even as Chibás baited Amado Trinidad, he never lost sight of his primary opponent—Carlos Prío. The new president was off to a fairly auspicious beginning, having collaborated more closely with Cuba's legislators during his first two months than either Grau or Batista in their entire terms. For the first time, the semi-parliamentary system envisioned by Cuba's 1940 constitution seemed to be taking shape. Prío's first initiative, the so-called Anti-Gangster Law, was approved in the senate with wide bipartisan support on November 10. The measure created a special court for prosecuting gangster-related crimes with the understanding that they would be severely punished. Moreover, it required clubs and associations to register with the government and obligated guntoting citizens to obtain a license. Explaining his vote, the Liberal senator Eduardo Suárez Rivas declared that "when the government proclaims that it would like to rid the country of gangsters, the opposition parties have an obligation to provide the president with the necessary instruments."[58] On the other hand, Chibás mocked the statute as a "lie and deception," alleging it would deprive law-abiding Cubans of weapons and leave them at mercy of *pistoleros*.[59] For emphasis he added that "the gangsters with ties to the presidential palace have received the law with happiness and enthusiasm."[60] Cuba's gangster problem, continued Chibás, was not due to a lack of laws but the fact that gunmen never seemed to remain very long in prison—usually because they had friends in high places. Indeed, much of Prío's anti-gangster rhetoric was undermined by the fact that he, like Grau, had filled the nation's security services with pseudo-revolutionary triggermen. For example, Eufemio Fernández, the new Bureau of Special Investigations chief, was a member of Acción Revolucionaria Guiteras (ARG).

Prío attained less ambiguous success when the chamber of representatives unanimously approved a law to establish the National Bank of Cuba on December 21. During negotiations in the senate, Prime Minister Tony Varona stressed the administration's desire for a "common effort" including opposition lawmakers that would produce the "most technocratic national bank in the world."[61] Even so, minority leaders such as Eduardo Suárez Rivas and his fellow Liberal Ramón Zaydín stalled the national bank statute, believing it would be useless without budgetary and accounting reforms. Chibás, who was no longer a senator, echoed their concerns. Without the necessary safeguards, he declared, the national bank may as well feature a "roulette wheel, baccarat, poker and Paco Prío."[62] In the event, creation of Cuba's National Bank was closely followed by the Organic Budgetary Law, which mandated transparent accounting practices. As a gesture of goodwill, Prío provided an itemized budget to Congress even before the law took effect—becoming the first president to do so in eleven years. Both the Organic Budgetary Law and National Bank fulfilled directives of the 1940 constitution that had been ignored by the previous two presidents. Moreover, Prío delivered on his promise to oversee a "technocratic" bank by appointing Felipe Pazos, a promising thirty-six-year-old economist, as its director. Pazos had been a member of the Cuban delegation to the Bretton Woods conference in 1944 and had just completed a three-year stint at the International Monetary Fund when he was nominated.

The education ministry seemed another preliminary triumph. During the interim between Prío's election and his inauguration, José Manuel Alemán had paid off some favors by handing out a "mountain" of education ministry jobs.[63] Aureliano Sánchez Arango, the new chief, rejected them. Sánchez Arango also cultivated a swashbuckling image by piloting his own plane to all parts of the island, showing up unannounced and conducting on-spot school inspections. Within two months, he fired a plethora of teachers who did not meet certification requirements. In a shocking move, Sánchez Arango even renounced the right to name teachers or school inspectors. Henceforth, they would be hired according to an objective set of guidelines issued, ironically, by Alemán in 1946. Chibás personally hated Sánchez Arango but nonetheless applauded this act as a "commendable rectification."[64] However, this compliment was not allowed to linger in the minds of his listeners. Moments later, Chibás confessed sarcastic surprise that Prío or his education minister had been offended by inciso K or BAGA-fueled appointments in the first place. After all, Prío had used them to win the presidency just as Alemán's designees had hoped to net an easy paycheck. "In other words," concluded Chibás, "from this mud hole and from such corruption the present government was born."[65] Heeding the advice of his friend Ignacio Mendoza, Chibás supplemented his criticism with a series of countermeasures. Specifically, he believed the massive teacher layoffs violated the principle of tenure and replaced the problem of indiscriminate hiring with the equally unsavory prospect of arbitrary dismissals. He also drew attention to the many teachers who had purchased their positions because, given the education ministry's venality, there was no other way to practice their profession. Rather than persecuting such figures, he urged Sánchez Arango to jail the high-level officials who profited from this practice.

Above all, the thousands of newly unemployed teachers were less interested in what was best for Cuba's education ministry than they were in recovering their jobs. Six weeks into Sánchez Arango's term, their growing clamor led Eduardo Suárez Rivas to submit a motion of interpellation. Sánchez Arango appeared before the senate on December 15 and connived, with the approval of Senate President Miguelito Suárez Fernández, to fill the visitor's gallery with sympathizers. This was more a matter of comfort than necessity, as the education minister advanced his case for reform by ruthlessly detailing the abuses of his predecessors. Special attention was reserved for the schemes of José Manuel Alemán, which included manipulating tax collections, the employment of ghost workers, and outright theft of ministry funds. The onetime "monarch of inciso K," who had pulled out all the stops to avoid appearing before the senate in April of 1947, was now brutally exposed in absentia by a barrage of incriminating documents. While Sánchez Arango emerged unbowed from these proceedings, they stirred the displeasure of Grau, who believed Alemán had been his best minister.

Grau's fury was also aroused by an investigation into administrative corruption during his term, announced by Pelayo Cuervo Navarro on November 8. That afternoon, at around 4:30 p.m., Cuervo Navarro requested that Finance Minister Antonio Prío appear before the senate and explain why more than 100 million pesos were missing from the treasury. Speaking in the Capitolio to a rapt audience of journalists, members of the public, and fellow senators, Cuervo Navarro revealed a wealth of scandalous tidbits. Chief among these were the disappearance of one million pesos from customs service coffers the day before Prío's inauguration and indications that Grau had daily stowed away 60,000 pesos from illicit sources during his years in power. A *Carteles* correspondent reminded readers that "this is not the rumor of a mosquito."[66] Rather, it was Pelayo Cuervo Navarro, one of Cuba's most honest men, pointing the finger. Determined to avoid a potentially embarrassing scenario, the Auténtico senator Lomberto Díaz and his Republican counterpart Santiago Rey lamely asserted that the finance minister was working long days and could not spare even a moment of his time. When pressed, they were blunter—informing Cuervo Navarro that his motion of interpellation would never gain majority approval. Despite this setback, Cuervo Navarro doggedly continued his inquiry and revised the amount of stolen funds upward as he gained possession of new documents. In effect, the former Ortodoxo and current Liberal senator's crusade was an advertisement for the benefits of pragmatism. Contrary to PPC isolationists who cherished the prospect of an ideal government sometime in the future, Cuervo Navarro argued for the best possible one immediately. His abandonment of the Ortodoxos had disgusted many party members, Chibás foremost among them, but Cuervo Navarro's activities presently represented the best chance of achieving something his old companions only talked about: putting government thieves on trial and delivering the guilty behind bars.

While a potential exposé of Grau's administration could prove awkward, especially as Prío had also pocketed significant sums, the new president's direst challenge involved the military. After eight years of civilian rule, Cuba's soldiers were as liable to violate the island's laws as they were to defend them. Genovevo Pérez Dámera, Grau's army chief, set the tone for his subordinates by periodically ignoring elected officials or judges. For example, he offered a public showing of the Orfila footage, gleefully overriding the interior minister's ban. Further, he had no qualms about contradicting Cuba's Superior Electoral Tribunal or defending the captain who murdered Jesús Menéndez in extrajudicial fashion. Even worse, Pérez Dámera showed scant concern for Cuba's precarious finances and demanded inordinate sums for the military. When the treasury ministry's head accountant objected, a confidant of Pérez Dámera gruffly informed some friends of Prío's that "this little guy doesn't realize that Genovevo can get rid of him and the president whenever he feels like it."[67] In opting to retain him, while dismissing all of Grau's cabinet ministers, Prío was most likely moved by two key factors. First, Pérez Dámera had been instrumental in coaxing Miguelito Suárez Fernández back into the Auténtico fold. In doing so, he had cleared the last hurdle facing Prío's presidential bid.[68] Moreover, he was a sincere enemy of Cuba's *pistoleros* and a useful counterweight to the gangster-infested police forces.

If Cubans were curious as to whether the irresponsible or prudent Pérez Dámera would show up first, they did not have to wait long to find out. Shortly after Prío's term began, a retired general named Abelardo Gómez, who lived in Miami, accused Pérez Dámera of embezzling 2 million pesos from the military retirement fund. On November 13, Pérez Dámera responded with a bizarre and disturbing rant against the island's media outlets.

> I urge, emphatically, from now on that those in the national press who assume such cowardly attitudes, for God knows what reasons, to limit themselves to

topics that rightfully correspond to publicity organs. They must understand that the obligation to nobly and disinterestedly serve the republic is more important than chasing after a few extra coins! We have had to make great efforts in order to contain the spontaneous impulses of the soldiers, who without exception have demonstrated their anger and a desire to go beyond the military barracks to attack those responsible for the insult. If mercenaries without conscience were to reach the Cuban public and commit imprudent or evil deeds, the responsibility would rest squarely with the press. We would like to advertise, once and for all, to anyone who would ignore our message, that we will not in any way tolerate those who question our prestige and reputation based on lies, because in that case we will know how, in a virile manner, to demand the respect we deserve without worrying about any consequences that may result.[69]

Needless to say, the island's journalists were horrified. Yet again, Pérez Dámera had disdained Cuba's laws and declared himself the ultimate arbiter of its public life. In the senate, Antonio Martínez Fraga demanded that the defense minister appear and personally explain the army chief's declaration. However, no official quorum took place the whole week because Auténtico and Republican legislators stayed away. During his radio show, Chibás read aloud Article 33 of the constitution, which provided for complete freedom of speech and confirmed that the judiciary alone had the power to determine whether charges were libelous. By now, however, the scandal centered less on Pérez Dámera's threats than Prío's reaction to them. On November 15, the president notified his cabinet that he had authorized the general's screed—adding that he personally had no intention of permitting the press to criticize his family. Chibás noted that many of Prío's relations were also public figures, including his older brother Paco, a senator from Pinar del Río; his younger sibling Antonio, the treasury minister; his brother-in-law Enrique Cotú Henríquez, a member of the chamber of representatives; and his father-in-law, Gerardo Tarrero, the director of Cuba's lottery. "According to this theory," said Chibás, "the day that all the president's ministries are occupied by relatives there won't be any opposition in Cuba because the sacred family of his majesty, Carlos I, is taboo."[70]

That same day, Prío exacerbated the situation by deciding to temporarily shut down the radio shows of Chibás and Salvador García Agüero, his two most popular critics, ostensibly because of "verbal excesses."[71] Suddenly, the man seeking to restore his party's good name was verging on tyranny and faced with mass protests. University and secondary school students joined ordinary citizens in the streets. The Federation of Radio Broadcasters, the Professional Journalists Association, the Cuban Press Bloc, the Federation of University Students, *Prensa Libre*, and *Bohemia* all weighed in with strong condemnations. Given the furor, Prío reversed himself within twenty-four hours. The erudite Manuel Bisbé quipped that the president was like Penelope, wife of Odysseus, who unraveled at night what she wove during the day. Chibás called this the "politics of zigzag," created by those who were "inebriated."[72] With a glint in his eye, Chibás added, "One is no longer allowed to say drunks because Virgilio (the communications minister) may deem it incorrect."[73]

THE RETURN OF BATISTA

On Saturday, November 20, armed with parliamentary immunity and personal guarantees from the president, Fulgencio Batista boarded a plane for Havana. Upon arriving, the ex-general was met by a throng of several thousand supporters whose fervor was such that he was able to reach his automobile only with the help of a military contingent. Ten days later, Batista appeared in the Capitolio where a less sympathetic audience awaited. Strangely enough for a man who had once ruled Cuba as a military strongman and an elected president, he was, according to a *Carteles* correspondent, "visibly embarrassed and suffering from stage fright like any debutant."[74] Batista was helped through his initial disorientation by the ex-Ortodoxo and former Democrat José Enrique Bringuier, who escorted him toward the Liberal delegation. Sensing everyone's eyes upon him, Batista rushed to sit down, but the place he chose belonged to Rafael Guas Inclán. He then settled into the adjoining seat, which pertained to Eduardo Suárez Rivas. Moments later, Suárez Rivas appeared, and Batista rose to greet him. Instead of informing Batista that the bench was his, the mischievous Suárez Rivas dropped a tie pin on it, causing the onetime military chief to jump up in pain and thereafter stand awkwardly in the aisle. Finally, Bringuier reappeared and shepherded Batista to safety in one of the back rows. However, he did not stay long. At his first opportunity, Batista fled the chamber. The *Carteles* reporter estimated that he had spent a mere eleven minutes among his fellow senators before leaving.

During his radio show, Chibás portrayed Batista in even more pathetic terms—describing him as "exhausted, bent under the weight of the millions he stole, subjugated by the president, full of prudence and fear, after asking Prío's government, very docilely, for permission to return."[75] As with most Cuban politicians, Chibás was a man of countless grudges. Three unforgiveable transgressions in his mind were murder, venality, and betrayal of the 1933 revolution. Usually, his enemies were guilty on one or two counts, but Batista was a rare figure who covered all the bases. On this occasion, Chibás wondered how the ex-military chief would assist Prío in undermining Cuba's revolutionary ideals. He noted that Batista, who had often commented on the island's politics while in Florida, was now mum "as if he had come from China or Siberia."[76] Chibás speculated that the ex-general had been allowed back as a ruse to divide the opposition. Needless to say, he felt this was the wrong way for Prío to pursue reforms, saying:

> In order to preach, with moral authority, the value of honest administration, the first thing that must be done, as a gesture of sincerity, is to incarcerate those who have stolen from the National Treasury beginning with Grau San Martín and Fulgencio Batista. Anything else is hypocrisy or complicity. These two men belong in jail not for political reasons but because they are thieves and that's where they would be if there were sufficient shame in this country. In the United States, in England, in Switzerland, in the Scandinavian nations, in any country where laws are respected, these two men would be in prison even if they had only robbed and damaged their people half as much as they actually have.[77]

Despite Batista's hapless senate performance and initial deference, Prío was also playing with fire. Batista commanded considerable admiration among the island's soldiers, whose respect for civilian authority remained uncertain. As if to underline the danger, a military junta in Venezuela toppled the democratically elected Rómulo Gallegos on November 24. Cuba already counted uniformed dictatorships to its east in Nicaragua and its west in the Dominican Republic. Now there was one to the south as well. Even worse, Cuba's northern neighbor, the United States, seemed perfectly inclined to recognize the new Venezuelan regime. During his December 5 broadcast, Chibás did not hesitate to sound the alarm. He accused Prío of "taking a siesta" while Batista cultivated enlisted men and Grau recruited army and naval officers in competing attempts to seize power. "What just occurred in Venezuela," warned Chibás, "and what happened in Peru can be repeated in Cuba. We are in great danger."[78] As proof, he noted that Prío was having a difficult time standing up to his overweight military chief. Recently, Pérez Dámera had replaced a respected general loyal to the president with one of his own devotees over a trivial infraction. Rather than protesting, Prío backed El Gordo. In an episode that inspired less confidence, Pérez Dámera placed Abelardo Gómez, the general who accused him of corruption, under summary arrest. General Gómez had arrived in Havana to challenge the acquittal of Pérez Dámera before a military court on charges of embezzlement, but only after receiving guarantees from Prío regarding his freedom and well-being. Pérez Dámera, obviously, had little use for such promises. Given these circumstances and the fall of democratic governments throughout Latin America, Chibás proclaimed: "Carlos Prío, remember the adage that says: 'when you see your neighbor's beard on fire, soak your own in water.'"[79]

Chibás spent the next few weeks drumming up support for President Gallegos, who had taken refuge in Havana along with many members of Acción Democratica—his political party. In fact, Gallegos was lionized by Cuban leaders across the political spectrum. Carlos Prío received Acción

Democratica exiles with open arms and permitted them to engage in conspiratorial activities on Cuban soil. Moreover, he withheld recognition of the military government. On December 18, a motley collection of political leaders and intellectuals organized a pro-Gallegos rally in Havana's Parque Central. The speakers included Fernando Ortiz, Manuel Bisbé, and Communist chief Juan Marinello, who blamed Gallegos's overthrow on the Truman administration. Chibás, who was an enthusiast of the US president, believed the coup was backed by Wall Street moguls interested in Venezuela's oil, but absolved Truman of any responsibility. Also, Chibás accused Cuban Communists of "unprecedented cynicism," for praising democracy during the gathering while their Venezuelan comrades were busy accommodating the military regime.[80] Above all, Chibás felt there was a lesson that Cuba must not ignore. The Ortodoxo leader, whose radio show reached the entire Caribbean basin, recalled that Venezuelan listeners had ridiculed him when he first underlined the influence of Perón and the threat of military dictatorship in late October. Weeks before Gallegos was ousted, a Venezuelan newspaper accused Chibás of "seeing visions" and asserted that the "epoch of military takeovers and dictatorship is gone forever."[81] Chibás worried that Cubans were similarly smug about the prospect of a barracks revolt.

Chapter Six

"I Would Proudly Go to Prison to Defend the Cuban People"

On the evening of January 1, 1949, Aurelio Álvarez died in a Havana Charitable Society hospital amid a coterie of companions, including Eddy Chibás and Liberal vice-presidential candidate Gustavo Cuervo Rubio. Chibás respected the sixty-seven-year-old Álvarez despite his vociferous belief in pacts and desertion of the Ortodoxos nearly eight months earlier. The PPC leader could forgive these faults because, over a long career that spanned Cuba's entire history as an independent nation, Álvarez had behaved honorably at each major turning point. He joined the island's liberation army at the age of sixteen, where his mettle caught the attention of Commander in Chief Máximo Gómez. In 1926, as a senator and president of the Conservative party, he rejected the policy of *cooperativismo* under which Cuba's political organizations agreed to slavishly follow President Gerardo Machado. After Machado's illegal reelection two years later, Álvarez and his son René actively struggled against the regime. The boy was killed by Machado's soldiers while the father suffered prison and exile. In 1933, Álvarez supported the "100 days" government of Ramón Grau San Martín and the next year became a founding member of the Auténticos. He was elected as a delegate to the constituent assembly that devised the island's constitution and as an Auténtico senator from Camagüey, Álvarez was among the first to denounce the venality of Grau's administration. Álvarez had also warmed Eddy's heart by accusing Prío of betraying the revolution.[1]

As a former legislator, Álvarez lay in state in the Capitolio. During the wake, which attracted present and former lawmakers of every party, a pair of hoary nabobs, Carlos Manuel de la Cruz and Carlos Miguel de Céspedes, discussed the two most talked about figures in Cuban politics—Fulgencio Batista and Chibás.[2] De la Cruz, an erstwhile Democratic parliamentarian who in 1934 had been a heartbeat away from Cuba's presidency, spoke first.[3] "Batista is finished," he said. "He will never again lift his head in triumph. He represents expedience. Those who want money and who took advantage during his years in power will support him, but no one else. If he didn't have the millions he stole from the treasury, he would be selling candy on the street right now."

Céspedes, the former public works minister under Machado and current senator from Matanzas, replied, "You are mistaken. In my opinion, Batista is the most interesting figure in Cuba since the war of independence. He became president after starting from nothing."

"Don't forget, Carlos Miguel, that the slogan 'Shame against Money' obtained 400,000 votes in the last elections. This is the seed that will flower one day! Perhaps tomorrow, in 1950. A new generation is going to judge everything, from the Batista dictatorship up to the present era of Prío."

"When this day arrives," answered the senator from Matanzas, "there will once again be student martyrs and property belonging to government figures will be sacked just as it was during Machado's era. And everything will happen very rapidly because today it's possible to mobilize people by radio, which was impossible during our time." He paused for an instant and then added, "Batista will play his part. Remember that all the colonels enriched themselves while he governed omnipotently and they won't sit idly by. As for Chibás, don't assume he will be able to take advantage of the situation. History shows that all the apostles who light bonfires are burned in them. He will be the instrument who shows the way but will perish."[4]

THE UNFAITHFUL DISCIPLE

While the death of Álvarez deprived Cuba's political scene of a pugnacious and upright pragmatist, another figure with comparable qualities kept his shoulder to the grind. On January 18, Pelayo Cuervo Navarro presented a thirty-three-page accusation to Cuba's Supreme Tribunal alleging 174,241,840 pesos and 14 centavos had been purloined during Grau's administration.[5] The case was subsequently passed along, "like a hot potato," to the Court of Instruction—which was deemed a more appropriate forum by reluctant Supreme Tribunal judges.[6] Lawsuit 82, as Cuervo Navarro's denunciation was officially known, provoked a flurry of speculation. Francisco Ichaso believed it contained "more than sufficient" evidence for criminal proceedings against Grau, some of his ex-ministers, and numerous government functionaries.[7] At the same time, he was realistic, asserting that "there is nothing more difficult in Cuba than punishing administrative corruption," especially as many citizens believed that stealing from the state was relatively harmless.[8] On the other hand, Cubans were beginning to question whether the government would be able to fund basic services. In a cartoon that encapsulated the fears of many, the satirist David portrayed a doubtful man telling his friend that "there will be a budget! But . . . will there be money?"[9] Prío guaranteed both while asserting the shortfall had "nothing to do" with his administration.[10] Chibás, however, begged to differ. On February 10, he visited the Court of Instruction and urged the judge assigned to Lawsuit 82, Antonio Vignier, not to spare Prío's appointees, saying: "To exonerate the thieves who occupy positions in the current government and throw all the blame on former employees of the previous regime . . . would be a monstrous miscarriage of justice and an example of incalculable cowardice."[11] For his part, Prío had followed Cuervo Navarro's relentless accumulation of evidence with dread since it began. The week before the senator submitted his complaint, a treasury ministry official called to ask whether he intended to denounce financial "irregularities" committed during the previous administration.[12] Cuervo Navarro, who responded affirmatively, saw this as evidence that the palace was monitoring his "steps."[13]

Specifically, Prío desired to know if he should brace for a scandal. Just as Cuervo Navarro had been patiently amassing documents, Grau had been collecting a list of grievances against his onetime prime minister. Above all, the former physiology professor had explicitly told Prío of his wish to avoid embarrassment over the treasury deficit—which he blamed on the 1948 election campaign and Prío's need to purchase the popularity he came by naturally. Prío had bent over backward to accommodate Grau, appointing a compliant finance minister and scuttling Cuervo Navarro's attempt at a senate hearing on the matter. However, he had been unwilling to prevent Cuervo Navarro's complaint from reaching the courts. Grau extracted swift revenge for this broken promise during a *Bohemia* interview published on January 31. To begin with, Grau dismissed Prío's attentiveness to the semi-parliamentary system—claiming his erstwhile disciple bought congressional support with stacks of lottery tickets, which were resold at a hefty profit. The former president, who had never needed to bribe the legislative branch since he ruled by decree, boasted of using lottery revenue for "superior objectives," such as hospitals.[14] He cast further aspersions on Cuba's semi-parliamentary model by saying it was an "invention" of Batista, who had charged Colonel Jaime Mariné with the task of cajoling lawmakers.[15] In general, Grau confessed, "If someone asked me now why I made Prío president, I would tell him I made a mistake."[16]

Although Prío had expected a reproach, he was stunned by the rawness of Grau's comments. Shortly after reading the interview, he sat down for lunch with his brothers Paco and Antonio, along with members of his inner political circle, such as Tony Varona, Virgilio Pérez, and the congressman Segundo Curti. Prío was livid but eschewed a forceful public rejoinder, particularly as Grau remained Auténtico party president and master of its machinery.

Instead, he remonstrated among his select but sympathetic audience in the presidential palace. In the first place, Prío bristled at Grau's charge that he was an "unfaithful disciple," saying he had always followed his "own impulses."[17] Further, Prío was irritated by the thefts from the treasury. "We have," he said, "shown extraordinary politeness in calling a deficit that which was really embezzlement, much of it realized after my election and, more concretely, between September 9 and October 10."[18] Lastly, Prío sensed something untoward in Grau's remarks. Like many Cuban politicians, he was acutely sensitive to possible signs of a coup. Grau, he opined, "thinks only of regaining power, but because he's old [his nickname was "El Viejo"] and must wait eight years in order to legally run for president, he's willing to try anything."[19] This sentiment was echoed by Miguelito Suárez Fernández, who told a *Bohemia* reporter that "Grau has been corroded by his ambition to re-conquer power through any means, except legitimate popular election."[20] Unlike Prío, who grumbled privately, the senate president was one of many Auténticos who spoke to journalists with alacrity. Aureliano Sánchez Arango deviously suggested that Grau's comments were rooted in "senility," and wondered whether this also explained the "disaster" of his final months as president.[21] Asked if he had read the Grau interview, Diego Vicente Tejera explained that "nobody believes in (Grau) anymore. The country has lost respect for him."[22] A survey commissioned by *Bohemia* seemed to confirm this view. If faced with a choice between Prío and Grau, 64.09 percent of Cubans preferred the current president while only 6.14 percent opted for his predecessor.[23] In many respects, this was a more devastating verdict than the jeremiads of Auténtico leaders—many of whom wished him ill for their own personal reasons.

Of all Grau's criticisms, the only one that remained unchallenged involved the Anti-Gangster Law, which, he declared, "has only served to encourage the very thing it seeks to avoid."[24] Grau, of course, had scarce moral authority in this case as he set the stage for gangsters during his own administration and had famously taken ill during the Orfila massacre. Nevertheless, Prío's law had done nothing to stem a recent outbreak of violence. On the evening of January 12, Rubén Darío González, a member of the National Police who also belonged to Union Insurreccional Revolucionaria (UIR), was shot seventeen times as he nursed a drink in Havana's seedy San Isidro district. In typical fashion, the bar's other patrons cowered on the floor until the getaway car had removed to a safe distance. The murderers were soon identified as Gustavo Massó and Juan Regueiro, both of whom were university students tied to Movimiento Socialista Revolucionaria (MSR) leader Rolando Masferrer. Masferrer's newspaper, *El Tiempo en Cuba*, praised them for eliminating the "assassin" González, who was implicated in the death of Manolo Castro.[25] Unfortunately, their celebration was short lived as their corpses turned up on the Havana Country Club's manicured grounds within seventy-two hours. During his January 16 broadcast, Chibás pointed out that Massó and Regueiro had last been seen entering police custody before their tortured and disfigured bodies were found. "It was the same way during the Machado era!" he shouted, anxious to make hay from the scandal.[26] Rather than pursuing justice in the courts, the National Police, with its strong UIR contingent, had apparently resolved the case in more drastic fashion. Not only had Massó and Regueiro been killed, but the latter's stepfather, Nemesio Fernández, had been interrogated and beaten with such ferocity that his wounds required treatment in the infirmary. The *Prensa Libre* columnist Néstor Piñango, who closely followed Cuba's gangster scene, explained that all National Policemen, even high-ranking figures, performed tasks for the UIR even if they did not formally belong to the group. Hence, National Police Chief José Caramés, who was unaffiliated, involved himself in UIR business although the actual killing tended to be done by members like Lieutenant Armando Correa.

Public outrage was compounded by the fact that another cadaver had already been deposited in the Havana Country Club earlier in the week. The victim, identified as Rolando Vázquez Contreras, was a construction worker belonging to Acción Revolucionaria Guiteras (ARG)—an outfit with close links to Carlos Prío.[27] Vázquez had been fingered in the shooting of Gregorio Martínez, an employee of the Havana Electric Company and UIR associate. By all indications, this was yet another gruesome case of gangland tit for tat. Trying to make the best of a bad situation, Prime Minister Tony Varona lauded the "zeal" of Havana's policemen in elucidating details of the Vázquez case. A *Bohemia* reporter offered a less optimistic assessment, noting that less than two weeks before, President Prío had announced that "the 'Anti-Gangster Law' has helped create the peaceful climate that Cubans are now enjoying."[28]

LEADER OF THE OPPOSITION

On February 3, 1949, Chibás scanned his advance copy of *Bohemia* with more than the usual anticipation. Inside was a public survey conducted among residents of Havana and its outlying suburbs, containing the following question: "If the opposition were able to unite, who, in your opinion, should be its natural leader, Chibás or Batista?" As it happened, a total of 42.73 percent of respondents preferred the Ortodoxo chief while 37.27 percent chose the former strongman. Moreover, Chibás owed this modest lead to women—who favored him by nearly 12 points (46.23 to 34.67). Among men, the two rivals were in a dead heat.[29] By any reasonable estimate, Chibás, whose popularity in Havana was well known, should have been the clear choice. However, he may have lost some support among pragmatists who looked askance at his distaste for pacts. Francisco Ichaso implied as much, claiming the Ortodoxos represented the most "sincere and vigorous" opposition to the current administration but their possibilities were hindered by a "lack of political realism."[30] Batista, who had imposed order during the turbulent years after 1934, may also have benefited from the spike in gangster violence. Even as Chibás boasted the most unconditional adherents in Cuba, the island's largest radio audience for a political show, and kudos from its highest circulation magazine, his position as opposition leader was precarious.[31]

As per custom, Chibás attempted to grab extra attention and prestige with his unique brand of muckraking. For most of January, this involved an escalation of the polemic with Amado Trinidad. The proprietor of RHC Cadena Azul and apologist for Argentine president Juan Domingo Perón had lately begun publishing a series of articles denouncing US policy in Latin America. Among those he considered "lackeys of Yankee imperialism" was none other than the Ortodoxo leader himself.[32] For his part, Chibás revealed that Trinidad had maintained regular contact with an Argentine spy named Guillermo Aikman. The two communicated via messages whose code Chibás had mysteriously managed to crack. Eddy thus treated his listeners to a detailed itinerary of the Argentine agent's activities, including worldwide travels, flight numbers, telephone conversations, hotel rooms, and even slight changes of plans. An impressed *Bohemia* reporter wrote that Chibás had turned himself into a "detective on a par with Sherlock Holmes."[33] Other media outlets were less gracious. Speculation abounded regarding how Chibás had come upon such sensitive documents and who had provided the key to encoded spy cables. The Communist daily *Hoy* angrily concluded that he was working for the United States Federal Bureau of Investigation and dubbed him "second in charge of the G-Men in Cuba."[34] Unfortunately for Chibás, the engrossing twists and turns of this case were overshadowed in the public imagination by bullet-filled gangster victims and Grau's sensational accusations.

Eddy would not play second fiddle for long, however. He, like most Cubans, had watched with alarm as the National Economic Board approved an increase in the country's already inflated electricity rates. In response, Eddy's friend Ventura Dellundé, who was president of the island's Consumers Association, appealed the measure before the Supreme Tribunal. After that, things became murky. Eduardo Salazar, a Cuban Electric Company executive, offered Dellundé 200,000 pesos to drop the case but was rebuffed. He then turned to the judges, who were importuned so relentlessly that one asked to be discharged from the case. Nonetheless, public opinion was buoyed by the knowledge that three of the five judges were known to oppose higher electricity prices. Cubans were thus "violently surprised" to learn the Supreme Tribunal had rejected the appeal on February 19.[35] The last-minute change of heart by Judge Francisco Torres Tomás, who had previously been critical of the Cuban Electric Company, was endlessly scrutinized. Chibás, whose radio show was scheduled for the next day, immediately realized he had a magnificent opportunity on his hands. The Cuban Electric Company, scorned by locals as the "electric octopus," was a perfect example of what he considered Wall Street imperialism. After all, its parent firm, Electric Bond and Share, was based in the United States, and gouging Cuban consumers had been company policy since 1902.[36] During Machado's administration, the Cuban Electric Company had been granted preferential tax rates and land rights superseding those of the state or private citizens. In 1927, Cubans paid seventeen cents per electric kilowatt even though production costs were only one and a half cents per unit.[37] Just over two decades later, the situation had improved but only somewhat. In January of 1948, citizens of neighboring Puerto Rico were charged $9.85 per electric kilowatt as compared to $16.45 for Havana residents.[38] Four months later, *Bohemia* reported that the Cuban Electric Company was using antiquated equipment requiring three times the petroleum to produce a kilowatt as similar utilities in the United States.[39] Currently, the "electric octopus" argued that more revenues were needed to offset higher expenses. However, this was exposed as a ruse by the US economist John Bauer and representatives of the engineering firm A. S. Beck, whose investigation found that the Cuban Electric Company's costs had risen 61 percent since 1936 but net income had doubled during that time.[40]

During his presidential campaign, Chibás had advocated "immediate nationalization" of the Cuban Electric Company, claiming this would benefit the commonweal rather than "egotistical money-making exploiters."[41] He had also asserted that exorbitant electricity rates precluded agricultural reform. While preparing for his broadcast, Chibás pondered these grievances and seethed at the latest insult perpetrated by the foreign-owned monopoly. Speaking into the microphones, he repeated the query ringing from every street corner. "What happened? What powerful force pressured this judge into changing his mind?"[42] Chibás knew the answer his audience expected and did not disappoint. According to his sources, Cuban Electric Company employees had paid $300,000 to ensure an agreeable ruling. "Once again," he said, "the Cuban people have been disgraced because money has overcome shame. The ever growing mud hole of corruption invading the country has now reached a place we never thought possible: to some of the Supreme Tribunal judges."[43] Given the verdict's unpopularity, others also offered denunciations. In some cases, they used terms strikingly similar to those of Chibás. The senate majority leader Lomberto Díaz lamented that "it's not just politicians anymore. It seems some judges have also entered into shady deals."[44] The Auténtico congressman Rogelio Regalado admitted, "It would be very bad for the country if the mud hole reached the judiciary."[45] Santiago

Rey, a Republican senator, proclaimed that "it appears a lot of money must have flowed" but added "some" of the judges were "responsible and honest."[46] For his part, Ventura Dellundé admitted the decision was "surprising" but rejected suggestions that bribery had been a factor and expressed "absolute faith" in the court system.[47] For a practicing lawyer rather than an officeholder, this was perhaps a wise tactic. He reiterated that under Law 5 of 1942 only the president could raise or lower electricity prices and eventually a majority of judges would recognize this fact.

Ultimately, Dellundé's stoicism placated neither Chibás nor the impugned judges. The latter merged their grudges into a single lawsuit and on February 25 Chibás was officially charged with defamation. After a brief hiatus, Chibás was once again the national focal point and seemed altogether pleased. In an interview with Luis Ortega, director of the Havana daily *Pueblo*, he claimed Carlos Prío had "inspired" the proceedings in order to jail him and thereby silence the "truths" he revealed every Sunday evening.[48] Besides a maximum two-year prison sentence, he was also liable for a fine of up to 360 pesos. Calling attention to this possibility, Chibás slyly said, "Since I never enriched myself in the government, nor did I rob, deal in the black market or enter into business arrangements with Grau's henchmen, I don't believe I'll be able to pay the fine."[49] These remarks were merely an opening salvo in a controversy he knew would play to his advantage regardless of the outcome. On March 6, Chibás published an article in *Bohemia* entitled "I Would Proudly Go to Prison to Defend the Cuban People," in which he excoriated the judges, the "Anti-Cuban Electric Company," and his favorite target, Carlos Prío. He noted ironically that the same three judges who declared themselves "incapable" of nullifying the recent increase in electricity prices had, in 1940, been quite "capable" of quashing a rebate some years earlier.[50] Regarding the despised utility company, Chibás railed against exorbitant fees that were the highest in Latin America and accused Prío of pushing through a 70 percent rate hike in September of 1947 while he was prime minister. Apart from this "embarrassing bit of graft," Chibás repeated his claim that a portion of the 174 million pesos missing from Cuba's treasury could be found in the bank accounts of Carlos and Antonio Prío.[51] Chibás also could not understand why he was the subject of a court case while the streets were thick with so many gangsters and embezzlers. Nonetheless, if convicted, Eddy promised to enter the hoosegow with "legitimate pride."[52] Curiously, the one thing Chibás neglected to do was provide any proof that the judges had actually accepted money in exchange for their votes.

Meanwhile, public ire against the Supreme Tribunal's ruling showed no signs of diminishing. The Federation of University Students "energetically condemned" the verdict in a public statement and incited Cubans to "fight against the oppressive electric octopus!"[53] Representatives from sixty-eight civic organizations throughout the island addressed an open letter to President Prío, urging him to ensure "efficient, abundant and cheap electrical service."[54] The provincial council of Oriente congratulated Ventura Dellundé and Chibás on their campaign against higher electricity prices, which "deeply affect the country's poor and its industry."[55] Chibás, who by now fancied himself a modern-day Galileo, stoked mass fervor at a series of nighttime rallies illuminated by candles and kerosene lanterns. On March 11, Chibás upped the ante by appearing before the senate and submitting a motion of impeachment against the three judges who had sided with the Cuban Electric Company. This gesture, provided for by Article 208 of the 1940 constitution, formed a symbolic contrast with the lawsuit against Chibás, which would be tried in the so-called Urgency Court created during Batista's military regime. The two cases crisscrossed four days later when the Urgency Court temporarily suspended its proceedings against Chibás in order to scrutinize the case pending before the senate. Chibás, who relished the gathering whirlwind, was buoyed by still more good fortune twenty-four hours later. Entering the studios of Unión Radio, Chibás enjoyed a chance encounter with the beautiful actress Carmelina Bandera—whom he found practicing her lines for an episode of a popular *radionovela* called *La Palabra de Mazorra*. The Ortodoxo leader duly confessed to being a fan of the show, demonstrating that stridency was a posture reserved for political opponents.

In April, Chibás learned that his family home, sold to pay for campaign expenses in 1948, had been converted into a funeral parlor. However, this inauspicious omen seemed more fitting for Carlos Prío—particularly as the Anti-Gangster Law seemed incapable of denting the brisk business of Havana's undertakers. On Saturday, April 2, a University of Havana student named Justo Fuentes was killed in a drive-by shooting. He was cut down at 12:45 p.m. on a busy Havana street near the studio of Radio COCO, where he had a daily show. Fuentes, who was vice president of the Federation of University Students, had once been a UIR member. More importantly, he had crossed a line by publicizing government attempts to discreetly exile the jailed MSR leader Mario Salabarría. Salabarría remained notorious for his role in the Orfila massacre and was one of the few gangsters actually serving a long-term sentence. Even so, his many contacts among high-level Auténticos nearly guaranteed an amnesty once conditions were right. Fuentes, in a fit of Chibás-style muckraking, had embarrassed the administration by revealing a passport had lately been issued to Salabarría. Shortly thereafter, friends began advising Fuentes to be careful because he was being "checked out."[56] Fuentes paid no heed to these warnings, and, given his separation from the UIR, there was little he could do to protect himself. The same hail of bullets that ended Fuentes's life also killed a nearby taxi driver. Interestingly, no policemen arrived on the scene but a watchman did, and he opened fire at the fleeing vehicle. He then drove the wounded Fuentes to the hospital.

Unfortunately, he was unwilling to identify the assailants. However, Fuentes confessed the names of his attackers to Fidel Castro, an old UIR companion, before losing consciousness. They included two of Cuba's most notorious gangsters: Rolando Masferrer and Orlando León Lemus. Aside from heading the MSR, Masferrer was an Auténtico congressman from Holguín. Lemus, commonly referred to as El Colorado because of his red hair, maintained close ties with the Prío brothers. In fact, during his final lucid moments, Fuentes had repeatedly said that "the redhead shot me on the ground."[57]

Chibás had sat near Fuentes the day before his death when both attended a rally against the Cuban Electric Company on the University of Havana staircase—known as *la escalinata*. During his weekly broadcast, he accused the government of "inciting and protecting the assassins" and Congress of "keeping the gangsters who reside among them from being prosecuted."[58] While Masferrer enjoyed parliamentary immunity, Lemus had been a fugitive since participating in the Orfila killings, and it was commonly believed he enjoyed official protection. In this vein, the journalist Ernesto de la Fé wrote, "The friendship between the Prío family and El Colorado is no secret."[59] A *Bohemia* reporter observed rising public anger at administration officials and their "guilty tolerance" of Cuba's triggermen.[60] By far, the bitterest expressions of outrage were those of Fuentes's classmates. The Federation of University Students issued a three-part declaration expressing a readiness to seek revenge if the murderers were not punished, urging Cuba's congress to rescind the immunity of Masferrer so he could be tried and accusing Paco Prío of personally sheltering El Colorado. Incensed students also intercepted passing trams and adorned them with posters insulting Masferrer, El Colorado, Paco Prío, and Police Chief José Caramés.

Two days after Fuentes's murder, the senate convened to discuss the accused Supreme Tribunal judges, the Cuban Electric Company, and electricity prices. The judges' fate initially rested with a five-man committee, which recommended against impeachment but backed a motion, proffered by Antonio Martínez Fraga, to create a senate commission charged with investigating the unpopular "electric octopus."[61] During the debate, Manuel Capestany emotionally vouched for Pedro Cantero, one of the indicted judges, who was also a childhood friend. Taking a less sentimental view, Varona opined that the motion for impeachment lacked "serious proof" and confessed that the government preferred to halt "Chibás's show."[62] Pelayo Cuervo Navarro, who admitted two of the judges were friends and believed all three were innocent, nonetheless felt a senate trial was the only means to exonerate them before public opinion. The Auténtico-Republican alliance, which held a majority, ultimately agreed to vote against impeachment and reject the proposed senate commission. Instead, they supported a project of the miguelista senator Porfirio Pendás—who planned to introduce a bill requiring lower electricity prices. This sop for the island's citizens was hushed up on the insistence of Varona, who claimed announcing it would "scare away" foreign investors.[63] The prime minister may have been feeling slightly fearful himself as a few days before he had received a visit from the Cuban Electric Company's American boss, known locally as "Mister" Wheeler. Leaving nothing to chance, the firm had also extensively lobbied members of the senate committee. Among other things, each man was provided with a thirty-three-page legal brief containing arguments in favor of the company. At least one committee member, the Republican Santiago Rey, mimicked these during the hearing. While pro-government parties guaranteed the judges would be spared, the indifference of opposition lawmakers turned the session into a rout. In the end, only Pelayo Cuervo Navarro and Federico Fernández Casas voted for impeachment. The following Sunday, Chibás blamed the senate's decision on prime ministerial "pressure" and an unduly cooperative opposition, which he compared to the cowed legislators of Machado's era.[64] However, even as the price increase was unjust and the legal reasoning behind it flawed, Chibás never offered concrete proof that the judges had acted improperly.

On April 10, Chibás opened a new front against the administration. In a *Bohemia* article, he commemorated Prío's first "semester" in office by enumerating all that was amiss. "Let us take a look," he wrote, "at the effect of his six months in power."

> Businesses are faltering, factories are closing, workers are being laid off, salaries are being cut, campesinos are being evicted from their lands by the army, public services are a mess, public transport is in chaos, telephone and electric bills are higher, there has been a notable drop in government revenues, illegal payments of spurious debts to United States citizens have taken place while Cubans are forced to tighten their belts, a 100 million peso foreign loan is being negotiated to replenish money embezzled from the treasury by figures who served the Grau administration and currently hold positions in this government (and lastly) student and union leaders have been serially assassinated.[65]

For Chibás, the most disturbing of these ills was the prospect of a foreign loan. Since January, rumors had been circulating that Prío would cover up Grau's "deficit" with borrowed money. Chibás had been among those stoking the buzz. He felt vindicated when the island's newspapers reported that President Prío and his brother Antonio, the finance minister, had recently received three representatives from Chase National Bank. As with the controversy over high electricity prices, Chibás was reenacting a drama from his years as a revolutionary. Just as Machado once extended preferential treatment to the Cuban Electric Company, he had also relied on Chase National Bank for economic support.[66] Nor did the coincidences end there. One of the financiers who had visited Carlos and Antonio Prío was Winthrop Aldrich, who had helped formulate the loans obtained by President Machado.[67] Given the sticky-fingered members of Prío's circle, especially his brothers Antonio and Paco, Chibás pointed out the danger of yet another parallel with the early 1930s—namely, that a foreign loan would enable graft of enormous proportions. In Machado's era, Chase National Bank had underwritten the construction of Cuba's 750-mile-long Central Highway, which spans the island from east to west. Although this project proved indisputably valuable, each mile, at a cost of 160,000 pesos, was ten times more expensive than reasonable estimates. "We will fight," concluded Chibás, "to keep the present government from mortgaging the republic once again."[68]

The following week, Chibás warned of an additional pending danger. On his radio show of April 17, he accused Carlos Prío, José Manuel Casanova, and the "known speculator" Francisco Blanco Calás of plotting to reap fabulous profits by manipulating sugar prices.[69] Casanova and Blanco had played comparable games in 1945, resulting in the infamous barter deal scandal. The feisty Liberal senator responded by labeling Chibás a "mental retard" in *Prensa Libre*.[70] Eddy countered with a *Bohemia* article that was equal parts wit and journalistic exposé. He irreverently compared the "Czar of Sugar" to his eighteenth-century Venetian namesake, contending that the latter, at least, had spent time in jail for his mischief while the "tropical" Casanova remained free to plague his fellow countrymen.[71] In this case, Casanova and Blanco had "fictitiously" lowered sugar prices a few months earlier by leaking "alarmist rumors" and utilizing their influence within the industry.[72] Afterward, Blanco purchased two hundred thousand tons and promptly began lobbying the government to prematurely end the sugar harvest in an effort to limit supplies. President Prío had thus far resisted such a move, knowing full well it would have resulted in mass unrest in the countryside. However, in February and March he issued decrees lowering the amount of sugar available for sale in Europe. According to Chibás, speculators, many with ties to the administration, would take advantage of the momentary shortage to vend their sugar in Europe at a huge gain.[73] Thereafter, the hoarded sugar would be released—flooding the market, fetching ruinous prices, and costing the Cuban treasury between 50 and 100 million pesos in tax revenues. The sixty-five-year-old Casanova reacted indignantly to these allegations and demanded a duel. Chibás chose Manuel Bisbé and Eric Agüero, the Ortodoxo party treasurer, as his seconds and dispatched them to negotiate terms with Casanova's representatives.

Carlos Prío had dueled with Chibás in 1947 after being similarly accused but was too tangled up with the island's gangster problem to respond. Six days after Fuentes had been killed, Prío received a delegation from the Federation of University Students in the presidential palace. The result was a ninety-minute meeting laden with tension and uncomfortable questions. Speaking on the students' behalf, Pedro Mirassou told Prío that "everybody knows" who killed Justo Fuentes but certain military and civilian authorities were "sabotaging" efforts to capture the perpetrators.[74] For instance, he found it "suspicious" that police and customs officials in Havana's airport had allowed Eustaquio Soto Carmenatti, one of those implicated by Fuentes, to board a Pan American flight for Miami—particularly as the suspected killer was using his own passport.[75] Confronted with these details, the cordial president attempted to win the students' confidence by revealing hitherto unknown information. Prío confessed that he had been notified "10 or 12 days" after El Colorado had secretly returned to Cuba but immediately sent a message urging him to leave so as not to "perturb" his government.[76] Rather than being placated, his audience was horrified. The medical student Orlando Bosch asked why Lemus had not been arrested. Prío lamely answered that such "elements" usually took refuge in the houses of senators, representatives, or "influential friends."[77] Finally, Mirassou informed Prío that if no "effective" measures were taken to prosecute the criminals, the students would "rise up in rebellion" after Easter.[78]

Despite this threat, Prío's options were limited as Rolando Masferrer enjoyed parliamentary immunity and Soto Carmenatti remained out of reach in Florida. El Colorado's whereabouts were uncertain, although murmurs on the street suggested he had fled overseas. On April 19, however, the truth turned out to be otherwise. That morning, in the working-class Havana neighborhood of Cerro, another university student with UIR ties was treated to a drive-by fusillade. The target, Luis Felipe Salazar Callicó, known as Wichy, was severely wounded in the head and neck. Upon arriving at the hospital, a commandant from the Bureau of Investigations asked who was responsible, but Wichy angrily replied, "Why should I tell you? Everyone knows the police protect assassins."[79] Once again, Fidel Castro was on the scene and extracted the information. He advised reporters that the car had been driven by someone wearing a police uniform and the shooters were El Colorado and Policarpo Soler. The latter was a Batista-era police chief and present-day mercenary. In early 1948, Miguelito Suárez Fernández had publicly accused Soler of seeking to kill him and his ally Diego Vicente Tejera. Consequently, Suárez Fernández had dispatched his UIR allies to neutralize the elusive Soler but to no avail. While Soler's reappearance was troubling, the continued presence of El Colorado posed a direct challenge to Prío. During his April 24 broadcast, Chibás singled out Lemus as part of a "tragic panorama" of impunity whereby gunmen "ride in the official automobiles of representatives, senators and ministers."[80]

Chibás had two other purposes that evening. First, he ceded the opening minutes to Pelayo Cuervo Navarro—allowing the self-styled "independent" senator to address his audience for the first time since their rancorous falling out. As luck would have it, Cuervo Navarro was also tangled up in Cuba's judicial system. The Havana Municipal Court had recently ordered him to pay a fine of 150 pesos and submit testimony before the Urgency Court regarding possible defamation of the justice ministry. Cuervo Navarro marveled at the "inconceivable paradox" of being the only man punished thus far in the 174 million peso corruption case.[81] Afterward, Eddy fulfilled a second goal: hyping his upcoming appearance before the Urgency Court. Having been denied an impeachment spectacle in the senate, he had every intention of embarrassing the government during this public forum, set for April 27. Chibás urged listeners to attend if possible and offered a preview of what they could expect, saying:

> I reaffirm tonight each and every one of my accusations against the Supreme Tribunal judges who ruled against the people, Gabriel Pichardo, Pedro Cantero and Juan Francisco Torres Tomás, who have shamelessly allied themselves with the Anti-Cuban Electric Company, the foreign monopoly, the international octopus of Electric Bond and Share. This is the truth. I proclaim it to the entire world. My sources include a high-ranking employee of the Electric Company itself along with four judges from the Supreme Tribunal and Havana Municipal Court. They can sentence me to 20 years in prison or even death but I will continue proclaiming the truth . . . Only an idiot could believe three judges of the Supreme Tribunal would dictate such an absurd and illegal sentence in order to bestow millions of pesos on a foreign monopoly and appease the magnates of Wall Street. The government is determined to see me defeated in the Urgency Court. The prosecutor will accuse me in the strongest terms. Nevertheless, if I am ordered to pay a fine, I will refuse. Nor will I allow the people to pay it or the president to grant me a pardon if I am convicted. I will go to jail.[82]

Chibás was in no danger of spending the next two decades behind bars or suffering capital punishment. His stretching of the particulars merely embroidered a situation whose outcome was a foregone conclusion. Chibás lacked parliamentary immunity and was not protected by a powerful patron. Moreover, his accusation was based on anonymous tips. Chibás was ticketed for prison, and he knew it. The prospect of martyrdom suited his temperament but was also shrewd politics. Many Cubans, especially the poor, would be tempted to associate Chibás with his dearest image of himself—namely, an honest politician who sacrificed to improve their lot. Nearly three months had passed since the *Bohemia* survey comparing him and Batista as potential opposition leaders. His popularity had surely increased since then and would climb still further if he were incarcerated. Chibás had labored relentlessly to gain a higher profile in the public imagination. Further, Eddy's crusade against the Cuban Electric Company offered an ideal showcase for his party. As Chibás headlined rallies in Havana and Santiago de Cuba, Ortodoxo rising stars like José Pardo Llada and Ventura Dellundé drew large crowds in Santa Clara and Matanzas, respectively. Meanwhile, President Prío seemed unwilling or unable to halt gangster violence and risked rebellion in the university. Batista, meanwhile, largely confined himself to Kuquine—his country estate on the Havana outskirts. Surrounded by a stew of sycophants, politicians, and journalists, he discussed goings-on and his prospects in 1952 but often seemed more interested in playing canasta or working out on his exercise machine. Prío's vice president, Guillermo Alonso Pujol, summarized the political panorama by telling a reporter:

> The opposition is composed of the popular thunder of Chibás and the tendency toward order represented by Batista. The first is an emotional opposition, of the youth, and the second channels sense and restraint. I've always believed the 357 thousand votes for Chibás mean something and if there is a great disappointment with the Auténticos, he will capitalize on it. . . . Only older people and traditional politicians will gravitate toward Batista.

After a pause, the wily Republican chief added, "But we are only in the sixth month of this administration. Who knows what will happen tomorrow?"[83]

PRISONER NUMBER 981

The Urgency Court met on Calle Tacón in Old Havana. Its surrounding alleys were congested with boisterous would-be spectators when Chibás arrived wearing his customary white suit and clutching a cigarette in his right hand. Ever mindful of public relations, he composed a statement for the press in the moments before the trial began—yet again deploring Cuba's scandalously high electricity prices. At 10:00 a.m., presiding judge José Cabezas asked the Ortodoxo leader to confirm his accusation, which he did. Chibás was no stranger to Judge Cabezas. In 1935, he had sentenced the young revolutionary to half a year in jail. Seeking to avert a similar fate, Eddy's lawyer, Francisco Carone, called a string of character witnesses—including the publisher of *Bohemia*, Miguel Ángel Quevedo, the Ortodoxo congressmen Manuel Bisbé, Roberto García Ibáñez, and Alberto "Beto" Saumell, along with the party's popular radio personalities José Pardo Llada and Guido García Inclán. Carone, who had participated in many anti-pact delegations during the Ortodoxo factional struggles, also defended his friend and client in a two-hour speech. Among other things, he argued the Urgency Court was unconstitutional, having been founded as the instrument of a military regime. A *Bohemia* reporter assigned to the case believed Carone was wasting his time, observing wryly that "the judges were so anxious to fulfill their duty that they scarcely listened to him."[84] This view was seemingly borne out when Judge Cabezas and his two colleagues announced their ruling of 180 days behind bars. Chibás responded with a signature phrase, yelling, "While the assassin of Guiteras lives unbothered in his finca and Alemán enjoys his millions, Prío has thrown me in prison for defending the people."[85] The pro-

Chibás crowd, which consisted of many who had traveled long distances to see their hero, erupted with indignation. From the visitor's gallery emanated whistles and cries of "Viva Chibás!" The prosecutor, Francisco Zayas, was escorted from the building under police protection. Another detachment of cops forcibly cleared the courtroom. Even Roberto Agramonte, whose bland personality had earned him the nickname "freezer bottle" among fellow Ortodoxos, found himself being attacked with a club.

Several hours later, the Urgency Court verdict inspired a heated debate in the chamber of representatives. Manuel Bisbé declared there had been a "prior agreement" between the prosecutor and judges that counted the president's blessing.[86] Predictably, he was contradicted by Segundo Curti, one of Prío's close advisors, who sang the praises of Cuba's independent judiciary. In contrast to Curti's lofty rhetoric, the minister without portfolio, Primitivo Rodríguez, joked that "today they have just crucified the Jesus of our present generation."[87] Reaching even lower, Rolando Masferrer, who was presently a larger headache to Prío than Chibás, proclaimed the Ortodoxo leader lacked the "courage" to confront Cuba's problems.[88] To this, Roberto García Ibáñez replied that Chibás walked the streets unaccompanied, a habit "tough guys" like Masferrer would never dare imitate.[89] The Auténtico-Republican alliance was unexpectedly delighted when Liberal and Democratic congressmen also defended the ruling. José Suárez Rivas, brother of the Liberal senate leader, asserted that "Ortodoxos exploit the psychosis of many citizens while Liberals limit themselves to crafting complementary legislation for the constitution."[90] This, of course, was quite untrue. Liberals had been in the ruling coalition between 1940 and 1944 and produced no such laws during that period. The real issue was that neither they nor the Democrats had any abiding love for Chibás, whose popularity threatened their perches in the opposition. The Communists, who were shunned by all and thus unencumbered by political calculations, offered the only outside support. Anibal Escalante, director of the Communist newspaper *Hoy*, said, "Everyone knows we have nothing in common with Chibás," but stressed that his first obligation was to defend the people against the Cuban Electric Company.[91]

In the senate, only twenty-seven members were present—which resulted in the session being canceled for lack of a quorum. Pelayo Cuervo Navarro had been among the most eager to comment but contented himself instead by chatting with reporters. From a strictly legal standpoint, he was indignant that a party leader could be incarcerated by a quasi-legal court on the periphery of the country's judicial system. He added that "I have no political relationship with Chibás, but his honesty and civic conduct are beyond dispute. While he sits in jail, professional assassins walk around with impunity, government officials encourage gangsters, illegal gambling is fomented and embezzlers of the public treasury are protected by the administration."[92] The Democrat Antonio Martínez Fraga was no Chibás admirer but nonetheless admitted the Ortodoxo chief had realized a "brilliant campaign" against the Cuban Electric Company.[93] Rather than consorting with the press, Miguelito Suárez Fernández visited Chibás in prison. The senate president arrived bearing a chicken pot pie courtesy of his wife, which he presented to Chibás and said, "Listen Eddy, I've come to tell you that I'm going to request a pardon. You shouldn't spend more time in jail . . . It's a political error to keep you behind bars."

"No, Miguel," responded Chibás. "I won't permit Carlos Prío to pardon me. What's more, I would consider it an injury to my honor if any supporter or friend requested such a favor from the president. I've already told everyone. Do you understand?"

Suárez Fernández was adamant. "I'm going to ask for a pardon anyway," he said, "and if you're offended you can demand a duel." This was a remote possibility, as Suárez Fernández well knew. The two men had an easy relationship and shortly thereafter they dissolved into smiles.

Later on, Chibás confessed, "Right now, the most important thing is to fight the foreign monopolies. I don't mind being imprisoned and in any case I've been here before."

"Don't worry," replied the senate president, "I assure you the electricity prices will be lowered."[94]

Suárez Fernández was not the only senator advocating a pardon. The Liberal chief Eduardo Suárez Rivas also backed the idea on behalf of his party. In the chamber of representatives, most Liberal and Democratic congressmen favored a similar proposal, as did the Auténticos Segundo Curti and Armando Caíñas Milanés. Even among legislators who disagreed with Chibás, many were uncomfortable with his sentence—which recalled a harsher era in Cuban politics, barely more than a dozen years in the past, when party bosses were routinely locked up. Others, like the Auténtico senate leader Lomberto Díaz, believed incarcerating Chibás was a "measure of dubious effectiveness."[95] In any case, Chibás was determined to wring every possible advantage from his situation. Mrs. Suárez's chicken pot pie notwithstanding, he ate common prison fare and used the same canvas folding bed as other inmates. With good humor, he told the journalist Mario Kuchilán that the view from his cell trumped that of his fourteenth-floor penthouse, which looked out over the Caribbean. The Ortodoxo leader added that he was content because "my being in prison assists the cause of national liberation."[96] Hence, Chibás asked Francisco Carone whether there was any legal way to prevent a pardon. Carone answered that the sentence could be appealed on the basis that it was unconstitutional. "Fantastic!" Chibás cried. "Submit it today and we will stop the government."[97] This tactic was unnecessary, however, as Carlos Prío showed no inclination toward leniency. Speaking for the administration, Prime Minister Tony Varona declared a pardon would represent a "slight" against Cuba's judiciary.[98] More importantly, the government looked forward to a respite from Eddy's Sunday evening harassment.

With the airwaves unavailable, Chibás resorted to his pen. On April 30, he published an article in *Prensa Libre* entitled "To the People of Cuba." The piece closely resembled one of his broadcasts—offering readers a familiar and titillating jumble of gossip, reminiscence, and criticism. Among other things, he questioned the Urgency Court's legitimacy, claimed Carlos Prío had mandated a guilty verdict in advance and that Judge Cabezas was happy to comply for personal reasons. Eddy noted that Cabezas was a cousin of Lieutenant Colonel José Eleuterio Pedraza, Batista's former second in command, whom he had often excoriated as an "assassin."[99] Judge Cabezas had been so bent on revenge that he had denied Chibás the chance to issue "revelations of enormous importance."[100] Had they been aired, he averred, convicting him would have been far more difficult, "in spite of the president's orders."[101] Chibás also pointed out that he had been sent to jail on two previous occasions, in 1929 and 1935, for "defending the people."[102] In each instance he was offered pardons by the tyrants who ruled Cuba, first Machado and later Batista, and had refused both offers—preferring the penitentiary to accepting favors from unsavory figures.[103] Presently, he was incarcerated by Carlos Prío, his former compañero from the Student Directorate, fellow political prisoner on the Isle of Pines, and erstwhile peer in the constituent assembly. Unlike the dictators Machado and Batista, Prío lacked the decency to offer him a reprieve (even though he would have rejected it), and this was because the president nursed a "grudge" against him.[104] Nevertheless, Chibás contended that he did not harbor "one drop" of hatred for his onetime friend, only "sadness" for what he had become.[105]

Eddy's modest bout of charity toward Prío was perhaps attributable to his choice of reading materials in the Castillo del Príncipe, which comprised the Bible and two religious tracts—"The Path to Salvation" and "Human Vanity Is the World's Natural Sin." On the other hand, Chibás devoured plenty of worldly literature as well, including verses from the nineteenth-century Spanish poets Gustavo de Núñez Arce and Gustavo Adolfo Bécquer, a biography of Alexander the Great, *Sugar and Population in the Antilles* by Ramiro Guerra—one of Cuba's foremost historians, and of course, the 1940 constitution. In addition, letters of support poured in from all reaches. Many echoed the sentiments of Victor Fuentes Castillo, the Ortodoxo president of Yateras, in Oriente province, who wrote, "Being in the Castillo del Príncipe is no affront for revolutionaries; we've been there before, many of us worshipping at the altar of Liberty and showing our contempt for tyrants."[106] Chibás mostly read during the evening, since he was allowed to receive visitors before 6:00 p.m. His secretary, Conchita Fernández, arrived on a regular basis to take instructions and keep him supplied with the cigarettes he smoked constantly. Francisco Carone often dropped by to discuss legal strategies and other Ortodoxos called to consult on matters dealing with the party. For example, the PPC planned a Saturday evening rally in Havana's Parque Central under the banner of "Bandits Are on the Street and Chibás Is in Jail." However, the interior ministry was loath to grant permission and dragged its feet—leading José Pardo Llada, Guido García Inclán, and Juan Amador to announce on their radio shows that the event would be canceled. Nonetheless, party members who spoke with Chibás were urged to press forward. They did, and the government relented at the last minute. Despite contradictory signals, the gathering attracted more people than the famous May Day parade twenty-four hours later. Chibás also saw a steady stream of journalists along with a record number of visitors, who arrived by the hundreds every Sunday.[107] In their presence, he cultivated an assiduously positive outlook, but privately, in letters to old friends, Chibás revealed hints of melancholy. Writing to his university pal José Chelala Aguilera, he lamented that "there are only a few of us left from the fight against Machado, because many of the 'crazy kids' from that era have already been assassinated, while others have assassinated themselves by betraying the ideals of the 'Generation of 1930' and renouncing their pasts."[108]

If Chibás was occasionally blue, he was also heartened by a slew of encouraging developments. Having always closely followed his portrayal in the press, Chibás was gratified to learn that most columnists and commentators backed him. Aside from his usual media allies like Miguel Ángel Quevedo and Sergio Carbó, Chibás was also supported by some longtime opponents. Notable among these was Ramón Vasconcelos, the minister without portfolio, who stated it was a "brutality" to "make an example" of a leader followed by "300,000 souls" while bloodthirsty gangsters enjoyed impunity.[109] Even more encouraging was the public reaction to those who were hardened against Chibás. Raúl Lorenzo attacked Eddy in such scathing terms during his show on Unión Radio that the station was deluged with angry phone calls and telegrams.[110] The fury was quelled only when José Pardo Llada, who hosted the popular program *La Palabra* (The Word), announced that the station did not agree with Lorenzo's opinions. Anecdotal evidence suggesting the people were behind Chibás was bolstered by statistical proof on May 6, when *Bohemia* hit the newsstands. According to a new survey, 93.82 percent of Cubans were aware that Chibás had been found guilty by the Urgency Court and 76.01 percent believed he had been wrongly convicted.[111] Further, 52.39 percent felt Eddy's accusations against the judges were true and 66.53 percent thought him worthy of a pardon.[112] This unequivocal rebuke almost certainly influenced Prío's decision, taken after a cabinet meeting the same day, to reduce electricity prices to their 1943 levels.

Bohemia also served up unpleasant reading for Fulgencio Batista. Chibás considered Batista more deserving of censure than ever—particularly as he once again resided in Cuba and was in the process of forming a new political party. Hence, Chibás delivered his latest vituperative attack on Batista by means of Cuba's most popular magazine. Chibás argued that Batista was unfit for politics because he had committed every imaginable abuse during his seven years as strongman and four years as president. Hence, he lacked the "moral authority" to address the nation's ills, including murders (he had sent plenty to the morgue himself), embezzlement (a Batista specialty), the lack of a formal budget (he had ruled without one), sleazy military men (he was the very embodiment of one), bloating the government payroll with friends and allies (a forte of his finance minister Anselmo Alliegro), abridgement of press freedom (Batista had closed unfriendly radio stations and persecuted individual journalists), failure to pass the 1940 constitution's complementary laws (this had never been a priority), the black market (a phenomenon that began during his time in power), and last but not least, the island's less than perfect democracy (Batista, after all, had engineered the impeachment of President Miguel Mariano Gómez in 1936, "managed" his successor, Francisco Laredo Brú, and imposed Carlos Saladrigas as his coalition's presidential candidate in 1944).[113]

Chibás believed Carlos Prío was discreetly helping Batista as a means to "place obstacles" in the Ortodoxos' path.[114] More conspicuously, the president shut down Eddy's radio show, hosted by Manuel Bisbé and Roberto Agramonte in his absence. The communication ministry, offering the flimsiest of pretexts, asserted the time slot must be sold to someone else if he personally could not use it. This was part of a larger assault against the media and demonstrated Prío's scant tolerance for public criticism. Earlier, the government had closed Radio COCO for three days after the station aired a scandalous interview between Néstor Piñango and the outlaw Orlando León Lemus. From his secret hideout, the redheaded gangster readily described his links with Carlos and Antonio Prío, which dated to the mid-1930s and continued still. The relationship was both deeply personal and convenient for both parties. For example, El Colorado had lent his support during the Auténtico registration drive of 1947 in the president's native province of Pinar del Río. He also provided a contingent of toughs during Prío's political standoff with Miguelito Suárez Fernández, who was backed by UIR roughnecks.[115] In return, Prío and his brothers protected Lemus from the authorities even though he was one of the most wanted men in Cuba.[116] Perhaps fearing this arrangement could one day break down, El Colorado expressed his desire to run for a senate seat and guarantee his impunity for good. Embarrassing as these remarks were, Piñango's own observations caused an even greater uproar. Among other things, the reporter noted that he had been driven to the meeting in a National Police squad car and upon arriving saw armed soldiers guarding the location—which appeared to be a finca just outside the city.[117] Prío privately fumed that he would "finish" Cuba's gangsters, but only journalists and the media felt his immediate wrath.[118] Aside from suspending Radio COCO, the government also apprehended Piñango and held him incommunicado until he recanted his comments about police and military involvement. Just before his release from the police station, Piñango offered what sounded like a rehearsed declaration to fellow reporters. "The authorities," he said, "have treated me with full respect for press freedom and an evident desire to bring to a close an era of crime in Cuba that, once finished, will resound to everyone's benefit."[119]

Even if this were true, the administration was on shakier ground after police conducting a "search" ended up sacking the offices of *Tiempo en Cuba*. The weekly newspaper, run by El Colorado's associate Rolando Masferrer, was a logical target for investigation. However, the officers who destroyed, overturned, and scattered everything in their wake aggravated the increasingly frayed nerves of Cuba's journalists. *Bohemia* published a photo of the grisly scene and asked, "Is this the new way of doing things?"[120] Of course, Masferrer was no run-of-the-mill reporter and represented a less than ideal poster child for press freedom. In the chamber of representatives, the Auténtico labor leader Emilio Surí Castillo pointed at Masferrer and yelled, "We need a dictatorship that will eliminate guys like this!"[121] Surí Castillo then requested Masferrer's immediate expulsion from the Auténtico parliamentary committee. However, he was mistaken in thinking gangsters could so easily be separated from the party. Rafael del Busto recalled that during the most recent Auténtico rally in Parque Central, his ticket to the grandstand had been stamped by none other than the elusive Policarpo Soler.[122] For his part, Masferrer explained what many already knew and the rest did not care to admit. "Gangsters exist for political reasons," he said. "Almost all political bosses arm their groups and use them for electoral purposes. It's not possible to ask favors of them one day and persecute them the next."[123] He added that the best way to disarm Cuba's gangsters would be to arrange an agreement with Miguelito Suárez Fernández and National Police Chief José Manuel Caramés—both of whom maintained ties to the rival UIR. Instead, Carlos Prío issued a decree creating the Group for the Repression of Subversive Activities, or GRAS, after its Spanish initials. This was to be an anti-gangster outfit commanded by the army. Though fears abounded that he was resurrecting Batista's hated Military Intelligence Service, which was disbanded in 1944, the president could no longer rely on gangster-infested security forces. Prío compared the situation to that of a patient who must submit to a risky operation in order to save his life and added, "If nothing else works, I'll use the same methods against these people that were once used against me."[124] Thus, Prío cast his lot with Genovevo Pérez Dámera. Masferrer would have to be content with repairing his broken printing press.

While Prío turned the screws on Cuba's gangsters, Communications Minister Carlos Maristany relentlessly attempted to bump Chibás from his soapbox. On May 15, CMQ director Goar Mestre denounced government demands that he cancel his contract with Chibás. After suspending Eddy's show the previous week, Maristany urged Mestre to wash his hands of broadcasts that were "harmful and disturbing to the nation."[125] When he refused, Maristany ordered radio frequencies to be changed in Pinar del Río and Camagüey in order to block CMQ and Unión Radio, which featured the popular Ortodoxo commentator José Pardo Llada, from reaching those areas. Mestre reminded Auténticos that they had heartily endorsed Chibás when the party was in the opposition and his criticisms were directed at President Batista. Many of the same figures who had applauded Chibás and the impartiality of CMQ were now sworn enemies of both. Miguel Ángel Quevedo griped in *Bohemia* that Maristany was a "Torquemada" who considered himself "owner and lord" of Cuba's airwaves even though the communications ministry was meant to be "purely technical."[126] In his weekly political comic strip called "The Little Cuban King," A.R. drew Liborio, the island's everyman, speaking into a microphone with Prío looking on in the background. At one point, Prío pulls a drawstring and the microphone disappears through a trapdoor. Eyeing the place where the microphone used to be, Liborio asks, "Is this cordiality or censorship?"[127]

Government pressure notwithstanding, Eddy's show was allowed to continue, and Manuel Bisbé reprised his role as surrogate. Rather than speaking himself, he read a statement written by Chibás that took the form of an open letter to the president. Eddy repeated his opposition to a pardon or provisional release, declaring he would only accept an amnesty voted by the senate and chamber of representatives. To those who believed his stubbornness was crazy, Chibás allowed he was an "abnormal case in a political climate where normal involved robbing, killing and selling drugs."[128] He also reminded Prío that his political slogans remained the same ones both of them had embraced as young revolutionaries:

> War against embezzlers of the treasury, corrupters of the people and gunmen! Continue the struggle for national liberation! Clean up the country's political culture! Freedom of the press! A judiciary free of government interference! Down with the Urgency Court! No more suspension of radio broadcasts! No Military Intelligence Service! Down with the lackeys of foreign monopolies! Down with abusive electricity prices, the Cuban Telephone Company and the consortium of overseas oil companies (Standard, Shell and Sinclair)! No more sellouts and gangsters![129]

As luck would have it, the last of these catchphrases proved especially timely and not only in terms of political point scoring. Some days following the broadcast, a group of prisoners who had been sentenced for gangster-related activities began planning to assassinate Chibás after rumors circulated that his presence among them was keeping the administration from granting a blanket amnesty. However, Gustavo Ortiz Fáez, the young agronomy student who murdered Manolo Castro, caught wind of the plot and notified Chibás—who defiantly exclaimed, "None of this worries me as I've never been the least bit afraid of dying."[130] Chibás added that if he were assassinated, he wished to clarify, for "historical" purposes, that the government was responsible.[131] As for Ortiz, he had not tipped off Chibás for altruistic reasons. He was a UIR member with close links to Fidel Castro. The latter was not only an Ortodoxo; he had also formed a youth splinter group loosely associated with the party called Acción Radical Ortodoxo (ARO).[132] Aside from publishing a newsletter and commenting on internal PPC matters, the organization was a stomping ground for the young and violent, many of whom were university students affiliated with UIR. This crowd no doubt horrified Ortodoxos who boasted of the party's "immaculate rank and file," but in this instance, at least, it may have saved Eddy's life.[133]

In truth, Ortodoxo purity proved maddeningly elusive as provincial party leaders and section heads continued to ferret out traitors and other undesirables. Throughout 1949, Chibás was regaled with accounts of unworthy or unsatisfactory partisans. Gloria Cuadras, who belonged to the Women's Wing, informed him that a certain Zoila Perozo had been ejected for "campaigning in favor of Carlos Prío" and "trying to corrupt the consciences of some *compañeras*, who civically denounced her."[134] Of course, the zeal with which such figures hunted the party's malefactors was matched only by their personal devotion to Chibás. Cuadras concluded that "all my sacrifices, all my efforts, all the minutes of my life are for the PPC and its honorable boss: my brother more than my friend, he who will bring a happy resolution to the great work for which many of our friends have shed blood or died."[135] In a similar albeit less florid fashion, the Ortodoxo municipal chief of Cárdenas sent Chibás a list of assemblymen who had crossed enemy lines during the presidential elections. According to some, such measures were not nearly sufficient. For example, the Youth Section of Sagua la Grande, in Las Villas province, demanded the expulsion of Ortodoxo congressman Félix Martín after he and fellow legislators voted themselves a raise in salary.

While Ortodoxo diehards schemed to dislodge real and perceived miscreants, the Auténticos purveyed drama on a grander and more public scale. The crux of the issue was Guillermo Alonso Pujol, the Republican chief and wily intriguer who also happened to be Cuba's vice president. His outsize influence had long been a source of discomfort, and Carlos Prío aimed to dilute his power by negotiating a pact with the Democrats. He entrusted the details to Tony Varona, but the prime minister was loath to offend El Gordo (a nickname Pujol shared with the similarly obese General Genovevo Pérez Dámera), who he hoped would support his presidential candidacy in 1952. With no results forthcoming, Prío asked Miguelito Suárez Fernández to head the discussions instead. Although the senate president was no great admirer of Prío, he was happy to undermine the Republican leader, saying, "I would rather deal with the devil than Alonso Pujol."[136] By May 13, the two sides had struck a bargain. Not only had the Democrats agreed to join the government, they also accepted a dissident faction of anti-Pujol Republicans into their party—thereby damaging the vice president even further. Suárez Fernández was ecstatic, telling a *Bohemia* reporter it was necessary to act against Pujol's "incessant plotting."[137] Certainly, Republican leverage over Prío had been substantially reduced. Moreover, the administration's congressional majority was now decisive. This was paramount for a president who took the semi-parliamentarian system seriously. Further, a handful of previously contrarian voices, such as Democratic senator Antonio Martínez Fraga, would now serve the government.

Prío was also in a stronger position to obstruct the amnesty law for Chibás proposed in the senate by Pelayo Cuervo Navarro and Federico Fernández Casas. Miguelito Suárez Fernández, who had earlier vowed to shepherd the measure, discreetly stalled while he and Prío worked together to lure the Democrats. When the amnesty was finally considered, the Auténtico majority leader Lomberto Díaz demanded the murderers of Aracelio Iglesias, the Communist organizer of Cuba's dockworkers, be covered as well.[138] In an interview for *Diario de la Marina* (whose editor, Gastón Baquero, was one of the few who agreed with Eddy's sentence), Díaz explained the government was against "personalized" laws and any amnesty would therefore have to be "general."[139] Closer to the truth was Prío's steadfast conviction that "nobody will remember" Chibás after six months in jail. However, the Liberal chief Eduardo Suárez Rivas astutely noted that Chibás had become a "permanent topic" in the street.[140]

Chibás also maintained his habit of answering those who disagreed with him in public forums. For instance, when former justice minister José Agustín Martínez wrote in *Prensa Libre* that Eddy's legal strategy seemed wanting, he replied that his was not a "regular case."[141] Rather, he stated that

> We have tried to stir the sleeping conscience of the Cuban people. If the knock has not been sufficiently strong to rouse them, we will redouble our efforts and sacrifices. They will not be in vain. We have faith in the noble and great destiny of our country, which occupies the gateway to the New World, the best strategic position in history. In the worst case, the day will arrive in fifty or a hundred years when others more fortunate than us will be able to wake the people. No one will be able to take away from us the glory of having been their precursors.[142]

While Eddy's arguments were unlikely to sway detractors, the political cost of keeping him behind bars was becoming manifest even to those who were close to the president. On May 29, Prío's public relations director René Fiallo published an open letter urging him to remove Chibás from prison "as soon as possible" because helping "the most insignificant little devil of the opposition" achieve martyrdom would be foolish.[143] Just over two days later, on the first anniversary of his election, Prío relented. He authorized a conditional pardon, effective on June 4, and a trio of lawyers informed the reluctant Chibás that he had no choice but to accept. A self-promoter to the last, he scratched the words "Chibás was imprisoned here for combating the electric octopus" on the wall of his cell.[144] Eddy also gave free rein to another of his manias, sending his faithful secretary Conchita Fernández to bring him a pair of socks that matched his bowtie in the minutes before he was due to be released.

When the gates were opened at midnight, Chibás was effusively greeted by a crowd of thousands—some of whom immediately hoisted him on their shoulders. The surrounding area shook with chants of "Shame vs. Money" and "Shame and Truth." As the throng accompanied Chibás to his car, the nearby thoroughfares of Carlos III and Infanta were so clogged with people that public transportation was paralyzed. By the time Eddy arrived home, his *guayabera* was in tatters from the many adherents who had been anxious to touch him. The next day, Chibás addressed an equally ebullient crowd in Parque Central. Describing these scenes, Francisco Ichaso wrote, "We are, without a doubt, in a mystical presence similar to that once aroused in the people by Grau."[145] He added that Chibás, like his erstwhile mentor, possessed certain "magical elements" and inspired a "quasi-religious fervor."[146] These intangible qualities were felt with particular keenness by Cuba's youth. Thus, it seemed apropos for twenty-three-year-old José Pardo Llada to warm up the Parque Central gathering while Chibás was flanked not by old friends, party bosses or even his lawyer but by two other Ortodoxos in their early twenties—Orlando Castro and Natasha Mella. Chibás counted this too in common with Grau, who had galvanized university students (such as himself and Carlos Prío) during the late 1920s. Nor was Ichaso the only one to see this parallel. Fulgencio Batista had also tabbed Chibás as the inheritor of "Grau-style messianism."[147] But the ex-general represented an even more pernicious paradigm, that of military rule.

Chapter Seven

"The Cave of Ali Baba and His 40,000 Thieves"

Carlos Prío was less worried about Grau-style messianism than by Grau himself. After lowering the temperature on his feud with Chibás and taming the untrustworthy Guillermo Alonso Pujol, he sought to make amends with the man who was perhaps his most formidable political opponent.[1] Hence, Prío summoned José Manuel Alemán from Florida to help arrange a meeting with Grau. Alemán arrived on a Pan American flight from Miami dressed immaculately in white and reinforcing his opulent reputation by leaving generous tips for those airport employees lucky enough to serve him. Nor did the regal gestures end there. The ex-education minister, who remained Cuba's premier political moneyman, also sent flowers to the wives of leading senators and congressmen. As a result, Alemán not only received the president at his finca outside Havana but also hosted a number of eager lawmakers—including Miguelito Suárez Fernández, Lincoln Rodón, Tony Varona, Eduardo Suárez Rivas, and Guillermo Alonso Pujol. Alemán's warmest welcome, however, awaited him in Grau's residence, where he was fervently embraced by his former patron and enabler. After a series of consultations, the summit was fixed for June 13 at "Rancho Alegre," the finca of Genovevo Pérez Dámera.[2]

On the appointed day, Prío nervously approached Grau—ready to hug the man who had bestowed the presidency on him but resented any display of independence. Grau, however, was in no mood for emotional gestures and stopped him short, saying, "What's going on, Carlos? How are you?" Prío began to explain some of their previous difficulties, but Grau waved them aside. "No. Nothing of the past," he said. "It's better not to speak about these things. What's done is done. We're here to discuss the present and the future." Alemán, who was standing nearby, added, "I came here to reestablish party unity. If we want to remain in power, we must stay together in order to win in 1952."[3]

Having dispensed with formalities, Grau seized control of the conversation. Specifically, he felt Prío needed to devise a public works program to create jobs. "As you know," said Grau, "the next sugar harvest will be disappointing. This means public revenues will be greatly reduced. I believe, Carlos, that you must cover this reduction and the best way to do so is through public works. Moreover, our government's success owes a great deal to rising salaries. As long as they keep going up, the purchasing power of consumers will too."[4] Rather than considering this advice, Prío gently pointed out that the term "our government" was a misnomer since he was now in charge. The ex-professor responded as if he were correcting a froward student. "When I talk about our government," said Grau, "in reality I am referring to you. You shouldn't forget that I was only the president while you were more involved in day to day operations as labor secretary and prime minister."[5] Following this enigmatic answer, which ridiculed Prío's attempts to distance himself from Grau's administration, the president proceeded to hold his tongue and listen politely in the name of party unity. This was clearly a shrewd strategy as Grau left the premises in high spirits. Speaking to some supporters later on, he pronounced the interview a "success," and deemed himself a "reverse Machiavelli" because of his knack for uniting rather than dividing.[6]

POLEMICS AND DUELS

Alemán's return to Cuba was a boon for most journalists, who dusted off old rants against corruption and famished schoolchildren. On the other hand, Humberto Rubio of *Pueblo* surprised fellow media types by lauding Alemán as a model citizen who used education ministry jobs to lower unemployment. Rubio even likened inciso K to the Home Relief Bureau devised by Franklin Delano Roosevelt during the Great Depression. This was too much for Jorge Mañach, who kindled a feud with his *Diario de la Marina* column entitled "Dialogue between Cynicism and Outrage." Mañach expressed "bitter anger" at Alemán for the "many millions" he embezzled as a public servant, particularly given his responsibility to educate the "Cuban people."[7] Perhaps no one was more acutely aware of Alemán's homecoming than Chibás, but he first had to settle some unfinished business. Shortly before his imprisonment, Chibás had agreed to a duel with José Manuel Casanova. On the morning of June 9, the two men touched sabers at a finca owned by the tobacco-growing Placensia family—whose patriarch was sympathetic to Casanova. Chibás had initially resisted the idea of settling his dispute with Casanova on the so-called field of honor, given his opponent's advanced age.[8] The fact that neither man incurred any wounds was most likely no accident. At any rate, Chibás had scarcely retired this dispute when he became embroiled in another with René Fiallo. Prío's public relations director initially chivvied Chibás for having reacted ungratefully to his pardon. Fiallo also chided Chibás for renewing his claim, shortly after leaving prison, that Prío owed his election "exclusively" to vote buying, inciso K, and doña Pastora—the term Cubans used to refer to money, ill-gotten or otherwise.[9] He then asked, tongue firmly in cheek, whether the only "valid" and "honorable" votes were those cast for the Ortodoxo party candidate. His most damaging charge was that Chibás was a hypocrite. He noted that Chibás had stood exultant on the balcony of the presidential palace in June of 1946, after the Auténticos had triumphed in that year's midterm elections, seemingly untroubled that the same tactics he now denounced had been employed. The most irritating passage for Chibás, however, was Fiallo's insistence that "Carlos Prío is conducting the best government that is humanly possible right now in Cuba, with the best intentions of any Cuban president in recent memory and the cleanest personal conduct one could ever demand from a chief executive."[10]

Chibás replied that "the good intentions of President Prío and his clean personal conduct" had not precluded him from visiting José Manuel Alemán, who he dubbed "the biggest embezzler in contemporary history." Rather than confronting the "great crook" and "demanding he take responsibility" for his "unprecedented" robberies, Prío, "to the shame of all Cubans," embraced him cordially and welcomed him back to the island. He added that "barely had the king of thieves landed in Cuba when all the principal figures of the government, beginning with the president of the republic, the prime minister, and president of the congress ran like crazy to greet and embrace him in a desperate race to see who would arrive first. The marathon, wrote Chibás, "was won by the president of the republic."[11] With that, the stage was set for a new polemic. This played out in the pages of *Bohemia*, where they took turns flinging accusations at each other. On July 3, Fiallo allowed that the president's reunion with Alemán and Grau had "perhaps" been a "weakness or error."[12] Nevertheless, he asserted that Cubans were less interested in such gestures than the actual substance of Prío's government. Fiallo noted that the president had made three significant appointments since the meeting took place and none of the new job holders were creatures of Alemán or Grau. Raúl Roa, Cuba's new culture director, was a respected University of Havana professor and eminent former revolutionary. Meanwhile, Carlos Ramírez Corría, the recently installed health minister, and Segundo Curti, who took over the defense ministry, were both close associates of Prío. Fiallo concluded that Prío was prone to mistakes, but his sensitivity to public opinion assured him these would never be irreparable. By contrast, he deemed Chibás a messianic demagogue whose party was endlessly obsessed with "ostracizing" and "excommunicating" those it considered unworthy. Fiallo claimed this guaranteed "audiences full of fanatics" but would never result in a national majority.[13] Noting Eddy's study of the Bible during his recent incarceration, he likened the Ortodoxo chief's self-righteousness to the Pharisees. Fiallo then recalled that Jesus pardoned adulterers, the men who sank a crown of thorns onto his head, the soldiers who nailed him to the cross, those who mocked his martyrdom, and even the repentant thief crucified next to him but never forgave the egotistical Pharisees who believed themselves in sole possession of truth and virtue.

Chibás had read the good book carefully while behind bars and was delighted to engage Fiallo on Biblical terrain. He observed that Prío's followers harbored abundant sympathy for the thieves crucified next to Jesus but pointed out that only the remorseful one was saved. The embezzlers of Prío's administration, those who spoke of rectifying previous ills but continued to rob and embrace José Manuel Alemán, more closely resembled the evil thief who was condemned. "Following the example of Christ," wrote Chibás, "I will also not pardon evil thieves."[14] Eddy left little doubt as to whom he considered unsalvageable. As evidence of presidential malfeasance, he offered Carlos Prío's latest real estate acquisitions on Havana's outskirts, including the fincas "La Chata" and "La Altura." On the latter, he alleged Prío used construction materials from the public works ministry to build roads, two regal mansions, a private wharf, and a personal airport. Chibás further charged that Prío had prepared the attacks against him that appeared under Fiallo's byline and the publicity director was happy to comply since he had been "born servile" and "sold himself" to the president.[15]

An exasperated Fiallo answered in kind on July 17. He argued that Eddy's dealings with Federico Fernández Casas constituted "servility" in their own right. In April of 1946, Chibás had denounced Fernández Casas as an "oppressor of the campesino," a "land thief" and "persecutor of needy veterans of the independence war."[16] This was after the sugar magnate demolished the hut and destroyed the crops of Eusebio Maceo, a peasant from Oriente province. These actions took on added significance as the man also happened to be a relative of Antonio Maceo, a revered general from Cuba's independence war. In June of 1947, Chibás seemed to reverse course, telling Fernández Casas in a letter that "destiny" had placed him in a position to "harmoniously" resolve Cuba's "campesino problem."[17] Fiallo contended that this turnabout was due to the "many thousands of pesos" Fernández Casas could provide for Eddy's fledgling party and his presidential candidacy. However, the attempt to paint Fernández Casas as an Ortodoxo version of José Manuel Alemán was marred by the fact that he no longer belonged to the party. Moreover, even though Chibás was not above expedience, the public knew he spent weekends in his Havana apartment writing radio speeches while Cuba's political and military brass luxuriated in country estates. In short, this was not the sort of argument Auténticos were equipped to win. Fiallo, though, had two trump cards. First, he repeated the charge, initially leveled by Aureliano Sánchez Arango in 1933, that Chibás had lived a comfortable exile in New York during the late 1920s and early 1930s thanks to his father's money but had been too mean-spirited to help fellow expatriates with fewer means. Thus, Fiallo asked why Chibás had refused to share his "opulence" with émigré compañeros.[18] The second accusation, which Fiallo asserted would "definitively shut [Chibás's] mouth," also dated from the 1930s. Specifically, he stated that Eddy's story of having been shot by an unknown assailant just before elections to the constituent assembly in 1939 was a lie. In fact, Chibás had wounded himself as a publicity stunt and claimed he was "never in any danger of dying."[19] He added that "everyone has taken notice of what extremes Chibás is capable of going to in order to assure a political objective. Faced with this grotesque spectacle everyone must arrive at the same conclusion: Chibás is a born clown, a born hypocrite, a born cheat—in other words: he was born vile."[20]

Eddy did not bother to pen a response. Rather, he sent Eric Agüero and Beto Saumell to discuss terms of a duel two days after the article appeared. This turned out to be a complicated matter. For one thing, Fiallo was unfit to clash swords or sabers as his arms were beset with cystic tumors. According to protocol, Fiallo submitted to a medical examination, which confirmed the limited use of his limbs. During the second round of negotiations, one of Fiallo's representatives withdrew and was replaced by Raúl Roa, Cuba's new culture director. Both sides agreed to pistols as the weapon of choice but did not concur on the exact type until a third meeting on July 22. After that, further wrangling ensued over whether a Spanish or French dueling book should be consulted. During a fourth meeting the following evening, at the Havana Yacht Club, Fiallo's seconds were replaced by the legislators Néstor Carbonell and Francisco Cairol. This was a common tactic given that dueling was illegal and lawmakers enjoyed immunity from prosecution. Finally, on July 24, Chibás and his adversary met at the finca "Milagros" outside Havana. Eddy violated the laboriously crafted rules straight away by loading one of the guns and firing a test shot into a tree. After a spate of head shaking and hand wringing, everyone settled down and the duel proved uneventful. Each man took aim twice, and no injuries were sustained.

Tony Varona was the next government official to try his hand at provoking Chibás. On October 12, he published an article in *El Mundo* entitled, "Chibás, the High Priest of Scandal and Intrigue." The piece was a mixture of epithets and family bashing. Chibás, however, did not take the bait right away. Instead, he professed shock and disappointment in the next day's edition of *El Mundo*, writing:

> As a Cuban, I feel ashamed by the miserable spectacle that the prime minister of my country has offered today, with his infamous declarations, which are a product of the corrupt and slimy atmosphere in which he operates, but I am not willing, out of respect for the Cuban people and myself, to descend into the filthy pond in which the premier of the government rolls about, without the least bit of shame, before the amazed eyes of the nation, which is already disgusted by so much cynicism and dishonor.[21]

For good measure and a bit disingenuously, Chibás added that "no man who is well born uses this sort of language to attack a political adversary."[22] Even as Chibás had mastered his emotions and responded moderately in print, he was furious. Unable to resist his ire, he telephoned Varona multiple times the next day, leaving a message and his number with the prime minister's secretary. On Saturday, October 15, Varona returned the call in the presence of two journalists—Carlos Lechuga of *El Mundo* and Ricardo Riaño of *Bohemia*.

"Who's speaking?" said the prime minister, "Chibás? Listen, this is Varona! Yes, Varona!"

"Be a man," replied Eddy, "and repeat the insults in your article to my face."

"Listen, Chibás," answered Varona, "you know very well I'm no coward but I don't have to do anything you say right now. I am going to wait until tomorrow when you answer me on your radio show so that later on I can unmask you publicly. You are a farce!"

"And you are a coward!" screamed Chibás. "Say those things to my face! I'm here in my house. Come find me if you dare!"

"I'm more of a man than you!" screamed the prime minister. "You're crazy only when it's convenient. Remember when you were in jail and you would leave the shower still covered in soap and would dry yourself off that way just to call attention to yourself?"

"You need to come find me," repeated Chibás.

"Enough of that!" said Varona. "Don't forget that I cut you in the right arm when we dueled in Camagüey!"[23]

After the conversation ended, Chibás lingered in his apartment, but Varona never showed. The following afternoon, Varona sent a representative bearing a letter. He hoped to unnerve Eddy shortly before his broadcast with yet more incendiary lines. "You need not beat or challenge me as I am not interested in exterminating cockroaches," wrote Varona. "What you must do is prove before public opinion that what I have said about you is untrue; explaining the usefulness of the things you have done in your life aside from injuring, defaming and living in luxury off the fortune you inherited but have not been able to conserve."[24] A *Bohemia* reporter lamented these increasingly caustic exchanges, observing that Chibás had unwisely shunned his "initially advantageous position" while Varona was being "insensible to his constitutional role" as the government's chief representative.[25] Nevertheless, Varona was very much doing Prío's bidding. The president had tried to marginalize Chibás by jailing him, banning his show, and harassing the owners of CMQ. Now, he attempted to discredit him through a series of polemics. Varona's intensely personal affronts were designed to elicit a wild response, something that would remind Cubans that Chibás was indeed unfit for high office. However, Eddy had composed a carefully written reply, recalling the style of Emile Zola's *J'accuse*, and did not deviate from it during his twenty-five minutes on the air. Avoiding ad hominem attacks, Chibás focused instead on his adversary's political shortcomings. For instance, he told his audience:

> I don't slander, Antonio de Varona. I accuse you concretely of criminal connivance with the government inspectors who defraud and extort money from industrialists and merchants, as proved by the case of Mr. Gabriel Rodríguez, owner of the furniture shop "La Venecia," in Camagüey. This retailer was foolish enough to heed the official exhortation to denounce government functionaries who deal in blackmail. He thus installed a microphone on the counter of his establishment and recorded the words of the inspector who tried to extort money from him, sending the disc to the police and informing the prime minister, Tony de Varona. The only thing he obtained was increased persecution from the inspectors who found all sorts of false violations and now he is trying to sell the store.[26]

Each paragraph began with the same litany: "I don't slander, Antonio de Varona. I accuse . . ." Besides doing nothing to help ordinary Cubans from being shaken down by their government, Chibás charged Varona with robbing the 100,000 pesos used to purchase his residence on Seventh Avenue and Twenty-Fourth Street in Miramar and illegally acquiring the finca "La Dominica," which was state property. He also alleged Varona was in league with Ramón Ruisánchez, who monopolized Cuba's dried beef market and artificially raised the price of this item. Furthermore, Chibás reminded listeners that his enemy had defended José Manuel Alemán in the senate in 1947 and subverted revolutionary ideals by investigating a pact with the Liberals to ensure support for the government's foreign loan.

On October 23, Varona answered Chibás in *Bohemia*. Among other things, he produced a letter from Gabriel Rodríguez, the everyman furniture store proprietor of Camagüey, which contradicted much of what Chibás said about him on the radio. Rodríguez had written to Varona the day after hearing the broadcast and revealed his problem with the government inspector occurred during Grau's presidency. He also denied sending his recording to the police or notifying Varona of its existence. Lastly, he admitted to selling his business but not because of official persecution or unscrupulous assessors but due to the law requiring retailers to keep fifteen years' worth of records on hand at all times. Rodríguez found this provision so onerous that he planned to seek greener pastures in a Latin American "sister republic" where maintaining only five years of records was the rule.[27] As for Chibás, he had obviously been sloppy. He had also been imprudent regarding his allegations of corruption against Varona. The prime minister lived well but not lavishly and was broadly considered to be honest. Rather than sleaze, his foremost shortcoming was placing party interests above Cuba's constitution. Chibás correctly excoriated him for defending Alemán over the senate's right to interpellate government ministers.[28] He was on shakier ground concerning Varona's Miramar home, which likely attracted his attention because its previous occupant had been Mirta Batista—the ex-general's daughter. At any rate, the prime minister contended his home had cost 75,000 pesos rather than 100,000 and supplied a document from Banco Gelats containing some details of his mortgage. Regarding the finca "La Dominica," Varona noted it was government property; Grau had stayed there periodically during his term in office, Chibás himself had visited on various occasions, and the premises were no more his than the presidential palace belonged to Carlos Prío. Having defended his own probity, Varona turned the tables on Chibás. He accused him of tax evasion and cashing false checks during his stint as a congressman. Above all, Varona still aimed to boil Eddy's blood. Thus, when Chibás protested against attacks on his family, the prime minister suggested he had none and deliberately impugned his manhood, writing:

> What I affirmed previously and I repeat now is that Chibás does not have his own household; he has no wife, nor does he have children and these are normal things for a man to have—this being a basic condition of his nature. And we can doubt his devotion and respect for the Cuban woman. He has not wanted to make one his wife and thereby recognize the virtue and goodness of our women. Chibás has not been able to find a good woman with whom to share his life and begin an honorable family—which is the basic unit of society.[29]

Chibás closed out the polemic a week later, reminding *Bohemia*'s readers that Varona had initiated the brouhaha to distract public attention from the administration's foibles. These included its treatment of Cuba's most famous furniture vendor, Gabriel Rodríguez, whose intent to leave the country represented "the most terrible accusation that has been made against a government."[30] Rather than "removing the filth," Chibás observed the Auténticos "aspire to muddy those of us who are clean."[31] He stated that the checks alluded to by Varona had corresponded to his regular congressman's salary and were in no way dishonest. Chibás added that his lawmaker's wages and inherited fortune had always been at the service of Cuba's people. Hence, while Tony Varona was buying the house of Mirta Batista, he was selling his cherished family home, with a "tethered heart," for half its value, in order to convert the island into a "great nation."[32] Nor was this the first time Chibás had sacrificed financially in order to change the island's politics. In 1944, he borrowed 20,000 pesos against the value of an apartment building he owned in Vedado, known as the Edificio Chibás, in order to assist the election of Ramón Grau San Martín. He claimed this money and the intense campaign it enabled were a "decisive factor" in the Auténtico victory.[33] With a distinct whiff of pathos, Chibás wrote that "when Grau San Martín became president of the republic, no one had more influence than I. But I did not ask nor did I accept anything for my personal benefit. I only urged him to fulfill the program of the revolution. I asked him on behalf of the campesinos and for Cuba."[34] Chibás, who lacked a steady income now that he was no longer a senator, then confessed he could no longer afford the monthly 133-peso payment on that loan and would probably lose yet another piece of his father's legacy. Despite his sporadically rash accusations, Chibás counted on two essential truths to maintain credibility and popular support. First, he was one of the few politicians who had become demonstrably poorer since entering politics—a fact not lost on many Cubans. While Chibás remained well off, the island's citizens were never regaled with accounts of his weekends at country estates or exclusive beaches. Second, even as his accusations of corruption against Tony Varona were off the mark, other Auténticos, notably the Prío brothers, were widely known to have profited from public office. Chibás sometimes played fast and loose with details, but the larger narrative was undeniable. "I entered power branded as a millionaire," he concluded, "but I left two years later poorer than when I came. In contrast, the current leaders entered power without fortunes but now enjoy many millions of pesos."[35]

DIVIDED LOYALTIES ONCE MORE

While Chibás tussled with Prío administration officials, trouble was afoot yet again within Ortodoxo ranks. During a tour of Camagüey province in mid-July, Chibás discovered that many members of the Workers' Wing also belonged to the proletarian-themed gangster outfit Acción Revolucionaria Guiteras (ARG). One of them attempted to play down his divided loyalties, saying, "Here in Camagüey, we do what we believe is right rather than following the orders of (ARG leader) 'El Extraño.'"[36] Sometimes, this included persecuting fellow Ortodoxo sugar workers in the area who also supported the Communist line. Isidro Figueroa, who headed the Ortodoxo Workers' Wing, admitted such "confusion" was detrimental to the party's development and lamented that various "distinguished" colleagues refused to understand the necessity of working toward "legitimate (political) independence."[37] This was never going to be easy given the long-standing competition for workers among ARG, the Communists, and Auténtico-sponsored labor organizations.

In Matanzas, the old question of whether Ortodoxos should cut deals with other parties was revived by a group devoted to the province's former governor, Pablo Vega. This effort was discreetly supported by José Manuel Gutiérrez, the former Ortodoxo boss from the region who had supposedly retired from politics. Tensions were further stoked by the fact that the local executive council remained peopled with traitors who had supported outside candidates in 1948. On July 17, Chibás used his bully pulpit to demand the ouster of double-dealers and press members of the provincial assembly to respect the national party platform. Chibás explained that "it's necessary to choose sides: those who are with (Pablo) Vega and the old tortured politics of horse trading and who would sell the party in exchange for government jobs or those who follow the Ortodoxos' moral rectitude. There is no room for middle ground or transactions."[38] Chibás was also tested by Guarro Ochoa, the Ortodoxo mayor of Holguín in Oriente province. Hoping to bolster his reelection prospects, Ochoa roiled the waters by mulling an offer of support from Fulgencio Batista's Partido Acción Unitaria (PAU). Chibás had no intention of allowing such a move and informed Ochoa that he would have to resign from the party if he struck such a deal. This, in turn, raised the ire of Guarro's brother Millo, the Ortodoxo vice president. He claimed provincial assemblies were autonomous and told a *Bohemia* reporter that "I sacrificed myself once already for the party and I'm not prepared now to follow the independent line. I consider it suicide."[39] Despite his brother's fiery words, Guarro Ochoa backed down. On July 23, he notified Chibás that the agreement with Batista was off.

The debate over pacts was not confined solely to the provinces, although at the national level there were fewer dissident voices. At a meeting of Ortodoxo heavyweights in Roberto Agramonte's house, Chibás claimed the party's independent line had "perfectly translated" popular sentiment.[40] He mentioned the "warm ovation" he had received during a reunion at his old high school, the elite Jesuit-run Colegio de Belén, along with the enthusiastic crowds that greeted him upon his release from prison and the rally in Parque Central in which Ortodoxo principles had been reaffirmed by a "human wave."[41] Chibás, who always loved a good metaphor, compared public opinion to large quantities of oil tucked beneath a thin layer of soil. "One only needs to drop a match," he said, "in order to create a blaze."[42] Chibás subsequently ceded the floor to Roberto García Ibáñez, the congressman from Oriente province, who argued for a less rigid policy. He cited the case of Pepillo Hernández, the Ortodoxo mayor of Victoria de las Tunas, who was offered support from outside parties. "What should we do?" asked García Ibáñez. "Should we sacrifice Pepillo to maintain our independence?"[43] Manuel Bisbé allowed that independence had been largely tactical before the

1948 elections, but the party's encouraging showing enshrined it as a guiding formula. The host, Roberto Agramonte, suggested a historical analogy from the region—noting that in Argentina the sustained intransigence of the Radical party, which was also an outfit dedicated to constitutionalism and clean politics, had eventually led to the election of its leader, Hipólito Yrigoyen, in 1916.

Closer to home, Chibás almost certainly must have recalled Auténtico factional struggles during the late 1930s between "revolutionaries" and "realists." The former had been dead set against compromise with Batista and advocated militancy in combination with acts of violence to defeat him while the latter, which included both Grau and Chibás, had sought the party's legalization and participation in elections. While the circumstances obviously differed this time around, Chibás now enforced the more radical path, having watched Auténtico realism mutate into moral turpitude. At the same time, discontented whispers and outright accusations of dictatorship made their way, as they often did in Cuba, to the press. The columnist Jorge Martí of *El Mundo* gave voice to some of these and was immediately graced with a letter by Chibás. He wrote that

> Liberty in the political sphere is not incompatible with discipline in individual political parties. . . . I will defend the right of any citizen to found a monarchical party, a communist party, an annexationist party or a party open to pacts in accordance with their own personal taste but no one has the right to join the Ortodoxo party, which has a very defined doctrine, and defend monarchy, communism, annexation to Spain or political pacts. Every citizen has the right to dip their head into the pond infected by traditional politics but they don't have the right to join the Ortodoxo party and push it into a corrupt swamp.[44]

Two days later, on July 31, Millo Ochoa appeared on Eddy's radio show and proclaimed his adherence to the independent line. A contented Chibás told his listeners that Ochoa embodied the Ortodoxo ideal of personal sacrifice for the greater good. Ochoa however had little choice but to submit. Since the 1948 elections, supporters of independence had gained control of the party. Ochoa disagreed with them but bowed knowing that circumstances were fluid. After all, the national assembly had endorsed pacts in the recent past as had five of the party's six provincial bodies. At any rate, Ochoa's attitude formed a marked contrast with that of José Manuel Gutiérrez. After failing to reorient the Matanzas provincial assembly, he bitterly declared that "this Eduardo Chibás has created a party that seems like those of Mussolini, Hitler, etc. in which every member must adhere to the unassailable truth, to the word and orders of the leader whether he's called Duce, Führer or Chibás."[45]

This view was most assuredly not shared by Carlos Márquez Sterling, the former president of Cuba's constitutional convention and erstwhile Liberal who was courting the Ortodoxos but had not yet become a member. From one standpoint, there was a certain poetic justice in Márquez Sterling, the biographer of Ignacio Agramonte, joining the party led by his subject's admiring descendant.[46] However, the man described by a *Bohemia* reporter as "the most intellectual of Cuba's politicians" was more interested in electoral reform than maintaining an isolationist posture.[47] Speaking of the 1948 contest, Márquez Sterling averred that "shame could not defeat the two large coalitions supported by bribery and electoral machinery, and the Ortodoxos finished in third place although they deserved to win."[48] This fact influenced him to believe that effecting changes in the electoral code, which unduly favored alliances, should be the party's first priority. While the old ways were still in force, Márquez Sterling advocated "temporary" pacts lest the Ortodoxos run the risk of losing their historical moment.[49] To be sure, these musings were purely theoretical for the time being. Even so, Márquez Sterling's dance with the party, which was very much encouraged by Chibás, indicated he was not quite the hard-liner suggested by his rhetoric.

A NEW ARMY CHIEF

On July 19, Chief of Staff Genovevo Pérez Dámera was alarmed by a broadcast from the Dominican station La Voz del Yuna warning him that his life was in danger. This threat resonated because the same announcer had correctly predicted the death by ambush of Colonel Francisco Javier Arana in Guatemala a day earlier. Nonetheless, Prío advised his army chief to ignore this provocation from the Dominican dictator Rafael Trujillo. After all, the tyrant was not only an enemy of the Auténticos, who sheltered anti-Trujillo exiles on Cuban soil, but of Prío's family as well. The president's brother-in-law, Enrique Henríquez, was an Auténtico congressman with Dominican roots who had helped organize a failed plot against Trujillo the previous month.[50] To place more stock in Trujillo's hints than Prío's assurances would thus represent a double and unforgivable betrayal. All the same, Pérez Dámera yielded to his anxiety. He sent two men on a clandestine mission to Santo Domingo, where they spoke with Trujillo and received information regarding the supposed peril. Pérez Dámera was sufficiently convinced by the evidence they brought back that he began surrounding himself with machine gun–wielding bodyguards, a fact that caught Prío's attention and aroused his suspicions. On August 22, the president learned the reason behind these precautions. His sources had uncovered Pérez Dámera's secret contact with Trujillo and revealed that one of the go-betweens was Colonel Camilo González Chávez, Cuba's air force chief. The next day, Prío obtained a copy of the document that had unnerved his top military man. Written by an agent of Trujillo posing as a renegade ARG gangster, the text described preparations to murder the island's top general in minute and obviously disturbing detail. These included five different schemes, developed during the past several years, all of which betrayed intimate knowledge of Pérez Dámera's habits. The forgery maintained that ARG leaders Jesús González Cartas and Eufemio Fernández were behind these plans as they believed Pérez Dámera would "always be a serious obstacle" to their organization.[51] Moreover, Fernández, who was a close friend of Prío, supposedly had a clear motive given Pérez Dámera's "betrayal" of the Auténticos' first effort to oust Trujillo—the Cayo Confites operation in 1947.[52]

After reading the phony letter, Prío declared, "Either the army is an institution or a political force. If it's the first, my presence in Columbia [the main military barracks] will resolve the problem; if it's the second, the country is lost and I will share its fate."[53] At 5:00 p.m., the president ordered Police Chief José Manuel Caramés to keep his men in their station houses. He then called Defense Minister Segundo Curti to the presidential palace. Prío was determined to relieve Pérez Dámera of his position, but two obstacles presented themselves. First, his decree required the prime minister's signature, but Tony Varona was abroad. Second, the prospective new army chief, Ruperto Cabrera, was vacationing in New York. Prío resolved the former by naming Curti interim prime minister. As for the latter, Cabrera arrived home at 10:00 p.m. that evening—whereupon he was immediately summoned to meet the president. Prío realized he was in a precarious position even after General Cabrera agreed to command the military. To begin with, Pérez Dámera had named the entire palace guard, and its loyalty could not be assured. Hence, Prío ascended to the third-floor living quarters, told his wife he was about to "take a very serious step," and bid her to leave for his mother's house.[54] At 11:10 p.m., Prío left for the Columbia military base accompanied by Cabrera and two other officers. They found the place subdued and quiet, presided over by a pair of guayabera-clad colonels playing dominoes. A farcical scene ensued when Prío demanded the keys to Pérez Dámera's office, but neither of the colonels had them. Luckily, an officer spied an open window and climbed through. Shortly thereafter, the soldiers were stirred from their slumber and assembled on the parade ground. Prío announced the retirement of Pérez Dámera and his replacement by General Ruperto Cabrera. He also urged his audience to cast off any lingering allegiance to their former leader, saying, "I hope that in the following days, Cuban military men will think more highly of the will they possess than the functions they carry out because the former is permanent while the latter is fleeting."[55] To his relief, the president's oratory was met by a round of applause, but there was still no time to relax. Prío's most critical task remained at hand, namely, to speak with Pérez Dámera himself, who was rusticating in "La Larga," his *hacienda* in Camagüey province.[56]

"General," said Prío, "I have called to inform you that you have been relieved as army chief of staff."

"As you order, Mr. President," answered Pérez Dámera, growing pale as his family looked on nervously. Moments later, he added, "Mr. President, but why?"

"You have lost confidence in me and when a subordinate does not trust his boss the situation doesn't go very well," said Prío coldly.

"Very well, Mr. President. May I speak with someone there?"

"With whomever you'd like, General," replied Prío.

The telephone was passed to one of the colonels present.

"What has happened, colonel?" asked Pérez Dámera.

"You have been replaced, General, just as the president has informed you."

"What do the officers say?"

"All are at the president's orders."

"And you?"

"I also, General."[57]

Pérez Dámera was caught unawares and had no choice but to yield yet he plainly doubted the president's authority. Shorn of his command and suspected of treason, Pérez Dámera adopted a more humble demeanor. Thus, he told an intimate, ironically named Trujillo, to notify the president that he was willing to leave Cuba immediately if his presence was considered "prejudicial."[58]

For a moment, Carlos Prío basked in a hero's glow. The corpulent and opulent Pérez Dámera was no darling of the people nor was he a favorite of journalists, most of whom lionized Prío for defending the prerogatives of civilian government. Even the usually hostile Enrique de la Osa registered his approval, albeit by means of an anecdote. He noted that US embassy officials were among the first to detect something had happened. When informed that Pérez Dámera had been unseated, they requested permission to send observers. Gushing with pride, de la Osa described how they "verified with amazement" that a Latin American army chief could be removed without setting off an insurrection.[59] On the other hand, Chibás could not resist portraying the situation in negative terms. Asked by a reporter for his opinion, Eddy initially expressed surprise that Prío had waited until "three o'clock in the morning" to exercise his constitutional right instead of doing so "in broad daylight like any other normal government activity." The most dramatic man in Cuban politics added that the episode had developed, "theatrically, like a horrifying melodrama episode, where the president's fear constitutes the main character." Considering the matter a bit further, Chibás concluded that "what has occurred seems more like a surprise attack from one band of gunmen against a pack of rivals based on differences over how to divide their loot rather than the constitutional substitution of an army chief realized by the chief of state."[60]

Although ungenerous, Eddy's reference to gangsters turned out to be prescient. On the afternoon of September 1, Havana played host to yet another lurid scene as Wichy Salazar and Francisco Fernández Cristóbal were murdered in a drive-by shooting. Salazar's sister Efigenia was also wounded in the attack, but the enterprising Ortodoxo Juan Amador persuaded her to grant an interview from her hospital bed—which was broadcast live on Radio Progreso. Efigenia Salazar described how they had been walking toward Wichy's car, parked near their home in Havana's Cerro district, when bullets began flying from a vehicle in the distance. She later clarified that there were two automobiles filled with "around 12" triggermen along with some others on foot. "I recognized Policarpo Soler," she said, "who got out of the car with a machine gun. . . . Policarpo killed my brother on the ground. He was wearing dark glasses and a guayabera. I screamed: 'Assassin, don't kill him!' He then opened fire on me and believed I was dead. Ah! El Colorado was also in this automobile."

"You know him?" asked Amador.

"Of course! Since the era of Batista. I saw him perfectly. Later on, the police pretended to chase the fleeing assassins. The truth is that I don't know why they can't capture these individuals since they too have machine guns."[61]

As a gang member with a violent past, Wichy Salazar was not an ideal repository for sympathy.[62] Rather, the shocking aspect of this story was Policarpo Soler's attempt to murder an unarmed woman. During his Sunday evening broadcast, Chibás compared this outrage to Aurora Soler's execution at Orfila and noted that both had received "a bullet in the belly."[63] Moreover, Chibás incited anger at the apathetic lawmen who had watched in a nearby patrol car while Policarpo Soler descended from his vehicle and finished Salazar off. He also reproached them for their halfhearted pursuit of the perpetrators once they fled the scene. This last accusation was not entirely accurate, however. In fact, police trailed a pair of shooters to the University of Havana's agronomy school. This was one of many safe havens, including the houses and country estates of legislators, which dotted the capital's landscape and were off-limits to the authorities. Under intense pressure to act after this latest outrage, Carlos Prío set aside the university's autonomy and ordered police to occupy the agronomy school. They duly arrested the wanted gunmen along with twelve other suspicious characters. Among these was the agronomy school's student president, José Buján, who apparently had been doing more than keeping questionable company. By all indications, he had cut a deal with MSR gangsters to help win the presidency of the Federation of University Students (FEU).[64]

Buján was also using the agronomy school and adjacent botanical garden, known as the Quinta de los Molinos, as his own personal fiefdom. Buján resided with his wife and two small children in one of the school's buildings and cut down trees from the botanical garden as if they were his own, selling the lumber for profit. In an even cheekier maneuver, Buján had removed a wooden house, piece by piece, from the botanical garden and reconstructed it on land he owned on Havana's outskirts. Altogether, Buján seemed to possess the same nerve as his patron and benefactor, José Manuel Alemán. Many students believed Alemán was supplying weapons stockpiled in 1947 for the canceled expedition against Trujillo as a means to bring the university under his control.[65] Perhaps even more scandalous was the arrest of Juan Acosta, a member of the presidential palace secret service. Enrique de la Osa claimed this proved, "for the man on the street," that Prío had known all along what was going on in the agronomy school.[66] This theory was bolstered by documents confiscated during the police raid indicating that Buján and his MSR sponsors were closely monitoring the student campaign against Prío's attempt to secure a foreign loan. On his radio show, Chibás lamented that most students repudiated gangsters but were defenseless against gunmen who were "armed to the teeth, present everywhere, enjoying immunity, mocking the courts and boasting government support."[67] For Prío, the issue was particularly dicey because party reorganizations were scheduled for October. At that time Prío would need some of the same gangsters he now harassed to help secure friendly delegates in Auténtico assemblies, particularly as he hoped to propose his brother Antonio as a candidate for Havana's mayoralty. For this reason, most of those arrested were likely to find themselves back on the street before long. The case of Wilfredo Lara García, a drive-by shooter of Wichy Salazar nabbed in the agronomy school raid, more or less predicted this result. Lara already had murder and attempted murder charges pending against him, but was suspiciously free on bail when he joined El Colorado and Policarpo Soler on their deadly mission.

Unfortunately for Prío, the miasmal stew of gangsters, unprofessional policemen, and university violence continued to be a source of embarrassment. On September 13, José Pardo Llada announced during his radio show that a certain Mr. Manuel Caramés Monteagudo had been granted permission to construct a three-story house on Avenida Tulipán. Pardo Llada noted the name's similarity to that of Havana's police chief and wondered mischievously if they were the same person or whether perhaps there was a brother who had won the lottery. Two days later, the twenty-three-year-old Ortodoxo broadcaster found a man in uniform waiting for him and was escorted to police headquarters. He was quickly shown into the office of José Manuel Caramés Monteagudo. With nary a word, the latter closed the door, removed his gold-butted revolver from its holster, and cast it aside. Pardo Llada countered by taking off his glasses. Without further ado, Caramés punched Pardo Llada in the chest and received a glancing blow to the face in return. The two men grappled and hit each other for a short while before falling on the police chief's leather couch, whereupon Caramés bellowed, "You are a liar!" The affray then continued for another five minutes or so after which the exhausted belligerents began hurling curses at each other rather than fists. Finally, someone opened the door from outside and two legislators rushed in along with the journalist Humberto Medrano of *Prensa Libre*. "What's going on?" asked Medrano, looking at Caramés. "Are you crazy?"

"I couldn't allow what he said," answered the police chief. "It's a lie."

"This is foolishness!" said Representative Armando Fernández Jorva. "You can't fight with a reporter!"

The chubby Caramés, answering like a pouting schoolboy, said: "He attacked me! He's the one who fought with me!"

"Why then," remonstrated Pardo Llada, "did you put away your pistol?"

"And why did you take off your glasses?" asked the police chief.[68]

Finally, as the affair resembled a makeshift honor dispute, Medrano drew up a document, in accordance with the rules of dueling, which both men signed and thereby officially ended their conflict. By that evening, Caramés was such a laughingstock that the Puerto Rican singer Daniel Santos had already debuted a song dedicated to the incident. The island's cartoonists rejoiced as well. One sketch, entitled "Man of Prudence," portrayed a bare-chested figure wearing boxing gloves approaching police headquarters and saying, "Caramés wants to see me in his office and I have to be ready just in case."[69]

Aside from his imprudent and well-nigh illegal behavior, the Havana police chief had chosen poor timing for his ill-advised loutishness. September 15 represented the second anniversary of the Orfila massacre, and UIR militants were certain to commemorate the death of their boss with an attack. Instead of preparing for this eventuality, Caramés had spent the afternoon pursuing a personal quarrel. In light of what would happen later, this lapse was both reckless and unforgivable. Shortly after 7:00 p.m., a group of UIR triggermen opened fire on Rolando Masferrer as he left the Capitolio. A gun battle ensued on the marble staircase, and legislators who found themselves nearby hit the ground and tried to crawl discreetly toward safety. The MSR leader saved himself by shooting his way back into the building, but two of his gangster friends were gravely wounded and another died from a bullet to the head. As usual, no assailants were detained at the scene. A *Bohemia* reporter snidely observed that "the so-called Anti-Gangster Law had no effect even in the parliamentary realm, where the police showed themselves to be just as incompetent as they are in the university."[70] For Masferrer, this was the fifth time he had escaped unharmed from an assassination attempt since June of 1948. As with Wichy Salazar, public sympathy for Masferrer was scant but there was considerable fury that gangsters had yet again crossed a line—this time for bringing their conflict to Cuba's congress.

This sense of pervasive lawlessness was aggravated five days later when Gustavo Mejía Maderne, the vice president of the Association of Social

Science Students at the University of Havana, was shot eight times in the back. Mejía had been a third-year law student with no ties to the armed thugs on campus. Rather, he managed the university's swimming pool area and noticed its canteen was purveying drugs and attracting dubious characters who were not students. Moments after denouncing this state of affairs to the university deans, he was riddled with bullets by Modesto González del Valle, who owned the canteen. Raúl Roa, dean of the social sciences faculty, told grieving professors and students at the hospital, where Mejía had been delivered dead on arrival, that he had seen González del Valle brandishing a pistol and overheard him saying, "Blood is going to flow."[71] Heeding the popular uproar, Roa resigned his post and vowed to help rescue the campus from shady figures. The victim's uncle, Feliciano Maderne, who had fought Machado in the 1930s, hoped this episode would call attention to the "tolerance and protection that the present government reserves for gangsters" and said that criminals would continue to kill "peaceable citizens" until the police began catching them.[72] Speaking to reporters in the packed emergency ward that contained his nephew's body, Maderne added an emotional plea: "I summon President Prío to grant me an audience so I may ask him to fulfill his responsibilities and demand the guarantees and respect the honest citizens of my fatherland deserve!"[73]

While violence raged in Havana, assassins with government links plagued Cuba's countryside as well. On September 21, the Communist leader Lázaro Peña denounced the murder of two workers' leaders in the Francisco sugar mill of Camagüey province. Speaking in the chamber of representatives, he accused the Auténtico congressman and labor leader Emilio Surí Castillo of sponsoring the killings. Manuel Bisbé also blamed the administration for these deaths, adding that "in Cuba human life has no more value than that of an insect!"[74] The more immediate focus, however, involved Havana and its beleaguered police chief. Armando Caíñas Milanés declared that "everyone, from the president of the republic to the most insignificant policeman, knows who the gangsters are, where they work, where they live and where they spend their time."[75] He then called for the resignation of Caramés, who he claimed was incapable of maintaining order. Hardly one to remain silent during a lively debate, Rolando Masferrer artfully told the assembly that administration officials should follow the example of Aureliano Sánchez Arango—who had removed (mostly MSR) gunmen from the education ministry payroll. Specifically, he urged Miguelito Suárez Fernández and Interior Minister Rubén de León, both of whom sustained UIR militants, to follow suit.

For his part, Carlos Prío bowed to public opinion and unleashed GRAS. The so-called green flies arrested fifty men including Masferrer's private secretary, but as Enrique de la Osa noted, these were "third category" suspects.[76] "The big gangsters," including El Colorado and Policarpo Soler, "remained untouchable."⁷⁷ More compelling was the news that Caramés resigned his position under pressure from the president on September 22. Shortly thereafter, the ex-police chief agreed to an interview with two *Bohemia* reporters in which he connected each of the island's action groups to their respective Auténtico factions. For example, he claimed the government used ARG gunmen to win control over Cuba's labor unions. Caramés also stated that Miguelito Suárez Fernández provided "moral and material" support for gangsters and had helped the UIR boss José de Jesús Jinjaume flee to safety in New York. He further averred that the senate president had employed armed toughs in his electoral campaigns "before and after" the third front.⁷⁸ "Each time (the thugs) committed their misdeeds," concluded Caramés, "I sent them to the courts. In spite of the evidence I contributed, they were exonerated. This occurred with all the groups time after time."⁷⁹ Given all the negative publicity, Carlos Prío was lucky in at least one respect; namely, that Chibás had passed the week campaigning in Matanzas and Las Villas. This strenuous six-day tour, which encompassed trips to villages, towns, and sugar mills of every size, was undertaken during the island's rainy season—meaning he was subjected not only to intense downpours but also impassable country roads, which were dirt paths during the best of times and had now become car-swallowing brown muck. Chibás returned to Havana so exhausted that he dashed off only a quick condemnation of the Mejía shooting, which was read over the air by a minor Ortodoxo official.

As the first anniversary of Prío's inauguration approached, Raúl Gutiérrez conducted a public survey regarding how Cubans viewed his performance to date. The news was encouraging despite recent chaos in Havana's streets and university. In what was perhaps the most telling question, citizens were asked whether they preferred Prío over Grau, Chibás, or Batista. In the event, they opted for Prío over El Viejo by seven percentage points, over the Ortodoxo leader by nearly eight percentage points, and over the ex-general by almost nine percentage points. One of the main reasons for this could be found in something Chibás had regularly denounced during the latter half of Grau's presidency but had largely stopped talking about since Prío took office. That is, prices were falling for basic goods and the black market was receding. As Chibás and others had pointed out, this was a worldwide phenomenon rather than a local one, driven by increasing production in the United States and countries devastated by World War II.⁸⁰ Nonetheless, Prío and Commerce Minister José Andreu reaped the political benefits. Asked what was best about Prío's administration, the fact that he had "lowered the cost of living (and) ended the black market" was ranked first by respondents.⁸¹ They also chose Andreu as the government's best cabinet member. On the other hand, Prío remained unpopular in Cuba's interior. For example, more than 53 percent claimed the president had done "nothing good" during his first year in office.⁸²

Chapter 7

THE GOVERNMENT LOAN

The June 26 issue of *Bohemia* featured an interview with Treasury Minister Antonio Prío. Asked by Mario Kuchilán whether the government was preparing a loan, he opened his eyes wide and replied, "I would rather not talk about it."[83] Three weeks later, Francisco Ichaso noted that the president and his prime minister remained mum on the subject but found it telling that the government did not offer any denials. Even as the administration stonewalled about the loan, two related issues—namely, the pillaged treasury and its capacity to support an ever-expanding bureaucracy—could not be so easily minimized. Government jobs were the Auténticos' lifeblood, and Prío had insisted the so-called deficit would not endanger them. Hence, there was palpable shock when twelve thousand public employees received pink slips in July. Auténtico congressmen were particularly outraged. Some suspected that Grau's "deficit" had diminished the funds available for government work.[84] Moreover, the positions being cut had specifically been handed out by Auténtico representatives—some of whom counted more than one thousand places at the public trough at their disposal. Teodoro Tejeda Setién, a congressman from Las Villas province, was thus being quite honest when he referred to the displaced as "our employees."[85] Invited to address the Auténtico-Republican parliamentary committee, Tony Varona euphemistically explained that Cuba was suffering a "post-war crisis."[86] Predictably, those who complained loudest regarding the government's newfound penury were legislators loyal to Miguelito Suárez Fernández. The real question, then, was whether the administration was prepared to antagonize them less than a year before midterm elections.

Ichaso, in his *Bohemia* column, mentioned the persistent rumor that Prío planned to obtain a "river of gold" in order to bring back the go-go epoch of Grau.[87] This would maintain Auténtico unity at the cost of abandoning one of the party's last remaining principles. Having been formed during the late 1920s and early 1930s when President Gerardo Machado negotiated loans on what they considered exploitive terms, Auténtico founders, including Prío, had considered them anathema from the start. For this reason, Manuel Fernández Supervielle had campaigned for Havana's mayoralty in 1946 on a platform of bringing water to the city without foreign money or concessions. Of course, Supervielle's chief propagandist had been Eduardo Chibás, who was opposed to a loan then and remained steadfastly against one now. Asked by a reporter for his opinion, Chibás recalled that he had accused the government of attempting to borrow foreign money six months earlier on his radio show. Eddy also could not resist one of his traditional crowd-pleasing refrains, saying:

> What President Prío has to do now if he wants to behave honorably and logically is not to look for a loan of 100 or 200 million pesos to replace the millions that have been stolen from the public treasury but to throw the thieves in prison and confiscate the money they robbed. But he cannot do this because he would have to begin by incarcerating the majority of those who surround him.[88]

Chibás sprinkled his rhetoric with some sobering facts as well. He observed that Cuba had taken out 422 million pesos worth of loans in its history and had paid 205 million worth of interest on that amount. The most egregious case of abuse had been a loan for 35 million contracted by the island's first president, Tomás Estrada Palma, in 1904, to pay veterans of the independence war. This was finally retired forty years later, with the government forking over almost 43 million pesos in interest.[89] Chibás was not the only political leader who opposed the loan. Grau declared that borrowing foreign money was "totally contrary" to Auténtico doctrine while Fulgencio Batista deemed the prospect of a loan "inconceivable" and an "ominous weight" on the Cuban people.[90] Notable in his dissent was Miguelito Suárez Fernández, who stood to gain from an infusion of cash and argued against dismissing a loan out of hand. He mentioned that Cuba was in danger of "depression" and referred to the Marshall Plan and President Harry Truman's "politics of reconstruction" as evidence of crisis on a world scale that should be solved by creative rather than rigid thinking.[91] No doubt, Suárez Fernández was also considering the present crisis of patronage that would disproportionately affect his disciples without a new revenue source.

For Chibás, the loan was further evidence that Prío had become "a servant of imperialist interests."[92] His erstwhile friend had bowed to Wall Street through preferential treatment of the Cuban Electric Company and was doing so again by seeking to borrow money from US banks. Just as Chibás had pressured Prío into withdrawing the rate hikes for electricity, he hoped a similar campaign would scuttle the loan before it was consummated. Although the subject remained officially taboo, Prío had begun preparing the ground by touting his own personal honesty and that of his cabinet. Chibás scoffed, reminding Prío that he had known him as a university student who "lived very modestly."[93] He challenged Prío once again to explain how he acquired so many choice properties since entering politics. As for the president's ministers, Chibás accused Antonio Prío of lining his pockets by directing tax inspectors to shake down Cuba's merchants and industrialists. He also pointed out that an ethical cloud hung over Agriculture Minister Virgilio Pérez, who had manipulated the price of coffee by importing 15 million pounds even as the country was already well stocked. According to Chibás, this "affaire" netted 1.5 million pesos for Pérez and his cronies while "ruining" twenty-three thousand domestic coffee farmers.[94] Chibás concluded that

> Every time a government has requested a loan, they play the same tune: "the loan is for paving streets and constructing aqueducts in interior cities," "the loan is for improving the island's sanitation," "the loan is for stimulating agriculture," "the loan is for building a new sewage system," etc., etc. Nevertheless, in the shadow of these loans the one thing that has always been constructed is great personal fortunes.[95]

While Chibás steadfastly disapproved of any loan, he felt borrowing money domestically represented the lesser of two evils. He noted that Cuba possessed 300 million pesos worth of gold in New York's Federal Reserve Bank and more than 600 million pesos in national bank deposits. The onus of repayment would still hinder industry, business, and the general population—all of whom would endure higher taxes, but at least this money would stay on the island. Foreign loans were not only a "bloodbath for the national economy," they also begat an inevitable swarm of outside accountants, engineers, and other technocrats sent from overseas to ensure compliance.[96] In this vein, he warned Prío that "you know very well that loans constitute the imperialist instrument of penetration, the favorite weapon of 'dollar politics' in order to economically subjugate the people of Latin America."[97]

By now, the loan was such a charged topic that Raúl Gutiérrez, Cuba's public survey guru, was commissioned to produce a new poll. His research revealed a trio of interesting findings. First, 75.56 percent of respondents were aware of the government's semi-clandestine project. Second, more Cubans seemed to think borrowing cash could be beneficial or conditionally beneficial (45.56 percent) than those who felt it would be prejudicial or conditionally prejudicial (37.58 percent). This was no surprise as many Cubans hoped renewed public works employment would cover the loss of jobs caused by a 20 percent reduction in the sugar harvest. Did this mean Eddy's instinct for what was popular had deserted him? Not quite. Asked whether the loan should involve money from the United States or capital raised domestically, only 2.96 percent preferred the former while an overwhelming 77.46 percent opted for the latter.[98]

Apart from fanning patriotic feelings and impugning Prío's credibility or that of his ministers, Chibás began using the government's attempt to cadge foreign funds as an all-purpose cudgel to hack away at his rival's political failings. In an August 28 *Bohemia* article, he utilized the loan as a metaphor for the administration's neglect of everyday Cubans. Chibás was particularly galled by Prío's plan to build a tunnel beneath Havana's harbor and a tourist area on the other side's surrounding land. He claimed the tunnel would connect capital dwellers more easily to the beaches but would do nothing to help rural farmers, who lacked decent roads, bring their products to market. Regarding the future sightseeing zone, Chibás predicted it would be a "new city overflowing with wealth for the recreation of tourists and rich Habaneros" while the rest of the island was "abandoned."[99] To underline his point, Eddy inserted a photo of an overcrowded tenement in a ramshackle Havana neighborhood. Underneath, the caption asked, "Will the tourist city in eastern Havana be built before this situation is remedied?"[100]

Chibás also believed the loan flowed from Cuba's overly deferential legal system. Rather than enforcing the law, judges permitted venal government employees to steal without fear. As a result, those who normally pilfered "up to their elbows" now did so "up to their shoulders."[101] The lamentable status quo was encapsulated by Pelayo Cuervo Navarro's lawsuit. At first, the case seemed destined to reverse decades of impunity for sleazy officials. Aside from Cuervo Navarro's detailed thirty-three-page brief, the Ortodoxo congressman Félix Martín had provided documents proving José Manuel Alemán had bribed legislators from the Auténtico-Republican alliance. Given this profusion of evidence, Special Judge Antonio Vignier admitted at the time that "there's enough here for an indictment" and "people will wind up in jail."[102] Cuervo Navarro, however, began to express pessimism—telling reporters that Carlos Prío had offered Vignier and District Attorney Jesús Coll positions on the soon to be created Tribunal of Constitutional Guarantees if they would ease up. As luck would have it, Vignier and Coll eventually concluded there was not enough evidence to prosecute. Chibás found this odd since Alemán, secure in his parliamentary immunity, had told the journalist Mario Kuchilán that he had filched "a little more" than 20 million pesos between January and October of 1948.[103] While the ex-education minister and current senator was untouchable, some of his accomplices were vulnerable. The most obvious was Grau. In fact, a *Bohemia* reporter had recorded Carlos Prío implicating the former president in February of 1949, and hundreds of thousands of Cubans had read about it for themselves. "I wonder," asked Chibás, "what Judge Vignier has to say about this?"[104]

Just as the lawsuit appeared fated to languish, Carlos Manuel de la Cruz entered the fray unexpectedly. The grizzled lawyer and erstwhile Democratic lawmaker submitted a motion to revive the case and allow time to adduce further proof of wrongdoing from treasury ministry archives. De la Cruz also sought to initiate a criminal investigation regarding the disappearance of books, papers, and documents relating to the case—especially as Antonio Prío had publicly admitted to removing them. As the unsympathetic Coll and Vignier were away on vacation, so his appeal was received by District Attorney Rafael Trejo instead. Trejo immediately placed the matter before Cuba's Supreme Tribunal. In a grave tone, de la Cruz asserted this was the "last opportunity" for the island's judiciary to demonstrate respect for the law but also expressed optimism given the "irreproachable conduct" of the judges on its highest court.[105] Nonetheless, this flicker of hope was promptly snuffed out by an unfavorable ruling. Appraising the situation, a *Bohemia* reporter remarked that Grau had scorned Cuba's judiciary but Prío, himself a lawyer, preferred cajolery. Neither man seriously considered Article 170 of the constitution, which mandated "independent" judges who owed obedience "only to the law."

Of course, the nation's most pliable judges occupied the Urgency Courts—which existed outside the constitution altogether and were despised as instruments of political repression. In 1947, a lawyer named Emilio Maza brought a suit before the Supreme Tribunal seeking their extinction. The case was decided after Prío assumed office, and its resolution reflected the new president's wheedling style. At the outset, Presiding Judge Julián de Solórzano and a majority of his peers agreed the Urgency Courts should be abolished. Later on, Solórzano was suddenly withdrawn in favor of the more amenable Judge Francisco Chaves Milanés, who convinced enough colleagues to keep the Urgency Courts. Prío wanted them to handle those accused of violating the Anti-Gangster Law and held out the prospect of nominations to the Tribunal of Constitutional Guarantees to those who complied. On the other hand, Cuba's court system did not always bend to the whims of power. The Supreme Electoral Tribunal ruled with commendable impartiality during the island's voting season but in general the judiciary had thus far proved incapable of standing up to the island's presidents. In this vein, the philosopher Mario Llerena indicated that "our constitution is admirable, the laws are good, the form of government is satisfactory," but the problem is one of "spirit." In other words, "the evil is not in the law but IN THE JUDGES WHO MUST ENFORCE THE LAW."[106] For Chibás, this failure was at the root of the administration's loan proposal.

By October 10, when Carlos Prío addressed the nation on the first anniversary of his inauguration, Chibás had been intermittently railing against the foreign loan for ten months. Since being released from prison in June, Eddy's criticism had evolved into an all-encompassing monomania. During Prío's speech, broadcast from the presidential palace, he attempted to deflect some of the criticism—promising the loan would be used to create jobs rather than covering Grau's deficit. At the same time, Prío warned Cubans against "someone" who "portrays himself as a national hero by insulting the chief of state on a daily basis."[107] He added:

> Guard your home, Cubans, from the man who slanders me so crudely because what he does against me, knowing that as president of the republic I cannot hold him to account, he will one day do against you, because the slanderer is a slimy type who cannot master his own criminal weakness![108]

The identity of this mystery figure, already quite obvious, became even more discernible when Prío inveighed against "irresponsible and shrill voices that have been attacking the public works plan based on funds from the loan."[109] He did not explicitly refer to Chibás because of his constitutional responsibility as Cuba's "moderating power" and source of "national solidarity." More importantly, the great unknown remained the loan itself rather than the name of Prío's principal foe. When the island's citizens turned off their radios that evening, they still had no idea when the loan would be contracted, how much money was involved, who was doing the lending, and what terms were being discussed. Chibás echoed these and other concerns in a public reply to the president on October 16. With typical pizzazz, he claimed the government's vaunted public works program was so hopelessly vague that "a child in kindergarten" could produce something "equal or better."[110] Chibás maintained that construction projects required long months of planning by engineers and other technical personnel, none of which was being carried out. Moreover, Prío's assertion that the loan would not be arranged with any institution requiring oversight of the money or detailed building schemes seemed like a recipe for massive embezzlement. Chibás concluded that

> If a bank exists that will lend the money under these conditions, it better not hope later on that the Cuban people will pay back, with interest, the millions of pesos it gave the members of this administration to spend on elections or rob outright. This would be a political debt for them but never a debt of the republic.[111]

Regardless of its parameters, the loan would require two-thirds approval in Cuba's senate and chamber of representatives.[112] This set the stage for the legislature's most pivotal moment since 1941, when it narrowly approved a $25 million credit from the United States Export-Import Bank. Back then, Auténtico lawmakers including Carlos Prío and Tony Varona had vigorously opposed the measure in terms similar to those now being used by Chibás. Prío had questioned whether public employees who flaunted "costly luxury items" could be trusted to administer the funds honestly while Varona proclaimed that "we will only be truly free when we have our own economy."[113] Chibás gleefully turned their previous words against them in what was now an all-out campaign. Apart from denigrating the loan from behind his microphones every Sunday, Chibás also used the regular space in *Bohemia* offered by his friend Miguel Ángel Quevedo to do the same. On October 23, Chibás lambasted Prío's preliminary message to congress—claiming the president's promises to build country roads and irrigation canals were insincere because he offered no specifics. He also wondered why there was no mention of rural electrification or an agricultural lending institution. Once again, Chibás asked whether the government was only serious about allocating resources to Havana's tunnel, which he had long since dubbed "the cave of Ali Baba and his 40,000 thieves," and the tourist city.

The following week, Chibás emphasized a new wrinkle. He noted the president's loan proposal was in the hands of José Manuel Alemán, who headed the senate's finance and budget committee. "This means" that Alemán, as "the biggest embezzler in history," would be charged with deciding if the loan was "honest and convenient to the republic's interests."[114] Chibás also compiled quotes from Cuba's pantheon of heroes from previous generations, all of whom had bequeathed warnings against foreign loans. These included José Martí, the island's foremost poet and essayist whose thoughts on almost any subject were usually considered definitive; Antonio Maceo, a venerable general from the independence wars; and Enrique José Varona, the father of Cuba's educational system. In addition, Chibás reproduced a snippet from his ex-nemesis, Ramón Grau San Martín, who had recently told an ad hoc student group, known as the University Committee Against the Loan, that

> They have asked me not to talk about the loan, to remain silent and be quiet. But faced with this nonsense that could sink the republic I cannot just cross my arms. The loan goes against the national interest and combating it is a duty of the entire citizenry. I would be against any loan, even if it were only for one peso.[115]

University of Havana students, in fact, were among the loan's fiercest opponents. Since being created in August, the University Committee Against the Loan had gained support from all twelve faculties. As the congressional debate approached, the outfit began organizing a march on the Capitolio. Aiming for the largest possible crowd, invitations were extended to each of the island's political leaders. This did not sit well with some committee members, notably the Ortodoxo youth leader Max Lesnik, who objected to courting Batista and Grau, both of whom he dubbed "traitors of the university."[116] His was a minority voice however even among fellow Ortodoxos. Chibás himself backed a truly mass demonstration. In this vein, students visited the Liberal leader Eduardo Suárez Rivas in his law office and Ramón Grau San Martín in his home on Miramar's Quinta Avenida. Suárez Rivas denounced the loan in its present form as "anti-constitutional" and "anti-scientific."[117] As such, he promised to expel any Liberal who voted in favor of the measure. Nevertheless, he was not opposed to the loan per se, only its current dearth of detail and thus refused to attend the rally. Grau was more sympathetic, but he too declined to show his face. The ex-president, who overrated his popularity, feared the government would claim people had shown up to support him rather than to protest the loan. He thus promised to send the Auténtico legislator Humberto Becerra as his representative. Batista also demurred, but his party, PAU, eagerly agreed to participate.[118]

In the early evening of October 31, as senators met the quorum call, an estimated eighty to one hundred thousand people paraded up Old Havana's grandest thoroughfare, the Paseo del Prado, toward the Capitolio. Students led the procession, but an honorary place among them was given to Enrique Loynaz del Castillo. Loynaz del Castillo had been a general during Cuba's independence struggle but was also famous for having written the text and music of the Himno Invasor, or marching theme of the 1895 war against Spain. Behind them followed the political parties: the PAU sans Batista, the Ortodoxos headed by Chibás, and the Communists led by Juan Marinello. The throng also contained a substantial number of women, which drew the attention of *Bohemia*'s correspondent. Their collective chants were heard inside the Capitolio, and many lawmakers could not resist the temptation to have a gander at the crowd outside. Given the magnitude of their votes, the session was unusually well attended but there were some notable absences nonetheless. Despite his stated opposition to the loan, the habitual truant Fulgencio Batista remained at his country estate. José Manuel Alemán, another regular absentee, stayed away as well. According to the Auténtico senator Rubén de León, Alemán was actually opposed to the loan and had "given orders" to his legislative adherents to vote against it.[119] This likely explained why Alemán's acolytes in the senate, Carlos de Arazoza and Pancho Grau Alsina, were no-shows. Liberal ranks were missing José Manuel Casanova, who was in London, along with Alfredo Hornedo and Eduardo Zayas Bazán. Among these, Casanova was known to support the loan and had signaled his willingness to return if his vote was needed.

Sixty minutes into what would be a twenty-hour session, Pelayo Cuervo Navarro offered the simplest and most direct criticism of the loan. Namely, the president refused to provide "detailed information" that would allow legislators to vote responsibly.[120] This was part of an ongoing pattern. He reminded his peers that the senate had requested documents regarding the nation's finances a year ago and Carlos Prío had refused to comply despite repeated appeals. Cuervo Navarro promised to combat this latest round of obfuscation with a lawsuit if the loan were approved. The Liberal boss Eduardo Suárez Rivas was equally feisty but far more partisan. Among other things, he accused the president of using the loan as a vehicle to finance his brother Antonio's campaign for mayor of Havana. In any case, after myriad delays, recesses, motions, and speeches, the weary senators voted 37–9 in favor of the loan at 2:10 p.m. the following day. The measure was now confronted with one final obstacle, Cuba's unruly chamber of representatives. While gaining the senate's assent for the loan had involved a fair amount of drama, the government's pact with the Democrats had largely ensured the necessary votes for a two-thirds majority. This was not the case in the lower house, particularly as many Auténticos harbored reservations. Such renegades were dealt with harshly. For example, eight public employees who owed their positions to Rafael del Busto were fired after he withheld support. Thereafter, del Busto adopted the government line. Victor Vega Ceballos was more willing to bend at the outset but only up to a point. He told Prío he would vote for the loan but declined to defend it in the chamber of representatives, saying the bill was unconstitutional and its justification did not merit 2 million pesos, let alone the 200 million the administration was seeking.

On November 11, a session was initiated in Cuba's lower house. While opposition representatives such as Manuel Bisbé and the Communist Anibal Escalante denounced the loan, pro-government legislators feverishly negotiated to increase their vote totals. Tony Varona tirelessly coursed through the Capitolio's nooks and crannies, alternately wheedling and threatening potential targets. After seventeen hours, it was clear the majority would fall three votes short of the necessary two-thirds. Hence, the Auténticos postponed the proceedings until November 15. This ensured at least one more vote as the Republican Manuel Orizondo, who had been vacationing in Paris, was due to return by then.[121] The government also managed to lure two Liberals during the hiatus. Hence, when the chamber of representatives reconvened, the result was already a foregone conclusion. However, members of the public were still treated to a show. The excitement began when José Suárez Rivas asked for a recess so the party could expel its treacherous legislators, whom he deemed "men without honor."[122] This delighted the crowd, which burst into spontaneous applause. However, chamber president Lincoln Rodón was in no mood for theatrics and ordered the visitor's gallery to be emptied—prompting even more noise along with shouts of "traitors," "thieves," and "*botelleros*."[123] Once they were gone, only representatives, journalists, and a handful of politicians remained. During the interminable speeches, which lasted into the following afternoon, lawmakers whiled the time by playing poker, taking naps, or gossiping. At one point, Grau's ex-interior minister Alejo Cossío del Pino approached the Communist Joaquín Ordoqui. Referring to the common cause made by Ortodoxo and Communist congressmen in censuring the loan, he said, "Listen, Joaquín, when Chibás is president he is going to let the Communists use the radio frequency 1010 once again. He may even give you a second frequency as well."

"*Chico*," said the gray-haired Communist leader, "but that won't be for a while."

Chibás, who happened to be nearby, said, "Only two more years. By 1952 we'll already be in power."

Cossío then touched on the juiciest topic among Cuban politicians besides the loan; namely, the attempt by Carlos Prío to position his brother Antonio as Havana's next mayor and possibly as a future presidential candidate. Alluding to the Prío family's thin skin and willingness to shut down critical broadcasts, Cossío added, "The worst scenario would be if you had to wait for Antonio to grant you a radio frequency."[124]

With the loan now a certainty, Raúl Gutiérrez conducted a second public opinion poll, which showed that a majority of Cubans were now against the measure. This was a tribute to Chibás, whose denunciatory broadcasts and *Bohemia* articles reached a larger combined audience than any other politician. The survey revealed that 46.28 percent of Cubans believed borrowing money would prove prejudicial while 34.87 percent felt it would be beneficial or conditionally beneficial. Even more damaging, when Cubans were asked who would administer the loan more honorably, they chose Chibás over Prío by a margin of nearly fifteen percentage points.[125] Thus, even though the Ortodoxo leader had lost his campaign against the loan, the issue would remain a potent weapon against Prío going forward—particularly if questions of mismanagement were raised in the future.

CASTELLANOS FLIRTS WITH THE ORTODOXOS

Since leaving the chamber of representatives in 1948, Alejo Cossío del Pino bought Radio-Cadena Habana and devoted himself part-time to journalism. He had become somewhat marginalized among the Auténticos after serving Grau as interior minister but remained close to Havana's mayor, Nicolás Castellanos. Castellanos, for his part, was increasingly worried by Carlos Prío's attempts to install his younger brother Antonio as the Auténtico mayoral candidate.[126] He thus began to consider alternative options, which included switching parties and running under a new banner. Cossío, who maintained ties with Grau, the Communists, and Guillermo Alonso Pujol among others, was an ideal emissary. On October 12, 1949, Cossío happened upon Millo Ochoa at the funeral of Peru's ambassador, José Bernardo Goyburu. Cossío pulled the Ortodoxo vice president aside and begged him to arrange a meeting with Chibás. Just over a month later, Cossío addressed Chibás, Ochoa, Luis Orlando Rodríguez, and Orlando Castro in the Ortodoxo vice president's hometown of Holguín. Cossío informed them that Castellanos was prepared to adopt the party's independent line and face Cuba's voters without pacts. Chibás expressed doubts that Castellanos fully understood the party's "new political style" but promised to consult its higher-ups and return with a definitive answer.[127] Eddy saw Cossío next on November 16, in the Capitolio, during the legislative session on the foreign loan. He handed over an envelope with his reply, which dismissed Castellanos as little different from fellow mayoral candidates Antonio Prío and Panchín Batista—both of whom were widely considered to be corrupt.[128] For good measure, Chibás sent a copy of his remarks to the press.

The matter was far from decided, however. At noon on November 18, José Pardo Llada set the nation abuzz when he broadcast that Chibás and Castellanos had broached the possibility of the latter leaving the Auténtico party and running for reelection as an Ortodoxo. A *Bohemia* reporter noted that "it's been a long time since an event has been able to excite the man on the street to such an extent."[129] Castellanos had met Chibás the previous evening, having insisted on an audience regardless of the Ortodoxo leader's declarations. During their talk, Chibás asked numerous questions regarding the mayor's conduct, his efforts to build a new aqueduct, and how he responded to meddling from the central government. Castellanos offered detailed answers that began to peel away his interlocutor's skepticism. Playing on the Ortodoxo leader's fondness for honest administration, Castellanos proclaimed that "43 million pesos have passed through these hands over the past three years and look, Eddy, they are clean!"[130] The mayor also offered up Havana's municipal electoral apparatus, which would provide a considerable boost to a party notable for its lack of organization. While some of his misgivings had been assuaged, Chibás expressed a reluctance to withdraw the mayoral candidacy of his friend Manuel Bisbé. At any rate, he promised Castellanos that his appeal would be placed before the party's executive council.

A spirited meeting ensued in the home of Roberto Agramonte. As party bigwigs discussed Castellanos in the second-floor library, delegates from the Ortodoxo municipal assembly fluttered nervously downstairs. Many could not hide their enthusiasm for the Havana mayor, who offered control of Cuba's capital without compromising the party's much-disputed independent line.[131] Conversely, Chibás made no attempt to conceal his reservations. Aside from his reluctance to retire Bisbé's nomination, two things gnawed at him. First, Chibás feared backing Castellanos would give the impression he was a hypocrite, particularly as he had publicly censured him a few days earlier. Second, the Havana mayor's campaign already counted the outright support of Grau and Guillermo Alonso Pujol—two toxic figures whom Chibás preferred to avoid. Eddy's doubts were shared by Isidro Figueroa, the Workers' Wing boss, and Orlando Castro, the Youth Section head. Castro claimed the current popularity of Castellanos would be fleeting, akin to "the foam of a newly poured beer."[132] On the other hand, Castellanos found fervent support among Beto Saumell and Roberto García Ibáñez. Saumell addressed his colleagues in a passionate tone, saying:

> Compañeros, the party has now been presented with its best opportunity to strengthen itself. This may involve a concession of principle but it will be repaid by winning the island's second most important position. It is my understanding that we are a political party that must confront reality rather than a conclave of cherubs or Franciscan monks. If we follow the path of rigorous Puritanism, the moment will arrive in which every Ortodoxo will be obligated to be a saint with a halo among other attributes. By this avenue, we will never be a majority party nor will we ever win the presidency of the republic. Let's not deceive ourselves: the people of Havana support Castellanos against Prío's attempt to impose his younger brother.[133]

García Ibáñez confirmed the last portion of this comment with an anecdote. He related that he had been eating in a Vedado restaurant recently and the waiters, who were all Auténticos, approached him to say they would vote for Castellanos.

Meanwhile, one floor below, Agramonte's residence was filling up with telegrams from Ortodoxos on every corner of the island imploring the party leadership to welcome Castellanos.[134] Unlike previous wrangles, intrinsic aspects of the party program were not at stake. Essentially, the question was whether Castellanos was moral enough to be an Ortodoxo. For men like Saumell, Millo Ochoa, and García Ibáñez, this was crossing the line between a new political style and electoral hara-kiri. As such, García Ibáñez added:

> We are a political party, different though we are from all the others, and not a sect of monks. We have to conquer power by political means and we will never do so if we maintain this religious aura that some would like to impose on the Ortodoxo movement. The incorporation of Castellanos would represent a second rebellion from within the Auténtico party. This offers a tremendous opportunity for us. If we nominate Castellanos, we will march at the front of popular opinion.[135]

Luis Orlando Rodríguez, who opposed Castellanos but allowed that Manuel Bisbé was a weak candidate, tried to break the impasse by suggesting Chibás run instead.[136] Eddy, however, demurred. As the meeting stretched past 4:00 a.m., Chibás spoke one last time before committee members would cast their votes and stagger home to sleep. He observed that

> There is no doubt Castellanos has offered us the mayoralty on a silver platter. It's true that by nominating him the independent line wouldn't be jeopardized but the morals of our movement would certainly suffer. Any other party would accept his nomination because this would bring in the *jamón* and everyone would be anxious for their share. But we don't do such things. And even though winning the mayoralty could guarantee victory in 1952 the people would doubt our conduct and would lose faith in us. It's preferable to wait with our prestige intact rather than to arrive in power quickly and discredit ourselves.[137]

Shortly thereafter, the groggy assemblage had its say. When news that Castellanos had been vetoed was communicated downstairs, an audible groan spread through the house.

According to preliminary polls, Chibás had passed up an excellent opportunity. Raúl Gutiérrez's public survey of November 22 showed that 57.91 percent of Havana residents preferred Nicolás Castellanos as opposed to 12.87 percent for Antonio Prío, 10.43 percent for Manuel Bisbé, and 8 percent for Panchín Batista—the PAU-style nepotism candidate. In addition, 66.91 percent of Auténticos declared themselves ready to buck party discipline and vote for Castellanos.[138] Nevertheless, Chibás was content to demonstrate that he, unlike other Cuban politicians, was willing to sacrifice expedience in the name of principle. Thus, he told the *Bohemia* reporter that "they won't be able to brand me as a vulgar aspirant for the presidency because everyone now knows that I have scorned my chances in '52 by rejecting Castellanos."[139] At the same time, many members of the Ortodoxo municipal council remained partial to Castellanos, and some publicly called on Bisbé to step down. The professor of Greek duly satisfied them by publishing a letter resigning his candidacy. This touched off a new round of jostling for the party's nomination along with recriminations from Bisbé's closest adherents, including Chibás himself. The most likely replacement was Ventura Dellundé, who had distinguished himself in the campaign against the Cuban Electric Company. He was also affluent and demonized by hard-liners as the "BAGA of the Ortodoxos" for alleged delegate buying.[140] For his part, Dellundé led a group protesting "favoritism" toward their leader's closest confidants. Chibás, however, argued that he was not prepared to sacrifice Bisbé for "one who has arrived at the last minute with a bag of money."[141] The Ortodoxo executive council agreed and restored Bisbé. Further, pleas to place the matter before the municipal assembly, which would probably have contradicted this decision, were dismissed. Ironically, this was the sort of chicanery Ortodoxos ascribed to "traditional" parties. At any rate, Chibás had demonstrated once again that he feared the wrath of history more than the ire of his party's rank and file. On the other hand, Millo Ochoa was warier of irrelevance, telling a reporter from *Pueblo* that "if we don't enter into any pacts, I invite you to the burial of the PPC on June 1, 1952, at 6 p.m."[142]

"Carestia de la vida." This sketch, by the cartoonist Ozón, depicts Liborio, Cuba's everyman, being pummeled by high prices while President Grau San Martín smiles in the foreground. Many Cubans blamed Grau's commerce minister, Cesár Casas, for the raging black market that forced them to pay dearly for everyday goods. *Carteles*, April 13, 1947

"La policía no se mete en estos líos." This drawing by Ozón depicts a shootout among Cuba's notorious "hombres de gatillo" or triggermen, while a bystander blithely explains that the police do not bother with such messy situations. *Carteles*, September 14, 1947

"A quien no quiere caldo, tres tazas." This cartoon by Ozón shows a smiling President Grau forcing three servings of his highly unpopular and corrupt education minister, José Manuel Alemán, on a disgusted Liborio. *Carteles*, October 19, 1947

"No harán nada pero cobran." This sketch by Ozón depicts a pair of smiling legislators leaving Cuba's Capitolio with bags of cash. The caption, reflecting popular opinion, reads, "They collect their salary but do nothing." *Carteles*, November 2, 1947

"Y esta es la república que concebimos?" This cartoon by Ozón portrays a disappointed veteran of Cuba's independence war reading all manner of negative news about the island and asking himself, "And this is the republic we had in mind?" *Carteles*, February 29, 1947

"Dónde aprendiste decir malas palabras?" This drawing by Ozón depicts a young girl innocently asking her father, "Papá, what is a politician?" The question is so disturbing that the man drops his cigar and bellows, "Young lady, where did you learn to say bad words?" *Carteles*, April 11, 1948

"Evite que ésta, sea la próxima Estatua." This Auténtico advertisement, which appeared three weeks before the 1948 presidential elections, suggests Liberals would build a statue to the abhorrent dictator Gerardo Machado if their coalition proved victorious. It urges Cubans to "ensure peace" by electing Carlos Prío Socarrás. *Bohemia*, May 9, 1948

"Verguenza contra dinero." This Ortodoxo advertisement appeared two weeks before the 1948 presidential elections and highlights the party slogan of "Verguenza contra dinero" or "Shame against Money." The ad also exhorts Cubans not to sell their votes for cash, annul their ballots, or trade their votes for favors. Otherwise, they would "lose their right to happiness" by allowing a corrupt political system to flourish. *Bohemia*, May 16, 1948

"Trinomio de integridad moral." This advertisement, which appeared one week before the 1948 presidential poll, underlines the "moral integrity" of a Liberal-Democratic threesome—namely, presidential candidate Ricardo Núñez Portuondo Portuondo, vice-presidential candidate Gustavo Cuervo Rubio, and senatorial candidate Manuel Dorta Duque. It notes that all are "illustrious" University of Havana professors of "irreproachable" conduct who can be counted upon to run an honest government. Ironically, Dorta Duque would later join the Ortodoxo party. *Bohemia*, May 23, 1948

"Cubano, escoge tu camino!" This Ortodoxo advertisement, which appeared a week before the 1948 presidential poll, presents Cubans with a stark choice. On one side, there is the "stormy" past of "bloodshed" represented by the Liberal party and its many former supporters of Gerardo Machado. The present, marred by Auténtico corruption and an oppressive black market, is equally gloomy. By contrast, Chibás offers a future where the "sun of honesty and decorum" shines brightly. *Bohemia*, May 23, 1948

Eddy as a child holding a gun. Photo courtesy of Marissa Chibás Preston

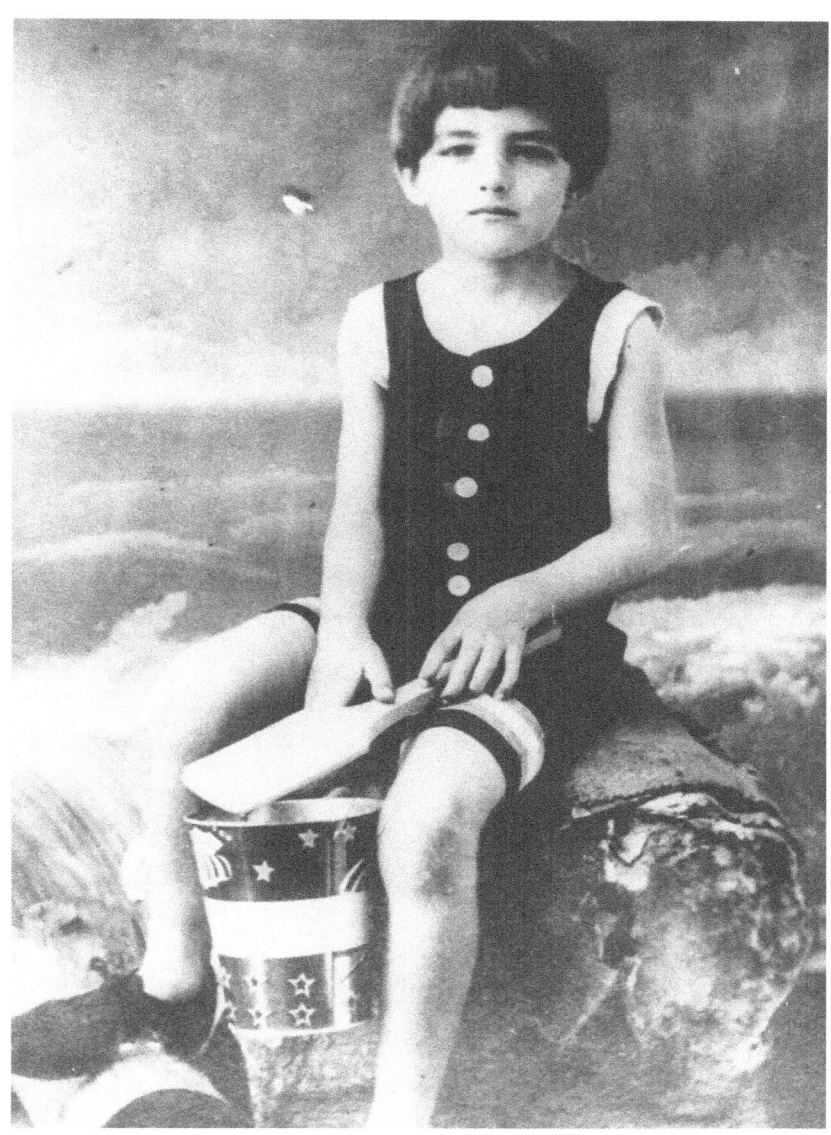

Eddy as a young boy. Photo courtesy of Marissa Chibás Preston

The building in Santiago de Cuba where Eddy was born. Photo by Ilan Ehrlich

The plaque, which is currently affixed to the building in Santiago de Cuba where Eddy was born, reads: "He lived and died for his people." Photo by Ilan Ehrlich

Eddy as a young revolutionary. Photo courtesy of Marissa Chibás Preston

Eddy broadcasting his popular Sunday evening radio show on CMQ. Photo courtesy of Marissa Chibás Preston

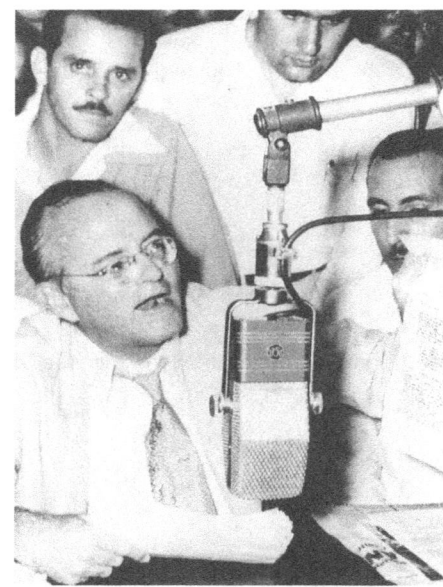

Eddy broadcasting his weekly show sitting next to his friend Luis Orlando Rodriguez. Photo courtesy of Marissa Chibás Preston

Chibás looking out from the Empire State Building's observation deck during his visit in 1950. Asked by a reporter about the view, Eddy quipped that he preferred to gaze at the "incomparable" Caribbean from from his penthouse apartment in Havana. *Bohemia*, October 8, 1950. Photo by Isaac Astudillo

An animated Chibás speaking into the microphone. This photo appeared in the June 6, 1948, issue of *Bohemia*, which trumpeted his surprisingly good showing in that year's presidential election. Photo courtesy of Marissa Chibás Preston

Eddy's casket being carried by a multitude of grieving followers from the University of Havana toward the Colón Cemetery. Photo courtesy of Marissa Chibás Preston

The procession reaching the entrance of Havana's Colón Cemetery. Photo courtesy of Marissa Chibás Preston

Chapter Eight

"I'm Not One of Those Generals Who Die in Bed"

On January 1, 1950, the cartoonist Carlos Vidal published a satirical take on Cuban politics entitled "What Will the New Year Bring?" "Will it bring happiness?" asked one drawing, in which Uncle Sam handed Carlos Prío a bag of (loaned) money. "Will it bring political liberty?" inquired another frame in which a gun-toting, well-dressed "political sergeant" traded cash for the vote of a barefoot peasant. "Will it bring sacrifices?" posited a further sketch in which Carlos Prío gamely shares his jamón, the emblem of political goodies, with his brother Antonio. "Will it bring struggles?" asked yet another in which the Republican chief Guillermo Alonso Pujol and the Liberal leader Eduardo Suárez Rivas fought over the very same jamón—in reference to the latter party's negotiations to join the government. "Or," asked the final portrait, which portrayed a hungry guajiro dreaming of a full plate, "will it be exactly the same as last year?"[1] While Chibás was nowhere to be found in this comic strip, he too was the subject of a pressing question as the new year dawned, namely: Would he continue to defend political independence at all costs? The latest figure to test this conviction was Eduardo Suárez Rivas, who visited Chibás on the evening of January 11. Arriving at Eddy's penthouse apartment, the Liberal boss offered to delay the pact he was discussing with the Auténticos and see whether an agreement with the Ortodoxos could be reached instead. In this vein, he informed Chibás that the Liberal assembly was ready to nominate him as the party's presidential candidate in 1952. Intransigent as ever, Chibás rejected the proposal but left the door slightly ajar by suggesting the Liberals dissolve themselves and join the Ortodoxos as the ABC party had done in 1947. This was an unlikely prospect but represented the only way Chibás could imagine squaring his conscience with Cuba's political realities. However, this solution presented a host of intractable problems. Much to their horror, the Ortodoxos found that numerous ABC members remained loyal to their former leaders even after the party had ceased to exist. Many had abandoned the Ortodoxos in 1948 after Joaquín Martínez Sáenz joined the Liberal-Democratic coalition. Absorbing the Liberals now would have proved far trickier. For one thing, how could Chibás agree to merge with President Machado's old outfit? Even if those with ties to the tyrant were excluded, the symbolism would have been crushing. Further, the Liberals had brought Fulgencio Batista out of retirement in Daytona Beach. Suárez Rivas himself had lobbied for the move. Having committed this unholy sin, how could he hope to fare in a party whose executive committee had refused the relatively benign Nicolás Castellanos?

Admitting an influx of Liberals became all the more impossible on January 28, when the Ortodoxo national assembly convened in Havana. This gathering, which took place on the ninety-seventh anniversary of José Martí's birth, reelected Chibás as party president and produced a strikingly self-righteous document. One motion, which was introduced by Chibás and approved unanimously, proclaimed:

> It is evident that the Ortodoxo party, the only true opposition party, would be diluting the ideals that gave it life and would betray its reason for existing if it were to enter . . . into understandings with the men and organizations of the present and past who are responsible for the existing corruption and therefore squander the Ortodoxo moral revolution and its historical destiny in order to embrace immediate electoral opportunism.[2]

Rather, the Ortodoxos pledged to "sweep away the putrefaction of national politics."[3] As a result, there was an obligatory dig at Nicolás Castellanos, who had loomed so large in the party's imagination lately and whose acceptance of support from Grau, Guillermo Alonso Pujol, and José Manuel Alemán was exhibit A of the sort of politics they intended to eschew.[4] Chibás and the Ortodoxos added an extra dollop of legitimacy to their position by including a maxim from the Apóstol himself that dovetailed nicely with the party slogan, namely: "Shame must become the fashion while shamelessness should go out of style."[5]

For the time being, however, shamelessness was very much in vogue. Nowhere was this more visible than in the nomination of Antonio Prío for Havana's mayoralty. "Little brother Antonio," as he was irreverently known by many of the capital's denizens, was proclaimed the Auténtico candidate in a Sunday morning ceremony in the National Theater. This event was open to the public and widely advertised, but most of those in evidence were conscripted public servants or the quarry of political sergeants. Employees of the customs service were not only ordered to attend but were told exactly where to park their vehicles.[6] Further, while an understanding with the Liberals had yet to be consummated, they helped the Auténticos rustle up spectators in a gesture of goodwill. Antonio Prío's inability to attract a large audience without government intervention was due to his unpopularity but also to the 9:00 a.m. start time, an hour when plenty of Habaneros preferred to sleep. Among those who were awake, quite a few directed insults at the caravan drivers offering free rides to the National Theater. But inside the neo-baroque edifice, a mere stone's throw from the Capitolio, an entirely different atmosphere reigned. Cabinet members were out in force to commend the president's younger brother, including Education Minister Aureliano Sánchez Arango, Foreign Minister Carlos Hevia, Public Works Minister Manuel Febles, Interior Minister Rubén de León, minister-without-portfolio and all-purpose yes-man Primitivo Rodríguez, and Antonio's successor as treasury minister, Pepín Bosch.[7] When his turn to speak was at hand, Antonio had no trouble wringing an ovation from the assemblage of bullied government workers, well-fed political operatives, rural laborers bused in from the countryside, and random pickups from the streets lured by curiosity or the prospect of favors.[8]

Encouraged by this warm reception, Antonio Prío visited the Palacio de los Deportes later that evening, where Havana residents often spent Sundays participating in raffles. He sought to elicit some cheers by telling the announcer he would sponsor a prize of one hundred pesos. However, this overture did not stop the thousands of raffle players from whistling derisively when Antonio appeared before them. When he tried to speak, the whistles grew louder. Others stood on their seats and shouted, "Out!" or "Go away!" The raffle announcer ventured to settle the crowd by shouting, "Gentlemen, Cubans are famous for being civilized."[9] Unfortunately, the restive throng responded by smashing chairs against the floor. Not knowing how to respond, the conspicuously upset and pale-faced candidate for Havana's mayoralty remained on the scene. The mayhem subsided only when a recording of Cuba's national anthem was played. This not only tranquilized the seething multitude and allowed the raffles to continue but also provided "little brother Antonio" with a chance to discreetly escape his most embarrassing moment in politics.[10] The cartoonist Vergara was one of many who reveled in the incident, drawing a bedridden Antonio Prío flanked by an advisor who tells a colleague, "Since going to the Palacio de los Deportes he's been sick with the whistles."[11] Of course, Chibás attempted to disparage Antonio even more forcefully during his radio show by comparing him to another former treasury minister who had been nominated for mayor in the very same National Theater four years earlier. Unlike Antonio Prío, though, the martyred Manuel Fernández Supervielle had never pilfered state funds. "In today's event," said Chibás, "not one of the speakers referred to the honesty of the Auténtico candidate. His only merit consists in being a brother of the president of the republic!"[12] Chibás then proceeded to explain why Antonio was never extolled for his probity. For one thing, he had lied to Judge Antonio Vignier, who was investigating Lawsuit 82, by swearing the nation's finances were in perfect order even though he had publicly admitted there was a deficit upon taking office. Chibás also accused him of ordering subordinates to torch a building in Old Havana which, "coincidentally," contained documents proving the previous government had embezzled 174 million pesos.[13] In addition, he alleged Antonio had shortchanged the newly founded National Bank and increased the money supply in exchange for "private commissions."[14] Summarizing Antonio's fifteen-month tenure as treasury minister, Chibás told listeners, "This has been the worst and least efficient administration the republic has ever had," adding that his management had been characterized by "jokes, *santería*, gambling and corruption."[15]

While Chibás seemed feisty as ever in his politics, he had recently appeared emaciated and lacked his usual verve. Unusually for him, he skipped an Ortodoxo rally in Sagua la Grande due to vomiting and intense abdominal pain. This situation deteriorated further until the morning of February 12, when Chibás was hospitalized for a diaphragmatic hernia that doctors linked to his much-disputed gunshot wound from November of 1939. Apparently, the bullet that had nearly ended his life just over ten years earlier had relaxed the muscles of his diaphragm, which in turn was harming his stomach and digestive system. This condition required immediate treatment as the hernia could otherwise become strangulated and potentially life threatening. Eddy's close friends debated whether he should travel to the United States as diaphragmatic surgery was uncommon in Cuba. Chibás, however, insisted on staying and chose an eminent local doctor, Vicente Banet, to perform the procedure. That evening, Chibás gamely said a few words over the air and ceded his remaining time to Carlos Márquez Sterling. The latter had recently heated up his flirtation with the Ortodoxos by writing a series of flattering columns for *Bohemia* but continued to shun outright commitment. Nonetheless, Chibás was shrewd in his choice of understudy as Márquez Sterling spoke about the looming threat of fraud in Cuba's mayoral vote. He accused Antonio Prío's henchmen of filching one hundred thousand identity cards from the communications ministry, which would be strategically "managed" on election day.[16] Another scheme entailed arranging city residency for fifty thousand rural dwellers who would cast ballots for the president's younger brother.

Meanwhile, Chibás spent the next two days preparing for surgery in Havana's Sagrado Corazón hospital. This in no way implied a hiatus from politics. On the contrary, Chibás kept tabs on the Ortodoxo municipal assembly to ensure they would nominate Manuel Bisbé as the party's mayoral candidate. After the vote was taken, Bisbé and a group of Ortodoxo councilmen visited Chibás at his sickbed to deliver the good news. These were hardly the only guests who graced the clinic. Apart from friends and family, Eddy was mobbed by anxious supporters. Some assuaged their fears by fastening religious pins and medallions to his pajamas or praying to Cuba's patron saint, the Virgen de la Caridad. On the morning of February 15, Chibás passed two and a half hours under the knife. When he emerged from the anesthesia, his friend and personal doctor Pedro Iglesias Betancourt greeted him by saying, "Shame vs. Money!" The bleary Ortodoxo leader responded with "We must fight for Cuba!"[17] Although the initial prognosis was promising, Chibás remained in the hospital during the following two weeks so doctors could monitor his diet and shoo away most callers. Afterward, he convalesced in Roberto Agramonte's residence—where he was attended to regularly by his cousin's family, his younger brother Raúl, and his secretary Conchita Fernández. All the while, he was instructed to avoid strenuous activities of any sort. Even reading was proscribed. Chibás paid scant heed to the ban as he was a notorious bibliophile and habitual devourer of newspapers and magazines. Worse still, the famously fidgety Ortodoxo chief, who chafed under these restrictions, granted an interview to a *Bohemia* correspondent. Having already been dubbed "the impatient patient" by a journalist, Chibás further justified this nickname by greeting his interlocutor with a barrage of questions and series of mini-sermons.[18] Chibás was particularly eager to comment on Carlos Prío's pronouncements regarding *nuevos rumbos*, or new directions, for his presidency. This was Prío's catchall phrase for a "break with the past" that would involve respect for the constitution, administrative honesty, economic development, and an end to gangsters.[19] Chibás pointed out that Prío's negotiations to bring the Liberals, with their Machado-era holdovers, into his government was hardly a step forward. He also questioned whether Pepín Bosch, the new treasury minister and former head of the Bacardí Company, could run an honest outfit while thieves and smugglers were among his subordinates.[20] Attempting to allay concerns about his condition, Chibás exclaimed, "I am not one of those generals who die in bed!"[21] Just the same, the interview petered out because he eventually became too exhausted to continue.

As the weeks passed and Chibás remained in poor health, his doctors began to fret. They sent copies of his X-rays to the Mayo Clinic in Rochester, Minnesota, for a second opinion. The medical staff there replied that Chibás was in serious danger and should check himself in immediately. Meanwhile, Eddy was consumed by the idea that he had stomach cancer. He begged Pedro Iglesias Betancourt and the other doctors not to conceal the truth from him. Above all, he was frightened by the prospect of dying in the United States and refused to make the trip. Despite these worries, Chibás projected an impishly cheerful façade for public consumption. When a reporter from *Alerta* called, he claimed to be "perfectly well" and confessed to having eaten chocolate ice cream, black beans with rice, and fried pork—much to the horror of his doctors.[22] Chibás also forsook his sickbed now and then. On one occasion, he snuck out of the Agramonte residence in order to attend a meeting of the Ortodoxo municipal assembly. News had reached him that a potential candidate for city council was being vetoed by hard-liners because of his wealth. Chibás, who found this unfair, wished to argue in his favor. Lastly, and most predictably, Chibás would drag himself out of bed to visit *Bohemia* headquarters at 6:30 a.m. every Thursday so he could receive his advance copy of the magazine.

THE DEATH OF JOSÉ MANUEL ALEMÁN

Chibás was not the only prominent Cuban politician whose well-being was in doubt. On the evening of March 24, José Manuel Alemán lost consciousness at his home in Havana's exclusive Alturas de Miramar district. He had been suffering from Hodgkin's disease since 1942 and tried a variety of treatments, including radiation therapy, mustard gas injections, and urethane. However, medical science was largely helpless in the face of this ailment, and those afflicted usually lived between two and ten years. When Alemán regained his senses, he was overwhelmed by pain. Sensing the end was near, he summoned Guillermo Alonso Pujol and entrusted him with his final political instructions. Although he had seldom fulfilled his duties as a senator and prized the office mostly for its parliamentary immunity, Alemán insisted on a state funeral in the Capitolio. The ex-education minister's desire for a grand public ceremony was slightly odd given his tendency to work behind the scenes while he was alive. However, this may have owed something to his eminent father and a wish to be acknowledged for his own achievements—even as these seemed dubious to most Cubans.

He had spent the first twenty-five years of his life under the shadow of José Braulio Alemán, a general during Cuba's independence struggle, delegate to its 1901 constitutional convention, and governor of Santa Clara province. During his lengthy career in the Liberal party, José Braulio had also been named ambassador to Mexico by President Gerardo Machado and later served as education minister. The latter position allowed him to arrange a plum job for his young son, José Manuel, who had graduated from West Chester Normal School in Pennsylvania with a degree in accounting. Given his connections, José Manuel rose quickly within the education ministry and soon became chief of personnel. At the same time, Alemán was not without talent nor was he content to coast on the basis of his father's credentials. He mastered the ministry's bureaucratic minutiae so thoroughly that he became indispensable to successive education ministers and finally to President Grau himself. In the words of Enrique de la Osa, he was also an "astute psychologist."[23] This allowed him to cultivate and accommodate men of vastly different personalities and political ideas. Thus, during the mass strikes of 1935 against Fulgencio Batista's de facto military regime, Alemán ran the education ministry while its chief, Leonardo Anaya Murillo, sought to deal with the three hundred thousand students, teachers, and university employees who had joined the demonstrations. His support for one quasi dictator did not preclude him from attempting to overthrow another in 1947, especially as he was now an Auténtico and his new boss, Ramón Grau San Martín, hoped to oust the Dominican strongman Rafael Trujillo. Hence, Alemán organized and bankrolled the ultimately unsuccessful Cayo Confites expedition.

Alemán's pliable principles and penchant for opportunism were by no means exceptional. Neither was the fact that he had pinched public money. Alemán's notoriety derived from unprecedented larceny and his creation of a blunt political instrument out of cash designated for Cuba's schoolchildren. Certainly, prosperous figures had always swayed politics and underwritten friendly legislators. Alemán took this a step further by diverting the nine-centavo tax on every bag of sugar sold toward a slush fund whose name became synonymous with corruption. In the years 1946–1948, BAGA subsidized Auténtico campaigns, including Carlos Prío's presidential bid; purchased lawmakers, who were colloquially known as *baguistas*; co-opted the interior, treasury, and health ministries; financed MSR gangsters; bought friendly press coverage, notably in *Pueblo*; and won Alemán a place in the party's highest reaches. Alemán also pursued personal enrichment with more zeal than any of his predecessors. In September of 1949, a *Miami Herald* reporter named Bert Collier estimated Alemán's Florida real estate empire was worth between $70 and $200 million. This included luxury hotels and residences on Collins Avenue in South Beach along with apartment buildings in downtown Miami. He was also a player in the land development business, buying up much of Key Biscayne through his Ansan Corporation. Alemán's dearest possession, however, was "Il Mío Castello," his mansion on Pine Tree Drive acquired toward the end of 1947. Its amenities included a bronze gate, marble staircases, a dock for his yacht, and a six-car garage. Moreover, Alemán invested in three construction companies owned by Anselmo Alliegro, a former Machado supporter and Batista ally who had been his boss in the education ministry between 1940 and 1944.

Shortly after Alemán's death, the journalist Manuel Hernando Torres attempted to calculate the value of his Cuban holdings. Among Alemán's known possessions was a cargo transport company called Línea Cuba Aeropostal, which counted a fleet of seven planes and whose primary route was Havana–Miami. Almost certainly, Alemán sought to capitalize on those like himself who pilfered things in Cuba and aimed to place them beyond the writ of local authorities. As in Florida, he acquired great quantities of land for future development—chiefly on Havana's outskirts, where he hoped to construct an international airport and build new towns. Alemán also cultivated Cuba's primary cash crop, having procured and remodeled the sugar mill "Portugalete" near San José de las Lajas. His tentacles even extended to the island's national pastime as he purchased the Marianao Bears, one of Cuba's four professional baseball teams. Last but not least, as with any man of means, he presided over a luxuriously outfitted finca, the "América," on which he had spent more than a million pesos in renovations. After surveying these and other assets, the author believed Alemán's fortune was impossible to calculate but remained certain his heirs would gain "the most fabulous inheritance" any Cubans had ever received.[24]

In political circles, there was less interest in Alemán's lucre than his senate seat. The Liberal lawmaker Carlos Miguel de Céspedes declared that his party should wage a sincere effort to capture it, especially as the death of José Manuel Casanova in January had raised the danger of losing a seat in Pinar del Río. However, the Liberals lacked a natural candidate and occupied a nebulous middle ground between the government and opposition. Meanwhile, the compulsive intriguer Guillermo Alonso Pujol encouraged Grau to run as a means of fortifying the motley coalition of Republicans, Communists, and Batista's PAU known as the Coincidencia. However, El Viejo politely refused their entreaties, citing his determination to avoid seeking parliamentary immunity.[25] Alonso Pujol's second choice, Pepe San Martín, turned him down too, despite heavy lobbying by Grau. This left the ad hoc group with little choice but to nominate the nondescript Guillermo Belt—who had served as unelected mayor of Havana under Batista during the 1930s and had also been Grau's former ambassador in Washington.

As for the Ortodoxos, they deemed this a perfect opportunity for Chibás, despite his health woes. At a meeting of party higher-ups in Manuel Bisbé's residence, the host argued that candidates for congress and the city council (not to mention himself) would benefit from Eddy's considerable coattails. Luis Orlando Rodríguez put the matter in starker terms, demanding that Chibás reward the party for its loyalty to his principles by giving it a presence in the senate. After all, he said, "We have accepted, despite its risks, the heroic line of political independence."[26] Millo Ochoa added that Eddy's prestige would allow him to win from his sickbed if necessary. Leonardo Fernández Sánchez chimed in that Alemán's seat "historically corresponded" to the one Chibás relinquished in 1948 and implied it was bound to return to its rightful owner.[27] The uncharacteristic harmony of this session, which must have surprised its normally disputatious participants, reflected Eddy's rare combination of the ethical credentials craved by Ortodoxo hard-liners and the political viability cherished by realists. Nevertheless, their gusto was tempered by Pedro Iglesias Betancourt, who informed Eddy's Sunday evening radio audience on April 2 that its idol was seriously ill even if his life was not directly in danger. Iglesias Betancourt also confessed that the "impatient patient" would require another operation. He concluded by saying, "I beg Ortodoxo compañeros to set their desires aside and oblige Chibás to rest for the good of his health."[28] This plea not only failed to convince the party faithful, it was dismissed by Chibás himself—who delighted in discounting or ignoring nearly every recommendation provided by his medical handlers. On April 8, Chibás attended the party's Havana provincial assembly meeting. This took place in the home of Heriberto del Porto, an Ortodoxo candidate for Havana city hall, because the party, always short on cash, had sold its headquarters. Chibás was greeted with typical euphoric fervor but also by solicitous shouts and instructions. Some voices urged supporters not to embrace him too tightly, while others bid Chibás to sit down and preserve his strength. All the while, his friend Iglesias Betancourt stood nearby carrying a small briefcase containing an emergency injection in case he faltered. When Leonardo Fernández Sánchez nominated Chibás as the party's senatorial candidate, he praised him as "the man without fear and without defects" who "showed the way in 1948 with an intense campaign that resonated in the conscience of the Cuban people."[29] Shortly thereafter, Chibás rose and addressed the packed salon—promising to serve the Cuban revolution and fulfill his party's orders by winning. The excitable José Pardo Llada subsequently exclaimed that "we will fill the most dishonest of vacancies with the most honorable of all Cuban politicians!"[30]

The nomination of Chibás was met with a mixture of fear, resignation, and eagerness among Auténticos. Some, like Alberto Inocente Álvarez, believed he was too formidable an opponent. The venal former commerce minister, who was contesting the vacant seat in Pinar del Río, told reporters, "I wouldn't dare challenge Eddy. To go against this monster of popularity would be political suicide!"[31] Other potential nominees declined for different reasons. Foreign Minister Carlos Hevia believed the moment was inopportune while Education Minister Aureliano Sánchez Arango, who was urged to run by René Fiallo, was loath to abandon his current post. This left two keen but unloved contenders. The first was Agriculture Minister Virgilio Pérez, who was dogged by sparse personal appeal and copious dirty laundry. He had dishonestly managed Cuba's Institute of Coffee under Grau and been a policeman during the Machado era. His rival was minister-without-portfolio Ramón Vasconcelos, who was also director of *Alerta*. In the latter capacity, he had disgruntled Carlos Prío for lambasting the imprisonment of Chibás in 1949 and thus ruined his chances of garnering any favors. Vasconcelos further realized the bleakness of his prospects when he spied Pérez-for-senate posters on his way back from Alemán's funeral. Even as Pérez seemed to have the inside track, Miguelito Suárez Fernández was determined to put forward a more distinguished contender lest Chibás win in a romp and use the victory as a springboard for 1952. He therefore suggested the party try three of the island's best-known brand names—Pepe San Martín, Miguel Mariano Gómez, and Raúl Menocal. Grau's cousin, whose lack of political enthusiasm had rendered him very much in demand, reiterated his desire to remain a private citizen. Gómez, who was the son of Cuba's second president and had occupied the top office himself in 1936, also declined, as did Menocal, the child of a two-time president and former Democratic boss.

MIDTERM ELECTIONS

With midterm election campaigns already in high gear, Raúl Gutiérrez published a survey measuring the "political sympathy" for Cuba's primary movers and shakers.[32] The questionnaire guru asked respondents who, among Carlos Prío, Ramón Grau, Guillermo Alonso Pujol, Fulgencio Batista, and Eduardo Chibás, they believed was "most beneficial" for Cuba.[33] Despite an uneven record, Prío topped the list with 23.86 percent. Chibás was next with 20.74 percent. Batista registered 17.17 percent, and Grau followed in fourth place with a mere 12.82 percent. Alonso Pujol had the worst showing by far, rating an embarrassing 0.67 percent nationwide and zero in the province of Pinar del Río. Prío's relative popularity was in marked contrast to that of his government. In a different query, where Cubans were asked to judge his administration, 23.19 percent replied that it was "good," 29.71 percent said it was "bad," and 35.06 percent answered it was "average."[34] The most notable finding was that Grau, who had been so revered in 1944 and whose smile still tickled the masses in 1948, had seen his standing sink lower than Batista's. This owed much to the sensational revelations of José Manuel Alemán's vast and varied shopping spree with state funds. If Pelayo Cuervo Navarro's Lawsuit 82 against Grau and those who sacked the treasury during his term seemed somewhat abstract or politically motivated, as El Viejo himself liked to believe, there was no facile explanation for the seemingly endless possessions of his favorite minister. The columnist Francisco Ichaso styled these a "new and forceful blow to Grau's solar plexus," adding that the former physiology professor could no longer claim, "It wasn't me."[35]

The timing of this poll may have appeared curious since, among all these figures, only Chibás was seeking elective office in 1950. However, the others were fixtures of Cuban politics and each was running a proxy in the pivotal Havana mayoral race. Antonio Prío's demoralizing experience in the Palacio de los Deportes had sketched the limits of his brother's boosterism. The only question was whether he could buy off his unpopularity or frighten Habaneros into voting for him. In advertisements, Antonio promised to build a "true" aqueduct, suggesting his proximity to the president would facilitate this project. His slogan was thus "Whatever Havana Needs, Havana Will Have." Also, having failed to lure the Communists himself, he derided his rival Nicolás Castellanos for accepting their support. One poster showed a pair of children praying at their bedside under a portrait of the Virgin Mary while the ominous shadow of Joseph Stalin hovered above them. Castellanos remained the front-runner despite being supported by two men, Grau and

Alonso Pujol, who were held in low public esteem. Most importantly, he relied on incumbency and the fact that he was not Antonio Prío. His campaign emphasized all manner of "tangible achievements," including renovated day care centers, improvements in city hospitals, and new schools. Hence, Castellanos proclaimed himself "A Mayor Who Shows the People His Works." Lastly, there was the well-meaning but grayish Manuel Bisbé. He boasted the moral stature of Chibás sans charisma, but this was not an auspicious formula according to polls. His candidacy would test whether Cubans were willing to vote for the upright but often bland figures proposed by Ortodoxo fanatics. Bisbé's announcements stressed his revolutionary credentials, including expulsions from teaching jobs by Machado and Batista. They also lionized the fact that his current position at the University of Havana had been gained through an "open competition" rather than favoritism. Moreover, he was touted as an industrious congressman, who proposed numerous bills, and a man of principle, who had spent seven hours combating the president's foreign loan. His motto declared that "His Clean and Useful Life Guarantees That He Is the Best Candidate."

On April 16, Bisbé was featured in a *Bohemia* series called "Twenty-Four Hours in the Lives of the Mayoral Candidates." Readers of the magazine and potential balloters were offered a photo essay of Bisbé at his steady best. As such, he was shown inscribing Greek phrases on the blackboard of his university classroom, sitting with sympathizers at his campaign headquarters, and chatting with colleagues who were also respectable Ortodoxos, such as Herminio Portell Vilá, Vicentina Antuña, and Roberto Agramonte.[36] While these portraits portrayed a decent man who associated with an honorable crowd, Bisbé's main liability was highlighted by something missing in the captions. Pictured next to Chibás in one frame and José Pardo Llada in another, his companions were both described as "popular" while Bisbé was attached to laudatory but less handy adjectives like "honest" and "trustworthy."[37] In fact, the twenty-five-year-old Pardo Llada was shaping up as the party's newest superstar, having built his following, like Chibás, through a popular radio show and charismatic, scandal-mongering style. Pardo Llada first drew national acclaim in 1944 with his commentary on the vastly destructive hurricane that wrecked Havana harbor and killed an estimated three hundred people. Like Chibás, he championed causes dear to the island's rural and urban working classes. For example, he advocated higher salaries for sugar workers and denounced a rise in bus fares. While Pardo Llada was far from unique in espousing these stands, he also possessed what the journalist Walfredo Vincente called a "contagious popularity."[38] This was reflected in the top ratings of his daily afternoon broadcast, which outperformed all other news shows of its kind.[39] In addition, he could neither walk nor drive through Havana without being stopped and effusively greeted by people of every sort. His run-in with former police chief Caramés notwithstanding, even officers of the law happily paused and chatted with him. Aside from his magnetism, Pardo Llada's background as a schoolteacher's son and his generally modest personal habits pleased Ortodoxo moral guardians.[40] His closeness to Chibás, whom he saw nearly every day, also stood him in good stead. Although he was still quite young, the party astutely nominated him to run for congress, and the enthusiasm aroused by his candidacy was second only to that of the man he so consciously emulated. With no need for a political machine, Pardo Llada gathered tremendous momentum using his radio popularity, the genuine affection of Havana residents, and endorsements from respected men like the independence hero Enrique Loynaz del Castillo and Cuba's foremost public intellectual, Fernando Ortiz.

In this too, Pardo Llada was treading a path previously blazed by Chibás. For the party's established luminary, however, this would be a different campaign given his physical limitations. Ecstatic rallies culminating with leaps into the arms of aficionados were out of the question. Nor could Chibás tour the numerous towns and villages of Havana province to personally state his case. The Ortodoxo leader still had his wits about him though and on April 9 delivered a blistering contumely against his two opponents. In his first live and complete radio address since February, Chibás recalled that Virgilio Pérez, the erstwhile judicial policeman, had arrested him in April of 1929 and sent him to prison for four months, thereby rendering a valuable service to President Gerardo Machado. He also accused Pérez of raiding Cuba's Institute of Coffee and agriculture ministry to the tune of 5 million pesos. Moreover, just as Pérez had succeeded José Manuel Alemán as Auténtico party boss in Havana, he also desired to replace him in the senate using the same methods favored by the late education minister—namely via "large scale bribery."[41] Chibás referred to his second opponent as "Mister William Belt." This was a reference to his American roots as the grandson of John Benjamin Belt, who had settled in Cuba after the United States Civil War. In this vein, Chibás wondered whether Belt aspired to represent Cubans or "Boston aristocracy."[42] In the end, Belt did boast one Cuban trait, although it was the disappointing one of opportunism. Hence, in 1935, while serving as Batista's appointed mayor of Havana, he placed a medal of honor around the neck of José Eleuterio Pedraza for suppressing the mass strikes of that year.

Besides returning to the airwaves full-time, Chibás also took up his pencil.[43] As always, his friend Miguel Ángel Quevedo happily ceded him space in the island's most popular magazine—which was already running regular pro-Ortodoxo columns by Jorge Mañach and Carlos Márquez Sterling. On April 23, Chibás published an article entitled "Message to the Cuban People," which reiterated and amplified his earlier criticisms of Virgilio Pérez and Guillermo Belt. Apart from painting Pérez as a pro-Machado stooge and abuser of public office, he provided an embarrassing anecdote. Chibás related that after Machado was ousted and angry mobs sought revenge against government agents, Pérez had "hidden behind the skirts of female family members and friends" who begged revolutionary leaders to pardon his "wickedness."[44] Chibás lacked similar juicy details about "Mr. William Belt," dismissing him instead as an "unconditional servant" of Wall Street who would feel more at home in Washington's Capitol than Cuba's Capitolio.[45] Finally, Chibás reserved some harsh words for a newcomer—the Communist Anibal Escalante. Unlike Pérez, whom he deemed a crook, and Belt, whom he called a lackey of US bankers, Chibás considered Escalante a flunky for Moscow's "despotic" empire—which he termed "the most dangerous and bloodthirsty" of the current century.[46] In presenting his own case for election, Chibás recycled choice bits of rhetoric from his presidential campaign. Paraphrasing his classic speech from 1948, he asked, "What are we counting on to win Havana's vacant senate seat?"[47] Rather than a political machine or money, Chibás answered, "My history as an incorruptible combatant during a quarter century of incarcerations, persecutions and constant sacrifices."[48] He reminded readers that the Prío family, Nicolás Castellanos, Virgilio Pérez, and Alberto Inocente Álvarez had all enriched themselves in public office. Conversely, he had refused to "exchange shame for money" and was now measurably poorer.[49]

Chibás also reprimanded the government for abetting an epidemic of "siblingism" in Cuban politics. This began at the top with Carlos Prío's imposition of his younger brother Antonio as the Auténtico mayoral candidate of Havana, his sister Mireya as a congressional hopeful from Oriente, and his sister-in-law's brother, Tino Fuentes, as a prospective representative from Las Villas.[50] Those who followed suit included Tony Varona, who had his brother Roberto nominated to run for mayor of Camagüey; Virgilio Pérez, who tabbed his brother Gerardo to fill the congressional seat he was vacating; Diego Vicente Tejera, who lined up a congressional bid for his brother Titi in their home province of Matanzas; Senator Octavio Rivero Partagás of Pinar del Río, whose brother César was up for reelection as a congressman; and the infamous Rolando Masferrer, who placed his brother Kiki on the congressional ticket in their native Oriente. On the other hand, Chibás was not immune from the tendency toward nepotism—which was pervasive in all of Cuba's political parties. He conveniently neglected to mention that his cousin Roberto Agramonte had been elected Ortodoxo party boss in Havana at his behest and that the two delegates who had raised charges of favoritism had been expelled.[51]

As Chibás pressed on in characteristic style, the Auténtico senator and Prío confidant Lomberto Díaz described a different though no less captivating panorama. While Chibás railed against the status quo from outside, Díaz detailed the thinking of those who ruled the island. Having invited a *Bohemia* reporter to his country house in Pinar del Río province, Díaz spoke frankly, assisted by several drams of *guayabita*, a local guava-infused liquor. Among other things, he stated that Carlos Prío rather than party assemblies would choose the Auténtico presidential candidate for 1952. As a consequence, legislators loyal to the president were anxious to modify the electoral code and eliminate the veto currently wielded by provincial bodies over party nominees. Apart from being anti-democratic, this change would cause considerable rifts within the party—particularly among followers of Miguelito Suárez Fernández.[52] As to whom Prío would actually select, Díaz said the president was awaiting the midterm election results. If Antonio were to win the Havana mayoralty "by an ample margin," as many in the party expected, he would be the standard-bearer in 1952.[53] In the event that Antonio lost, the field would be more wide-open. Díaz claimed Carlos Hevia would have the inside track as the president held him in "great esteem."[54] However, circumstances were still fluid. For instance, if Virgilio Pérez upset Chibás at the polls, he could reasonably expect the party's laurels, although Díaz recognized the Ortodoxo leader was a "fearsome" opponent and would probably prevail.[55] Even in the likely event of his defeat, Pérez was "lending a great service to the government" because no one else had been willing to challenge Chibás.[56] In fact, for an Auténtico nabob, Díaz offered a surprisingly nuanced assessment of his party's bête noire. The standard Auténtico appraisal portrayed Chibás as an irresponsible rabble-rouser who was unfit for high office and a ruinous influence on the nation. On the contrary, Díaz allowed that Chibás alone among opposition figures "had something to say."[57]

If his campaign advertisements were any indication, Chibás was saying the senate was a den of iniquity and vowed to construct a wall against "vile exploiters of the people" if elected.[58] He thus urged voters to "place their brick" by marking their ballots for him. Another poster limned a battle scene and proclaimed that Chibás would be the people's "trench."[59] As there were no Ortodoxos in the senate and only two open seats there, he would have scarce opportunities to introduce any bills. However, because he was a party chief and future presidential candidate, the press was understandably interested in his legislative proposals. One afternoon a reporter stopped by the Agramonte residence to ask Chibás about his program and found him still in pajamas. A smiling Eddy related that he had attended a rally in Cárdenas (seventy-five miles east of Havana) the night before and gone to bed at 4:00 a.m. This had not been a campaign stop, as Cárdenas was in neighboring Matanzas province and nobody there could vote for him. Rather, he had felt obliged to support a local Ortodoxo candidate and made the trip despite violent objections from Pedro Iglesias Betancourt. Chibás answered the journalist's questions with gleeful good humor and offered, with consummate showmanship, to pose at the desk where he wrote his Sunday radio speeches. At one point, he turned on the radio and said, "Permit me to listen to Virgilio [Pérez] so I can amuse myself."[60] Soon enough, Chibás dived into a lecture on nepotism, as he explained that all four Pérez brothers were elected officials or state employees, and dishonest ones at that.[61] Regarding his legislative agenda, Chibás mentioned passage of the 1940 constitution's complementary laws. He was especially keen on imperatives that would curb corruption, such as a general accounting law, establishment of a national comptroller's office, and an act that would establish defined standards for state employees. Chibás also wished to tinker with the electoral code so that senators would be elected based on majority vote rather than by coalition. His most ambitious scheme was a crowd-pleaser and classic campaign staple that involved handing "thieving functionaries" over to the courts for prosecution and devising legislation that would recover stolen funds and invest them in "urgent" projects, including aqueducts, hospitals, country roads, and rural schools.[62] This project was timelier than ever in the wake of Alemán's lavish accoutrements but had no chance in an Auténtico-controlled senate.

Shortly after this interview, Chibás began feeling the effects of his ill-advised trip. Besides staying out until the wee hours, Chibás had insisted on delivering a speech and passing through the gigantic crowd on foot, accompanied by José Pardo Llada. Within days, Chibás began vomiting after meals and required regular infusions of saline, blood, and plasma. Moreover, his weight plummeted since he could not digest solid food. On April 27, he had planned to commemorate the first anniversary of his incarceration by addressing an Ortodoxo throng next to the Castillo del Príncipe. That morning, however, Chibás fainted multiple times. Pedro Iglesias Betancourt told him to stay home, warning he could die in the middle of his speech otherwise. Chibás spent the afternoon in his room pondering the counsel of his friend and doctor, but by 7:00 p.m. he had decided to forsake sound medical advice yet again. This seemed foolish, particularly as Chibás threw up twice before leaving the house and three more times as he waited his turn at the pulpit. When the Ortodoxo leader finally stood to address the multitude, he was interrupted by concerned voices begging him to stop. Chibás marveled that never before had "his people" asked him not to speak.[63] Later on, having safely returned to the Agramonte residence, he asked his cousin's wife, "Don't you think the Cuban people, who are so good, deserve what I just did?"[64]

On April 30, the Havana senate contest swerved in a highly unexpected direction. That evening, Chibás offered breaking news to his Sunday audience. Shortly before he began broadcasting, Cuba's Superior Electoral Tribunal had disqualified Virgilio Pérez from running because of an erroneous coalition agreement. Specifically, he had sought to be listed on the Auténtico, Democratic, and Liberal ballots, but the Liberals had never formally nominated him, and the pact was thus invalid according to the island's electoral code. Upon learning the verdict, Prime Minister Tony Varona announced over the radio that the court had initiated a "coup" and claimed, with notable indelicacy, that it "could not do this to a government party."[65] The ornery

Varona thus expressed officially what most Auténticos had long assumed—namely, that they were entitled to rule and the law was a useful cudgel against opponents but did not apply to them. Virgilio Pérez echoed the belief that Cuba's courts were a government plaything by wondering how the judges had dared to "rebel against the president of the republic."[66] For his part, Carlos Prío telephoned one of the magistrates and accused him of "negligence" for not clarifying the rules pertaining to special elections.[67] This was a disingenuous gripe since the electoral code had not changed. Further, Pérez had been the only candidate to run afoul of the regulations. The real problem was that he had trusted his bungling advisor and lawyer, Rigoberto Ramírez, to submit the paperwork. Chibás, who was no stranger to legal disputes, convened the Ortodoxo executive committee for a consultation. In a dig at Varona, the party conveyed "support" for the electoral tribunal's decision to "apply the same legal precepts to the government parties as those that oblige everyone else."[68]

The government, of course, was not inclined to stand pat and submitted an appeal that was considered on May 2. Judge Eloy Merino, who had been extensively lobbied by the president, seemed ready to change his mind. He argued the court had created "public anxiety" and urged his peers to grant an extension allowing the Auténtico, Democratic, and Liberal parties to put their pact in order.[69] His revised criteria drew a strenuous and verbose objection from the court's Ortodoxo observer, Joaquín López Montes. Speaking for ninety minutes, López Montes denied the existence of any public anxiety—claiming the only citizens suffering unease were the prime minister and friends of Virgilio Pérez. He concluded darkly that "a state of public anxiety will reign only if the people, who have respectfully accepted the Supreme Electoral Tribunal's egalitarian sentence, now contemplate its retraction and thus lose faith in the courts."[70] Regardless, Judge Merino and Judge Aurelio Álvarez Maruri reversed course, and their votes swung the majority in favor of repeal. Weighing in as a "responsible citizen," Chibás deplored the government's "brutal coercion" and pronounced himself "profoundly ashamed" by this turnabout.[71] At the same time, he had relished the prospect of "soundly defeating" Pérez and confessed to feeling a certain "personal satisfaction" that the race would continue. Chibás repeated and expanded on these thoughts in a subsequent *Bohemia* article. Eddy asserted that he was "sure" Cuba's Court of Constitutional Guarantees would invalidate Pérez if given the chance.[72] However, his party had decided to forgo this route:

> because everything that the ex-*porrista* Virgilio Pérez represents—stolen money, political machinery, vote buying, fraud, shady political deals—all this corruption is going to be swept from public life in the six provinces, not by means of legal appeals but through the clean and incorruptible votes of the

Cuban people, in an avalanche of ballots without precedent in Cuban history.[73]

The obsession of Chibás and the Ortodoxos with vote buying seemed to be gaining traction not only among hard-core followers but also for the island's shapers of opinion. During the second week of May, the theme was taken up by Francisco Ichaso in *Diario de la Marina*, Rafael Estenger in *Alerta*, Carlos Lechuga in *El Mundo*, and Prío's minister-without-portfolio Ramón Vasconcelos. A *Bohemia* correspondent quipped that even sleazy politicians were none too happy with the situation as the price of purchasing their positions was becoming onerous.[74] Buying votes had not always been part of Cuba's electoral process, but the practice boasted a long and varied history—dating from at least 1914, when two unpopular politicians found success by bribing those who marked ballots for illiterate citizens. In those days, they tore one hundred–peso bills down the middle and provided one half to their accomplices prior to elections and the other once victory was assured. Given the multitude of choices on each ballot, including candidates for congress, provincial government, and city council, voters could opt to sell their votes in bulk (a ploy known as the pineapple) or keep one or more for themselves. In Havana, this enabled an early political vehicle known as the Cenáculo, or Circle, which entrenched Liberals in the city's bureaucracy and elective offices. During Gerardo Machado's presidency positions were auctioned from the presidential palace, often costing up to 100,000 pesos. With the advent of BAGA in 1946, a joint venture between José Manuel Alemán and Francisco Grau Alsina to capture senate seats snowballed into the most powerful political machine in Cuba's history—capable of co-opting entire municipal assemblies. BAGA's essentially unlimited funds, siphoned directly from Cuba's treasury, provided Carlos Prío with approximately 30 million pesos for his 1948 election campaign. Alemán spent an estimated 10 million pesos on his senate seat. This infusion of money raised the ante for everyone else, including fellow Auténticos, some of whom had paid upward of 300,000 pesos for places in Congress.[75]

Alemán's demise and the dissolution of his political apparatus did not diminish the preeminence of mammon. On the contrary, costs inevitably climbed. This was nowhere more evident than in the Havana mayoral race. Aside from trying to buy the city's hostile denizens, Antonio Prío also needed to appease his coalition partners and other useful individuals. With habitual indiscretion, he admitted to shelling out 350,000 pesos for Liberal support. The amount paid for Democratic fealty was undoubtedly substantial as well. Panchín Batista, the governor of Havana province and an erstwhile mayoral candidate himself, was lured to the Auténticos through a generous cash reward. Moreover, Antonio supplemented his budget by distributing an endless supply of lottery tickets—which served as a form of currency. While the precise extent of his expenses remained unknown, he bragged to an adherent of Nicolás Castellanos that "the money I'm spending resembles a tale from *A Thousand and One Nights!*"[76] Needless to say, the legislative races involved similar tactics. Alberto Inocente Álvarez, the Auténtico senate contender for Pinar del Río, told the press he expected to spend a million pesos on his campaign. Moreover, the average bid for an Auténtico congressional seat, which often surpassed 900,000 pesos, required only slightly more modest outlays.[77] A *Bohemia* reporter blamed these swelling prices on candidates who "brilliantly" manipulated the "bribery industry," including Edgardo Buttari, Prío's ex-labor minister; Armando Da'Lama, a venal treasury ministry official; Gerardo Pérez, brother to the unscrupulous Virgilio; and Guillermo Ara, who employed UIR gangsters along with Cuba's dubious political sergeants to harvest votes.[78]

While vote buying proved phenomenally successful over the years, Cubans had usually been willing to forgo the extra lucre if they felt strongly about a candidate. Hence, the sports journalist Victor Muñoz topped the list for Havana city council in 1920 because he was adored by the island's myriad baseball fanatics.[79] Ramón Grau San Martín achieved the same result in Cuba's constituent assembly elections of 1939 by riding a wave of popular emotion and messianic fervor. The man who placed second in that contest, Eduardo Chibás, was currently headlining what a *Bohemia* reporter called "an historic duel between opulence and civic-mindedness."[80] A public survey by Raúl Gutiérrez, published on May 14, suggested most Cubans would vote their consciences rather than selling them—at least in his case. The poll indicated that 33.14 percent of Havana residents preferred Chibás, while 20.11 percent favored Virgilio Pérez. Third place belonged to the Communist Anibal Escalante, with 8.25 percent, and Guillermo Belt of the ad hoc Coincidencia, who lacked both riches and devoted followers, placed last with 4.10 percent.[81] These statistics, while not encouraging for Pérez, nonetheless implied that vote buying was having an impact. This was especially true in rural parts of Havana province, where Pérez led Chibás by more than seven percentage points. Pérez, whose policies as agriculture minister had proved disastrous for coffee farmers, was no darling of country dwellers. Rather, poverty and desperation inclined them to sell their votes more than wealthier urban inhabitants. In fact, every candidate except for the well-heeled Pérez counted less support in bucolic areas.[82] Then again, this advantage was offset by Pérez's unpopularity within his own party and coalition partners. Only 37.64 percent of Auténticos showed a willingness to vote for him, and 27.01 percent were prepared to mark their ballots for Chibás. Among Democrats, Eddy led Pérez by more than ten percentage points. Liberals also opted for Chibás by a lesser but still decisive margin of almost five percentage points.[83]

While Chibás was among the handful of Cuban politicians whose popularity could surmount a well-financed pro-government opponent, his friend Manuel Bisbé lacked the same crossover potential. Unlike the Ortodoxo leader, Bisbé encountered no significant backing outside his party. According to the public survey of May 14, only 4.95 percent of Auténticos intended to vote for him. Bisbé registered similarly dismal figures with every other political grouping except his own—never surpassing single digits for any of them. Even worse, 26.51 percent of Ortodoxos preferred Nicolás Castellanos.[84] Bisbé was not entirely without appeal, given his election to Cuba's chamber of representatives, but he was in no way capable of overcoming the municipal machine of Castellanos or the prodigal spending of Antonio Prío. Bisbé did not blame his projected third-place finish on either of these things, however. Rather, he irascibly accused Raúl Gutiérrez of distorting the results and claimed his numbers would improve if he could afford to pay for his own research. If anyone had the resources to co-opt Cuba's premier pollster, it was Antonio Prío, but his second-place showing, more than twenty-two points behind Nicolas Castellanos, implied his wallet was being utilized elsewhere. In many respects, he resembled Virgilio Pérez, given his huge war chest and meager likability. Even as he bought votes and slowly rose in the polls, the distaste many Havana residents harbored for Antonio was a poor omen. Since the last public survey in March, his overall rating had increased from 20.53 percent to 26.32 percent.[85] This reflected the unwillingness of Auténticos and members of pro-government parties to back him uniformly. For instance, 40.09 percent of Auténticos and 38.70 percent of Democrats favored Castellanos. Even worse, 58.82 percent of Liberals preferred Castellanos even though the party hierarchy had been bought off by the government.[86]

With election day looming, the moment for eleventh-hour surprises was at hand. Despite his comfortable lead in the polls and uncooperative diaphragm, Chibás set to work on a new *Bohemia* piece featuring sensational revelations about Virgilio Pérez. From back issues of *Diario de la Marina*, *El Crisol*, *Información*, and *El País*, he reconstructed a lurid incident from March 19, 1934, in which Pérez shot and wounded his vaudeville actress girlfriend during a lovers' quarrel and then murdered a man who crossed his path as he fled through Old Havana's streets. Pérez was accordingly arrested and tried in the city's Instructional Court, where his defense lawyer happened to be Miguelito Suárez Fernández. Chibás declared that "enormous pressure" had been exerted on the judges to absolve Pérez, and they duly complied. He also found it "curious" that Pérez's file had been subsequently "robbed" from the court's archives. Chibás concluded that "anyone who does not believe what I am saying about Virgilio Pérez can visit any public library, request the newspapers I referred to in this article and verify the truth for themselves."[87] Not surprisingly, Pérez was livid. He threatened violent reprisals against the magazine's director, Miguel Ángel Quevedo, its staff, and even their premises. Pérez also denounced *Bohemia* before Cuba's Association of Journalists, albeit to little effect. The following week, *Bohemia* ran a defiant editorial stating it would not be "frightened" by "boasts" of an "ex-servant of Machado and modern 'revolutionary' millionaire."[88] On the other hand, Carolos Lechuga, writing in *El Mundo*, upbraided Chibás for exposing Pérez's former paramour to unwarranted scrutiny. The woman, whose full name and home province had been furnished by Chibás, appeared to agree. She published an insulting public letter to him in a wide swath of Havana's newspapers. Undaunted, Eddy charged Pérez with having ghostwritten the abusive missive and forcing his old sweetheart to sign or forfeit her government job. In fact, so many rumors emerged regarding this affair that Chibás felt compelled to refute some of the more scurrilous ones. He acknowledged that people were saying his article had ruined the woman's marriage, that her husband had vowed to kill him, and her small grandchildren were crying desolate tears. In a last *Bohemia* column before the elections, Chibás explained the lady was actually single and childless. The incessant hearsay, he averred, was nothing more than a government-sponsored "farce."[89]

As the campaign drew to a close, Chibás continued to exasperate his doctors. On May 30, he attended an event honoring him in the Hotel Inglaterra but was so weak he could hardly say more than a few words. Since his diaphragmatic hernia was diagnosed in February, Chibás had dropped fifty pounds from a frame that had never been stout to begin with. Twenty-four hours before the polls closed, looking wan and ghostlike, he toured Havana's neighborhoods with Manuel Bisbé and planned last-minute strategies with Ortodoxo candidates for congress and city hall. Dressed in a white guayabera and bowtie, he contemplated updated surveys by Raúl Gutiérrez indicating his polemic with Virgilio Pérez had damaged his case but still showed him ahead "by a nose."[90] Pérez's gains, which may have been the result of frenzied ballot buying as well, were not enough to carry him past Chibás—who won by just over seventeen thousand votes.[91] Chibás blamed the closer-than-expected result on concerted attacks by the Communists, who were strong in Havana and barely mustered a peep against Pérez. The Ortodoxo leader allowed that he disagreed with the Communists on international matters but noted his vigorous protest when Jesús Menéndez had been murdered. "Do they believe Virgilio would have done the same as me?" he asked. "[Virgilio] would have supported the government against any transgression against our democracy."[92] At the same time, Chibás obtained an unexpected boost from Mayor Francisco Orúe of Marianao, who gladly accepted cash from Pérez to deliver votes but ordered his constituents to support Chibás instead. Commenting on Eddy's victory in *Diario de la Marina*, Francisco Ichaso wrote

> Electoral machines and money are losing the dominance they once possessed. The Ortodoxo candidate has won on the basis of his superior personality, his influence with the masses (and) the respect his behavior has awakened. . . . The people see in Chibás an implacable critic, a prosecutor who fearlessly attacks shamelessness and iniquity wherever he finds them. In a sphere where silence, dissimulation and complicity are the norm, he represents an exception.[93]

The government absorbed an even greater blow when Nicolás Castellanos was reelected as Havana's mayor by a margin of 16.5 percentage points. While Virgilio Pérez was amply assisted by the Auténtico apparatus and his own personal affluence, he was not a member of Carlos Prío's inner circle nor had he been the president's preferred choice to succeed Alemán. By contrast, the administration spared neither expense nor effort to elect Antonio Prío. Ignoring polls that predicted a distant second-place finish, Auténtico operatives fancifully viewed a landslide victory in the offing.[94] When the bad news became evident, Carlos and Antonio Prío covered assorted advisors with epithets.

These prominent setbacks notwithstanding, electoral bribery continued to yield fruit more often than not. Despite losing in Havana, and also in Camagüey, Cuba's third-largest city, where Tony Varona's brother Roberto was defeated, the Auténticos snagged more than one hundred mayoralties.[95] Some of these were won by genuinely popular candidates, such as Luis Casero in Santiago de Cuba, but many others resorted to shady methods. The government also added to its congressional majority. In Las Villas province, the Auténticos spent approximately 500,000 pesos to elect six representatives. One of these, the president's brother-in-law Tino Fuentes, was accused of funding his campaign with government checks meant for road construction and selling pardons to criminals via the justice ministry.[96] The midterm elections thus offered consolation along with dollops of bitterness for each of the island's political groupings. Guillermo Alonso Pujol and Ramón Grau San Martín reveled in the victory of their protégé, Nicolás Castellanos, who retained Cuba's second-most powerful political office. However, Castellanos, who had been an obscure Havana city councilman before the suicide of Manuel Fernández Supervielle, won because he was not the president's brother. Other Coincidencia nominees such as Guillermo Belt and René Benitez, who ran for senate in Pinar del Río, finished poorly in their respective races. As for the Ortodoxos, they regained a presence in the senate after a two-year hiatus, and Chibás, who had conducted a heroic campaign, showcased his presidential bona fides for 1952. Ortodoxos advanced in the lower house as well. In particular, José Pardo Llada provided a spectacular boost by collecting seventy-two thousand votes—more than any congressional candidate in Cuba's history. He thus established himself as the island's most dynamic young politician. Pardo Llada represented a new generation that had neither fought in the independence war nor tussled with Machado. His credibility derived from being a Chibás-style muckraker who was always, in the words of a *Bohemia* reporter, "risking his life in daily combat for the public benefit."[97] Ortodoxo fixtures such as Luis Orlando Rodríguez and Millo Ochoa were also elected. While these men embodied the Ortodoxo ideal of relative poverty, not all the party's winners fit this profile. In Las Villas, an Ortodoxo coffee baron named Aurelio Nazario Sargent rode to victory on a flotilla of jeeps that crisscrossed the countryside and blared his message. Even more enterprising was the prosperous Gerardo Vázquez, who accrued the highest vote total in Camagüey by hiring a dozen airplanes to spread Ortodoxo slogans across the skies. These successes were tempered by the poor showing of Manuel Bisbé, who could not muster even 10 percent of the vote in a party stronghold.

With the elections over, Chibás acquiesced to his doctors and remained inactive for nearly all of June. His devotees, however, busied themselves with letters of congratulations. A "great admirer" from Panama who read Eddy's articles in *Bohemia* and commended his "righteous conduct" requested an autographed photo.[98] A thirty-year-old sugar worker from Las Villas province who had previously shown negligible interest in politics wrote that he was now enthusiastic about campaigning for him. A Cuban man residing in New York City related that "I pray for the triumph of [your] party and your ideals and also for your personal health, knowing that you are my country's salvation."[99] Ricardo Pareja Lodosa, a member of the Young Ortodoxos in Matanzas, claimed Chibás was bound by a pact "with the entire nation and our martyrs to care for your well-being." He added that "you must not abandon your health and cannot forget that you are the only and supreme hope of the entire Cuban people, which trusts in you alone."[100] Chibás read these missives and others with great satisfaction, underlining as always his favorite passages with a red pencil. He was further gratified by a fresh opinion poll published on June 25 that confirmed him as Cuba's leading presidential contender. Asked who they preferred in the island's highest office, 26.25 percent of respondents chose Chibás. His nearest rival, Fulgencio Batista, trailed in second place by nearly eight percentage points. The third-place candidate, Miguelito Suárez Fernández, was just over twelve points behind. In addition, Chibás led in five of Cuba's six provinces, including the three most populous ones: Havana, Oriente, and Las Villas. Chibás was also undoubtedly pleased that his erstwhile adversary, Virgilio Pérez, gleaned a measly 0.84 percent.[101] Asked by a journalist for his view, Chibás said, "This clearly indicates that in Cuba space is being cleared for shame in the face of political machines and the government's corruptive money."[102]

CAUSA 82

In the simplest terms, Chibás and the Ortodoxos aimed to change Cuban politics by offering honorable candidates for public positions. For Chibás this was not merely a political strategy but a duty to the country's founders. Responding around this time to a letter from a young aficionada, he noted, "Our forbearers, who knew how to write pages of glory and bequeathed us a free and sovereign republic, deserve something better than what our present unscrupulous rulers have delivered. This," he concluded, "is the task to which the Ortodoxo party has pledged itself."[103] Although the organization's civic-minded gestures had aroused considerable enthusiasm, these tactics by themselves were not a blanket solution. Reform also required curbs on the ability of politicians to fund campaigns and buy votes from the national treasury. Reasonably effective deterrence, involving prosecution and incarceration for embezzlers, was therefore essential. Hence, on June 30, Chibás submitted a brief avowing that approximately 50 million pesos had been pilfered from the Sugar Workers' Retirement Fund during the Grau and Prío administrations. Chibás proclaimed that

> Justice should reign for everyone. The weight of the law should fall equally, without favoritism, on all those who have put their hands in the till and not only the ones who are less influential or powerful or have lost proximity to executive power. It is neither civic-minded nor brave to accuse only ex-President Grau San Martín and not his ex-prime minister and the current president of the republic Carlos Prío; the same goes for he who was director of rents and taxes under Grau and who was treasury minister in this administration. Both (Prío) brothers were as responsible for these outrages as Grau.[104]

However, it was one thing to make denunciations before the courts and quite another for them to be acted upon, as Chibás well knew. In this sense, the fate of Causa 82, the lawsuit brought by Pelayo Cuervo Navarro against thieves from Grau's administration, was highly significant. During its initial go-round, the case yielded little except a fine against Cuervo Navarro for publicly criticizing the lethargic and reluctant judiciary. Special Judge Antonio Vignier had actually closed the indictment and recommended the lawsuit be discontinued. In a rare display of independence, the Havana Municipal Court disagreed and reassigned the case to Judge Arturo Hevia with instructions to investigate more than thirty potential instances of malfeasance. Before Judge Hevia could pursue this mandate, however, he was recused on a ridiculous pretense. Specifically, a man named in the lawsuit, who had fought in the independence war, claimed Hevia was prejudiced against veterans. The next judge appointed eventually recused himself as well, this time because Grau's ex-finance minister, Isauro Valdés, alleged personal enmity. In truth, Valdés worried that an honest magistrate would send him up the river. Toward late May, Judge Federico Justiniani took over, and within a month he filed charges against the men he deemed "scoundrels."[105] These included Valdés and four associates who were arraigned for stealing nine and a half million pesos from the Havana customs office. Asked by a reporter for his opinion, the usually stern Pelayo Cuervo Navarro pronounced himself "very satisfied" that the "dignity" of Cuba's judicial branch had been salvaged. Addressing the customary unwillingness of government officials to pursue these cases, he said, "the justice minister should not forget that the state is harmed above all by such crimes."[106] Judge Justiniani expressed fewer doubts about the process, affirming that "criminal lawsuits are like a sudden storm. You walk outside one day to sun and a fresh breeze and just like that you are soaked!"[107]

Unfortunately, these exultations proved premature. In the early morning hours of July 4, six masked men toting machine guns appeared at the courthouse in Havana's La Víbora neighborhood, where the Causa 82 documents were stored. Although Judge Justiniani had instructed the guards not to open the door for anybody, one of them insouciantly ignored his orders and moments later he and his companion were bound, gagged, blindfolded, and had their ears plugged. Wasting no time, the burglars forced open a cabinet and removed all 6,032 relevant pages. Such surgical efficiency was curious, as the folders holding them were unmarked. Further, not a single piece of paper pertaining to any other case was taken. Even an adjacent civil suit concerning a certain purveyor of frogs legs remained undisturbed. After stowing their precious loot in a sack, the villains fled without further ado. Thus, rather than an unexpected tempest of justice, there was only more scandal. José Pardo Llada, who was informed right away by a police reporter, called it "the news of the year" and rushed to the courthouse with Pelayo Cuervo Navarro in tow.[108] One of the guards, Julio Gutiérrez Santana, told his version of events to a *Bohemia* correspondent. Speaking with visible unease, he disclosed that he and his partner had unlocked the door because they believed the intruders were night patrolmen. He also confirmed that the robbery was an inside job, indicating that one man seemed to know exactly what they were looking for. Judge Justiniani, who was justifiably livid, contributed his own more extensive commentary. He refused to forgive the guards, particularly as they had been warned not to admit anyone during strange hours, not even himself. This was because there had already been an attempt to tamper with the evidence. Some days earlier a man impersonating Pelayo Cuervo Navarro had tried to enter the courthouse after midnight. Justiniani also revealed that his phone had been ringing incessantly of late. The callers, who universally claimed to be journalists but who were probably political operatives, always sought information regarding the next round of indictments so they could plan accordingly. Exactly whom they represented was a matter of feverish speculation. Popular suspicion implicated Humberto Becerra, Grau's close friend and ex-interior minister, who was arrested that afternoon. In custody, Becerra glibly maintained that he and Grau were anxious to see the case go forward in order to ascertain "who had robbed in Cuba."[109] He blamed Carlos Prío for the break-in and maliciously wondered how "two unhappy policemen" could have been the lone custodians of such important documents.[110]

The eminent lawyer and retired Democrat Carlos Manuel de la Cruz, who had recently joined the prosecution of Causa 82, estimated that only seven people were familiar enough with the case to know the exact folders that contained its pages. These were Judge Justiniani, his secretary, the court clerk, Pelayo Cuervo Navarro, Justice Minister Oscar Gans, State Prosecutor Jesús Coll, and de la Cruz himself. He thus believed someone from that group had supervised the assailants. Otherwise, the precision and speed of their operation would have been impossible. De la Cruz suspected Coll, who had been added to the legal team just seventy-two hours before the robbery. He avowed that stealing the documents was "ridiculous" since copies could be had from the various ministries within twenty days. Conversely, he allowed that powerful figures would aim to thwart any such effort.[111] These included Antonio Prío, who had served in the Grau-era treasury ministry and was among those "most compromised" by the case.[112] For his part, Pelayo Cuervo Navarro guessed that Coll and perhaps Gans had a hand in the burglary. Given his pro-government orientation and previous efforts to smother the case, Coll certainly possessed a compelling motive. At any rate, Cuervo Navarro admitted he was already preparing a brief for the Supreme Tribunal to assist in reconstructing the lawsuit. The press was also anxious to hear from Chibás on this matter. In his statement, the ailing yet spirited Ortodoxo leader saw an irrefutable link between the stolen documents and a meeting on July 1 between Grau and emissaries from Prío. He claimed they discussed reconciliation so as to present a common front against the threat of legal investigations involving both sides.

During his July 9 broadcast, Chibás, as he often did, reiterated what was already being said in the newspapers and on the street. Unlike Carlos Manuel de la Cruz and Pelayo Cuervo Navarro, both of whom pointed implicit fingers at the president, Chibás opted for a more unequivocal tone. He told his audience:

> Tonight, before the people of Cuba, we concretely accuse the president of the republic, Carlos Prío Socarrás, of being the intellectual author of the armed assault against the courthouse where the lawsuit against the embezzlement of 174 million pesos is being processed and which was perpetrated in order to save his brother Antonio . . . who was about to be indicted by Judge Justiniani.[113]

For good measure, he added that the Causa 82 fiasco demonstrated the government was unworthy of foreign credit. "When we announced more than a year ago that American bankers should not provide one cent to the Prío government," he said, "the president's paid spokesmen disparaged us as slanderers and demagogues. Once again, time has proven us right."[114] Chibás then contrasted the "corruption" and "incapacity" of Prío's administration with the probity of Ortodoxo congressmen, who had recently agreed to forgo their parliamentary immunity.[115] At the government's behest, State Prosecutor Rafael Trejo sent a transcript of the radio show to the Urgency Court and recommended that Chibás be charged with defamation.[116] Relishing the prospect of another popularity-boosting row, Chibás shunned his election certificate—which would have exempted him from being tried.

On July 16, Chibás took to the airwaves and excoriated Trejo for doing the administration's dirty work. Trejo's lack of backbone also served as a potent allegory since his son of the same name was a revolutionary martyr who had been murdered by Machado's policemen in 1930. Chibás noted that

> Judge Trejo has passively watched, without pressing any charges, as hundreds of assassinations have taken place in full public view and hundreds of millions have been impudently robbed; the only thing he has bothered himself with is accusing me of denouncing the thieves by their first and last names and for uncovering the intellectual author of the famous Causa 82 burglary; in brief, his indescribable behavior is offending the memory and civic example of his son Rafael Trejo.[117]

Chibás also accused the government of attempting to use his delicate health against him. Since he required a second operation, and soon, any jail sentence would essentially prove fatal. Chibás told his listeners the president hoped to silence him by effectively threatening his life. "But Carlos Prío made a mistake," he said defiantly.[118] Chibás not only refused to recant, he offered a detailed narrative of the Causa 82 thefts. He alleged that Antonio Prío and Oscar Gans had directed the operation in accordance with the president's orders. Moreover, he claimed Miguelito Suárez Fernández had offered "advice" and the Bureau of Investigations Chief had provided "technical support."[119] Looking forward to his day in court, Chibás chose the juridically nimble Carlos Márquez Sterling as his legal counsel—who likened the action against his client to the false accusations against Captain Dreyfus in France. If the administration insisted on bringing the case to trial, a public relations disaster beckoned since both Pelayo Cuervo Navarro and Carlos Manuel de la Cruz were eager to testify. By far, the surest indicator of government complicity was the fact that all the initial suspects had been released and the case was in danger of being dropped due to a lack of indictments. This situation was mercilessly lampooned by Cuba's cartoonists. Carlos Vidal sketched a boy asking his father, "So, Chibás is the only one who will be prosecuted for the Causa 82 robbery, is that right *papi*?"[120] Determined to avoid this eventuality, Cuervo Navarro submitted a denunciation against Ernesto Figueras, the guard who had opened the courthouse door and seemed curiously untroubled by the whole affair. Specifically, Cuervo Navarro suspected him of having been planted and believed he had let the criminals in without them bothering to knock.

Judge Justiniani did not rest either. Citing the indictment Chibás had submitted in June, he petitioned the Urgency Court to consider criminal charges against Carlos Prío for raiding the Sugar Workers Retirement Fund. Since the president could only face prosecution before Cuba's Supreme Tribunal, the Urgency Court was essentially deciding whether to elevate the case. As often happened when so much was at stake, one of the magistrates, Eugenio González, apparently had trouble making up his mind. In a move that hardly inspired confidence, he spent July 20 at "La Chata," Prío's finca, where he received less-than-objective instructions and perhaps an inducement or two. Not surprisingly, González voted no as did his colleague Fidel Vidal. This excused the president from the awkward and unprecedented spectacle of appearing as a defendant before the nation's highest court. Somewhat unexpectedly, however, the verdict was not unanimous. Chibás hailed the dissent of Antonio Barreras as a "glorious achievement for Cuba's judiciary."[121] As for his own prospective date with the Urgency Court, Chibás was disappointed to learn that Havana's Provincial Electoral Authority had sent his credentials to the senate and he was therefore immune from prosecution. This by no means ended the proxy war waged by Prío against Chibás via the Urgency Courts. During his July 30 broadcast, Chibás contended that Carlos Prío met secretly with Fulgencio Batista at the finca of Senator Manuel Pérez Galán—Cuba's pineapple king.[122] Prío roundly denied this and resorted to the Urgency Court once again, which requested a waiver of the Ortodoxo leader's parliamentary immunity. Chibás complied with alacrity, but as his second operation loomed this new skirmish would have to wait.

THE SECOND SURGERY

Given the failure of his operation in February, Eddy's doctors and many of his supporters urged him to schedule his second surgery in the United States. Nevertheless, Chibás flatly refused, holding that if he were going to die, he preferred to do so in Cuba. Thus, on August 1, he checked into the Miramar clinic—one of Havana's newest and most advanced hospitals. Chibás would need a few weeks of rest and close monitoring by his medical staff before going under the knife. Almost immediately, he required two blood transfusions. In the early going, at least, the Ortodoxo leader's repose was strictly enforced and only his brother Raúl, his cousin Roberto Agramonte, and his secretary Conchita Fernández were allowed to visit.

While Chibás was indisposed, Communications Minister Sergio Clark issued the controversial Decree 2273, guaranteeing a "right of reply" to anyone singled out for censure during radio transmissions. This measure, which became known as the "gag decree," had actually been devised by Justice Minister Oscar Gans. He justified it as a remedy for the "great number of citizens" whose "prestige" was being "compromised" on the island's radio shows.[123] Under the new rules, radio stations were obligated to cede space for the injured parties so they could personally rectify any insults directed against them. Enrique de la Osa claimed the justice minister's real aim was to curry favor with Carlos Prío, especially as a cabinet reshuffle was in the offing. That Prío desired a new instrument for suppressing media criticism was undeniable. Just before the midterm elections, he had told a crowd in the town of Bauta that "soon, Cuban women will no longer suffer attacks on the radio."[124] This allusion to the feud between Chibás and Virgilio Pérez during their senate campaign hinted at the decree's real purpose. After being publicly accused of responsibility for the Causa 82 robbery, Prío proved willing once again to compromise the island's constitution for imagined political advantages over Chibás and José Pardo Llada. The decree almost certainly violated Article 33, which guaranteed freedom of expression, and absolutely breached Article 24, which prohibited the confiscation of property without payment. Perhaps worst of all, Cuba's radio director, a functionary in the communications ministry, was granted the power to decide whether a complaint merited the right of reply rather than the nation's courts. This contradicted Article 170, which declared that "justice may be administered only by persons who permanently belong to the judiciary."

Despite these imperfections, Gans crowed that he had extended free thought and expression to all of Cuba's five million inhabitants. He further declared that "to deny a citizen the right to defend himself against distorted claims would be a manifestation of ambitious totalitarianism."[125] In a swift response, the Ortodoxo radio host Guido García Inclán stated,

> The five million citizens Gans refers to have no need to protect themselves from radio attacks but rather against the government itself. Isn't it true that hospitals lack thousands of beds and many poor people die due to a scarcity of medical assistance? Isn't money robbed from the people in order to build luxurious apartment buildings? Does the farmer feel secure in his land and does he have access to roads so he can sell his products? These things that are denounced on the radio constitute an effective defense of the citizens against the government's outrages.[126]

Goar Mestre, the director of Circuito CMQ, concurred, affirming that radio campaigns generally defended the "great masses" against the "egoism, ambition and venality of our politicians."[127] Alejo Cossío del Pino, who owned Radio Cadena Habana, asserted that men who had illegally enriched themselves wished to avoid the embarrassment of being called thieves. In fact, the decree was reviled among reporters of all political stripes and every independent press organization. More to the point, Cubans already exercised the right to defend themselves against all manner of accusations—doing so vigorously in the many polemics conducted via radio, magazines, and newspapers. The government's objective, gussied up in fancy garb, was to intrude on the broadcasts of Chibás, Pardo Llada, or any other opponents.

Although he was ostensibly out of commission, the Ortodoxo leader was planning a surprise—which he hinted at during a visit by Carlos Márquez Sterling. Chibás swore he would return to the radio "very soon" and indeed, on August 13, he escaped from the hospital and broadcast an open letter to the president.[128] While journalists made much of his flair for the dramatic, Chibás was also convinced he could die in surgery and felt the need to condemn Prío's "gravest" error.[129] His strong voice belying a faltering body, he pointed out that Cubans had no reason to expect anything constructive from an "evil machadista" like Oscar Gans.[130] Chibás also mentioned that Goar Mestre offered the government a thirty-minute time slot on CMQ immediately after his show in order to rebut any prospective inaccuracies, but it had refused, insisting instead on replying, if need be, during his own half hour. "This," he said, "demonstrates the hypocrisy of Decree 2273, which the people, with their formidable intuition, have baptized the gag decree from the first moment."[131] Chibás further noted that the president had all of Cuba's media at his disposal while he possessed only a single show. "And this half hour, once a week, on one radio station floor," he declared, with rising indignation, "you want to take from me with tricks, using my illness to your advantage."[132] Lastly, Chibás reminded Prío of their time as delegates to the constituent assembly in 1940, where they had advocated the creation of Article 40. This nullified any provisions by the government or courts impinging upon constitutional guarantees and condoned "adequate resistance" against them. Thus, he concluded, "Whenever you attempt to violate public liberties, you will have to confront me, your incorruptible adversary."[133]

As if to demonstrate the needlessness of Decree 2273, Antonio Prío fulminated on Unión Radio later that night against José Pardo Llada, Carlos Márquez Sterling, and Goar Mestre. Further, Humberto Medrano, the editor of *Prensa Libre*'s evening edition, responded in print to an offensive remark by Chibás. This included an invitation to duel once the Ortodoxo chief recovered from his surgery. As the insulted party, Medrano had the right to choose the weapon—a fact that caused panic among Eddy's friends since the *Prensa Libre* editor was a champion marksman. Nonetheless, Chibás told his seconds, Luis Orlando Rodríguez and Pardo Llada, to accept whatever terms were proposed. As a result, both men withdrew, saying they refused to "lead

Chibás to the slaughterhouse."[134] Impervious to all pleas, Chibás named new seconds, who were relieved when Medrano's representatives opted for sabers. Having settled this matter, Chibás finally gave the go-ahead to his medical staff. On August 17, Dr. Antonio Rodríguez Díaz sutured the hernia and signs of success abounded almost immediately. Chibás began gaining weight within days. On August 26, for his forty-third birthday, the doctors allowed him to eat steak fillet and roast chicken. As proof that political disagreements did not always constitute grudge matches, Commerce Minister José Andreu was among those who visited Chibás in the hospital. Miguelito Suárez Fernández also inquired about Eddy's health.

On the afternoon of September 1, Chibás checked out of the Miramar clinic with a provisionally clean bill of health. Amenable at last to his doctors' orders, he agreed to depart for a recuperative vacation in Canada and the United States that evening. Before setting off, however, he supervised an Ortodoxo meeting in the house of Manuel Bisbé. While Chibás had been convalescing, the administration had ventured into dubious legal territory once again by arbitrarily closing the Communist daily *Hoy*. Instead of seeking a court order or legislative approval, the government favored a ministerial resolution. Unfortunately, Labor Minister José Morell Romero, whose signature would have been required, expressed serious qualms about its legitimacy. Tony Varona thus proposed that Morell Romero feign illness so he could temporarily assume control of the labor ministry and shut down the newspaper. The prime minister warned cabinet members that "the next loan we will be requesting, which we need so badly and will guarantee us victory in 1952, depends on what we do now against the Communists."[135] Minister-without-portfolio Ramón Vasconcelos, who had attended the meeting and vehemently opposed the prime minister's reasoning, subsequently resigned in protest. Speaking to reporters, he pointed out that even the US government, which currently was at war with Communist North Korea, did not restrict publication of the *Daily Worker*.[136] Chibás, whose thinning locks had grown noticeably grayer since enduring two surgeries over seven months, informed the assembled Ortodoxos he feared the government was "on the road to dictatorship" but remained confident the party would thrive during his absence.[137] He added that the Ortodoxos were the only party with the moral standing to criticize the closing of *Hoy*, which he termed "unjustifiable" and a "flagrant aggression," because they had never cut any deals with the Communists.[138]

Even as the Ortodoxos in attendance were grateful to see Chibás, many disagreed with him. The newly elected Havana city councilman Herminio Portell Vilá spoke first, asserting that *Hoy* was not really a Cuban newspaper like *Diario de la Marina* or *Alerta* but rather an "organ of Moscow."[139] As evidence, he pointed out that *Hoy* reproduced the same articles that ran in Communist dailies from throughout the world. Portell Vilá also challenged the official Ortodoxo posture that the attack against *Hoy* endangered political freedom, believing the government was focused solely on the Communist threat. The onetime Communist José Chelala Aguilera agreed, saying he knew better than anyone that Cuban Marxists were "puppets of Moscow."[140] Gerardo Vázquez, the recently elected congressman from Camagüey, urged the party to outflank the administration by demanding an outright ban of the Communist party. On the other hand, Joaquín López Montes, the Ortodoxo delegate to the Supreme Electoral Tribunal, explained that seizing *Hoy*'s offices without compensation contravened Cuba's constitution. Then, abandoning his legal emphasis for a moment, he declared, "Closing a newspaper means closing an idea and we cannot fully develop our democracy without allowing opposing views."[141] Beto Saumell and Luis Orlando Rodríguez concurred, with the latter claiming Ortodoxos were, above all, "militants of democracy."[142] By 6:00 p.m., time was running short as Chibás would soon have to catch his flight. In his closing appeal, Chibás referred to a *New York Times* editorial that argued that banning Communism in the United States would betray the principles of freedom espoused by its Founding Fathers. When the vote was taken, a majority supported his position. He thus boarded the plane with an air of contentment.

As Chibás was whisked northward, a *Bohemia* reporter conducted an unconventional interview with Diego Vicente Tejera, the quintessentially quotable Auténtico party boss of Matanzas, and his lieutenant Sergio Megías. Having been granted permission to sit in the back of Tejera's Cadillac and discuss politics with the two bigwigs, the journalist was treated to numerous intriguing snippets. Regarding the 1952 presidential race, Tejera averred that the only Auténtico candidate capable of being elected "without difficulty" was the ostensibly retired Pepe San Martín.[143] If Prío chose someone else, which was likely, he stated, the party would merely "utilize certain procedures" to ensure victory.[144] Asked what he meant by this phrase, Tejera frankly replied, "It's foolish to think we will hand over power the way Batista did in 1944."

"And what about the popular will?" inquired his interlocutor.

"What popular will?" responded Tejera with obvious contempt. Motioning to the sidewalk, he said, "Do you think we will permit that man, for example, who is waiting for the bus to decide our future? Don't even think about it!" In this vein, he confirmed that "life in Cuba is becoming increasingly difficult. For me, the voter who seeks to resolve his personal problems on election day is more valuable than the one depositing a ballot influenced by hysteria on the radio." Tejera concluded that "we will follow the lead of Mexico, where the government party always wins even as it takes some work to obtain votes from the opposition."[145]

IN NORTH AMERICA

Eddy's doctors had prescribed a vacation abroad with the idea that he would avoid the strains of Cuban politics. However, during the course of his journey, Chibás was never far removed from the island's hustle and bustle. For one thing, he remained informed through constant telephone contact with Conchita Fernández. During one call in late September, she told him that MSR gangsters had murdered Tulio Paniagua Recalt—a treasury ministry official and confidant of Miguelito Suárez Fernández.[146] He subsequently denounced the killing during a wide-ranging press conference. As part of his talk, Chibás invited the popular Communist radio commentator Salvador García Agüero to join the Ortodoxos and promised to nationalize the Cuban Electric Company and Cuban Telephone Company if elected president. Chibás was also more than happy to discuss politics with reporters from New York's Spanish-language daily, *La Prensa*. For every bit of tourism he indulged in, including visits to the Empire State Building observatory and the Bronx Zoo, there were politically oriented excursions to places like the United Nations or NBC studios in Rockefeller Center, where Chibás recorded a message for his compatriots. Even his modest room in the Hotel Edison near Times Square was no sanctuary. Once Cuban expatriates learned of his whereabouts, he was besieged by would-be callers. On October 10, Chibás addressed the Cuban Athenaeum of New York and lambasted the Prío administration before a packed house. Further, Chibás eagerly contributed to a *Bohemia* survey regarding the views of Cuban politicians on the second anniversary of Prío's inauguration. Swollen with ire over Decree 2273 and convinced that Prío had dishonorably exploited his infirmity, Eddy was decidedly ungenerous in his assessment. He affirmed that Prío's government "could not have been more negative for the republic."[147] The man who usually exalted his country and told reporters he preferred the Caribbean vista of his bedroom window to the panorama from New York's tallest building then cast Cuba as a land of gangsters, nepotism, rural misery, urban decay, red-baiting hysteria, and untrammeled venality. Further, Chibás mocked the president's long-awaited cabinet reshuffle. He observed that the "prelude" to these changes, which included replacement of the widely disliked Tony Varona as prime minister, were the gag decree and "hypocritical attacks" against the press.[148] Fellow Ortodoxo Jorge Mañach was asked to comment as well, and he furnished a more nuanced analysis. Among other things, he praised Prío for wriggling free of the men who made him president—namely Grau, Guillermo Alonso Pujol, and José Manuel Alemán. In addition, Mañach lauded him for dismissing the crooked army chief Genovevo Pérez Dámera and purging the education ministry of thieves. The National Bank, Tribunal of Guarantees, and new University of Oriente were also tangible achievements. Mañach, whom Chibás had designated as his future culture minister, qualified these positives by confirming that many of Cuba's "great necessities" remained unsatisfied and lamenting the "tone" of its political life.[149]

Despite Eddy's frenetic schedule and inability to abstain, even fleetingly, from Cuban politics, his condition swiftly improved. When Chibás left Cuba, he weighed a mere 119 pounds. By the first week of October, he had reached 143 and seemed finally to fill his clothing. Chibás had planned to return on October 14 but extended his stay so he could pass through Washington, DC, where he had lived with his father in 1932, and Tampa, home to a substantial émigré community. In the latter city, Chibás paid homage to an elderly matriarch who possessed two quasi-sacred artifacts. These were a gold ring bestowed by José Martí and a revolver that had belonged to Máximo Gómez, the commander-in-chief of Cuba's liberation army. The woman was so moved by Chibás that she offered to make a present of them, but he demurred, requesting only to borrow the ring. Thereafter, he told a gathering of more than five thousand people in the local baseball stadium that he would keep it if he continued to pursue the work of Martí. "But if I frustrate the longings of my people," he said, "if I am unfaithful to revolutionary ideals, please señora do not send Martí's ring, send instead Gómez's revolver so I may castigate the brain that has betrayed my heart."[150] As in Cuba, the multitude fervidly hugged and touched him as he exited—many with tears welling up in their eyes.

OPEN DOORS

Chibás arrived in Havana on October 28, allowing him sufficient time to prepare for his Sunday radio broadcast the next day. After a year in which he had rejected a deal with the Liberals and shunted aside Nicolás Castellanos, Eddy attempted to present a more inclusive message. He declared that

> The Cuban People's Party is not a closed sect that cultivates hate, vengeance and grudges but rather a party of open doors. No decent, honorable and honest Cubans—be they Liberal, Democrat or Auténtico—will find among us a single voice of censure. This is a place for those who aspire to consolidate the republic and to eradicate crime, thievery and vice.[151]

Later on in his speech, Chibás took this idea a measured step further, announcing that

> The Ortodoxos do not discriminate against anyone willing to serve the nation and lose their life for it if necessary, even if they have previously committed political errors involving tactics or strategy. Proof of this can be found within our ranks, where those who once marched under different banners and who, on occasion, were our bitterest opponents now work together . . . The only ones

who have no place in the Cuban People's Party are those who have mocked the people's trust, unseemly politicians, thieves of all epochs and people who only pretend to believe in democracy.[152]

After the show, Chibás headlined a rally in Parque Central where he addressed masses of broom-wielding supporters. He reiterated that Ortodoxos welcomed all Cubans with clean hands and concluded by reprising a version of the ritual he had debuted in Tampa. In a deliberate swipe at the last three Cuban presidents, Chibás swore before the statue of José Martí that after being elected in 1952 and serving his term, he would possess no more gold than the ring he had been entrusted with in Florida.

On November 9, Chibás arrived at the house of Roberto Agramonte—where he presided over his first Ortodoxo meeting since returning. The agenda was particularly important as Pelayo Cuervo Navarro, José Manuel Gutiérrez, Agustín Cruz, Federico Fernández Casas, and Carlos Márquez Sterling had recently asked to join the party. Eddy's rhetoric had almost certainly been a factor in their decision, and he argued strenuously for their acceptance. He related that other politicians had expressed a willingness to sign up as well, suggesting the party's softer tone could broaden its appeal.[153] First, however, some men who had once been considered traitors would have to be readmitted into the fold. Chibás himself had feuded acrimoniously in the past with Cuervo Navarro, Gutiérrez, and Fernández Casas but now claimed he was beyond grudges or pettiness. He also pointed out that none of the five applicants had stained their reputations with blood or stolen money. Lastly, Chibás sold the advantages of having three Ortodoxo senators rather than one. Above all, he emphasized that "we just affirmed that (our) doors are wide open to Cubans of goodwill so how can we reject them?"[154] The most obvious reason to do so was that each had a fondness for pacts but so did the party's vice president, Millo Ochoa. In the end, this did not prove to be an obstacle. José Chelala Aguilera proposed they sign a declaration recognizing the independent line but was waved away. Several expressed reservations about Fernández Casas, whom they considered ethically suspect, but the vast majority agreed with Chibás, and the final vote was unanimous. In fact, the combination of Eddy's restored health and the prospect of adding five political big shots inspired a feeling of giddiness among the attendees, one of whom blurted out that "we ought to win the presidency because we are going to save everyone!"[155]

Similar emotions bubbled over after Raúl Gutiérrez conducted his latest opinion poll. The results, which fittingly arrived on Christmas Eve, were greeted with euphoria by Ortodoxos as they contained all manner of encouraging news. Asked to rate Carlos Prío's administration, only 17.97 percent of Cubans nationwide volunteered that it was "good." By contrast, 34.50 percent answered "bad," and 37.09 percent said "average."[156] Questioned which electoral block they preferred in general terms, an astounding 58.63 percent chose the opposition against 31.40 for the government. In part, this reflected disillusion among Auténticos, 36.70 percent of whom were willing to vote against their party. Regarding those who planned to run against the government in 1952, Chibás was easily the most popular contender—more than nineteen points ahead of Fulgencio Batista.[157] Further, Chibás retained the crossover appeal that proved decisive in his election to the senate. For example, 25.34 percent of Auténticos backed him, as did 24.24 percent of Democrats, 30.72 percent of Republicans, and 25.52 percent of Liberals.

Chapter Nine

"Time Will Prove Me Right Once Again"

The period between December 24 and January 6 was traditionally a dead spell in Cuba. Havana's middle class temporarily drifted toward seasonal culinary delights or the circus, with its elephants, dwarves, lion tamers, and alluring equestriennes performing in the Palacio de los Deportes. The *Bohemia* columnist Néstor Piñango opined that the season, ushered in with roasted pork on Christmas Eve and ending with the clank of toys received on the day of the Three Wise Men, was best withstood by "enjoying it—if possible—or just letting the days pass."[1] Chibás, a restless workaholic with few interests outside politics and no family of his own, showed little inclination for such customs. The *Carteles* columnist Virgilio Ferrer Gutiérrez, with blithe sarcasm and a dollop of truth, described a nation contentedly indulging in Christmastime delicacies ranging from cassava with sour garlic sauce and oven-cooked turkey to succulent *congri* and hazelnuts. In the midst of such bliss, among the gifts left under the bed by the Three Wise Men, next to the mended shoes, were the "frightful" declarations of Chibás that suddenly and unexpectedly jolted Cubans back into reality.[2]

These were based on the government's decision, on December 21, 1950, to secure a second public loan of 25 million pesos, coupled with the fact that the pro-government majority in the senate voted down a motion to investigate possible embezzlement of funds from the Sugar Workers' Retirement Fund. Moreover, the loan had been concluded while the Supreme Tribunal was still considering whether the law authorizing it was constitutional.[3] To Chibás, the strategy was obvious. Prío's new loan would be used to cover up peculation of the Sugar Workers' Retirement Fund just as the $200 million the administration borrowed in 1949 had mitigated the "deficit" left by Grau. Lastly, an article that appeared in the November 12, 1950, real estate section of the Sunday *New York Times* provided just the right kindling for Eddy's imagination. It reported that "Havana interests" had been purchasing choice Manhattan properties, the latest of these being the twenty-five-story Heckscher Building on the southwest corner of Fifth Avenue and Fifty-Seventh Street, whose value was estimated at $5 million. In a tantalizing twist, the buyer's identity was not revealed. The only certainty was that "Cuban plantation money" was involved.[4] On January 7, *Bohemia* brought this irresistible story to the attention of its readers, running a suggestive piece called "Cuban Millionaires Make Mysterious Investments in New York Properties."[5] Aside from reprinting the brief *New York Times* article, close-up photos of Manhattan skyscrapers now in Cuban hands were splashed across the magazine's pages. The journalist Baldomero Álvarez Ríos reported that Havana residents were already guessing which of the nation's parvenu politicians would turn out to be the new José Manuel Alemán. Chibás, of course, already had his own ideas.

> Who are these Cubans of the capital who are buying gigantic buildings, immense skyscrapers, whole blocks in the heart of New York, on a colossal scale that is only comparable to the acquisition of Rockefeller Center, and surpasses those of Henry Ford, Vanderbilt and J.P. Morgan? It is a mystery. Nevertheless, among the real estate agents of the Babel of Iron, who are shocked, it is insistently rumored that the principal axis of the new New York empire in valuable properties is none other than the President of the Cuban Republic, Carlos Prío Socarrás.[6]

After leveling this explosive charge, Chibás recounted that such "fabulous" acquisitions easily superseded those of Batista, Anselmo Alliegro, and José Manuel Alemán in Miami—the three of whom had previously set the gold standard for purchases of foreign real estate using stolen taxpayer funds. Chibás reminded his readers that the rightful recipients of this money were the nation's sugar workers. But if part of Prío's loan were meant to replenish the Sugar Workers' Retirement Fund, the real victims would be Cuban taxpayers. As such, Chibás asked, "Do the bankers of the government of cordiality believe the Cuban people are such idiots that they will later spend many years paying them the money they lent to Carlos Prío so he could buy skyscrapers in New York?"[7]

Curiously, Chibás did not revisit any of the above themes during his broadcast of January 14. Even more peculiar was the fact that Eddy's article was never discussed during his appearance on *Ante la Prensa* (Meet the Press), a televised political talk show hosted by CMQ. The panel of questioners included distinguished journalists such as Rafael Estenger, Ángel Pubillones, and Miguel de Marcos, whose bylines graced the political sections of Cuba's premier newspapers and magazines. Surely each had read Eddy's article accusing the president of buying New York skyscrapers with stolen cash. Perhaps they believed more serious issues, such as when and under what terms Cuban troops should participate in the Korean War, trumped their guest's foray into rumor and hearsay. In any event, Chibás benefited from the omission and his performance demonstrated why this "candidate of the street" was also favored by so many of the island's intellectuals. Eschewing the tone he had so recently employed, his answers were largely well considered and rational with only an occasional whiff of stridency—as when he referred to the Prío administration as "eminently putrid."[8] At one point, Miguel de Marcos was so impressed by a rapid and prudent response to a query regarding the "average provisional sugar price" that he wryly said Chibás was "becoming more of a statesman than a shrieking man."[9]

From an Auténtico perspective, few images could have been more harrowing than that of a statesmanlike Chibás transmitted on national television with excerpts of the show being disseminated in the press.[10] As the 1952 presidential elections loomed, Auténtico bigwigs considered Chibás far more dangerous than Batista in their quest to retain power.[11] At the same time, in confronting Eddy's multiple political personalities, they much preferred the irresponsible shouter and reckless accuser to the man who provided compelling answers to the island's problems.[12] Despite the injunction of Cuba's 1940 constitution that presidents serve as a "moderating power of national solidarity," Prío addressed his adversary personally over the national airwaves on January 17. Prío dismissed Eddy's charge that he had bought New York skyscrapers with the loan money as a "frightful invention." He also argued that Eddy's threat to repudiate the loan would sacrifice "the honor and credit of Cuba" on the altars of political advantage and personal resentment. Further, Prío claimed Chibás had waged a campaign of "incessant defamation and injury" against him since he became president. Nevertheless, his credentials as an anti-Machado revolutionary allowed him to value "public liberties" over the Ortodoxo chief's "excesses." Lastly, Prío summoned the "responsible organs" of the PPC to declare whether they supported their chief's threat to disavow the loan.[13]

The island was transfixed by this "gigantic" new polemic. Even commentators who covered non-political topics offered opinions. For example, the literary critic Juan J. Remos devoted his column of January 20 in *Diario de la Marina* to the issue, despite confessing that he found political polemics "too debased."[14] Nonetheless, he claimed the need to weigh in because Eddy's accusation represented an attack on the nation itself. At the same time, Remos, a longtime associate of Batista, could hardly claim to be unbiased.[15] Certainly, objectivity was in short supply on all sides. A *Bohemia* reporter claimed Prío's "involuntary" pro-Chibás propaganda had provided Eddy with "the greatest resonance of his career." He also wondered dryly how "one more political paragraph" was such a threat to the republic in an era marked by a surfeit of scandals and robberies.[16] Francisco Ichaso allowed that Chibás had the potential to be Cuba's "Savonarola," but warned that he should "accentuate his feeling of responsibility, of not making false steps, of rigorously monitoring his words and deeds."[17]

After two days of unrelenting press coverage and behind-the-scenes maneuvering, the controversy reached a spectacular denouement over the weekend. On Saturday, January 20, Orlando Puente, the secretary of the presidency, appeared on Unión Radio Televisión wielding an affidavit from a "certain American businessman," signed in the presence of a New York notary. The document averred that, to the best of his knowledge, neither Carlos Prío nor any member of his family, nor any Cuban government employee nor anyone who represents them, was involved, directly or indirectly, in the purchase of Manhattan skyscrapers.[18] Then, in a tirade reminiscent of Eddy's most exaggerated moods, Puente claimed the Ortodoxo leader harbored a "monstrous aspiration . . . to sink all that exists in order to achieve power on the ruins of the fatherland."[19] Chibás, whose gambit of arming a scandal and drawing the nation's attention had already proved a fantastic success, responded immediately. Utilizing the radio slot of José Pardo Llada, he proclaimed that the government had launched "the most intense campaign of defamation ever realized in Cuba against any political leader." Moreover, his accusations in defense of the "impoverished masses" had so incensed government honchos that he now faced expulsion from the senate, the dissolution of his party, and, yet again, incarceration. Eddy, who reveled in the avalanche of attention, swore he would not be swayed by threats of any kind and that the party slogan of "Shame vs. Money" resonated now more than ever.[20]

Later that day, Luis Orlando Rodríguez appeared on the televised news show of Unión Radio. "What matters to the country," he began, "is not to know whether, through an American affidavit, Prío has or doesn't have buildings on Fifth Avenue in New York but to know whether it is true that he has them in general, whether in New York or in Havana." Then, addressing himself directly to the secretary of the presidency, he continued:

> Tell me it's not true, Dr. Puente, that the current president of the republic won't be the richest ex-leader once his term has finished; that no other man who has governed Cuba permitted his brothers to become millionaires to such an extent . . . I'm not going to show a New York affidavit but rather a televised photograph of a building that isn't on New York's Fifth Avenue but on Fifth Avenue in Havana. Show me, Dr. Puente, a new affidavit that proves that this monumental building costing 300 thousand pesos isn't the property of Francisco Prío Socarrás. The essential thing, what you aim to avoid, is the accusation that the Príos embezzle public money, not how, not where the stolen funds are invested; that the current administration enriches itself at the cost of the country and that there is a national conscience that repudiates, with disgust, this farce.[21]

In the same vein, a *Bohemia* editorial from January 28 stated that "the country has been living for some time in a period of bonanza and if the treasury runs into difficulties this is not due to a lowering of revenues—which have never been higher—but poor management of public funds."[22] Néstor Piñango asserted that Chibás may have been crazy once, but his attack on the loan demonstrated that he was now "perfectly well in the head." After all, his censure was directed at the most "momentous and scandalous" of the administration's shortcomings—namely, the borrowed millions. These were not being robbed, in his opinion, but neither were they benefiting the Cuban people in any tangible manner.[23]

Of course, Saturday's recriminations were a mere prelude. The following day, Tony Varona read a statement on behalf of pro-government legislators in both houses of Congress charging Chibás with attempting a "parliamentary golpe de Estado."[24] Varona's solemn performance was complemented by a frothy jeremiad courtesy of Antonio Prío. The president's brother, sensing the momentum tipping toward Chibás, railed against his foe's "diabolical genius" for wiggling out of "compromised situations."[25]

Normally, Chibás spent all day on Sundays preparing for his evening radio show. On some occasions, when additional rumination or research was required, Saturday was also devoted to this endeavor. This time, Chibás and various Ortodoxo higher-ups began deliberating on Thursday, January 18, in the residence of Roberto Agramonte. The assembly was delayed until 11:00 p.m. that evening as it awaited the arrival of Carlos Márquez Sterling, who was charged with formulating the Ortodoxo reply. Chibás opened the meeting by claiming "knowledge of a vast plan" hatched in "La Altura" by the president, Aureliano Sánchez Arango, and others.[26] Eddy believed his rivals' threefold objective involved destroying him as a presidential candidate, fomenting divisions in the Ortodoxo party, and forming alliances in the provinces so as to minimize the chances of PPC victories in senate races.

After Eddy's remarks, everyone read Márquez Sterling's memorandum. A debate soon ensued between those who approved of the text or advocated only minor changes and a group, consisting of Luis Orlando Rodríguez, Herminio Portell Vilá, Pelayo Cuervo Navarro, and Jorge Mañach, who felt thorough revisions were necessary. In particular, they objected to the personal tone employed by Márquez Sterling. For example, Rodríguez singled out a paragraph describing Prío as "having used all the resources of power" to help install his brothers Antonio and Francisco in high places and his desire to do the same for his sister Mireya in Oriente province—eventually preparing all three for positions in the Senate, a "fantastic" prospect that would be "a first in the history of nepotism." He argued that the Ortodoxo response should aspire to "great historical importance" and thus needed to remain on a more intellectual plane.[27] Mañach, taking a similar position, maintained that the final document should "express the party's political doctrine of order and constructive sentiment."[28]

The preponderance of intellectuals in Agramonte's house was a feather in the cap both of Chibás and the Ortodoxo party. More impressive still was the lengthy intraparty debate, permitted and encouraged by Chibás, during a time when his political future hung in the balance. The vituperative position paper of Márquez Sterling could easily have been written by Chibás himself and certainly embodied his pugnacious style. However, Chibás proved receptive to a moderate stance and a new committee, composed of Rodríguez, Mañach, Márquez Sterling, and Cuervo Navarro, was assigned to write the final draft. Perhaps most importantly, excerpts of this internal discussion were reproduced in *Bohemia* and *Carteles*—allowing the Cuban public a glimpse of the goings-on. Among these was a change of venue on Friday morning to Cuervo Navarro's home on Fifteenth Street in Vedado. There, he and his three partners began working on the final draft. At noon on Sunday, January 21, the Ortodoxos convened again at Agramonte's house to vote on the completed document, which was approved unanimously.

At 8:00 p.m., Chibás took to the airwaves. Speaking for the party rather than himself, Chibás affirmed that the Ortodoxos believed the loan had been "imposed on the nation without necessity" and had passed Congress on a narrow partisan basis. For this reason, the Cuban people, in accordance with international law, retained the future right to review and repudiate the loan if, in addition to being unnecessary, it had also been squandered or dishonestly managed.[29] For the moment, Chibás appeared to be the most statesmanlike figure in Cuba, bolstered by the full support of a party that had often proved unruly but now sensed, with good reason, that its leader's popularity would carry it to power in 1952. Guillermo Alonso Pujol noted that "Chibás has succeeded. No one would dare deny it."[30] Without a doubt, the eminently fickle Alonso Pujol had reasons for praising Chibás. Specifically, he was interested in aligning with whoever seemed likely to rule Cuba. He had thus assured José Manuel Gutiérrez of his willingness to "make viable an understanding between [Nicolás] Castellanos and Chibás."[31] At the same time, Eddy's waxing appeal could do nothing but strengthen his conviction that pacts, like the loan, were unnecessary and distasteful—an attitude perfectly summed up by the political cartoonist Antonio Prohías. In a sketch entitled "Insinuation," a smiling, cigar-chomping Alonso Pujol appears at the door of Eddy's home bearing a shoe-shine kit and says, "Listen Chibás, can I be of use in some way?" Rather than respond, Eddy turns his squinting, disgusted face to the side and prepares to plunge his finger down his throat.[32]

The Liberal boss Eduardo Suárez Rivas also continued to pursue an agreement. In public declarations, he proclaimed the Liberals' willingness to consider an "understanding" with the Ortodoxos, which would include support for Eddy's presidential candidacy. Rafael Guas Inclán affirmed that

Liberal senators had negotiated with Chibás regarding a possible alliance. Chibás, however, had merely advised them to change sides in order to run as Ortodoxos in the next election.[33] In any case, the newest overtures of Alonso Pujol and Suárez Rivas, if nothing else, were evidence of the PPC's growing power and surely must have bolstered Eddy's confidence.

Above all, Chibás basked in the supportive telegrams and letters that flowed toward his office from every part of the island. For instance, a missive from an Ortodoxo councilman of Central Chaparra in Oriente province conveyed the following greeting, most of which Eddy underlined with his trusty red pencil: "I want you to know that I'm with you unconditionally and it pleases me to inform you that the majority of the people are with you."[34] Another letter from Elida Mallea Sánchez of Central Adelaida in Camagüey province articulated the rage felt by many rural Cubans against the government loan. While listening to Chibás on the afternoon of January 20, she heard a knock on her door and upon opening it saw two poor guajiros, a father and son from the neighboring region of Santa Clara, who had arrived for the sugar harvest. Unfortunately, the harvest had not yet begun, so the men were without work and going from house to house asking for food in order to keep from starving. Mallea Sánchez relates that their faces were "pained and ashamed" and the scene filled her eyes with tears. Gravid with frustration, she wrote: "And the current government hopes to force unhappy fellow countrymen like these two to carry the heavy bundle of the debt which they will have to pay later." A few sentences later, exasperation yields to anger as she exclaims, "No, a thousand times no, Senator Chibás!"[35]

Despite the unsolicited advice of Alonso Pujol, who proclaimed, "If I were Carlos Prío, I would leave the controversy right here," the administration pressed its case one last time.[36] Hence, the director of the National Bank, a deputy of the Agricultural and Industrial Development Bank, the minister of finance, and the director of the National Development Council were drafted to defend the loan.[37] While this tactic was sensible, given the rectitude of these figures, all lacked charisma (which made for a boring spectacle) and none could quash the national uneasiness. Afterward, Carlos Prío appeared and boasted of "attempting to do an effective job in the economic field" and expressed a desire to "turn the page on this unfortunate chapter."[38]

Two evenings later, Chibás demonstrated once again why, despite periodic lapses into recklessness, he was a force to be reckoned with. Abandoning the caution he displayed the previous week, Chibás averred it was "logical" to believe Carlos Prío was somehow involved in the purchase of New York skyscrapers by unnamed Cubans. Why else, he asked, would their identity remain such a closely guarded secret? Eddy then reminded his listeners that six years before, when he was the first to accuse Batista, Anselmo Alliegro, and Jaime Mariné of buying properties in Miami and Venezuela, he was called a liar, but in time he was proved right. When, three years ago, he accused José Manuel Alemán of robbing public funds, he was called a calumniator, but in time he was proved right. In 1949, when he accused Carlos Prío of owning "La Chata" and "La Altura," two lavish country estates, he was denounced, but later proved right. In this instance, cried Chibás, "Time will once again prove me right! History will repeat itself!"[39] Chibás then invoked José Martí, who had been born on that day ninety-eight years earlier, and summoned the government to appoint a special senate commission that would investigate the personal finances and property holdings of himself and the president in order to see how each had acquired what they presently own. Hence, Chibás not only gave the Cuban people a compelling show, his discourse, laced as it was with a catchy mantra and straightforward challenge, easily surpassed the droning, technocratic rambling of Friday evening. A *Bohemia* reporter quipped, with good reason, that Chibás remained "the incorrigible man of Cuban politics."[40]

CAPORAL

Even as Cubans were engrossed by January's polemic, politics remained a distant second to baseball as the island's consuming passion.[41] Cuba's professional baseball season reached its zenith each February, and in 1951, the pennant race was particularly intense. The Almendares Scorpions, known as the "Blues" for their azure uniforms, and the Habana Lions, known as the "Reds" for their incarnadine duds, completed their schedules with identical records. This unprecedented result required an extra game between the two archrivals to decide the championship. First, however, the league had to alleviate suspicions that the tie had been fixed beforehand as a money-earning gambit. It therefore agreed to donate the proceeds of the game's ticket sales to the city's Casa de Maternidad y Beneficencia—a Catholic charitable organization that housed orphans and abandoned children.

The contest was scheduled for Monday afternoon, on February 19. By all accounts, this was a most unproductive workday. The famed sportswriter Eladio Secades acknowledged that "all the island" was anxious to know the result.[42] The Havana city council, which customarily met each Monday and Thursday, canceled its afternoon session so members could attend the game. A *Diario de la Marina* reporter noted that the incessant arguments between Auténtico and Ortodoxo town councillors, which mirrored those on the national stage, were fleetingly superseded by "baseball fanaticism."[43] He also stated that a majority of the councilmen, along with Mayor Nicolás Castellanos, were Almendares fans although none would confess their preferences publicly out of fear of upsetting supporters of other clubs.[44] In any event, the "Reds" eked out a win by a score of 4–3. Afterward, Habana's manager was overcome by tears and confessed that he had just experienced the most profound happiness of his long life dedicated to the sport. The team's fans enjoyed a less introspective brand of satisfaction, many of whom stormed the field waving red banners after their team's victory. An overly enthusiastic handful even tried to lower the blue flag of Almendares, which flew over the stadium in recognition of the club's championship the previous year, and raise the red Habana standard in its place. The next day, a cartoon by José Roseñada satirized the consequences of life without baseball. Entitled "Realities," the sketch depicted Liborio, Cuba's everyman, confronted by an unattractive woman whose black dress was adorned with the word "politics." Full of disgust, he exclaims, "The baseball season is finished; now I have to deal once again with this!"[45]

Despite playing second fiddle to the island's national pastime, Chibás managed to remain newsworthy. On Saturday, February 3, Chibás indulged in a rare bit of leisure, visiting "Buena Vista," the estate of his high school friend Miguel Ángel Quevedo. A number of other Chibás intimates were there as well, including Enrique de la Osa and his brother Tony, along with José Chelala Aguilera. At one point, Chibás was good-naturedly needled about not being able to roller-skate. Eddy claimed he could, only there were no roller skates that would allow him to demonstrate. With a smile, Chelala Aguilera walked to his car and produced a pair. Chibás promptly laced them up and commenced darting about with ease, delighting all those assembled. Fresh from this triumph, Chibás insisted on mounting Quevedo's horses. First, he climbed onto an Arabian steed and subsequently set his sights on an "indomitable" white stallion named Caporal.[46] Ignoring the advice of his host, he made the horse rear up on its hind legs. Shortly thereafter, Caporal dashed off at top speed and crashed into a tree. Chibás was hit in the face by a branch and knocked to the ground. Fortunately, he was not badly wounded. In fact, Chibás proceeded to eat lunch with an undiminished appetite and then bowled and played pool with his pals.[47]

The following evening, during his radio broadcast, Chibás thanked everyone who had expressed concern for his well-being. He then provided a fanciful account of the previous day's accident, claiming he had mounted a "wild horse" that had been unable to buck him despite thirty minutes of trying and finally resorted to "throwing itself against a tree trunk, breaking its head, while I lightly scraped my nose and face against a tree branch." Then, in a statement bordering on self-parody, he proclaimed, "I never fall from horses."[48] Regardless, the term "Caporal" became the newest condiment in a Cuban vocabulary always on the lookout for piquancy. The feisty steed himself graced the cover of *Bohemia*'s March 11 edition, evidence that Quevedo had an ampler sense of humor regarding his friend than Chibás had in relation to himself.

Of course, plenty of Cubans were dismayed by Eddy's shenanigans in "Buena Vista." A peasant mother of ten from Cruces in Las Villas province, whose common sense far outweighed her knowledge of syntax, wrote, "you must live in order to save us, the guajiros, who I can tell you are tired of suffering and as the only hope of my Cuba."[49] Xiomara Serra of Cascorro, a village in Camagüey province, reminded Eddy that he had recently been operated on and urged him to take better care of his health.[50] These expressions of concern, sprinkled as they were among Eddy's mail in the weeks after he became an unwitting national punch line, were likely a source of comfort. This was especially so given that many were from humble Cubans, the apple of Eddy's eye and quintessential pueblo in the Partido del Pueblo Cubano. Learning they were worried rather than disappointed was surely a relief.

Far more than mere solace was offered by a letter of February 5 from Daniel Cortina of La Grifa, a hamlet on the outskirts of Guane in Pinar del Río province.[51] Cortina recently had the good fortune of purchasing ten winning lottery tickets, each of which was now worth 1,000 pesos. He enclosed five along with the letter so that "I will have the satisfaction of contributing to the great PPC with something more than my physical, mental and emotional energies."[52] While reading the missive, Chibás underlined most of this sentence, presumably with enormous satisfaction. To put this donation in perspective, the average salary in Cuba was $378 in 1957.[53] By all appearances, Cortina, who handwrote the letter on a sheet of notebook paper, was very much an ordinary Cuban of the provinces. For such a man, donating $5,000 to a political party, an amount equivalent to more than twelve years' salary, seems astounding—particularly as he expected no favors, jobs, or anything else in return. At the same time, Cortina's letter embodies a significant phenomenon of the era. That is, the degree of faith placed in Chibás by peasant and working-class devotees was unrivaled in Cuban politics. Supporters expressed a desire to do anything for the party, even die if need be. Many considered Chibás a family member. An even larger number believed he represented the nation's only chance for salvation and prayed to the saints or Virgen de la Caridad whenever Eddy's health faltered. René Ayala Pomares of Santa Clara echoed the sentiment of these Chibás adherents when he declared:

> I joined the Partido del Pueblo Cubano for two reasons; first, because I have absolute faith that you will fulfill your promises, because you are among those who fought in the past for sincere ideals that, disgracefully, have still not been recognized by the politicians we have suffered through and whom we are still suffering through; and second for the tenacity, constancy and self-denial that you continually demonstrate before the people of Cuba, showing that nothing or no one is capable of making you renounce your resolutions.[54]

THE POLEMIC WITH MASFERRER

At noon on February 8, Roberto Agramonte received an anonymous telephone call, asking whether an Ortodoxo meeting would take place that evening as planned and specifically if Chibás would attend. Receiving no answer, the caller hung up. At 10:00 p.m. that night, Agramonte's servant, a young girl named Margarita Pérez Martín, was leaving after the day's work, and on her way out she spied a strange-looking package in the walkway covered by a page of dampened newsprint. Apparently, the rainy weather was the only thing that kept the ten sticks of dynamite contained inside from exploding and thereby destroying the library of Agramonte's house.[55] Chibás seized on the situation to underscore another Auténtico failure: namely, the inability to control violent action groups whose spectacular murders embarrassed the government and enraged the capital's middle class. During his Thursday spot on Unión Radio, Chibás attacked the administration's Anti-Gangster Law, claiming it only served to disarm law-abiding people. He concluded by saying that "the voice of dynamite will never be able to silence the voice of truth."[56] On his Sunday broadcast of February 11, Chibás blamed Rolando Masferrer. Eddy lacked evidence, but he rarely passed up an enticing target and Masferrer was an ideal foil. Also, Chibás almost certainly was stirred by *Bohemia*'s recent coverage of the Auténtico gangster.

The magazine described Havana's latest crime wave, featuring the signature murders, kidnappings, and tortures that the government had promised to end.[57] This had begun on January 10, when Antonio Bayer, editor of the political page for Masferrer's mouthpiece, *Tiempo en Cuba*, was killed in a hail of twenty-nine bullets. He and three coworkers had been drinking a few blocks from the paper's offices in the seedy neighborhood of Colón. Interior Minister Lomberto Díaz had recently designated the area a centerpiece of his anti-vice campaign. After all, he said, "We can't allow a place so central, that's a short distance from the presidential palace and where many decent families live to continue to be infested by prostitution and public scandal on a daily basis."[58] Policemen were now conspicuous on every street corner and the sordid figures that formerly prowled the area had all but disappeared. At the same time, the city's gangsters were clearly not intimidated, nor did they appear to show any fear of being apprehended. Rather than vacating the scene immediately, the man who shot Bayer approached his victim, who was lying on the floor, and pulled the trigger again at point-blank range. The three other gangsters accompanying him then paused to fire their weapons in the air before driving away in the car they had parked just outside. Enrique de la Osa noted that "for the thousandth time" the police arrived on time to pick up the wounded but too late to arrest the criminals.[59]

Bayer himself was a rather "turbulent" figure.[60] He had been affiliated with ARG until being expelled as a traitor and fleeing to Argentina, where he remained for a few months. Upon returning to Cuba, Bayer joined the rival MSR, offering inside knowledge of his old comrades in exchange for protection. Just before his murder, he had also spent a year in prison for possession of an illegal firearm. In any case, Bayer's death set in motion an unsavory series of events. The day after his murder, a tearful woman rushed into Havana's seventh precinct police station. In a voice thick with desperation, she shouted, "Masferrer has just kidnapped my husband and will surely kill him!"[61] Identifying herself as the wife of Humberto Huguet Domínguez, a docks worker and ARG member, she related that witnesses had seen Masferrer and four cronies force her husband into a car at gunpoint. Toward midnight that same evening, a young man, "with a singular air of suffering about him," entered Havana's Bureau of Investigations and asked to see Chief Sigfredo Díaz Biart.[62] This turned out to be none other than Humberto Huguet, who related that Masferrer had indeed abducted him. He had been brought to the Havana Forest, threatened with death unless he divulged the names of those who had murdered Bayer, and tortured. At one point, his assailants placed a noose around his neck and told him that if he didn't confess, he would be hung—a death that could easily be made to appear as suicide. Finally, having convinced themselves that Huguet knew nothing, they freed him on the condition that he not reveal any details of his ordeal. Otherwise, he would be killed, "like a dog."[63]

The following evening, a boy burst into the military barracks at Jaimanitas and blurted out, "Run, corporal, run! Near my house there's a group of men beating two captives and I heard one of them say that if they didn't talk, they were going to bury them."[64] The captain and some enlisted men quickly drove off in a pair of jeeps and approached the spot, where they observed various figures arguing in the darkness—one of whom carried a machine gun. Quietly, they encircled the suspects, whereupon the captain shouted at them not to move, that they were surrounded by the army. Immediately, they raised their hands and dropped their weapons, except for two men, one carrying a pick, the other a shovel, who fled. When the captain threatened to shoot, they turned around. Realizing they were no longer in danger, one of them, trembling, thanked him for saving their lives. In any case, the entire group was brought to the barracks for questioning. The two men who had been digging were Salvador Hernández Garriga and Luis Díaz Duque. According to the former, Masferrer and his group had appeared at their houses claiming to be police officers and forced them into his automobile. Later on, in their formal statement, the victims asserted that Masferrer pointed a gun at them and demanded to know who was responsible for Bayer's murder. Eventually, the car stopped in a secluded location. The two men were beaten for a while until Masferrer decided on a different tactic. They were given a pick and shovel and forced to dig their own graves.

Masferrer marveled that he had been surprised and captured by "a simple little corporal."⁶⁵ At the same time, he declared the above testimony to be "completely false."⁶⁶ He was also quick to point out that as a legislator he could not be detained or tried. However, an official reminded Masferrer that according to Article 127 of the constitution, parliamentary immunity did not apply in cases where suspects were caught in the act of committing a crime. Regardless, Masferrer was released at 4:00 a.m. that morning, while his henchmen and their two victims were sent to Castillo del Príncipe—the latter as suspects in the murder of Antonio Bayer. Later that week, Masferrer explained himself. He averred that Bayer was killed on orders from the ARG leader Jesús González Cartas. Bayer's published accounts of his "scandalous depredations," which appeared in Masferrer's newspaper, had enraged him. In revenge, he had rounded up a bunch of "common delinquents" to do his bidding.⁶⁷ These included Salvador Hernández and Luis Díaz, who feared further embarrassing accounts by Bayer could result in their expulsion from the unions they belonged to—where they served as gunmen for the Auténtico senator Eusebio Mujal, the Auténtico congressman Francisco Aguirre, and other unscrupulous figures of the so-called workers' movement. Further, Masferrer contended that the kidnappings of January 11 and January 12 were part of a plan, hatched in conjunction with the Bureau of Investigations and GRAS, to assist in the interrogation of Bayer's murderers. Their identities had already been revealed "privately" to him, and he claimed that psychologically, encouraging them to believe they were about to die was far more effective than physical violence.⁶⁸ In fact, this method had been yielding some very useful information when the Rural Guard interrupted him. Asked to respond to this version of events, González Cartas claimed his group sought only to advance working-class interests and "is the first to regret, combat and repudiate acts of bloodshed such as those which have recently happened in the capital."⁶⁹

Chibás accused Masferrer of planting the bomb under Agramonte's library exactly one month after he and his underlings had dominated the news. Confronting him would afford Chibás the opportunity to underscore Auténtico links with gangsters, hardly a new revelation, but one that rankled residents of the capital. Moreover, such a fight promised to further invigorate his party and attract new adherents. This strategy, assisted yet again by government missteps, succeeded beyond all expectations. First off, Masferrer responded by invoking the much-derided gag decree. Among those who immediately denounced this measure were Goar and Abel Mestre, owners of the radio station CMQ. To quell the initial uproar over Decree 2273, Prío had arranged a private compromise with the Mestre brothers shortly after it was issued. In exchange for dropping their campaign against the decree, the president promised it would never be implemented.⁷⁰ The fact that Masferrer had done so after consulting with the secretary of the presidency indicated the administration remained very nervous about Chibás. Thus, Communications Minister Sergio Megías assigned the first ten minutes of Eddy's broadcast to Masferrer so he could respond to the accusation.

On February 14, Chibás released a brief statement. He claimed the right of reply was the gravest of all recent Auténtico "provocations" against his party, including the bomb placed under Agramonte's library—which he now believed was planted on orders from the defense ministry. Chibás also pointed out that Ortodoxos never attempted to interfere with the administration's radio transmissions. Citing Articles 33 and 40 of Cuba's constitution,[71] which guaranteed individual freedom of speech and authorized resistance against government acts that abridged rights guaranteed by law, he declared Masferrer "will not speak under any circumstances during the Sunday radio hour of the Partido del Pueblo Cubano."[72] The following day, a "manifesto" by the Ortodoxo National Executive Committee was distributed to the press and printed by *Diario de la Marina* and *Bohemia*, among other publications. The text underlined the party's unequivocal support for Chibás and chastised Auténticos for "attaching themselves to the most irresponsible elements" in an attempt to silence Cuba's "only existing opposition."[73] The gag decree was thus portrayed not only as an attack on freedom of speech but also as a boon to gangsters. Adding to the commotion was a statement by Masferrer, who revealed the existence of a "diabolical plan" to murder Chibás and blame his death on the government. According to him, this situation would benefit the estranged Auténtico, Miguelito Suárez Fernández—who would assume leadership of the opposition. Masferrer thus bizarrely claimed he would convert himself into Eddy's bodyguard for the foreseeable future.[74] This did not mean, however, that his opinion of the Ortodoxo chief had improved. On the contrary, Masferrer referred to Chibás as a "libidinous satyr" and "old homosexual." Nor was his invective reserved exclusively for Chibás. For example, he charged that Manuel Bisbé "exchanged passing grades in his classes for the caresses of young girls in the faculty of philosophy."[75] Needless to say, such statements, some of which were issued during radio appearances, made a mockery of the government's intent to muzzle Chibás.

On February 16, an Ortodoxo plug for Eddy's Sunday broadcast called for an "imposing popular demonstration" in front of CMQ's headquarters on Twenty-Third Street and Avenue L in Vedado.[76] With tensions mounting and the public anticipating yet another extravagant row, Sergio Megías informed the press that he had approved the "pages" Masferrer was set to read over the airwaves. He observed that they would expend a paltry eight minutes, hardly worth all the fuss.[77] On the other hand, he affirmed the government would not tolerate "unauthorized street actions" that threatened to impede the proprietors of a radio station from fulfilling their legal obligation.[78] Lomberto Díaz added that a heavy police presence would be called upon to guarantee public order and prevent the owners of CMQ from being coerced or endangered. Police Chief Quirino Uría thus prohibited "masses of people" from forming near the station.[79] This rhetoric conveniently ignored the actual directors of CMQ, Goar and Abel Mestre. In an official press release, they reiterated their opposition to the right of reply from its inception as "unconstitutional" and "disturbing in many respects."[80] Meanwhile, a new advertisement by the Ortodoxos reproduced an excerpt from Article 40 of the constitution that read:

> Government laws or any order that regulates the exercise of the rights guaranteed by this constitution will be nullified if they diminish, restrict or adulterate them. Adequate resistance for the protection of these individual rights is legitimate.[81]

The ad invited Cubans to congregate in front of CMQ's offices at 6:00 p.m. in order to defend the constitution and block Masferrer from speaking during the party's broadcast. It also taunted Oscar Gans for his machadista past and warned the gag decree could provoke another August 7—the day in 1933 when Machado's reviled police chief, Antonio Ainciart, oversaw the massacre of eighteen people during an anti-government demonstration.[82]

On Sunday, February 18, the National Police and army cordoned off a five-block radius surrounding CMQ's studios beginning at 1:00 p.m. The show of force was such that a *Bohemia* reporter remarked that "to someone who didn't know what was going on, it would seem the city feared a foreign invasion or imminent social revolution."[83] One beleaguered man, who lived within the prohibited area and attempted to return home, was brusquely told to "go to the movies and stay there until 9 p.m.!"[84] Seemingly, only the deceased merited lenience, as a funeral procession was allowed to pass through—albeit after some discussion. Before setting out for CMQ, Chibás addressed his followers from the top of a news truck. He implored them to remain calm, come what may, and refrain from violence. "We are not gunmen," he said. "We are directing a movement of moral and political renewal."[85] At 7:15 p.m., in the dark winter evening, a vast throng headed by Chibás and his party's parliamentary contingent began moving southeast along Avenue L. As the demonstrators approached the main thoroughfare known as Línea, or Ninth Street, they found the intersection obstructed by a patrol car.[86] Once the crowd began to bypass the vehicle, its lights began flashing. Immediately, a group of sirens wailed as police cars rushed to block the next intersections. Soon thereafter, officers bearing machine guns, rifles, and pistols blocked the assemblage. Their commander, Rafael Casals, yelled, "Stop! Not one step further! Back! Back!"[87] Nonetheless, the multitude continued forward. In response, the policemen fired warning shots into the sky. Even so, the marchers kept going. The police then lowered their aim and fired once again, but this too had no effect. Finally, they targeted the mass of protesters. As people fell to the ground, wounded, many carried on, but others fled in the direction of a nearby park or the hospital on Thirteenth Street and Avenue L. The police, however, did not allow them to escape. Rather, they battered them with machine guns. The main group stopped and waited for instructions from Chibás and also assisted the wounded. One of these, a young Ortodoxo worker named José Otero Ben, had been shot in the eye.

Quirino Uría, the police chief, appeared in the midst of this grisly scene clad in civilian clothes and requested a meeting with Chibás. The two briefly conversed while bullets still flew in all directions and those who attempted to escape were manhandled. Uría calmly said he had been ordered not to permit the demonstration. Only Chibás and the Ortodoxo legislators could proceed to CMQ headquarters. Chibás shouted that the rally was supported by Cuba's constitution and the police should be protecting defenseless men and women rather than knocking them around. Uría offered to personally escort Chibás and his party's lawmakers to CMQ's studios if the Ortodoxo chief would tell the crowd to congregate outside the nearby López Serrano building and stay there. Chibás discussed this proposal with Millo Ochoa, Pelayo Cuervo Navarro, and José Pardo Llada. A few minutes later, he climbed onto the hood of a police car and advised his supporters to wait for him at his residence. Despite loud groans of disagreement, Eddy's supporters heeded his instructions. Among the thousands who had been assaulted or wounded were Pelayo Cuervo Navarro and the Ortodoxo congressman Manuel Dorta Duque—both of whom had been beaten with clubs. Another Ortodoxo congressman, Andrés Nazario Sargent, had been jabbed in the chest with a machine gun by the overzealous Rafael Casals. Carlos Márquez Sterling had been attacked by a group of vigilantes. Orlando Castro, director of the party's Youth Section, was roughed up by a particularly determined policeman who was called off only at the behest of Police Chief Uría himself. In addition, members of the press attempting to cover the demonstration were harassed and threatened. Reporters and photographers who ventured near CMQ's offices risked being "splashed" by soldiers manning water cannons.[88]

In a twist worthy of the island's soap operas, the Ortodoxos reached the radio station just as an Auténtico motorcade arrived bearing Rolando Masferrer, Tony Varona, Rubén de León, Sergio Megías, and other party stalwarts. Chibás chased after them but was detained by Millo Ochoa and Luis Orlando Rodríguez. Moments later, when the Ortodoxos entered the building, they encountered Lomberto Díaz. "Give my respect to the police," shouted Chibás, "who have followed their orders!"[89] As the Ortodoxos continued down the hallway, they passed studio 3, where Masferrer was preparing to broadcast. Chibás and Luis Orlando Rodríguez directed a final unflattering remark at him before entering studio 4. Pelayo Cuervo Navarro reminded

Chibás to compose himself, as he would address the nation shortly. While Chibás paced impatiently back and forth in the studio, Masferrer was on the air next door. The MSR chieftain undermined the government's case for the gag decree by inviting the audience to tune in to his 9:00 p.m. show that evening on RHC-Cadena Azul, in which he would give a "complete response, in his own language, to Senator Chibás."[90] As a *Bohemia* correspondent noted, "It was clear [Masferrer] had a radio space to utilize his 'right of reply.'"[91]

When Chibás was cleared to speak, he did so in a voice trembling with indignation.[92] He asserted that the police and army were not responsible for the bloodshed, as they merely followed orders. Those who were truly culpable before the Cuban public were President Prío, Defense Minister Rubén de León, Interior Minister Lomberto Díaz, and, of course, Oscar Gans. Chibás concluded that

> While the government protects the gangster Masferrer with a grand show of force in order to rob us of our radio time and the right to disseminate our thinking, a right guaranteed by the constitution . . . honest and decent citizens were not permitted to arrive here as they have done every Sunday evening for seven years. Neither Batista nor Grau restricted these rights despite the fact that we combated them tenaciously. Carlos Prío was the first to do this![93]

Chibás lacked the time or perhaps did not feel the need, given its obviousness, to mention what many residents of the capital were almost surely contemplating. Namely, these very police who were so miserably incompetent on January 10, who proved incapable of stopping gangsters from committing murder in broad daylight or making an arrest even though they were clearly nearby, seemed perfectly assured when faced with a group of unarmed citizens devoid of political connections. The next day, with the island's attention diverted by the championship match-up between Almendares and Habana, José Otero Ben died from his wounds. On Tuesday afternoon, February 20, an "uncountable" crowd of Ortodoxo leaders and supporters attended his burial. A *Bohemia* reporter described with unmistakable irony how the funeral procession passed along Twenty-Third Street, which had been so aggressively guarded two days earlier, on the way to the cemetery and how the event came off with nary a single "accident."[94] During the eulogy, Chibás praised the deceased and painted his party as a beacon of legality and coolheadedness. He observed that Otero Ben had fallen "defending the constitution" and promised Ortodoxos would remain loyal to his "magnificent example" by seeking redress in the courts because "we are not gangsters and are against criminality." Chibás added that "when we are in power, we will present your assassins before the tribunals of justice so they may be sentenced to prison. The constitution prohibits the death penalty and we respect it and the law." He concluded by saying, "José Otero Ben, to you as with the people of Cuba, we will bring justice."[95]

With this affair seemingly at an end, the government braced for the nation's wrath. Carlos Prío, who had opposed precisely this sort of brutality as a member of the 1930 Student Directorate, had seriously blundered. Further, the administration could expect no quarter from journalists given the disdain with which they had been treated by policemen. In an article published by *Prensa Libre*, the Republican senator Santiago Rey claimed, "President Prío didn't have a single friend at his side."[96] Sadly for Cuba's chief executive, this piece had been published before the mass beating had taken place or José Otero Ben had died. His situation had certainly taken a turn for the worse since then. Nonetheless, the Auténticos pleaded their case. Interior Minister Lomberto Díaz rejected the accusation, put forth by Roberto Agramonte, that he had ordered the police to fire on the crowd. Moreover, he claimed armed protesters had assaulted the police and injured some of them—although he failed to produce any wounded officers. Tony Varona opined that Chibás "declared an insurrection against the government and incited the people to attack it."[97] He also argued for more stringent measures that would allow the president to shut down any radio station, newspaper, or magazine whose behavior was deemed disrespectful. The columnist Nick Machado replied that "Varona is in love with press censorship. In Argentina, he would collaborate very well with Perón."[98] Ramón Vasconcelos, who had resigned his cabinet post over government attacks on free expression, signaled his dismay in the form of a parable. He said,

> I have just seen two contrasting scenes on television regarding the events of a few days ago. In one Rolando Masferrer appears smiling, conceited and self-satisfied after having had his way. He was accompanied by the ministers of defense, interior and communications along with the senate president and Senator Tejera. All of them seemed satisfied as if they had won a great battle in favor of democracy or Cuban brotherhood. In the other scene, an injured man appears in a bed, wounded and suffering from terrible pain. A doctor is trying to save him. At his side, their faces filled with indignation and sadness stand various Ortodoxo leaders who are worrying over the patient's fate. They are Chibás, Márquez Sterling [and] Agramonte. The first group descends jovially from the staircase of a radio station. The second visits a hospital room. All are Cubans but behold the moral chasm separating them! On one side are those who persecute their countrymen who have differing opinions and confront them with trigger happy police. The others, by contrast, defend the people's rights to express themselves freely.[99]

Ortodoxos rallied around their party's first martyr, collecting money in some instances to raise a monument to him. Within days of the funeral, an Ortodoxo from the town of Santo Domingo in Las Villas province declared that Otero Ben had died "at peace" as he never "sold or tried to make money from his ideal."[100] Others, while lamenting the "assault," were almost delirious at the prospective political advantages they would reap from the government's heavy-handedness. Ernesto Buch López, a lawyer from Santiago de Cuba, wrote to Chibás claiming the party would gain one hundred thousand extra votes because of the incident. Eddy, with presumable delight, underlined this phrase with his red pencil.[101] The administration's excesses in other areas, particularly its fervor for shaking down wealthy citizens, were also potentially as harmful. In this vein, Ramón Grau San Martín, who always reveled in pointing out Prío's mistakes, told an anecdote about a prosperous farmer in Camagüey province who had been forced to pay 10,000 pesos to corrupt treasury ministry inspectors. Furious, the man, who was not an Ortodoxo, told him, "I am voting for Chibás because things can't continue like this!"[102]

Chapter Ten

"I Am Going to Open My Briefcase"

In late February, Chibás was confronted by a potentially embarrassing situation. At that time, a group of campesinos appeared in Havana and claimed they were being exploited. This was fairly commonplace but these peasants also happened to be employees of a coffee plantation near Guantánamo, whose part owners were none other than the Chibás family. Eddy had inherited a one-sixth share of the property from his father, which meant the self-styled protector of Cuba's rural poor was apparently profiting from their misery. Curiously, these oppressed laborers did not direct their complaints to him, as Chibás had always urged on his radio show, but rather they spoke with reporters from the capital's major newspapers. This raised suspicions among Ortodoxos that the government had staged the entire affair. Regardless, Chibás sensed an occasion for a grand gesture. On February 24, Chibás announced he would donate his earnings from the plantation to found and maintain a free school for the farmers' children so they could "learn to read and defend their rights." He added, "May this example spread among the new rich of our politics."[1] That evening, he journeyed to Guantánamo, signed the divestment papers, and paid a visit to the plantation in question. Chibás and a retinue of Ortodoxo eminences, including Millo Ochoa, Leonardo Fernández Sánchez, and Beto Saumell, also used the trip to inaugurate party offices in the town. Although an impending scandal had been defused and even turned to an advantage, the fact that midsize Guantánamo, with more than sixty thousand inhabitants, was only now gaining a public headquarters proved Ortodoxos were still lagging in their attempts to build a national party apparatus.

THE AUTENTICO-LIBERAL PACT

For more than a year now, Eduardo Suárez Rivas had been seeking a home for the Liberals. Their traditional electoral partners, the Democrats, had long ago signed up with the government. Ever since, Suárez Rivas had spent much of his time flitting between Ortodoxo and Auténtico representatives. With presidential elections on the horizon, talks had intensified in recent weeks. On February 27, Chibás sent Suárez Rivas a missive that all but settled the issue. He pronounced himself unwilling to engage in further negotiations, underlined his commitment to independence, and, as he had done numerous times before, welcomed Liberals with clean records to join the party on an individual basis. Suárez Rivas was thus nudged toward the Auténticos and settled preliminary terms with Prime Minister Félix Lancís and Senate President Tony Varona. In exchange for Liberal support, he demanded three cabinet positions immediately along with nine senate seats, two to three provincial governments, and the vice presidency on the 1952 ticket.

Upon hearing these conditions, Auténtico bigwigs let out a collective gasp. Miguelito Suárez Fernández was the first to object, saying the agreement was "premature" and "imprudent."[2] He claimed the party would gain popularity with campesinos after Congress approved the Agricultural Development Bank. To everyone's alarm, Antonio Prío also argued against the understanding, asserting it was needless in light of guarantees by Suárez Fernández not to bolt the party. He also noted that "new directions" policies discouraging corruption meant there was less cash and other incentives to lure additional coalition partners. In fact, he observed that Democrats were already chafing because they had fewer goodies than promised. These opinions were refuted by a red-faced Diego Vicente Tejera, who responded in a voice taut with urgency and anger. He protested that

> I have heard . . . Miguel Suárez talk of revitalizing the party through its collateral sections, organizing the workers, the campesinos, the women (and) the youth; but this makes me laugh. It is true, for reasons we are not here to analyze that we can longer portray ourselves as great social reformers nor anything of the sort. No one believes in us any longer after having been in power for six years . . . Gentlemen, let's not pretend. We are among family and can tell the truth.[3]

In Tejera's view, the pact was about winning and all other considerations were secondary. "On the first of June in 1952," he concluded, "I don't want to find myself in limbo! I want the Auténticos to have won yet again."[4] Tensions rose further when Paco Prío denounced the pact, leading some to believe the president was less enthusiastic about it than they had imagined. This impression was swiftly and heatedly dismissed by Tony Varona. A visibly perturbed Félix Lancís wondered why, if there was no consensus, he and Varona had wasted their time. "This is ridiculous," he huffed, "and I'm too old for this!"[5] When news leaked out that the agreement was on hold, Eduardo Suárez Rivas fumed and publicly scuttled the bargain. This prompted Carlos Prío to send his presidential airplane for the Liberal leader so they could talk things over in "La Altura." After plying his guest with a sumptuous breakfast, Prío assured him a deal would go through "regardless of what happens" in the Auténtico executive committee.[6] At the same time, Prío advised Suárez Rivas to be flexible in his demands as he hoped to bring Grau and Castellanos into the fold before election time.

For his part, Chibás wasted no time condemning what he called a "pact of renegades."[7] This was the ultimate cynical combination, and Chibás delighted in identifying the hypocrisy of both parties. The Auténticos, as everyone knew, had incessantly vilified their Liberal opponents in the 1948 presidential campaign—equating their possible victory with a Machado-style restoration. Indulging in some brazenness of his own, Chibás scolded the Auténticos for belittling Ricardo Núñez Portuondo without recognizing his "undeniable personal prestige."[8] Chibás, after all, had leveled more devastating attacks against Núñez Portuondo and placed him closer to Machado than any other candidate. Relying on the short memories of his fellow Cubans, he advertised that Ortodoxos distinguished between Machado loyalists and regular Liberals who were "deceived and exploited" by the party hierarchy.[9] Chibás was more effective at highlighting the growing divide between Auténtico and Liberal chieftains and their rank-and-file supporters. "What," he asked, "will the thousands [of] Auténtico party members say after having been taught for the past 15 years to hate anything that smells Liberal?" In the same spirit, he inquired, "What will Liberal masses say about being used as a trampoline by the Auténticos so they can retain power for four more years?"[10] Eddy's intuition on this matter was corroborated by a survey of Auténticos published on March 18. Asked which electoral partner would prove most valuable to the party's prospects in 1952, only 8.05 percent chose the Liberals. By contrast, 59.73 thought reuniting with Grau would greatly enhance their chances.[11] Further, a poll of the general population was equally discouraging as 42.69 percent of respondents believed the Auténtico-Liberal pact would damage Cuba. Conversely, a mere 13.27 percent held that it would benefit the country.[12] Among Liberals, evidence of discontent was more anecdotal, but the signs were ominous. For instance, the Liberal congressman Radio Cremata complained the party had "been turned into a cash cow" and predicted the agreement would herald its demise.[13] The Liberals suffered a symbolic blow on March 18, when Emilio Núñez Blanco, the young nephew of Ricardo Núñez Portuondo, appeared on Eddy's show and announced he was joining the Ortodoxos.[14] Other less prominent Liberals expressed their disgust in personal letters to Chibás. One man, who was a sugar worker, wrote:

> The person writing to you is a born Liberal who will die a Liberal, one who is not for sale and cannot be bought for any price contrary to what the party leaders believe and I want them and the people of Cuba to know that honorable Liberals with a sense of shame still exist and these Liberals will know what to do with their votes, getting rid of this heap of assassins, thieves and traitors to the fatherland and replacing them on June 1, 1952 with the only man who can honorably rule the destiny of Cuba, Eduardo R. Chibás.[15]

To underscore how bizarre the Auténtico-Liberal arrangement really was, Chibás reproduced various statements from Carlos Prío and Eduardo Suárez Rivas regarding each other and their respective parties. For example, in April of 1948, Prío asserted that Liberal higher-ups had "enriched themselves by pillaging the Cuban people."[16] The following month he said that

> The Liberal party, which arrived at its climax with the tyranny of General Machado, was characterized by its subjugation to Yankee imperialism and by the utilization of foreign loans to construct public works; the negation of fundamental liberties; the destruction of labor unions; (and) muffling freedom of speech, the press and assembly.[17]

Meanwhile, in September of 1950, Suárez Rivas told a journalist that "Prío wants to avoid supervision of the treasury so he can use the people's money according to his whims." A month later, he affirmed that the government "lacks a moral basis, violates rights, ignores the law and knowingly contradicts the constitution."[18] Vitriolic as they were, the above statements lost all significance once Suárez Rivas sniffed the jamón. Without further ado, he was named agriculture minister while Ramón Zaydín displaced Democratic chief José Andreu in the island's commerce ministry. Even as many everyday Liberals fumed, the party's nabobs were ecstatic and effusively congratulated their leader. When Suárez Rivas broke the news of his meeting with Prío in "La Altura," a *Bohemia* reporter snidely noted that his audience behaved as if "their souls had been returned to their bodies" because "there was still an opportunity to snatch a slice of the budget even if they would be last in line."[19]

THE INDICTMENT OF GRAU

The pact between Auténticos and Liberals occupied the nation's attention only a short time before being eclipsed by something astonishing. On March 17, Judge Federico Justiniani announced the indictment of Ramón Grau San Martín as part of the Causa 82 proceedings. As Justiniani had promised, the burglary of his office nine and a half months earlier had not derailed or even substantially delayed the case. In November of 1950, he had charged Eduardo Sánchez Alfonso, the former director of Havana's customs house, with illegally transferring roughly 9.5 million pesos to the national treasury—where they were ultimately siphoned off under diverse guises. Unfortunately, Sánchez Alfonso fled the country with his booty and was beyond the reach of justice. Grau, on the other hand, defiantly remained in his Miramar mansion and had refused to run for public office as a way of avoiding prosecution. Judge Justiniani answered his regular protestations of innocence with a carefully researched brief, covering seventeen pages, offering Cubans extensive evidence to the contrary. Much space was devoted to Grau's scandalous enabling of José Manuel Alemán. Ultimately, this was the crux of unprecedented and by now well-publicized acts of impudence. These included a bacchanalia of thievery during the final ten days of Grau's term in which 20,765,872 pesos, or approximately 10 percent of the national budget, disappeared. Also documented was Alemán's habit of selling teaching positions in Cuba's public schools for up to 2,000 pesos and using the education ministry as his personal piggy bank even after he had been replaced. Judge Justiniani averred that Grau was "principally responsible" for this conduct given that he "could have and should have put a stop to these activities."[20]

This was the most spectacular story in Cuba, and journalists descended upon Grau's home to hear what he had to say. Mostly, they were treated to a series of zany explanations and thinly veiled barbs. Among other things, Grau declared he had been tried under Machado and now history was repeating itself because Liberals were once again part of the government.[21] Subsequently, he asserted that Cuba's polytechnic schools had been the "pride of the country" during his administration. He thus staunchly defended Alemán, insisting his erstwhile education minister had "left behind many beneficial things for the people."[22] Above all, Grau was incensed with Carlos Prío. His reference to the Liberals was a case in point. Another was his assertion that

> I am willing to demonstrate publicly how I acquired my properties. They are a product of my own hard work, in caring for my patients and through long nights of study. By the same token, I will demand on the radio, in the press and on the street that everyone does the same as I! Let them show how they entered into official positions without a centavo and later on, how they enjoy lots of money![23]

Grau had been especially enraged during his arraignment, when Judge Justiniani informed him that Prío's presidency showed signs of dishonesty as well. This was precisely why the trial promised to be so tricky. Any investigation into corruption during Grau's rule would shed light on Prío's foibles and implicate the Auténtico party as a whole. For this reason, the Grau stalwart Alberto Cruz lamented that "we will no longer be able to campaign based on the positive advantages achieved during our government."[24] The party's ultimate pragmatist, Diego Vicente Tejera, spoke more bluntly when asked for his opinion—volunteering that "there were only two ways out of this: resolving the matter by paying everyone off or letting things play out as they have. And here you see the consequences!"[25]

As the scandal broke on a Saturday, Chibás readied himself to pounce twenty-four hours later. During his broadcast, he commended Judge Justiniani for "writing an exemplary page in the annals of Cuba's judiciary" by revealing how "modest public employees or politicians" including Alemán, Alberto Inocente Álvarez, Carlos Prío, and Virgilio Pérez had "magically" become "opulent businessmen."[26] Claiming thievery of state funds was a "crime against the *patria*," he said, "delinquency in government circles should be punished like any other offense" and stipulated that "sleazy big shots should also go to prison!"[27] In this vein, he urged Judge Justiniani not to forget Fulgencio Batista, saying, "While he was in power, Batista robbed everything he could. If he didn't steal more it was only because he presided over a less prosperous era."[28] Eddy's rant against Cuba's overnight millionaires did not go unanswered, of course. At 8:30 p.m., Antonio Prío appeared on Unión Radio with a rebuttal. Employing all manner of colorful language, he styled Justiniani a "venal judge," a "prevaricator," a "zombie," and an "automaton in the hands of Chibás and Pelayo Cuervo."[29] For good measure, he tapped him as a Communist sympathizer. Antonio had every reason to smear Judge Justiniani, for he would likely figure in future Causa 82 indictments. As a preemptive defense, the president's younger brother asserted that he had never behaved incorrectly in the treasury ministry and as proof of his innocence vowed never to abandon the country or seek refuge in parliamentary immunity.[30]

Curiously, Antonio's tirade made no reference to Grau. The reason for this soon became apparent when a coterie of Auténticos and ex-Auténticos, including Félix Lancís, Miguelito Suárez Fernández, Tony Varona, Nicolás Castellanos, and César Casas, appeared at Grau's house in an impressive show of solidarity.[31] Also present was the ever-protean Guillermo Alonso Pujol along with Carlos Arazoza, a former education minister and acolyte of José Manuel Alemán. Even Luis Caíñas Milanés was on hand. The Auténtico congressman was a living testament to the evils of parliamentary immunity, having murdered a fellow Auténtico legislator in broad daylight three years earlier. Everyone appreciated the danger Causa 82 represented for their political futures and set all grudges aside. However, as Grau issued a new public statement, the decision to surround himself with embezzlers, black marketers, and a known murderer seemed dubious. This was especially true since Grau based his defense on alleged ethical deficiencies of Judge Justiniani and the Ortodoxos. Rather than offering evidence for his charges, he resorted to folksy aphorisms, noting that "[The Ortodoxos] speak constantly of morality and honor but the truth resembles the Spanish proverb that says, 'Tell me what you possess and I'll tell you what you lack.'"[32] He also employed old-fashioned name-calling, describing Pelayo Cuervo Navarro as "acromegalic" and "abnormal" while likening Chibás to a howling monkey.[33] Later that day, a *Bohemia* reporter visited Eddy at home to hear his reaction. Chibás was in a jovial mood and received him with alacrity. Rummaging through his collection of old press clippings, Chibás withdrew a *Carteles* article from July 16, 1939, in which Grau was quoted as saying:

> Cuba must do everything it can to change the prevailing mentality so that the public believes robbing the treasury is infinitely more dangerous than robbing a bank. We cannot continue with the same moral dissolution our country has suffered since it became independent, in which government employees, after occupying their posts for some time, become fabulously wealthy. Such overnight fortunes at the treasury's expense must be adequately sanctioned.[34]

Grau, of course, never acted upon his lofty oratory. To illustrate the abyss between word and deed, Chibás produced the transcript of a radio broadcast by Carlos Prío from May 30, 1950. He called this "the most forceful reply to the grand corruptor of Cuban politics."[35] At the time, Prío announced that

> When I took office, the treasury ministry was the scandal of Cuba. It took me more than a year to clean up the embarrassments there. I received a nation in debt so extreme that no supplier was willing to provide medicine to the sick, food for the imprisoned and cement or treenails for public works. I received a country divided by hatred in which men hunted each other with guns in the streets. Upon becoming president, I found 101 unfinished construction projects whose completion required 205 million pesos. The public works ministry owed suppliers and workers 20 million pesos, of which two million was for salaries. Everyone in Cuba knows that on October 10, 1948, there was no money in the register.[36]

Later that week, *Alerta* columnist Rafael Estenger added a new wrinkle to the polemic. Shunning crude or eye-catching phrases in favor of lawyerly logic, he advanced a highly provocative argument. He indicated that Grau was basically being tried for tolerating José Manuel Alemán's sleaze. However, according to the constitution, the prime minister bore responsibility for the government's "general politics" and ruled hand in hand with the president.[37] This seemed to imply that Grau's prime minister, none other than Carlos Prío, was also culpable for Alemán's offenses.

On March 25, Grau appeared as the weekly guest on *Ante la Prensa* and offered another outlandish performance. Asked why he stubbornly defended a man like José Manuel Alemán, who had been "totally repudiated" by the Cuban public, Grau responded that his former education minister was, in fact, a darling of the masses. As proof, he cited Alemán's election to the senate. He then mused rather wistfully that "[Alemán] was accused of so many things but people showed up to his funeral, they came to be there with him!"[38] Grau was wrong on both accounts but did not allow reality to stain his logic. Alemán obtained his senate seat because he was on a winning party slate in 1948, not due to personal popularity. Regarding his burial, it was modestly attended as befit a man known for depriving schoolchildren of their breakfasts. Grau offered equally unsatisfying answers to ensuing queries. When asked if Alemán had embezzled state funds, Grau stonewalled. As to how Alemán could have amassed so many properties without robbing the treasury, Grau changed the subject. Forced to contemplate the possibility of Alemán's dishonesty, Grau waxed allegorical, saying, "It's as if you allowed a friend to stay in your house and he kidnapped your child. I wouldn't be responsible because I didn't put him there to kidnap. In this case, it's the same thing: I didn't put Alemán in the education ministry to enrich himself, I put him there to work."[39] Grau was no more forthcoming about other aspects of his administration. For example, questioned about gangsters, he rambled about how "many of them, although they behaved badly, were not bad people," and denied his administration maintained links with triggermen or allowed them to act with impunity.[40]

Despite this embarrassing spectacle, the Auténticos had no choice but to back him. The next evening, the party's executive committee praised Grau and rebuked Judge Justiniani in a public statement. In a similar gesture, Eusebio Mujal, chief of the Auténtico-controlled Cuban Workers Confederation, affirmed the "working classes" were behind Grau.[41] He also mimicked a favorite tactic of Chibás by declaiming the injustice of Grau's trial while known murderers such as Fulgencio Batista and "hundreds more" roamed free.[42] Eduardo Suárez Rivas conveniently forgot his long history of Grau-bashing by declaring Causa 82 "legally unjustified."[43] The Liberal chief, who wished to please his new coalition partners, also lamented that Cuba's courts were destroying "our great national leaders."[44] Responding to this barrage of official disparagement, fourteen Havana Instructional Court judges published an open letter in the press. They appealed for an end to "unjustified demagogic attacks against the prestige of the republic's courts" whose object was to "interfere with judicial independence."[45] Aside from its campaign against Judge Justiniani, the government availed itself once again of press censorship—this time against the Ortodoxo radio host Guido García Inclán. He had recently begun interviewing guests via telephone and broadcasting the conversations over the air. Unhappily, his choice of subjects, including Ramón Vasconcelos, Pelayo Cuervo Navarro, and Chibás, was not to the administration's liking, nor was their tendency to discuss Grau's impending trial and the Auténtico-Liberal pact. Thus, Communications Minister Sergio Megías all but banned the interviews by requiring their texts to be handed over for approval five days in advance. Conversely, Chibás was not obstructed in any way. He remarked that

> The uproar nurtured by the embezzlers against the courts of justice is even less justifiable given that the indictment handed down by the upright Judge Justiniani is notable for its moderation and prudence and shows extraordinary consideration to ex-President Grau. For example, he is not being held on bail but is free to enjoy his liberty. Nevertheless, followers of Grau, Prío, Batista and the Liberals who show support for embezzlers never think for a moment about the millions of senior citizens, women and children who have died in hospitals during the past ten years because thieves in the administrations of Batista and Grau robbed the money for medicines. The same thing is happening under Prío. These are the true victims; these are the real unhappy ones. These are the people defended by the Cuban People's Party, not the bandits, the impudent or the cynics who have become multi-millionaires and who have bought palaces and fincas with the money they have robbed and who now hypocritically pretend to be unhappy.[46]

On April 3, the administration's harassment of the judiciary sparked debate in Cuba's bar association. The topic was broached by Emilio Núñez Blanco, the recent Ortodoxo convert, who urged his peers to pass a motion backing Judge Justiniani against "inconsiderate attacks."[47] However, several members were reluctant to involve the organization in what they considered a partisan matter. Mario Lamar remarked that the bar association had remained mum when Chibás accused a judge of taking bribes after ruling in favor of the Cuban Electric Company. While not against a pronouncement, he argued the one submitted by Núñez Blanco should be shorn of its references to Judge Justiniani so as to be generic and apolitical. Another lawyer, named Ovidio Mañalich, disagreed, saying:

> What Justiniani has done is so exemplary that it has no parallel in the history of Latin America. The idea that the law should apply equally to the powerful as well as the weak will no longer be just another aspiration. This indictment means that Cuba can truly function as a complete and dynamic democracy. In defending Judge Justiniani, the judge who has tried for the first time in our hemisphere an ex-president, we are giving a great lesson to our citizens. This being the case, we can mention him by name and I don't have the slightest doubt the bar association will be fulfilling its duty by approving this motion.[48]

Humberto Sorí Marín added that the time was right to "define ourselves without half measures or euphemisms," especially while government figures such as Tony Varona, himself a lawyer, were assailing the judiciary so aggressively.[49] The naïve Núñez Blanco proved more pliable. He allowed bar association president Gastón Godoy to edit the document if he promised not to alter its fundamental spirit. In fact, this led to a heated row as Godoy rendered his motion entirely neutral after it was approved by majority vote. Even Núñez Blanco's signature phrase about justice applying equally to the powerful as well as the weak was removed because, explained Godoy, similar words appeared in the constitution. Sorí Marín tried to console his younger colleague by stoically saying, "This is the first time you have been disappointed here. I have suffered the same fate many times."[50]

This minor frustration would pale by comparison to what was in store. On April 27, Judge Justiniani received a complaint demanding that he recuse himself because a relative of his was among the defendants and contending this "intimate friendship" compromised judicial objectivity.[51] While this seemed a reasonable objection at first glance, its author was the infamous spoiler Froilán Núñez. The ninety-year-old veteran of Cuba's liberation army, who maintained close ties to Carlos Prío, had already gained the recusal of one Causa 82 judge on spurious grounds. A day later, Núñez added an additional charge—namely, that Judge Justiniani was an Ortodoxo "sympathizer" serving the interests of Pelayo Cuervo Navarro.[52] No one believed Núñez was acting alone, particularly as the Grau loyalist Carlos Estévez had been bragging between court sessions that he knew a way to save his political patron. Judge Justiniani responded that he was only distantly related to the man in question, Luis Arango Fumagalli, and claimed the two were not close. Even so, he had no recourse but to leave the case. An outraged Pelayo Cuervo Navarro observed that Núñez was a "front man" for the Prío family and a convicted criminal as well, having once murdered a man only to be pardoned by President Alfredo Zayas in the early 1920s.[53] Cuervo Navarro also derided Núñez's lawyer, Israel Algaze, who was on the public payroll as an agriculture ministry employee and always enthusiastic about serving his patrons. He concluded that "all these tricks, in total, are little more than a new plan, devised with the consent of the president of the republic, to hinder the implementation of justice in the most scandalous trial in our history as a republic."[54] Ramón Vasconcelos wrote that "every time there is an honest judge, the government looks for a stooge whom it can maneuver from behind the scenes by a minister of injustice."[55] For his part, Froilán Núñez said nothing to dispel the idea that he was a government pawn. In an interview with a *Bohemia* correspondent, he was asked to explain his decision to the Cuban public. Núñez replied:

> Let me be frank. When I saw that the presidents of the senate, the Cuban Workers Confederation, the Auténtico party and other responsible people signaled that Judge Justiniani sympathized with the party of Chibás and that he and other leaders of his party defended him, I felt that Judge Justiniani should not continue because he appeared partial.[56]

Cuba's cartoonists saw things rather differently. One sketched a beaming Grau driving a truck bearing a sign saying, "Froilán: Available for Rent."[57] Another drew a walking billboard that read, "You Don't Have to Go to Prison! Froilán: He Does All Types of Recusals for Modest Prices!"[58] Regardless of these jibes, there was rejoicing in government circles, but this was tempered by the Havana court's unanimous selection of Gilberto Mosquera as Justiniani's replacement. Known as an honorable man cut from the same cloth as his predecessor, Judge Mosquera was certainly no flunky.

Grau's lawyers were nonetheless optimistic that Judge Mosquera would prove more sympathetic. In short order, they submitted a brief requesting that the charges against their client be dismissed. As Grau was represented by José Miró Cardona and Carlos Menció, both of whom were among Cuba's leading attorneys, many who were familiar with the case anticipated a favorable verdict. Essentially, their argument was threefold. First, they invoked Article 145 of the constitution—which stated that presidents could only be judged by the Supreme Tribunal. Second, they asserted that Grau himself had not committed any crime. Lastly, they reasoned he was innocent of malversation since no public money had been under his personal control. On May 18, however, Judge Mosquera rejected their appeal. José Miró Cardona's logic had relied heavily on a Supreme Tribunal precedent from 1935, whereby a mayor and his treasurer were tried for fraud but only the latter was convicted. Judge Mosquera ruled this was irrelevant since it was based on a statute from 1870 rather than the current Code of Social Defense. The updated law cast a wider net of culpability, which Judge Mosquera explained to a *Bohemia* reporter in the following terms:

> The problem of profit is a question that should be very clear for a judge. From a popular point of view, profit suggests gaining material benefit from a deal regardless of whether the intent was good or bad, but for a judge, this concept has a wider meaning. If an individual, for example, steals a pair of glasses in order to make a gift to someone who really needs them, he's profiting from the interior satisfaction that comes from the act and even the good reputation he acquires for having done it. But it's a crime that should be punished even if people believe he was pursuing altruistic ends and not for his own private gain.[59]

Applying this to Grau, he allowed that the ex-president may not have personally robbed the treasury, but he certainly profited from Alemán's misbehavior. As for the contention that Grau was only subject to judgment by the Supreme Tribunal, Judge Mosquera noted this applied exclusively to sitting presidents.

No one relished this turn of events more than Pelayo Cuervo Navarro, who asked, "What will the government and Grau's defenders say about Judge Mosquera's decision now? Will they accuse him too of being an Ortodoxo and aspiring to a senate seat, the way Senate President Varona did, so irresponsibly (with Judge Justiniani)?"[60] The gravity of Grau's situation was beyond dispute, highlighted by a ruling stuffed with foreboding references. Point by point, Judge Mosquera demolished Grau's pleas, legal and otherwise, that he had stood aloof from the sordidness of his administration. He noted that Grau had reappointed Alemán as education minister and subsequently as minister without portfolio despite the "public scandal" provoked by his "well known" thefts.[61] Judge Mosquera also observed that Grau continued to support his favorite minister in the face of day-by-day press accounts, both in Cuba and abroad, of his "real estate acquisitions worth millions of pesos."[62] In addition, he affirmed that Alemán had utilized a portion of his ill-gotten gains to form BAGA along with the ex-president's "close relative," Francisco Grau Alsina.[63] Judge Mosquera was all but saying Grau should reserve a cell in Havana's Castillo del Príncipe. Given his expansive view of culpability, many high-level Auténticos, including all three Prío brothers, could easily find themselves behind bars. The administration thus did not tarry in seeking to remove Judge Mosquera from the case. By early June, he became the third consecutive judge to be recused on flimsy pretenses.

THE LATEST POLL

On May 17, Raúl Gutiérrez appeared as a guest on Guido García Inclán's radio show. Cuba's public survey guru had recently conducted a fresh round of interviews, and the results would appear in *Bohemia* shortly. With elections now barely a year away, and given the accuracy of previous forecasts, his conclusions were anxiously awaited. Gutiérrez related that his poll was "absolutely national," with rural and urban Cubans in every province consulted.[64] Lastly, he cautioned that his work was not a "prophecy" but rather "a register of current opinion."[65]

Questioned about Carlos Prío's administration, 22.80 percent of Cubans replied that it was "good." This represented a nearly five-point improvement on the president's rating from December of 1950 but was still quite low. At the same time, 35.00 percent of Cubans answered "bad," which was half a percentage point worse than the previous poll. An additional 25.22 percent said it was "average." Another troubling sign was that a mere 40.44 percent of Auténticos were pleased with Prío. His popularity among the party's coalition partners was much lower, as only 22.92 percent of Democrats and 18.23 percent of Liberals viewed him positively.[66] Among the 60.22 percent of Cubans who considered Prío "bad" or "average," their four biggest complaints were the poor economic situation, a lack of construction projects, corruption, and abuses against workers. In many ways, these problems were interrelated. Construction projects served as a prime source of jobs, but resentment simmered because they were not distributed evenly throughout Cuba.[67] Moreover, despite promises to improve the lot of country dwellers, their misery sometimes played to the party's advantage. After all, desperate peasants were more likely to sell their votes. Another sore point was the black market's resurgence, which raised the cost of living. The island's myriad sugar workers were also angered by the 1 percent tax levied on their salaries to fund the Cuban Workers Confederation, especially as that money was funding the government-controlled union's violent acts against rival outfits. Naturally, some of that cash was bound to disappear into venal pockets as well.

Not only were Cubans broadly dissatisfied with Prío, they showed scant enthusiasm for his probable successors. Carlos Hevia and Tony Varona, who were the president's favorites, polled 2.59 percent and 2.20 percent, respectively. Miguelito Suárez Fernández tried to portray himself as a more pragmatic choice but was unloved outside his native Las Villas. Paradoxically, the most desirable Auténtico was not even seeking the nomination. This was Pepe San Martín, the acclaimed former public works minister, picked by 7.73 percent of Cuban voters. As in December of 1950, the most popular candidates were Chibás and Batista. The Ortodoxo leader remained ahead by a wide margin at 29.70 percent, but this was five points lower than his previous rating. Chibás, who had benefited from an outpouring of sympathy after his surgery, may well have slipped now that he was once again in rude good health. At the same time, Batista had climbed four points to 19.03 percent, but Chibás led in all six provinces and was preferred by members of every social class.[68] He was also more admired by Auténticos than Pepe San Martín or Miguelito Suárez Fernández. His lone weakness appeared to be among Cubans over fifty years old. Even in this category, he trailed Batista by less than three points. This disparity was remedied by his dominant showing among the nation's youth, as Cubans aged twenty to thirty opted for Chibás over Batista by more than nineteen points.[69]

The poll was relentlessly parsed by commentators and common citizens alike. "What can be guessed from this survey?" inquired Ramón Vasconcelos. "What we already know: that the government has lost the street definitively."[70] Rafael Estenger ventured that the Auténticos would need a "miracle" to win in 1952.[71] The columnist Manuel Alfonso of *El Crisol* observed that Chibás was "deeply rooted" among the Cuban electorate.[72] Those with close ties to the president, such as Antonio Prío, Félix Lancís, and Aureliano Sánchez Arango, argued that respondents who classified the administration as "average" were actually supporters. By this reckoning, 48 percent of Cubans were behind them. This curious logic was also adopted by Gustavo Herrero of *El País*, the pro-Liberal broadsheet that now toed the government line. Raúl Gutiérrez himself arrived at a very different conclusion, telling viewers of Unión Radio-Televisión, "If elections were held tomorrow, Chibás would be president with majorities in all six provinces."[73]

Unlike his younger brother or other close associates, Carlos Prío did not publicly mention the survey or its implications. Instead, he took to the radio on May 22 and reminded Cubans of his achievements in a wide-ranging speech. Prío was especially proud of his work with Congress, which enacted laws creating the National Bank and Agricultural and Industrial Development Bank. He bragged that the newly minted Tribunal of Accounts and State Bookkeeping Law would transform embezzlement from an unfortunate habit to a common crime. Prío also crowed about tax increases recently approved by the legislature that would guarantee solvent retirement funds and raise judicial salaries. In a bid to mollify rural Cubans, Prío alluded to a special 4 percent levy on utility companies that would help purchase land for poor peasants. Further, he promised 5 million pesos for agricultural reform and 1 million pesos for a children's hospital. Of course, Chibás was unwilling to cede the momentum, and during his Sunday show he denigrated or denied each of these accomplishments with characteristic flair. He said Prío deserved no applause for the National Bank, Tribunal of Accounts, or State Bookkeeping Law as these were merely "demands of the constitution."[74] Chibás added that the latter two were actually Ortodoxo initiatives since Manuel Dorta Duque had introduced the bill to establish the Tribunal of Accounts, while Pelayo Cuervo Navarro designed the State Bookkeeping Law. These measures would not have been approved without the government's consent, but even this was turned against Prío, for Chibás claimed they would take effect too late to ensure honesty in the current administration. Thus, Prío seemed to be telling future presidents, "Do what I say, not what I do."[75] Regarding the other Auténtico policies, Chibás found them wanting or insufficient and concluded each criticism with pledges to do better. For instance, he noted that Ortodoxo lawmakers had attempted to amend the tax bill so retirees and veterans of Cuba's independence war would receive back pay on their pensions. Although rejected by the pro-government majority, Chibás said, "We will do this when we are in power."[76] In the same fashion, he observed that Ortodoxos tried to raise judicial salaries by half, but the administration held the line at 20 percent. Once again, he repeated, "We will do this when we are in power."[77] As for the 4 percent duty on public utilities, Chibás claimed the government would use the proceeds to subsidize electoral campaigns rather than acquiring lots for campesinos. "We will annul such tricks," confirmed Chibás, "when we are in power."[78] He also calculated that the 5 million pesos earmarked for agricultural reform amounted to just one percent of total government revenue—a proportion he deemed "ridiculous" and "humiliating."[79] By comparison, he pointed out that waiters never received less than 10 percent in tips. Finally, Chibás boasted that Prío could lay the first stone for a Havana clinic but the Ortodoxos would supervise its completion and also that of five other hospitals—one in each province.

THE FINAL LOUD KNOCK

In late May, the *Prensa Libre* correspondent Mario Lliraldi conducted an interview with José Pardo Llada. During their conversation, he inquired why Chibás never attacked Aureliano Sánchez Arango. As a close advisor of Carlos Prío and potential presidential rival, Sánchez Arango certainly seemed a ripe target. "Is there mutual respect?" asked the inquisitive reporter. "Fear, perhaps?"

"No, it's not fear," responded Pardo Llada, "because Chibás is not afraid of anyone."

"Well then?"

"Chibás will attack Aureliano when it's convenient for him, not when it's convenient for Aureliano."[80]

For the time being, there was no need to pick a fight. Sánchez Arango had a meager popularity rating of 2.01 percent, and Chibás felt he would not be chosen as the Auténtico standard-bearer. Further, the education minister was currently embroiled in a dispute with Batista's ex-police chief, Manuel Benítez. At a Causa 82 hearing, Benítez had accused him of spending 50,000 pesos in public funds to bribe Judge Justiniani against Grau. Benítez could not prove these charges, and a *Bohemia* correspondent called them "an example of irresponsibility."[81] Even so, there was plenty of anger against Sánchez Arango in some quarters—particularly among the thousands of teachers and education ministry employees he had fired. Many of those who had been displaced possessed links to José Manuel Alemán and were unqualified for their jobs. However, there were also grumbles about schools being shut down for political reasons. For example, in April of 1950 Sánchez Arango decided to close the highly regarded Holguín Normal School in Oriente province even though it covered its own expenses and cost the state nothing to operate. Similar schools in Guantánamo and Manzanillo met the same fate. In each instance, they were simply declared illegal. Regardless of whether their dismissals were justified, Cuba's vast pool of laid-off teachers and school inspectors eagerly believed the worst about Sánchez Arango. When the allegations of Benítez were reported, a group of ousted teachers from Camagüey wrote Chibás and urged him to take up the issue on his radio show. Above all, they were anxious to see the education ministry "dictator" ridiculed.[82] Chibás declined because he considered Benítez untrustworthy. At any rate, a full-blown polemic developed between Sánchez Arango and Batista's old chum.[83]

On June 1, Sánchez Arango interrupted this quarrel to launch a contumely against Chibás. The Ortodoxo leader was unruffled, but a spat ensued among his followers. This was because Jorge Mañach saw fit to praise Sánchez Arango in his *Diario de la Marina* column two days later. Mañach had not been impressed by Sánchez Arango's derogatory words but rather his sponsorship, through the education ministry, of diverse cultural events all over Cuba. Recently, the oratorio *Joan of Arc at the Stake* had been presented in Havana's oldest public square.[84] This piece of highbrow entertainment had so tickled the Harvard alum that he rhapsodized unreservedly in favor of its patron. He claimed Sánchez Arango had achieved nothing less than the "fertilization of the public spirit" and concluded that "we will never be able to thank him enough."[85] Naturally, these breathless compliments did not sit well with many Ortodoxos. Raimundo Lazo encapsulated their views in an *Alerta* article entitled "Dr. Mañach Exaggerates." Lazo, a University of Havana literature professor, observed that *Joan of Arc at the Stake* had beguiled its primarily middle-class audience, but few poorer citizens showed their faces. This was not a question of taste but learning. "How can we speak seriously of spreading culture to the masses," thundered Lazo, "when the government has spent three years ignoring the illiteracy and physical and moral misery of hundreds of thousands of children and adults?"[86] At any rate, this disagreement soon petered out because Mañach was poised to visit Paris in his capacity as a UNESCO representative.

Having caused no damage to Chibás and inciting only mild ripples among his followers, the government tapped Eduardo Suárez Rivas for its next round of broadsides. On June 17, the Liberal chief appeared on Unión Radio and accused Chibás of overcharging for the coffee produced at his family-owned plantation in Oriente province. Cubans had been up in arms lately over the rising cost of their favorite drink, and Suárez Rivas attempted to direct their anger at Chibás. Eddy not only defended himself but retaliated in spectacular fashion. He reminded listeners that all revenues from his share in the plantation paid for the construction and maintenance of an area school. Next, Chibás trotted out Emilio Núñez Blanco. The young ex-Liberal, who was now a zealous Ortodoxo, shared a "regretful episode" with his former colleagues and the Cuban people.[87] Specifically, he revealed that shortly before the 1948 elections, Guillermo Alonso Pujol had suggested an agreement between the Republicans and Liberal-Democratic coalition. Had the fine points been ironed out, this effectively would have assured Ricardo Núñez Portuondo of the presidency. Among those entrusted with negotiating the deal was Eduardo Suárez Rivas, but instead of doing everything possible to ensure its realization, he had notified José Manuel Alemán and urged him to scuttle it. To corroborate this charge, Núñez Blanco read an incriminating letter from Suárez Rivas over the air, which had been found among Alemán's papers after his death.[88] In a voice seething with indignation Núñez Blanco summed up the situation thusly:

> A traitor to Ricardo Núñez Portuondo; a traitor to the opposition; Eduardo Suárez Rivas now wants to win points with the government by attacking Eduardo Chibás but fortunately the people know him well and say, Suárez

> Rivas, enough already with your claims that there is no funny business going on with the price of coffee because you are at the center of it; you are the hero of *café con leche*, capable of making money from the drink of the poor, of the unhappy, of the majority of the Cuban people.[89]

This explosive revelation completely hijacked a senate session, ostensibly devoted to budget issues, less than twenty-four hours later.[90] Suárez Rivas was so visibly incensed that Chibás had been advised to summon some Ortodoxo legislators for his own protection. The Liberal chief, however, resorted to rhetoric rather than fisticuffs, and in a long-winded speech he blamed Chibás for poisoning the political climate. Chibás retorted that the polemic began when Suárez Rivas slanderously accused him of being a coffee speculator. Most importantly, five hours of recrimination and debate could not erase the scandalous letter to José Manuel Alemán from the public mind. Not only was Suárez Rivas's credibility damaged, but another exodus from his party now seemed a distinct possibility. As Chibás exited the Capitolio, he was congratulated by the always-pliable Santiago Rey—who told him he had just behaved like a "true presidential aspirant."[91] The Republican senator was not merely being polite. His party was currently moribund after losing its place at the government table and being abandoned by Guillermo Alonso Pujol, who had formed a new outfit with Nicolás Castellanos. He was thus on the lookout for his next meal ticket. As Chibás gained momentum, such overtures were certain to become commonplace.

Meanwhile, the failure of Suárez Rivas meant a new government champion was required. The role was energetically reprised by Aureliano Sánchez Arango, who renewed his quarrel with Chibás in an epithet-laden broadcast on June 24. Apart from repeating the spurious charge that Chibás was a coffee speculator, he used all the old pejoratives and a few new ones too. By now, Eddy was accustomed to terms like "demagogue," "slanderer," and "false prophet" being bandied about. On the other hand, Chibás, who rented his Havana apartment and conspicuously lacked a weekend retreat in the countryside, had never before been painted as a "feudal lord."[92] This was politics leavened by an extraordinary degree of mutual loathing. Chibás shot back that Sánchez Arango had embezzled education ministry funds and invested them in Guatemalan real estate. Two days later, the pugnacious Sánchez Arango upped the ante by submitting libel charges against Chibás in the Urgency Court. Sánchez Arango supplemented this classic gambit with a novel twist. Knowing quite well that Chibás could no longer be dispatched in a government-friendly Urgency Court, Sánchez Arango hoped to sway public opinion by proposing a "tribunal of honor," which would investigate his supposed Guatemalan properties. Sánchez Arango boasted the tribunal could look anywhere between "the North Pole and Patagonia" for his riches.[93] Nonetheless, Chibás insisted his opponent was corrupt just as Sánchez Arango stubbornly stated that his adversary was an exploiter of peasants and a coffee speculator. Eddy's next sally was a *Bohemia* article, published on July 1, in which he noted that the education ministry had budgeted two credits of 175,000 pesos each for "very mysterious services."[94] He also claimed the 644,000 pesos earmarked for free school breakfasts was being raided because it reached "very few students."[95] Lastly, Chibás asserted that he possessed a "private document," signed by twenty-five Auténtico congressmen, confirming Sánchez Arango's dishonesty.[96] Sánchez Arango replied to these sketchy charges with some of his own, estimating rather lamely that Eddy's "black market operation" in coffee had netted 2,027 pesos and 50 centavos.[97] While not a negligible sum, this was hardly the stuff of scandal. Further, he could not prove Chibás had pocketed the cash or played any role in managing the plantation. Finally, the education minister challenged Chibás to a debate in Parque Central to settle their dispute once and for all.

Chibás refused this proposition, but his explanation left him open to derision. On one hand, he claimed Cubans would lynch Sánchez Arango once they found out about the government's shameless behavior. At the same time, he asserted that citizens attending the event were likely to be injured or killed by government thugs. He also chafed at the debate's rigid format, which would examine only two questions—namely, whether Sánchez Arango owned Guatemalan real estate, and if he had bought it with education ministry funds. Chibás suggested the senate or education ministry as preferable venues and demanded that a wider range of topics be allowed. Miguel de Marcos, for one, was thoroughly unimpressed. In a *Prensa Libre* column, he wrote that "after launching a false accusation, Chibás has avoided trying to prove it."[98] He also dismissed Eddy's "absurd pretexts" and mocked the notion of him trying to save Sánchez Arango from an angry mob using his "short arms."[99] De Marcos was obviously not well disposed toward Chibás, but he hardly qualified as a government hack. Francisco Ichaso criticized Chibás as well. Not everyone in the press lined up against him, however. Carlos Lechuga of *El Mundo* sympathetically counseled Eddy to adopt a more temperate and conciliatory persona. In addition, he warned Chibás that treating politics as a "captivating spectacle" damaged his reputation among "people who think."[100] Chibás gratefully thanked his "friend" Lechuga in a personal letter but defended his brand of politics.[101] For one thing, he pointed out that opinion polls had consistently validated his style and methods. Moreover, despite living one of the "most turbulent epochs" of his life and fighting "practically alone" against "bad faith, slander and conspiracy," he expressed optimism regarding his prospects.[102] Thus, he explained:

> What is certain—and it bears repeating—is that the presidential palace is waging a campaign to scare the fearful and innocent, trying to make them believe in the myth of a Chibás incapable of exercising power, whose promotion to

high office would mark the start of grave public calamities and irreparable institutional disequilibrium. Don't let them fool you, Lechuga. Disgracefully for these figures, the Cuban people have reached the age of their political maturity and will not be frightened by ghosts. When one looks at the quality of those politicians, it is easy not to believe in them. And because the people have never seen Chibás engage in lies, profit from public office, support or exploit the black market, embezzle from the treasury, deal in contraband or any of the thousand hobbies of our adversaries, they will not mind accusations that I am strident, that I come on too strong or that I am overly combative.[103]

Eddy's confidence was bolstered not only by auspicious survey results but also because he had extricated himself from similar fixes. In many respects, the situation was shaping up as a rerun of Eddy's skyscraper accusation. He had escaped that bind by deflecting attention from his unproven charges toward the veritable dishonesty of Auténtico leaders. His intent to widen the debate with Sánchez Arango beyond its initial parameters indicated that he would utilize this strategy once again.

Chibás spent July 8 in Parque Central, but rather than confronting his foe, he led a rally against the reduction of Cuba's sugar quota and the closing of the Gulf of Mexico to the island's fishermen. Both developments were unwelcome and promised economic hardship, especially as sugar typically accounted for 80–89 percent of Cuba's exports by value.[104] The diminished quota also stung for political reasons. This was because the United States had elected to buy more sugar from the Dominican Republic and Peru, despite the fact that they were ruled by dictators. Besides being democratic, Cubans contributed to their northern neighbor's economy. During the years 1948–1950, an average Cuban bought eighty-three dollars in imports from the United States. By contrast, Dominicans and Peruvians purchased only twenty dollars and seven dollars, respectively, in the same period.[105] In short, Cubans had every reason to feel angered and betrayed. Sánchez Arango was loath to see Chibás rile up the populace and hastily organized National Song Day, hoping musical entertainment would trump Chibás-style political theater. This effort was largely for naught as ten thousand people showed up in Parque Central and several thousand others appeared on its outskirts. To maximize turnout and infuse the event with a nonpartisan flavor, many invited speakers were not Ortodoxos. Such generosity of spirit had limits, though. For one thing, Chibás rigidly excluded Communists. Further, while the purpose was to protest decisions taken by foreign governments, plenty of scorn was heaped on Cuba's rulers.[106]

Guillermo Belt, who had served as ambassador to the United States under Grau, was among those who blamed the president. He proclaimed the oft-heard motto that "without sugar there is no country" and told the audience that Carlos Prío bore "a responsibility so grave" for the diminished sugar quota that he was "resorting to every type of subterfuge, excuse and pretext to absolve himself."[107] Belt noted that Dominican and Peruvian efforts to raise their quotas had begun at the end of 1949, but the administration had responded halfheartedly. "They were notified in advance," he said, "but did not act in defense of our sugar industry."[108] Pelayo Cuervo Navarro used the occasion to denounce government manipulation of sugar prices in league with known speculators. Already this year, he declared, a pair of decrees had artificially lowered sugar prices. This benefited insiders and higher-ups who resold their purchases on the world market for a hefty profit. Chibás, who spoke last, suggested that his adversaries should reconsider their priorities. "While the government was busy wasting time with petty and counterproductive attacks against the Ortodoxos," he said, "it should have employed its energies in attempting to prevent the present assault on the stability of sugar exportation."[109] For good measure, he added that "Carlos Prío and his clique are obsessed with attacking us rather than defending Cuba!"[110] No doubt, Chibás was refining this argument for his polemic with Sánchez Arango. As Chibás implied in his letter to Carlos Lechuga, Cubans had always forgiven his foibles, but he knew they would be less indulgent with an administration that chipped away the island's economic pillar. As a cabinet minister and close presidential advisor, Sánchez Arango was guilty by association. In the future, Chibás could turn this failure against Carlos Hevia with even greater force. After all, the presumed Auténtico nominee had been foreign minister for most of Prío's term.

While Chibás tinkered with this strategy and cast about for other potential advantages, he nearly won his grudge match with Sánchez Arango by default. A few days after the spectacle in Parque Central, the education minister, who was an avid pilot, crashed his plane. He was carrying dental supplies to various towns in Pinar del Río province, but his landing was complicated by an aircraft inexplicably parked in the middle of the runway. To avoid a collision, Sánchez Arango steered clear of the landing strip and touched down in a patch of mud—whereupon his AT6 military plane promptly spun around and flipped over. Sánchez Arango, who very easily could have lost his life in the accident, emerged with only light wounds. Without delay, he immersed himself once more in the polemic. On July 15, he accepted Eddy's offer to debate in the education ministry and outlined nine conditions. The education minister recommended that each man argue his case for thirty minutes and a tribunal, staffed by the hosts of *Ante la Prensa*, would decide the winner. Chibás rejected this idea later that night on the radio, saying he was only accountable before the Cuban people.[111] Eddy also insisted on "absolute freedom of speech, without restrictions or gags," and claimed he needed "at least an hour" to expound on his points but bragged he could easily spend ten hours detailing the government's misdeeds.[112] In the days that followed, both men haggled over particulars. All the while, Chibás was giddy at the prospect of winning his greatest victory to date. To a group of intimates, he exulted:

> This publicity is worth millions of pesos! These people are offering me the presidency on a silver platter. They cannot claim before the country to be honest, that they have never embezzled money nor engaged in business deals prejudicial to the public. Every move they make is a new scandal and offers further proof of their clumsiness. For any citizen, the situation is clear: they have the money and we have the shame.[113]

The problem was that Sánchez Arango refused to provide Chibás with a forum for ridiculing government shortcomings. During their negotiations, they agreed to hold the debate on July 21 at 9:30 p.m. In addition, they concurred on a moderator, naming Francisco Ichaso. However, Sánchez Arango wanted only to discuss Guatemalan real estate while Chibás demanded free rein. Ichaso sought to resolve the impasse by composing a binding document for both men to sign. He too felt the dispute should focus solely on Eddy's accusations and included this among the terms. Sánchez Arango gladly affixed his name, but the Ortodoxo leader balked. Ichaso responded by resigning, leaving them without a moderator or an agreement twenty-four hours before their highly anticipated meeting. As the deadline drew closer, Chibás declared he would accept any conditions except those restricting his choice of topic. In other words, he barely budged. The same held true for Sánchez Arango, who entrusted his response to the new moderator, Octavio de la Suarée—director of Cuba's journalism school. He met Chibás, José Pardo Llada, and Luis Orlando Rodríguez at noon on July 21. All three Ortodoxos scoffed at the education minister's proposal to allow freedom of speech providing Chibás did not "stray from the only topic" or mention "the president, his family, or the government as an entity."[114] Nonetheless, Chibás remained eager to take advantage of what he felt was a singular opportunity. He thus signed the revised contract but modified the section circumscribing his choice of themes, which he called "a joke."[115] Predictably, Sánchez Arango nixed this amendment later that evening. After a last-ditch round of negotiations proved fruitless, an exasperated de la Suarée quit as well. At 9:30 p.m., Chibás appeared at the education ministry surrounded by an Ortodoxo coterie, trailed by photographers, and expecting his most sensational victory yet. Upon reaching the entrance, though, he was handed the identical set of rules from earlier that afternoon and ordered to sign.[116] When Chibás crossed out those he considered untenable, he was barred from entering. Sánchez Arango had no intention of engaging in a debate he could not control and was content to address the nation on his own terms.

Chibás was livid at being denied his chance to discredit the government, with all of Cuba watching or listening. Rather than returning home, he visited the offices of various Havana dailies to register his protest and issue a statement. He told *Alerta*, "Now Sánchez Arango and the government are on the run because they know I have documented, overwhelming, truthful and sensational proof in my possession, the most impressive evidence that has ever been presented in Cuba against a government functionary."[117] He appealed to CMQ for an hour of air time, boasting that "I am ready to open my briefcase and prove to the nation that funds for children's breakfasts and school supplies were stolen, that there is a shady land deal in Guatemala and other things even worse, to demonstrate that this administration of Carlos Prío is the most corrupt the republic has ever had."[118] During that week, Eddy's briefcase became the subject of rabid speculation. Sánchez Arango dared him to "open your briefcase and show your proof to the nation!"[119] Newspapers ran photos of a smiling Chibás brandishing the "famous" leather attaché case. Even Cuba's songwriters joined in, with one popular verse asking, "Where is the proof / where could it be?" and the chorus answering, "When the briefcase is opened / you will see."[120] Chibás also received telegrams and letters from all quarters criticizing Sánchez Arango's performance as education minister. A telegram from the village of Sitiecito in Las Villas province confirmed that none of its one thousand children received free breakfasts and parents were obliged to buy school supplies for their kids, who were taught in crumbling buildings. "We challenge the minister to investigate this," concluded the authors.[121] A couple from the town of Bejucal in Havana province wrote that their son received nothing more than a pencil during the entire school year and added, "[Sánchez Arango] cannot fool the people by saying he's keeping an eye on the schools."[122] From the Central Carolina, a sugar mill in Matanzas province, a man wrote that students at the local school not only lacked free breakfasts and school supplies but also had no desks.[123] Another man, from the town of Yarey de Vázquez in Oriente province, described the familiar dearth of desks, school supplies, and free breakfasts but also included another frustrating detail—namely that the local teacher was so overwhelmed by these difficulties that he sometimes disappeared for a month at a time.[124] Such missives reinforced Eddy's belief that money was being misappropriated in the education ministry.

On the other hand, Chibás was running a tremendous risk by hyping the contents of his attaché case. The subdirector of *El Mundo*, Raoul Alfonso Gonsé, claimed, "if the celebrated briefcase is not opened or lost or its contents defraud public opinion we can already begin publishing the Ortodoxo party's obituary."[125] Gonsé predicted taunts of "Chibás, open your briefcase" would replace "Shame against Money" on the campaign trail if the accusations proved baseless. Chibás also faced skepticism and derision from those within his party. Around this time, the Ortodoxo executive committee convened in Eddy's apartment. Most of those in attendance believed their chief had fallen into a trap and deceived them. Pelayo Cuervo Navarro was particularly critical. After much heated discussion, the general view was that Chibás should expect no help unless he could prove his accusations.[126] Hence, he once again faced the specter of a divided party. Afterward, Emilio Núñez Blanco offered to visit Guatemala and look for evidence. Having nothing to lose, Chibás authorized the mission, but nothing useful turned up.[127] If Chibás was dismayed by the executive committee's unwillingness to stand behind him, he remained publicly defiant and stoked the embers of his conflict with Sánchez Arango while awaiting his chance in the limelight.[128]

As expected, the owners of CMQ agreed to extend Eddy's upcoming radio show by half an hour at no extra cost. Chibás asked that his address be televised as well because Sánchez Arango had enjoyed the same courtesy a week before, but they declined, citing commercial obligations. In newspaper advertisements, Chibás promised to expose "the enormous corruption of the present regime and Education Minister Aureliano Sánchez Arango's culpability."[129] Meanwhile, Sánchez Arango heckled Chibás all week. Calling him "Renato," a play on his middle name, René, the education minister goaded him to open his briefcase before Cuba's Supreme Tribunal. Chibás emptied its contents instead for a packed room inside CMQ's studios on July 29. However, the island's consummate showman disappointed this audience along with his multitude of listeners by serving up a farrago of recycled charges and fresh unverified allegations. Ultimately, Cubans did not tune in to hear that Sánchez Arango may have held a ghost job under Batista or had been reprimanded by the bar association for slander. The ten photographs Chibás exhibited of ramshackle schools, while gripping, were more suitable for television than a radio broadcast. His display of a private document signed by twenty-five Auténticos accusing Sánchez Arango of fraud had been mentioned during recent broadcasts. As for the polemic's central accusation, he now said, again without proof, that Sánchez Arango owned a lumberyard in Guatemala rather than residential real estate. Chibás asserted that the venture's beneficiaries also included Carlos Prío, Guatemala's former president Juan Arévalo, and the current ambassador of that country in Havana, Raúl Oseguda. After being primed all week for a scintillating finale, the mass of citizens waiting outside the station trudged home disgruntled. Stating the obvious, Enrique de la Osa observed that the performance "was far from being what the people were anxiously waiting for."[130] He further detected "a different tone of voice" in Chibás.[131] This, no doubt, was because Eddy, who usually aroused his countrymen's passions with uncanny precision, lacked the means to do so on this occasion.

Half an hour after Eddy finished speaking, Sánchez Arango commenced with a meticulously planned homage to himself in a Havana theater called, with no lack of irony, Principal de la Comedia. The invitees were greeted by a colossal image of Sánchez Arango draped in Cuba's national colors of red, white, and blue. Nor could they miss assorted posters publicizing Sánchez

Arango's achievements in the education ministry, replete with documentation of free breakfasts and school materials distributed. Official approval was insinuated by a large portrait of Sánchez Arango next to Carlos Prío, but, as everyone knew, the former had challenged Chibás precisely because he was not the government's preferred candidate.[132] At any rate, Sánchez Arango lavishly promoted himself, and while there was no evidence this effort had been financed by Guatemalan timber, all signs pointed to Cuban taxpayers footing the bill. What they paid for was an extravaganza of calumny and bombast on a par with Chibás in his most reckless moments. One of the education minister's cronies accused Chibás of colluding with Argentina's President Juan Domingo Perón, a proposition both laughable and outrageous. When Sánchez Arango took the microphone, he engaged in a foul-mouthed tirade of such exaggerated proportions that it became fodder for Cuba's cartoonists. Afterward, Sánchez Arango promised to have Chibás expelled from the senate, deprived of his parliamentary immunity, and jailed "in the name of the superior interests of the Cuban people."[133] This torrent of self-righteousness was ill-advised given that his party harbored gangsters and murderers among its legislators. Nor did the holier-than-thou Sánchez Arango seem to mind counting a known embezzler like Antonio Prío among his guests and propitiators. Sensing an opportunity to regain the momentum, Chibás challenged Carlos Prío to convoke the senate so he could be judged. In the same breath, he added that "[Prío] won't do it because each and every one of my accusations, including those referring to the enormous thievery of Cuban authorities and those relating to their secret investments in Guatemala are true, rigorously true."[134]

Just as Chibás had never backed down from the allegation that Carlos Prío owned skyscrapers in Manhattan, he steadfastly clung to the notion that Sánchez Arango was conducting dirty business in Guatemala. At first glance, there was no reason to believe this stubbornness would damage him. Guillermo Alonso Pujol, who was no friend of Chibás but very politically astute, believed any fallout from the polemic would be both minor and transitory. Chibás seemingly agreed and appeared before the Supreme Tribunal on August 2 to formally charge Sánchez Arango with numerous counts of malversation. At the same time, there were signs that he was suffering a personal crisis. Chibás had always derived a great deal of satisfaction and well-being from his encounters with common people, but some were no longer pleased to see him—at least on his jaunts around Havana. On one occasion, Eddy and José Pardo Llada were walking down San Rafael Street, and instead of being mobbed by adoring citizens, which was usually the case, they were serenaded by chants of "*la maleta, la maleta*" (the briefcase, the briefcase).[135] For Chibás, this almost certainly recalled the harassment of Manuel Fernández Supervielle just over four years before.

"*I Am Going to Open My Briefcase*" 231

As he prepared his next radio address, Chibás summoned Millo Ochoa and the Ortodoxo youth leader Luis Conte Agüero to Havana. Chibás hoped to sound out Ochoa, the party's quintessential political realist. He also wanted to exchange impressions with the twenty-seven-year-old Conte Agüero, who had strafed Sánchez Arango in broadcasts emanating from his native Santiago de Cuba. Chibás consulted the polling expert Raúl Gutiérrez as well and was assured his recent dip in popularity was within the statistical margin of error. Above all, he was determined to press forward against Sánchez Arango and turn the tide of public opinion. Chibás thus accepted an invitation from *Carteles* to continue the polemic in that magazine's pages. On the evening of August 4, he delivered a new article to its director, Alfredo Quilez. While sticking to his story that Sánchez Arango kept sordid investments in Guatemala and "other Central American republics," Chibás added another more devastating line of attack.[136] Specifically, he reproduced two education ministry documents indicating that money had been diverted from the budget for acquiring school supplies to fund "propaganda" activities in February, March, and April of 1951.[137] He concluded that Sánchez Arango was depriving Cuban schoolchildren in order to pay for his presidential campaign. Even as the amount, which totaled 6,509 pesos, was fairly modest, Chibás had hit a soft spot. Sánchez Arango was not a notorious peculator, but his presidential bid required cash as did his enormous public relations effort against Chibás. In this vein, the Auténtico congressman Gilberto Leyva said, "If I were [Chibás], with the evidence of thievery and embezzlement in the education ministry, I would have published what Aureliano spends on banquets, parties and trips to Guatemala with money taken from the budget."[138] Sánchez Arango had succeeded by steering the debate toward favorable terrain, but he was vulnerable and could not circumscribe the polemic indefinitely. Once again, Chibás was betting that Cubans would forget his occasional imprudence in the face of government malfeasance.

The following day, on August 5, Chibás invited Luis Conte Agüero over to read a draft of his remarks for that evening. At one point, Chibás absentmindedly picked up the Colt .38 on his desk and inquired of his guest, "Listen, which one is the safety lock?"

"You don't know?" asked Conte Agüero incredulously. After a moment's pause, he proceeded to demonstrate how the gun functioned while remaining certain that Chibás was pulling his leg.

Looking out his bedroom window, with its Caribbean vista, Chibás then asked, "Why don't we try it out? If I fired from here do you think the bullet would reach the sea?"

"I don't think so," replied Conte Agüero. "Besides, the bullet might hit someone."

"Yes, that's true," said Chibás. As he holstered the pistol, a bullet fell to the floor. Conte Agüero picked up the projectile and advised him to reinsert it in the clip.

"That's all right," said Chibás. "I already have all I need."[139]

At 7:45 p.m., Pelayo Cuervo Navarro showed up with his driver, and Chibás, who customarily walked the five blocks to CMQ studios followed by a bulging throng, arrived this time via automobile. He ceded the first fifteen minutes to José Pardo Llada, who had lately caused a stir by resigning from his popular daily gig on Unión Radio. The station had recently changed hands, and the new owners had named José Luis Pelleyá, a close friend of Antonio Prío, as administrator. Pardo Llada accused the administration of masterminding the purchase as a means of censoring him. He claimed this was part of a larger scheme to "control all the organs of publicity" using the government's "millions of pesos."[140] By the time Chibás took the microphone, only ten minutes of airtime remained. Employing a favorite trope, he recalled the case of Galileo, who had been deemed a "liar" and "deceiver" for lacking "physical proof" that the earth revolved around the sun.[141] Chibás then reminded listeners that he had been called a "liar" and "slanderer" when he accused José Manuel Alemán of acquiring a real estate empire in Miami. "I did not have physical proof that he was robbing from the national treasury," said Chibás, "but I kept repeating, firm in my moral conviction: 'He's stealing! He's stealing!'"[142] Concerning the present situation, he explained:

> Last Sunday, during this same broadcast . . . I offered irrefutable proof of the enormous corruption of Prío's administration, including photos of schools and hospitals in miserable condition and contrasting them with ostentatious fincas and mansions of government officials who, not long ago, lived in poverty. Nevertheless, in spite of continual depredations, Machado, Batista, Grau San Martín and Carlos Prío have not been able to dull the Cuban people's moral sensibility, which speaks very highly of the firmness of its virtues, but still my words from last Sunday did not have the resonance required by such a grave situation. Cuba needs to wake up. But my knocking was not, perhaps, sufficiently strong. We will, however, continue to count on the conscience of the Cuban people.[143]

Afterward, Chibás reiterated two ideas that were familiar to his regular audience. First, he emphasized that Cuba's "historic destiny" had always been frustrated by the "corruption and blindness" of its rulers. Second, he affirmed that Cuba would never fulfill its "mission" under the current administration, nor would this be possible through Batista's "false opposition" or the "spiteful group" led by Grau.[144] Only the Ortodoxos, who eschewed "transactions" and "shady deals," would suffice.[145] Right about then, the transmission was cut as Chibás had exceeded his time limit. While the island's citizens heard an advertisement for Café Pilon, Chibás steamed ahead with his final call to arms. "People of Cuba," he yelled, audible now only to those surrounding him in the studio, "Rise up! People of Cuba, wake up! This is my last loud knock!"[146] He punctuated this statement by slamming down his left fist. With his right hand, he searched for something. Moments later, seemingly out of nowhere, a shot rang out. The studio was immediately thrown into confusion. No one had seen a gun as Chibás had fired from beneath the desk. Some Ortodoxos reacted by fleeing toward the exit, while others pushed forward, trying to make sense of things. In the first moments, neither Millo Ochoa, who sat to Eddy's right, nor Roberto Agramonte on his left knew what had transpired. Soon enough, Chibás slumped over, and his pistol clanged against the floor accompanied by freshets of blood. Voices urging calm were interrupted by orders to detain the supposed aggressor. The would-be assassin, of course, was Chibás himself. Finally, a band consisting of José Pardo Llada, Millo Ochoa, Pelayo Cuervo Navarro, Orlando Castro, and Luis Conte Agüero took charge. They carried the bleeding Ortodoxo leader to a nearby automobile and rushed him to the nearest hospital. Before going into surgery, Chibás told them, "I'm going to die, but the party has to unite now more than ever. It must confront the corrupt government and pseudo-opposition."

"Where are you hurt, Eddy?" asked Orlando Castro.

"In the belly. . . . What a shame it wasn't in the heart!"[147]

Although the shot had not been audible over the air, news of it traveled fast, and a sizable gathering soon formed outside the Vedado clinic where Chibás was being treated. Men and women from all walks of life lingered throughout the evening, waiting nervously for information on Eddy's condition. Many donated blood. Sitting on a nearby patch of grass, some wept openly, while others consoled themselves with prayer. At midnight, the medical staff finally provided an update. Chibás had suffered a punctured colon, eight perforations in his small intestine, and a fractured vertebra. His condition was critical and might have been worse but for a dash of serendipity. Antonio Rodríguez Díaz, the gifted surgeon who repaired his diaphragmatic hernia nearly a year earlier, had just returned from out of town and led the operation. The next day, Chibás told him in a frail voice, "Doctor, I was able to save myself from the other thing but I won't escape this time." Rodríguez Díaz responded by asking Chibás whether he hoped to survive. "The truth, doctor, is that yesterday I didn't but now I want to live."[148]

Eddy's newfound will to endure was confirmed a few hours later by Luis Orlando Rodríguez, who had checked into the same hospital with an aliment of his own. Entering Eddy's room, Rodríguez clasped his friend's hand and said, "Eddy, we have to win this battle!" Chibás smiled weakly and agreed.[149] As someone who had always reveled in attention, Chibás may have changed his mind upon learning how many of the island's most prominent men had arrived to wish him well. These included political figures of every persuasion, including Guillermo Alonso Pujol, Nicolás Castellanos, Emilio Núñez Portuondo, and Pepe San Martín, along with representatives of the exiled democratic governments of Venezuela and Peru.[150] The eminent hero of Cuba's independence war, Enrique Loynaz del Castillo, was in evidence as well. Of course, old friends such as Miguel Ángel Quevedo and the Mestre brothers also stopped by, as did his newer ally Ramón Vasconcelos. Chibás was surely gratified when Conchita Fernández, who had attended to all these guests, informed him of their visits. This proved they had heard his "loud knock" and sided with him against Aureliano Sánchez Arango.

As a supremely political deed, Eddy's suicide attempt was naturally pored over and spun throughout Cuba in a variety of fashions. During an Ortodoxo meeting immediately after the shooting, Joaquín López Montes called it "an act of historical grandeur" and claimed, "this is not the suicide of a depressed or disappointed man but a self-sacrifice by a great combatant who desired to hand over his life to a great cause."[151] On August 6, Roberto Agramonte, Luis Conte Agüero, and Guillermo de Zéndegui published a statement in *Alerta* that sought to inculcate this saintly vision in the public mind. They deemed Chibás "the most extraordinary, valiant and honest figure of the Cuban revolution" and "the grand titan of national honor."[152] With an eye on the present political situation, they added:

> No one tended to Cuba's historical destiny more carefully than Chibás and yet he was shamelessly plotted against by a vile and corrupt government and a pseudo-opposition bereft of virtue and stripped of all grandeur. In order to inflict a mortal wound on the skepticism spread by the dominant immorality, to shake up the people's souls and awaken Cuba's conscience made lethargic by apostasy and frustration, the great leader tried to take his life in a gesture of heroic idealism.[153]

Conversely, Auténticos close to Carlos Prío felt Chibás had engaged in yet another publicity stunt. Many believed he had shot himself in 1939 to amplify his vote totals just before the constituent assembly elections. For them, this was a reprise of the same old show, and they worried Chibás would emerge as an even greater threat than before. Asked for his thoughts, the perpetually irascible Tony Varona said,

> I see no reason why I should feel sorry. If the deed [had] been the result of aggression, of chance or a natural accident, then I would deplore it. But an act committed with political and electoral ends in mind and in the security that he would not die is in no way lamentable.[154]

The Auténtico labor leader Eusebio Mujal was even harsher, describing Eddy's suicide attempt as "an explosion of hysteria" and "a product of his mental state upon finding out that public opinion was fed up with his slanders and lies."[155] This dismissive attitude did not extend throughout the party, however. Miguelito Suárez Fernández and Félix Lancís ignored the president's wishes and visited Chibás in the hospital. So did the Auténtico congressman Luis Pérez Espinós, who declared that "I don't believe there is a single Cuban who doesn't fervently hope to see Chibás recover."[156] The Auténtico governor of Camagüey, Jorge Caballero Rojo, counseled his more partisan colleagues that the "humane and chivalrous" attitude would be to "cease their passions" and "consider the man himself" as he struggles for his life.[157]

While cooler-headed Auténticos aimed for a magnanimous posture above the fray of politics as usual, Chibás sought to seize every possible advantage for himself and his party. At a devastating cost to himself, he had placed the Auténticos in an uncomfortable position—not only by exposing their internal fissures but also because they could not criticize him now without appearing mean-spirited and contemptuous of public opinion. Even as Chibás overcame frequent brushes with death, he seemed more interested in what the newspapers were saying and was particularly anxious to read the August 12 edition of *Bohemia*. At one point, Chibás admonished Pedro Iglesias Betancourt to tell him when the end was near as he had final instructions for the Ortodoxo executive committee. Subsequently, Chibás notified Conchita Fernández that if he died suddenly, she should tell Millo Ochoa to organize a rally on the second Monday in September at the rural school built with the revenues from his share of the family coffee plantation. "Let the people see," he said, "that while the government has abandoned the schools, we founded one to benefit peasants."[158] On August 13, Chibás eagerly asked José Chelala Aguilera how the people viewed his gesture of self-sacrifice. He was gratified to learn that Catholic masses throughout the island had been dedicated to him the day before and Cubans were "fervently praying" for his recovery.[159]

With the passage of time, hopes that Chibás might survive gained traction. His doctors cautioned that the period between ten and fifteen days after the wound, which Chibás was then entering, promised to be tricky, but they remained guardedly optimistic. On August 15, Antonio Rodríguez Díaz brashly told Eddy's secretary that "I am ready to do anything, to operate on his lungs, even his heart. This man cannot die on me."[160] Just before midnight, however, Chibás complained to the attending physician of pain in his stomach. During surgery a hemorrhage was discovered, the result of blood thinners administered to ease a clot in his small intestine. He received multiple transfusions but to no avail. At 1:55 a.m., the man cherished by nearly one-third of Cuba's population passed into myth.

Epilogue

Having lived for years with an eye toward posterity, Chibás began his afterlife in auspicious fashion. An estimated three hundred thousand "women, men and children" followed his funeral procession which, fittingly for Cuba's idol of the youth, commenced at the University of Havana.[1] The outpouring of sorrow was such that Colón Cemetery's caretaker, who had occupied his post since 1908 and witnessed memorial services for war heroes, ex-presidents, and actresses, predicted there would be no similar demonstration of deep, collective mourning "for the next 1000 years."[2] *Información* was one of several news sources to claim Eddy's burial was the most highly attended in Cuba's history—superseding those of revered generals from the independence struggle such as Máximo Gómez and José Miguel Gómez. The turnout was even more impressive because

> Chibás . . . had never dispensed services or done favors as a public servant and could not expect the recipients to show up out of gratitude, nor was anyone forced or obligated to attend because they occupied government jobs, neither were members of labor unions mobilized or compelled by directives to make an appearance. On the contrary, those who were present arrived spontaneously and of their own free will. This is true beyond a doubt.[3]

During the eulogy, Leonardo Fernández Sánchez consoled those assembled by quoting the New Testament, specifically Luke 24:5, asking, "Why do you look for the living among the dead?"[4] Chibás had not quite been resurrected, but endured in "our conscience," "our hearts," and as "an august symbol of self-sacrifice for the good of the patria."[5] While flattering, Chibás had spent more time poring over José Martí than the Bible and preferred the martyrdom of Ignacio Agramonte to that of the prophet of Galilee. In this sense, José Pardo Llada's tribute was more in line with how Chibás longed to be remembered. Far from a mere revolutionary or political leader, he claimed Chibás "transcended historical circumstances" and possessed a "moral attitude" that placed him in the pantheon of Cuban greats.[6] Of course, encomiums of this sort were expected from Eddy's closest friends and allies. However, a similar line was taken by many who had previously viewed Chibás with suspicion or disdain. For example, an editorial in *Diario de la Marina* portrayed him as "the constant moral force [and] visible link between today's generation and that of [Cuba's] founding fathers."[7] Even *Pueblo*, which had long been a mouthpiece for José Manuel Alemán, allowed that "the upright and unforgettable Chibás [was] one of the most vigorous and exemplary men in the history of our republic."[8]

In the days and weeks following Eddy's death, his tomb hosted myriad pilgrims. A group of peasants unable to reach Havana in time for the interment paid silent homage while holding aloft a sign that said, "Exemplary Cuban." Lines of women covered tear-strewn faces with fists or concealed their emotions behind sunglasses. One of the many who felt strong personal connections to Chibás told a *Bohemia* correspondent that "I will always miss Eddy. Nobody understood me like he did. Just by looking at me he knew if something was wrong."[9] Worshippers also turned out in large numbers, caressing rosaries while reading from the New Testament. One of them, a Spanish-born mother of six named Antonia López, said she hoped her children would "learn from the example of this good man" and then said a prayer so Chibás would rest in peace.[10] Middle-class children wore elegant dresses adorned with black ribbons while their rural coevals mourned in simple shirts and slacks. Men in suits solemnly crossed their arms, flanked by humbler types sporting guayaberas. Some dropped everything and spent hours on end in the cemetery. All were surpassed in their allegiance by María de la Paz Fonseca, who by August of 1959 had spent 2,920 consecutive days at Eddy's grave and vowed to maintain this habit for the rest of her life. A founding member of the Ortodoxos, de la Paz, who was by then fifty-seven years old, appeared early each morning to wash the marble sepulcher, prune flowers left by devotees, and sweep the surrounding area. Steadfast in her loyalty, even eight years after Eddy's demise, she told a reporter from *Carteles* that "we must teach the children of tomorrow about the man who founded the Ortodoxo party, how he worked tirelessly for the Cuban people and knew how to die for them."[11]

Apart from achieving glory as Cuba's newest martyr, Chibás hoped his death would achieve a raft of more quotidian objectives. Most importantly, he wished to unify his party and ensure pacts would always be shunned by its leaders. In the burst of emotion following his suicide, hardly any other posture seemed imaginable. Millo Ochoa, the party's archetypal pragmatist, declared during Eddy's memorial service that "we swear to fulfill and make a reality the independent line [and] . . . pledge to offer not only the sincere tribute of our tears but also to remain firmly united and continue to fly the flag of his ideals."[12] Less than two weeks later, the Ortodoxo executive committee unanimously nominated Roberto Agramonte as the party's presidential candidate for 1952—thereby avoiding a potentially damaging leadership struggle in the run-up to Cuba's presidential elections.

Chibás also bet that his passion play would "wake up" Cuba's populace and dramatically alter the political landscape. An aroused nation, snapped from its slumber would presumably support his party in overwhelming numbers. Nothing less would do, in fact, as the Ortodoxos required historic vote totals to win the presidency without election partners. A random sample of Havana residents, taken in the weeks after Eddy's suicide, suggested this might be possible. Speaking to a journalist from *Bohemia*, one man on the street said, "I don't belong to any political party but I will vote for the Ortodoxo candidate . . . and I hope he will fulfill the legacy of Chibás."[13] A soda jerk named Ramón Rodríguez expressed a similar view, declaring, "I will vote for whomever the Ortodoxos nominate, regardless of who it is. If he's an Ortodoxo he must be good."[14] In the same vein, a bus driver stated that "[despite Chibás's death] his party won't disappear. We have to pick up the flag of Chibás and keep it flying high."[15] Cuba's youth was perhaps the widest awake of all potential constituencies. Thus, a group of teenagers in Parque Central proclaimed that only José Martí surpassed Chibás in historical significance. Their leader, a boy named Sergio Bauzá, indicated they would support "Agramonte or whomever else [the party nominated]."[16]

Of course, Havana was an Ortodoxo stronghold—at least in part because its relatively prosperous and sophisticated inhabitants were less inclined than rural dwellers to sell their votes. For this reason, the detested but well-financed Antonio Prío had failed to win Havana's mayoralty in 1950. Effectively, the question was whether Eddy's immolation would sway hundreds of thousands of peasants in Cuba's countryside. They were not only tempted by cash payments at election time but usually lacked contact with live Ortodoxos given the party's absence from remote areas and even some midsize towns. Chibás thus gambled that his martyrdom and the attendant burst of sympathy it unleashed would overcome the party's limited reach.

THE MILITARY COUP

There is no way to know whether Eddy's calculations were justified, as the island's democracy survived him by less than seven months. On March 10, 1952, Fulgencio Batista, assisted by a cabal of junior officers and retired military cronies, toppled the government. The plot originated among a group of young officers who were disgusted by Auténtico corruption and out-of-control gangsters.[17] They were also influenced by rumors that the Auténticos planned to retain power forcibly as a means of preventing electoral defeat. The young officers felt a preemptive takeover to restore order and oversee honest polls was in the country's best interests. Auténtico depravity had offended them all the more given their training at Cuba's War College, where they had been schooled in the virtues of professionalism and sound administration. In fact, their professors included prominent Ortodoxos such as Roberto Agramonte, Herminio Portell Vilá, and Rafael García Bárcena.[18] While the conspirators were sympathetic to Ortodoxo ideas and many imagined their intervention would guarantee an Ortodoxo electoral victory, they recruited one of that party's archenemies, Fulgencio Batista, to guide them. This reflected both pragmatism and naïveté on their part. In order to ensure the coup's success, they sought a leader with national stature who counted prestige both inside and outside military circles. No one fit the bill better than Batista, who was a dyed-in-the-wool soldier and accomplished civilian politician.

They first approached Batista in June of 1951 but he demurred, hoping to secure an electoral victory instead. He had been encouraged by a four-point surge in the polls one month earlier, but as time passed Batista gained no further momentum. While the Auténtico and Ortodoxo candidates vied for first place, he languished far behind in third.[19] In January of 1952, Batista sought to improve his chances by negotiating a pact with Guillermo Alonso Pujol's newfangled Cuban National Party and Grau's semi-independent vehicle, Cubanidad. Neither of these entities could furnish many votes and in any case the talks came to naught over Batista's insistence on leading the coalition. Having exhausted all legal means of returning to power, Batista received the junior officers once again in February and entertained their entreaties more seriously.

After a dozen years of constitutional rule, the specter of a golpe de estado had never quite receded. Indeed, Cuba's army remained a hotbed of intrigue throughout this period despite its 20 percent slice of the national budget, ever increasing salaries for enlisted men, and an indulged officer class. Certainly, many officers accepted the new order, but they continued to treat civilian authorities with disdain. When the conspirators recruited Army Chief Ruperto Cabrera, he refused to join them but also failed to alert Carlos Prío. After a colonel named Lázaro Landeira suggested an investigation was warranted, Prío consulted Cabrera, who assured him nothing was afoot. Just like that, Cabrera hoisted a sin of omission atop one of commission—doubly betraying the man who had appointed him to his post.[20]

Shortly after 1:00 p.m. on March 10, with the plotters in full control, they issued a public statement via radio. The twenty-four young officers declared their intention "to save Cuba from the shame of a bloody and corrupt regime that disintegrated institutions and created disorder and anarchy in the republic."[21] They also repeated the unlikely rumor that Carlos Prío had "reached an agreement with some military men" to hatch a coup in early April after realizing his party would lose the June elections.[22] The last straw, apparently, involved "news" that attempts to murder "well known" opposition figures were being prepared by the administration—which would blame them on the very gangsters it armed and protected.[23] Portraying themselves as "soldiers loyal to the republic," the young officers concluded by announcing their confidence in Fulgencio Batista, in whose hands they had placed the "destiny" of their "revolution."[24]

Flush with victory, the junior officers exulted in their choice of Batista to lead them. Aside from devising a shrewd plan to oust Carlos Prío and anticipating most eventualities, Batista had also charmed the troops by promising to double their pay. Lamentably, he would prove less accommodating toward the young officers' second objective—namely, calling for elections and handing power to responsible civilian authorities with all due speed. Indeed, the youthful captains and first lieutenants would shortly rue their decision and realize they had been poor judges of character. Batista had not risked his life to guarantee an honest poll, which he was destined to lose. In addition, Batista was hardly anxious to vacate the perch he had so artfully seized. He thus postponed elections until November of 1953 and banned all political parties pending further notice.[25] Meanwhile, Batista named himself prime minister and recruited a cast of civilian characters to gild the new regime. The first order of business involved finding a respectable yet pliable president. Batista's top choice was the historian and ex-senator Emeterio Santovenia. However, Santovenia turned down the job.[26] After a slew of other candidates refused, Batista eventually took on the position himself. Regarding the cabinet, Batista tapped a blend of loyalists and opportunists. Among the former was Andrés Rivero Agüero, the new education minister and a veteran apologist for Batista in the pages of *Bohemia*.[27] Another was Miguel Ángel Campa, a career diplomat who had served as foreign minister under Batista's front man, President Francisco Laredo Brú, during the years 1937–1940 and now occupied that same job once again.[28] As for opportunists, Chibás had learned to his chagrin that they were never in short supply on the island. Thus, a handful of Ortodoxo "traitors" from the 1948 electoral campaign joined the dictator. These included Pablo Carrera Jústiz as communications minister and Joaquín Martínez Sáenz as head of Cuba's National Bank.

Batista cultivated other useful collaborators from the unlikeliest corners. His prize catch was Eusebio Mujal, the Auténtico senator, union leader, and signer of the now-defunct 1940 constitution. During Carlos Prío's presidency, Mujal had often abused Batista with unflattering public proclamations. Now, he called off a general strike after being assured Cuba's labor laws would be respected. The coup designed to rid Cuba of triggermen also lured Rolando Masferrer. He conveniently shed his Auténtico connections and placed his thugs, thereafter dubbed Masferrer's Tigers, in Batista's service. A further improbable candidate was Nicolás Castellanos, who offered assistance despite being dismissed as Havana's mayor. If nothing else, his accommodation confirmed the doubts Chibás had always harbored regarding his character. Had Chibás not opposed his attempt to run for mayor on the Ortodoxo ticket in 1950, Castellanos would have been the party's highest-ranking elected official before the coup.

More in keeping with Ortodoxo morals was the behavior of Eddy's childhood friend Ventura Dellundé. In late March, he visited New York and Washington, DC, where he lobbied the United Nations and Organization of American States for help against Batista. This was precisely the sort of appeal to legality often favored by Ortodoxos. As the man who had once sued Cuba's predatory electric company, Dellundé was perfect for this admirable but ultimately fruitless mission. For his part, Pelayo Cuervo Navarro dropped Causa 82 and began investigating Batista's manipulation of Cuba's sugar industry for his own personal gain. His exposé of the dictator's misconduct graced *Bohemia*'s pages in November of 1952. Of course, Dellundé and Cuervo Navarro were established men of principle and neither required Chibás as a rallying cry. Conversely, Cuba's youth appropriated the deceased Ortodoxo leader with gusto—invoking his name whenever and wherever possible. On March 16, they congregated at Eddy's tomb to find a measure of solace and express their indignation with the coup. At a May 20 rally to mark the fiftieth anniversary of Cuban independence, the University of Havana campus shook with chants of "Chi-bás! Chi-bás! Chi-bás!" During a celebration of Antonio Maceo's birthday on June 14, students decided to mourn Caporal, the recently deceased white stallion that had famously bucked Chibás. On August 16, Ortodoxos and students gathered to commemorate Eddy's death in his hometown of Santiago de Cuba. This boasted all the hallmarks of a political gathering, which was illegal, and the police duly arrested many participants—including Roberto Agramonte, Raúl Chibás, Luis Conte Agüero, and Luis Orlando Rodríguez.

By October of 1952, when Batista issued updated ground rules for political activity, it was clear he intended to revisit a dark epoch of Cuba's history. Under the new provisions, parties would be allowed to operate but risked persecution if they criticized the regime. This was reminiscent of the years 1934–1940, when Batista circumscribed political life on the island and opponents were subject to violence or intimidation.[29] Acts of brutality typical of this era were already being perpetrated against journalists. For example, Mario Kuchilán, a frequent contributor to *Bohemia*, was roughed up by Batista's agents in August. They were seeking information about Aureliano Sánchez Arango, who had also reverted to past habits by founding an underground military outfit, known as AAA, dedicated to overthrowing Batista by force.[30]

SPLINTERS

Sánchez Arango's group was not the only one dedicated to forcibly ejecting Batista. In May of 1952, Rafael García Bárcena bolted the Ortodoxos and founded Movimiento Nacional Revolucionaria (MNR)—packing its ranks with students, young professionals, and junior officers. These had been prime constituencies for Chibás, but García Bárcena was ideally placed to appeal to them too. He was a popular moral philosophy professor at the University of Havana and, until recently, military psychology at Cuba's War College.[31] García Bárcena had been an Ortodoxo hard-liner from the beginning, which also endeared him to Cuba's young people. Moreover, his revolutionary trajectory was eerily similar to that of Chibás. Both had belonged to the Student Directorate during Gerardo Machado's presidency. In the mid-1930s, he and Chibás were members of a left-leaning anti-Batista squad called Izquierda Revolucionaria. Later on, they joined the Auténticos but were disillusioned by Grau. García Bárcena was also a charismatic figure in his own right, although he was less of a natural crowd-pleaser than Chibás. Rather, he was a poet and public intellectual in the mold of other Ortodoxo professor politicians such as Carlos Márquez Sterling, Jorge Mañach, and Herminio Portell Vilá.

On Easter Sunday in 1953, an MNR contingent tried to seize Havana's central garrison, the Campamento Columbia, and thereby decapitate Batista's regime with a single crushing blow. A group of officers inside were García Bárcena's adherents, and they planned to simultaneously revolt from their end. However, word of the plot leaked out, and it was foiled when García Bárcena and twenty-one others were captured attempting to enter the base. In short order, he was tortured, tried, and given a two-year sentence. His movement endured but lost momentum. Many followers, including the young lawyer Armando Hart, who vainly defended García Bárcena in court, along with an eighteen-year-old student from Oriente Teachers College named Frank País, began looking elsewhere for ways to resist Batista.

In time, both alighted on a member of their own generation who had been plotting something comparable. Eschewing Cuba's largest and most impregnable military fortress, Fidel Castro looked instead to attack softer targets in Santiago de Cuba and Bayamo. Santiago de Cuba's Moncada Barracks was second in size only to Campamento Columbia but defended by undisciplined troops. Castro enhanced his odds by striking during carnival season, when soldiers would be carousing. His immediate objective was to overrun Moncada and distribute arms to the civilian population in preparation for a mass uprising. Meanwhile, occupying the modest Bayamo fortress would block government reinforcements. At 4:00 a.m. on July 26, just before the operation would commence, Castro told his 131 followers that

> In a few hours you will be victorious or defeated, but regardless of the outcome . . . this Movement will triumph. If you win tomorrow, the aspirations of Martí will be fulfilled sooner. If the contrary occurs, our action will set an example for the Cuban people, and from the people will arise young men willing to die for Cuba. They will pick up our banner and move forward.[32]

In its embrace of sacrifice and wish to "set an example" for Cubans, this speech was vintage Chibás. His audience was familiar with such rhetoric, as most had been recruited from the Ortodoxo party's working-class and peasant wings. As an added touch, Castro carried a recording of Eddy's final broadcast into battle. If successful, he intended to incite the local populace by playing it over the airwaves.

Castro, who like many young Cubans had learned the power of radio from Chibás, also intended to regale listeners with a nine-point "Moncada Manifesto." Written by a twenty-five-year-old poet and fellow Ortodoxo named Raúl Gómez García, the manifesto claimed to speak for "the youth of Cuba who love freedom and man's dignity."[33] Essentially, this was a blueprint for political life after Batista. Gómez García not only invoked Chibás by name, he also expounded on many themes dear to the martyred Ortodoxo chief, including "absolute and reverent respect for the constitution of 1940" and "theft of the national treasury."[34] In another echo of Chibás, he asserted that educational and agrarian reform could be funded partly though reductions in corruption. Of course, Gómez García would only win a public soapbox if the mission succeeded. To cover all bases, Castro instructed his mistress, Naty Revuelta, to distribute copies of the manifesto to *Bohemia* and other Havana dailies.[35] However, it was uniformly rejected or disregarded.

Despite Castro's weaker choice of targets, his endeavor remained the longest of shots. Besides being outnumbered nearly four to one, Castro's men were short on firepower. Regardless of their inadequacies, the troops guarding Moncada were well equipped with modern .30 caliber Springfield rifles. Castro's band, which was chronically broke, could only muster an assortment of hunting and sports rifles. Further, Castro lost the element of surprise almost immediately when his group was confronted by a patrol jeep as they were about to enter Gate 3. The ensuing firefight lasted several hours and killed eight of Castro's men. Another fifty-three were taken prisoner and subsequently murdered by soldiers enraged at the deaths of their comrades.[36] Castro and his younger brother Raúl were among the forty-eight who escaped only to be captured later on during an intensive manhunt.

At his trial that fall, Castro, who was a lawyer by trade, defended himself. During his two-hour speech, the twenty-seven-year-old revolutionary and part-time Ortodoxo borrowed liberally from Eddy's bag of tricks. His opening statement, for example, appropriated one of Chibás's favorite ruses—

namely that any measures taken against him were wholly unprecedented and totally outrageous. Hence, Castro asserted that

> Never has a lawyer had to practice his profession under such difficult conditions; never has such a number of overwhelming irregularities been committed against an accused man. In this case, counsel and defendant are one and the same. As attorney he has not even been able to take a look at the indictment. As accused, for the past seventy-six days he has been locked away in solitary confinement, held totally and absolutely incommunicado, in violation of every human and legal right.[37]

Castro also learned from Chibás that reckless accusations or hyperbolic claims are permissible in the service of a righteous cause. Hence, he argued that his followers were vanquished due to being outnumbered "fifteen to one," which was clearly an exaggeration.[38] More than anything, Chibás was fondest of portraying himself as a humble defender of Cuba's interests against sleazy and unscrupulous rulers. This was the essence of "Shame vs. Money," the Ortodoxo slogan and siren song. Castro, who understood the appeal of this tactic, thus declared that

> The politicians spend millions buying off consciences, whereas a handful of Cubans who wanted to save their country's honor had to face death barehanded for lack of funds. This shows how the country, to this very day, has been governed not by generous and dedicated men, but by political racketeers, the scum of our public life.[39]

Although Castro absorbed much from Chibás, his gangster links contravened Ortodoxo ideals of legality and civic responsibility. Castro's longstanding feud with Rolando Masferrer, for instance, was common knowledge during the late 1940s, and a single spectacular indiscretion on his part would have undermined Ortodoxo criticisms of Cuba's triggermen. Conversely, Castro's affluent father provided an excuse to tolerate him. Millo Ochoa, for one, appreciated the old man's ability to deliver campaign contributions and votes in rural Oriente province. He therefore nominated Castro as a delegate to the Ortodoxo national assembly in 1948.[40] Calculations of this sort were nothing new. After all, Chibás had overlooked the shortcomings of another prosperous but compromised figure, Federico Fernández Casas, not once but twice. After helping Chibás campaign during the 1948 presidential campaign, Castro distanced himself even further from the party's ideas when he founded Acción Radical Ortodoxo. This group of UIR ruffians was not officially affiliated with the party but remained a public relations nightmare in waiting. For this reason, Castro was kept away from Ortodoxo broadcasts. Among his peers, Castro's friends José Pardo Llada and Luis Conte Agüero boasted greater followings and more currency within the party. For this reason, Pardo Llada was tapped to succeed Chibás on the airwaves. He was also the top candidate of his generation to one day lead the Ortodoxos.

Castro's attack altered this calculus, converting him from Ortodoxo renegade to national figure within the space of a few months. This was partly due to a photo essay published in *Bohemia*, which depicted the appalling fate of Moncada attackers unlucky enough to have been taken prisoner. The resulting public outrage not only damaged Batista but also guaranteed that Castro, who was then still at large, would be spared similar treatment. Further, while Castro began serving a fifteen-year sentence on the Isle of Pines, a version of his courtroom speech circulated clandestinely throughout Cuba—enhancing his renown.[41]

THE UNHAPPY ORTODOXO FAMILY

Chibás had unified the fractious Ortodoxos in auspicious moments and hoped his martyrdom would hold them together permanently. However, with no opportunity to press their advantage at the polls, Ortodoxo cohesion began faltering during the spring of 1953. Once again, the point of contention was pacts—not the electoral sort, of course, but rather an Auténtico offer to join them in a civic front against Batista. Millo Ochoa, who had succeeded Chibás as party president, favored the idea. He was vigorously opposed by Roberto Agramonte, who headed a bloc of Ortodoxo diehards.[42] Disregarding his objections, Ochoa, along with José Pardo Llada, José Manuel Gutiérrez, and Isidro Figueroa, met Auténtico leaders in Canada. On June 2, they signed the Montreal Pact, which expressed agreement on several basic principles. To begin with, they demanded the reinstatement of Cuba's 1940 constitution. Both parties also concurred on the need for Batista's ouster as he was incapable of presiding over honest or legitimate elections. Once Batista was removed, a provisional government would restore Cuba's Electoral Code of 1943. Moreover, the assembled Ortodoxos and Auténticos embraced nonviolence as a means of political struggle. As a sop to purists like Roberto Agramonte, they even stated that the two sides were not an electoral coalition. Nonetheless, hard feelings persisted and boiled over in October when Agramonte challenged Ochoa to a duel—which was called off at the last minute.[43] From a personal standpoint, the thought of Ortodoxos negotiating with archenemies of his dead cousin, particularly men like Carlos Prío, Tony Varona, and Guillermo Alonso Pujol, must have nagged terribly at Agramonte.[44] Further, many rank-and-file Ortodoxos were leery of any agreement with Carlos Prío, as they suspected he was merely after his old job. Thus, less than two years after Eddy's suicide, his party reverted to self-destructive habits.

Impressive as it was that figures like José Pardo Llada and Carlos Prío could set aside past squabbles, there was no guarantee nonviolent opposition would sway Batista. Prío, for one, covered all possible bases by using his ill-gotten fortune to fund violent resistance groups. Less affluent Ortodoxos such as Pelayo Cuervo Navarro needled Batista in the press instead. While the dictator told anyone who would listen that his "liberation movement" had averted a civil war and scrubbed the nation of corruption, Cuervo Navarro's *Bohemia* exposés provided compelling evidence to the contrary.[45] In May of 1953, Cuervo Navarro charged the army with rigging Cuba's lottery much as it had under Grau and Prío. In a rebuke to those who signed the Montreal Pact, he added that only violence would dislodge Batista. This time, Cuervo Navarro had overstepped the limits and landed in jail for provoking insurrection.

With elections looming in November of 1954, the Ortodoxos sustained yet another fracture. Nearly all party members agreed that Batista should be resisted, but they diverged on the means. However, a modest faction, led by Federico Fernández Casas, flirted with collaboration by registering with the Superior Electoral Tribunal. Eventually, Fernández Casas and his acolytes balked after learning the restrictions under which they would be forced to campaign. Chief among these was Decree Law 997, which greatly suppressed freedom of expression. In fact, the upcoming polls divided most of Cuba's political organizations but none more so than the Auténticos. This was because Ramón Grau San Martín and a sizable cluster of Auténticos opted to run for public office despite the onerous conditions imposed by Batista. Grau defended his decision by claiming he was offering Cubans an alternative. Auténtico president Tony Varona begged to differ. Throughout 1954, he excoriated Grau as a "contributor to the great deceit" of fraudulent elections and charged that El Viejo shared "equal responsibility" with Batista for Cuba's miserable situation.[46] Grau weathered these jabs with aplomb, particularly as his desire for a third presidency outweighed the esteem of Varona—whom he had long ago grown to dislike. More importantly, Grau became increasingly convinced that Batista would manipulate the election boards.[47] As a result, he withdrew on October 30, one day before the balloting was set to begin.

Batista thus ran unopposed and was spared the inconvenience of having to cheat. Understandably, Cubans stayed away from the polls in droves.[48] On the other hand, while Grau had removed himself from the race, many Auténtico legislative candidates remained. Hence, the Auténtico haul of eighteen senators and sixteen congressmen allowed Batista to claim some semblance of legitimacy. Even better, his inauguration in February of 1955 coincided with the killing of Orlando León Lemus, the trigger-happy redhead and poster boy of Auténtico-sponsored gangsters. Batista's new cabinet testified that fickleness remained alive and well among Cuba's political class. Raúl

Menocal, who in 1948 had gasped in horror when Chibás had raised the possibility of a coup, now served serenely as Batista's commerce minister. Santiago Rey had backed Carlos Prío as a member of the Republican-Auténtico coalition and cultivated Chibás when the Ortodoxo leader's fortunes were on the upswing. Currently, he was Batista's interior minister. Neither man could match the contortions of Communications Minister Ramón Vasconcelos. He began his career as a Liberal, serving President Gerardo Machado as commercial attaché to the Cuban legation in Paris. During the mid-1930s, Vasconcelos was such a staunch ally of Batista that revolutionaries attempted to assassinate him. In 1948, he forsook the Liberals and joined Carlos Prío's administration. Frustrated at being bypassed for a senate nomination in 1950, he resigned as minister without portfolio. At around this time, the Havana daily *Alerta*, which he directed, began publishing highly positive commentary about Chibás. Most ironic of all, the lifelong journalist who had deplored Carlos Prío's "gag decree" was now in charge of censoring Cuba's reporters.

Between the elections and Batista's official installation as president, Ortodoxo bosses attempted to mend their rifts. As a goodwill gesture, Millo Ochoa announced that he and his followers would abandon the Montreal Pact—thereby eliminating an obstacle to unity. Given the raw feelings between Ochoa and Agramonte, finding a party president who appealed to all factions was also paramount. For this reason, the top job was offered to Raúl Chibás. Eddy's thirty-nine-year-old younger brother seemed a sensible choice as he was not a career politician and possessed no abiding links to any of the Ortodoxo camps. This would allow him to act as a neutral arbiter. In addition, his surname imbued him with more authority than a mere referee. These same benefits were also potential liabilities, however. Raúl was a private-school headmaster and lacked his brother's charisma and political credibility. If Eddy had sometimes been taxed beyond his capabilities by refractory Ortodoxos, Raúl would be even less likely to bend them.

Initially, though, the results were encouraging. After lengthy negotiations, the Ortodoxos restored political independence as their centerpiece and placated wayward or estranged party members by awarding them plum positions. Thus, the Ortodoxo executive committee was enlarged from sixty-seven to more than eighty—with spots bestowed on the eternally mercenary Federico Fernández Casas and the perpetual separatist Carlos Márquez Sterling.[49] In addition, invitations to join the executive committee were extended to the insurrectionary Rafael García Bárcena and Fidel Castro, along with the illustrious historian Herminio Portell Vilá. By May, with nearly all their errant partisans in tow, the Ortodoxos issued a public manifesto rejecting Batista's government as illegal and demanding restoration of the 1940 constitution. This show of unity was largely superficial, however. In fact, quite a few Ortodoxos lacked confidence in the younger Chibás and pursued separate agendas. José Pardo Llada and Jorge Mañach paid lip service to Ortodoxo intransigence as part of the executive committee but had collaboration in mind when they founded Movimiento de la Nación. This outfit was designed to contest midterm elections in November of 1956 and already counted some of the opposition Auténtico congressmen among its ranks. Millo Ochoa was less openly brazen than Pardo Llada and Mañach, but he also considered participating in the 1956 polls in exchange for "minimal" guarantees regarding their fairness.[50] Fidel Castro, who was now free courtesy of an amnesty law, hailed the choice of Raúl Chibás as party president, but showed no inclination to abide by Ortodoxo policies.[51] Rather, he was busy recruiting and training another rebel force in Mexico with funds provided by Carlos Prío. In August of 1955, Castro sent a message to Ortodoxo militants in Cuba describing his violently inclined followers as "the revolutionary apparatus of *chibasismo*."[52]

With the prospect of party unity becoming "increasingly unreal," Raúl Chibás opted to resign as Ortodoxo president in August of 1956.[53] Pelayo Cuervo Navarro filled the breach, but presided over a substantially diminished party. By now, José Pardo Llada and Carlos Márquez Sterling had abandoned the Ortodoxos. In September, Millo Ochoa's group followed suit. Each of these defectors, along with Federico Fernández Casas, who nominally remained an Ortodoxo, felt midterm elections offered the best way forward. Cuervo Navarro, who had shown similar pragmatic tendencies before the coup, continued to believe Batista must be opposed tooth and nail. Nor did he rule out violence as a means of ejecting the dictator, which put him at odds with Ortodoxo doctrine. When Fidel Castro and his band reached the Sierra Maestra Mountains of Oriente province in January of 1957, Cuervo Navarro did not hesitate to laud their courage. According to Raúl Chibás, he also developed the habit of telling intimates and political allies that Batista should be assassinated.[54] Raúl considered such talk dangerous as it usually found the prying ears of military intelligence. Ironically, something of the sort was actually being prepared, albeit unbeknownst to Cuervo Navarro, by a group called Directorio Revolucionario.

A collection of university students, Spanish exiles, and Auténticos backed by Carlos Prío, the Directorio Revolucionario aimed to murder Batista though a frontal assault on the presidential palace. Besides cash, Prío provided them with detailed blueprints of the edifice he once inhabited. As was often the case, Batista's agents caught wind of the scheme beforehand. When they struck, on March 13, 1957, Batista took refuge on the third floor—which was accessible only by elevator. After the attack was foiled, Batista's forces took revenge on all manner of real and imagined adversaries. Raúl Chibás feared for his life and slept in his office at the Havana Military Academy. Batista's wrath was directed instead toward Cuervo Navarro, whose corpse was found in the Havana Country Club's lake early the next morning. This outrage, which recalled the morbid days of Gerardo Machado's tyranny, represented a tipping point. Faced with a "total lack of personal guarantees," opposition figures, even those favoring peaceful methods, were forced to rethink their positions.[55] For Raúl Chibás and Felipe Pazos, the erstwhile director of Cuba's National Bank, this meant joining Fidel Castro in the Sierra Maestra Mountains. Roberto Agramonte and Millo Ochoa chose exile instead. On the other hand, many carried on as before. In mid-1957, a government appeal to participate in elections the following year was heeded by Ochoa's acolytes, led by Luis Conte Agüero, along with Carlos Márquez Sterling and José Pardo Llada.

By 1958, evidence that the vote would be yet another farce pushed Ochoa's partisans and Pardo Llada's Partido Nacionalista Revolucionario to withdraw. Pardo Llada himself turned up in the Sierra Maestra Mountains that autumn. Even so, the field of presidential contenders was robust. Carlos Márquez Sterling ran at the head of his splinter party, Ortodoxia Libre. Grau once again led the collaboration-minded Auténticos. In addition, a pro-Batista newspaper editor named Alberto Salas Amaro entered the race. All three provided window dressing for the regime's official candidate, Andrés Rivero Agüero, whom the US embassy dismissed as a "yes man."[56] Under no circumstances would Batista permit a reprise of 1944, when fair elections resulted in the defeat of Carlos Saladrigas, his handpicked successor. The November 3 ballot was inevitably crooked and marred by a dismal turnout, estimated at 30 percent by the *New York Times* correspondent Ruby Hart Phillips.[57] Aside from having scant reason to participate, prospective voters had also been threatened by Castro's rebels. Rivero Agüero was declared the winner, but he inherited a dubious bounty. Only force could ensure his installation in the presidential palace. However, Batista's military was demoralized and nearing collapse. As part of a recent effort to discourage Latin American dictatorships, the United States had imposed an arms embargo in March. This was compounded by State Department demands that Batista stop using units sponsored by the US-sponsored Military Defense Assistance Program against Castro's guerrillas.[58] Most critically, Cuba's soldiers thrived in urban confrontations but proved ineffective in the Sierra Maestra Mountains.[59] In the midst of this situation, Batista learned that one of his commanders had met Castro on Christmas Eve and agreed to hand him over for trial and execution as a war criminal.[60] Batista realized he was finished and whisked his family, along with three planeloads of close associates, toward exile during the early hours of January 1, 1959.

REVOLUTION

When Batista toppled the government in March of 1952, many Ortodoxos felt he had denied them an electoral victory. Nearly seven years later, they filled the vacuum left by his departure. This was because Fidel Castro, the party's problem child, quickly consolidated control over Cuba and ensconced himself in Campamento Columbia as military chief. Key cabinet positions in the first revolutionary government were occupied by Roberto Agramonte, who became foreign minister, and Luis Orlando Rodríguez, who headed the interior ministry. Further, Manuel Bisbé was named ambassador to the United Nations. In a gesture fraught with symbolism, Castro offered the choicest morsel of all, Cuba's presidency, to Raúl Chibás. However, Raúl declined and refused a subsequent entreaty to run the treasury ministry. Instead, he accepted a decidedly nonpolitical job as director of Cuba's Western Railways.

In selecting these figures, Castro not only burnished his Ortodoxo credentials, but also paid a very personal tribute to Eddy Chibás. More than mere party members, they were Eddy's cousin, two of his closest friends, and his younger brother. Nor did the reverence end there. On January 17, 1959, Castro addressed a large crowd at Eddy's tomb. Speaking as an Ortodoxo, he referred to "humiliations" perpetrated by Batista's "ruffians" at the party headquarters on 109 Prado Street.[61] Castro then described the importance of Chibás to himself and his rebel movement, saying:

> Today is like a culmination of the whole story, the story of the revolution and the events of 26 July, which are so closely linked with the tale of this tomb, with the memory of the man who lies here, with his ideology, feelings and preaching, because I should say here that without the preaching of Chibás, without what he did, without the civic conscience and rebellion he awakened in the Cuban young people, the events of 26 July would not have been possible.
>
> It was mainly among the young people who followed Chibás that the combatants were recruited. If these young people had not existed, if that preaching had not existed, if that seed had not been sown, the events of 26 July would not have been possible, as they were the continuation of Chibás's work, the harvesting of the seed he planted in our people. Without Chibás, the Cuban revolution would not have been possible. His physical presence was taken from us, we all miss him, and we all said "if Chibás were alive" and we said it bitterly, as if we had lost hope, but yet, Chibás had not abandoned us, Chibás was with the people, Chibás made his presence felt, his work lay dormant in the people, and on this basis the triumphant revolution which is today in power was built.[62]

Castro also honored three other Ortodoxo martyrs: Pelayo Cuervo Navarro, Juan Manuel Márquez, and Raúl de Aguiar. Márquez had been a city councilman in Marianao before the coup and later joined Castro in Mexico. He had been among the eighty-two men who sailed to Cuba on the *Granma* in November of 1956 and was shot by Batista's troops soon after landing. For his part, Aguiar had been a delegate in the party's Havana municipal assembly and died during the Moncada attack. Castro began his peroration by invoking a phrase often heard at Eddy's funeral, namely, "We swear we will complete your work, which we will never betray."[63] He added:

> And now we can say: "You fought graft, Eduardo Chibás, and now there is no graft. You fought petty politicking, Chibás, and now there is none. You fought administrative corruption and it no longer exists. You fought force and now force is not used. You fought profiteering and there is none any more. You fought crime and crime is no longer found here, Chibás. You fought Batista and Batista is no longer here. Chibás, for the first time since your death, your people are happy again. For the first time since your death, Chibás, your people are happy again thanks to the seed you planted, the revolution you implanted, you began, and which your comrades Pelayo Cuervo Navarro, Juan Manuel Márquez and Raul de Aguiar continued, and for which an interminable list of your comrades, comrades in the party you founded, fell, along with men of all parties, because your cause, your ideals ceased to be the cause of one party to become the cause, the ideals and the ideology of a whole people."[64]

Castro thus proclaimed, "Eduardo Chibás, your last loud knock has finally echoed!"[65]

Castro's esteem for Chibás and respect for his popularity were manifested in other ways as well. He raised a statue to the martyred Ortodoxo chief in Santiago de Cuba, realizing a project that had initially been proposed in 1951 by *Bohemia*'s publisher Miguel Ángel Quevedo. Castro even hired Conchita Fernández, Eddy's private secretary and close confidant, to serve as his personal assistant. Despite these gestures, Castro was selectively faithful at best to Chibás, just as he had been while the Ortodoxo chief lived. They shared a deep sympathy for Cuba's peasants, and the First Agrarian Reform Law, promulgated in May of 1959, boasted many provisions touted by Chibás during his presidential run. These included restrictions on landholding (in most cases to 995 acres), abolition of latifundia, and distribution of expropriated plots to poor guajiros.[66] By the same token, Castro's National Literacy Campaign of 1961 and quadrupling of Cuba's health care budget during the early 1960s aimed at rectifying disparities between affluent urban areas and vast zones of rural misery. Chibás had touched on this theme with regularity during his radio broadcasts. Conversely, Castro's decision to call off elections on April 9, 1959, flew in the face of Eddy's deepest convictions. Chibás was guided throughout his life by the ideals of Cuba's 1933 revolution, which, among other things, ousted a tyrant who had illegally amended the constitution to remain in power. Castro's reluctance to restore the 1940 constitution, a document rife with Eddy's fingerprints, was an ominous sign. Other portentous omens soon followed. During a cabinet meeting on June 12, 1959, Castro, who had assumed the prime ministry four months before, dismissed Roberto Agramonte, Luis Orlando Rodríguez, and the other moderate members of his cabinet. Shortly thereafter, Che Guevara, one of Castro's chief lieutenants in the Sierra Maestra, established official contact with the Soviet Union.

Although Castro increasingly spurned Eddy's ideas, his debt to the Ortodoxo leader's political tactics endured. When Castro sought to discredit President Manuel Urrutia and force his resignation, he did so through a Chibás-style tongue-lashing on national television. On July 17, 1959, with much of Cuba watching, Castro claimed Urrutia lacked "a sense of duty" and censured him for accepting his entire $100,000 salary despite Cuba's economic difficulties.[67] In an unmistakable echo of Chibás, he contrasted Urrutia's supposedly luxurious home with his own poverty and lack of interest in material possessions. It was "Shame vs. Money" all over again. Finally, he accused Urrutia, who four days earlier had opined that Communists were "inflicting great harm on Cuba," of conspiring with American agents.[68] Seeing which way the winds were blowing, Roberto Agramonte headed for Puerto Rico in May of 1960. Three months later, Raúl Chibás put his wife in a seventeen-foot boat and fled to Key West. Shortly after arriving, he told reporters from *Life* that he was alarmed by "increasing Communist infiltration" and "a climate of class hatred."[69] By contrast, Luis Orlando Rodríguez remained on the island. In deference to their friendship, Castro allowed Rodríguez to revive a newspaper called *La Calle* that the latter had edited during Batista's dictatorship. However, *La Calle* was shuttered in 1960 after Rodríguez wrote a series of anti-Communist articles—whereupon Castro dispatched him to Venezuela as Cuba's ambassador.[70]

On April 16, 1961, Castro declared that Cuba was a socialist state. This, along with Castro's announcement on December 2 that he was a Marxist-Leninist, presaged the end of Chibás as an emblem for his revolution. Eddy's implacable opposition to Communism and the Soviet Union proved inconvenient for a regime that, by July of 1960, had signed a formal military agreement with Nikita Khrushchev. As a result, Chibás largely disappeared from Castro's speeches and writings until the 1990s. In recent times, Chibás has undergone a revival because corruption has once again taken center stage in Cuban politics. During 2007, the centenary of Eddy's birth was commemorated by a flurry of admiring articles in *Granma* and *Juventud Rebelde*—the government's two official dailies. Armando Hart, a politburo member, lauded Chibás for elevating the importance of ethics in Cuban politics. He concluded that the Ortodoxo founder "continues to be very present in our feelings, actions and thoughts."[71] Pastorita Núñez, the former Ortodoxo hard-liner and subsequent Castro devotee, twisted herself into a knot trying to reconcile her past and present heroes. She thus claimed Eddy "was not anti-communist" but rather "against the Communist party's leadership of the time."[72]

Since Cuba's independence, the island has bent to the whims of its political luminaries. In the late 1940s and early 1950s, Eduardo Chibás seemed destined to sway Cuba via the nearly infinite power of its presidency. His failure tantalizes because he was a true democrat, an honest politician, and a sincere constitutionalist. The fact that Chibás was never tainted by the compromises of ruling magnifies his virtues. In this sense, Chibás may well have chosen martyrdom not only to unify his party but also to keep perpetually quibbling Ortodoxos from ruining his reputation for posterity.

Notes

INTRODUCTION

1. Reinaldo Arenas, *Antes que anochezca* (Barcelona: Tusquets, 1996), 52.
2. Arenas, *Antes que anochezca*, 52.
3. Ramón Rodríguez Salgado, *Vergüenza contra dinero* (La Habana: Editora Política, 2007), 248.
4. Antonio Rafael de la Cova, *The Moncada Attack: Birth of the Cuban Revolution* (Columbia: University of South Carolina Press, 2007), 28.
5. Hill had been a respected newspaper reporter for two decades, but his career took off when he began broadcasting over the airwaves in 1931. *Time* observed that "his deep timbred voice, easy delivery, and intelligent interpretation of the day's news won him a tremendous following. His sentimentality was sufficient to endear him to the radio masses yet not so cloying as to annoy most critical listeners." See: "Press: Hill to Hearst," *Time*, June 5, 1933, http://www.time.com/time/magazine/article/0,9171,745657,00.html.
6. *UN Statistical Yearbook* (New York: United Nations, Department of Public Information, 1963), 684. According to this source, Cuba counted 575,000 radios by 1949.
7. "El Milagro de Chibás," *Bohemia*, June 6, 1948, 43.
8. Archivo Nacional de Cuba (ANC), Fondo Eduardo R. Chibás, Legajo 9, Expediente 285, 101.
9. ANC, Legajo 9, Expediente 285, 88.
10. "Testamento Político de Chibás," *Bohemia*, August 26, 1951, 96.
11. ANC, Legajo 6, Expediente 201, 26.

1. "AS LONG AS ANY CUBAN SUFFERS, I WILL FIGHT FOR HIM"

1. "En Cuba, Duelo," *Bohemia*, May 11, 1947, 43.
2. Humberto Vázquez García, *El Gobierno de la Kubanidad* (Santiago de Cuba: Editorial Oriente, 2005), 316.
3. ANC, Legajo 35, Expediente 1097, 104–106. Armando Mier Vega and Rafael Fernández Núñez, both of whom were present at the hospital where Supervielle spoke, reproduced his words from memory just over two weeks later. A slightly different account of the situation also appears in "En Cuba, Municipio," *Bohemia*, January 26, 1947, 38–39.

4. The Cuban peso during this period was interchangeable with the US dollar.

5. Financing the aqueduct through a loan from the Sugar Workers' Retirement Fund had been the centerpiece of Supervielle's plan, in large part for nationalistic reasons. President Grau had devised the refrain, "An aqueduct without concessions and with Cuban money," in response to a previous proposal under the mayoralty of Raúl García Menocal (1943–1946), who was a Democrat, and which called for concessions and foreign funding.

6. ANC, Legajo 35, Expediente 1097, 104.

7. ANC, Legajo 35, Expediente 1097, 105.

8. "En Cuba: Municipio," 39.

9. ANC, Legajo 35, Expediente 1097, 105.

10. The tenants' assembly approved the loan on the condition that Cuba's legislature pass a law establishing a Tribunal of Accounts. This, obviously, was outside of Supervielle's control. The landowners' delegation also desired something from Cuba's legislators. They demanded that the Sugar Workers' Retirement Fund, which had been established by presidential decree, must be formalized by an act of Congress. Supervielle was powerless here as well. The workers' delegation, perhaps swayed by the enthusiasm of Jesús Menéndez, approved the loan without reservations.

11. *Bohemia*'s weekly circulation at this time was 140,000. Subsequently, the magazine conducted a study in urban and suburban areas revealing that approximately six people read each issue. When *Bohemia*'s rural subscribers were taken into account, the number of total readers each week was "conservatively" estimated to be more than one million, or 20 percent of Cuba's population. See: "Un Survey de Bohemia Sobre Sus Lectores Adultos," *Bohemia*, March 7, 1948, 58–59.

12. "En Cuba, Municipio," 38.

13. "En Cuba, Política: Ni sangre ni agua," *Bohemia*, April 6, 1947, 35.

14. "En Cuba, Municipio: Supervielle el Irresoluto," *Bohemia*, May 4, 1947, 41.

15. "En Cuba, Duelo," 42.

16. "En Cuba, Duelo," 42.

17. "En Cuba, Duelo," 42–43. See also Luis Conte Agüero, *Eduardo Chibás, el Adalid de Cuba* (México: Editorial Jus, 1955), 502. When President Grau arrived at the Supervielle residence shortly thereafter, he told the mayor's wife, "Señora, the nation has lost one of its most illustrious sons. You were a great help to him." Without missing a beat, she replied, "And you helped him to end up like this."

18. For example, a letter to Chibás by Jorge González Rojas, of Havana, stated, "I admire your bravery, courage and incorruptible dignity and I'm sure that just as God chose Jesus Christ to save Christianity from the wave of perverts that exploited it, He has chosen you to realize a similar labor in Cuban politics." ANC, Legajo 34, Expediente 1089, 1. Another Chibás admirer sent him a poem, the opening lines of which read, "Like Jesus Christ, you tell the truth to men without scruples." ANC, Legajo 35, Expediente 1094, 155.

19. The first *radionovelas* in Latin America were written and produced in Cuba during the late 1930s.

20. Richard Pack, "Report from Havana," *New York Times*, April 28, 1946, II, 7.

21. "En Cuba, Duelo," 43. See also, Conte Agüero, *Eduardo Chibás*, 503.

22. Chibás also sent his letter to the newspapers. On January 21, 1947, *Diario de la Marina*, among others, printed it in its entirety.

23. The fact that Chibás now criticized Grau for fomenting the black market represented a complete about-face. During a broadcast of April 15, 1945, he had strenuously defended Grau's system for supplying Cubans with basic foodstuffs. He also excoriated Santiago Rey Perna, a Republican senator from Las Villas, for lacking the moral authority to criticize Grau—especially given his poor record as former governor of that province. Three days later, Chibás and Rey fought a saber duel in which the former was lightly wounded on the forearm and back.

24. Although the constitution forbade consecutive reelection, ex-presidents could run again after they had been out of office for eight years.

25. "El Gobierno y la denuncia de Chibás," *Carteles*, January 19, 1947, 25.

26. Conte Agüero, *Eduardo Chibás*, 488.

27. "En Cuba, Política: Conflicto Emocional," *Bohemia*, March 9, 1947, 40.

28. As part of the deal, Grau's vice president, Raúl de Cárdenas, was a Republican.
29. "En Cuba, Política: Conflicto Emocional," 40.
30. On July 14, 1946, the provincial assembly of the Auténtico party in Oriente, the largest and most populous of Cuba's six provinces, proclaimed Chibás their choice for the presidential nomination in 1948. This had been arranged beforehand, with Eddy's knowledge, by Millo Ochoa, the Auténtico party president of Oriente. That evening, Chibás addressed a grateful speech to his supporters via radio in which he claimed his popularity coupled with that of the party would guarantee a "definitive and crushing victory" without pacts or coalitions. See: Conte Agüero, *Eduardo Chibás*, 445.
31. "En Cuba, Política: Chibás el Marino," *Bohemia*, March 16, 1947, 43.
32. "En Cuba, Política: Chibás el Marino," 43.
33. "En Cuba, Política: Conflicto Emocional," 40.
34. "En Cuba, Política: Conflicto Emocional," 40.
35. "En Cuba, 'Balance,'" *Bohemia*, October 10, 1948, 125.
36. Alemán purchased the finca "America," formerly the domain of ex-president José Miguel Gómez (1909–1913)—another distinguished figure in the annals of Cuban political corruption. Gómez, affectionately known as El Tiburón (the shark), was a general in the war of independence and dominated the island's Liberal party until his death in 1921. He entered the presidency with little money and exited a millionaire, albeit one who took care of his friends. This gave rise to a refrain that played on his nickname, "El tiburón se baña pero salpica." (The shark bathes but splashes.)
37. Alemán's rise within the party was nothing short of meteoric. Having joined the Auténticos only after Grau's victory in 1944, he had become the party's president in Havana by December of 1947 and won a senate seat in 1948. In the sort of irony that abounds in Cuban politics, Chibás occupied this seat two years later after Alemán's death from Hodgkin's disease.
38. Hugh Thomas, *Cuba: The Pursuit of Freedom* (New York: Harper & Row, 1971), 743. The University of Havana was an ideal place for the action groups as it was off-limits to the police. On the other hand, Cuba's various police and security forces were themselves often run by members of action groups during Grau's presidency, so they flourished outside the university as well. For example, the chief of Cuba's Servicio de Investigaciones was Mario Salabarría, a friend of Grau and member of MSR. Havana's police chief, Fabio Ruiz, belonged to MSR's bitter rival, Acción Revolucionaria Guiteras (ARG). Ruiz was made police chief in exchange for ARG support in the 1944 elections.
39. On November 20, 1946, Senator Millo Ochoa of the grupo ortodoxo submitted a motion to investigate irregularities at the polytechnic school of Holguín, his hometown. Alemán responded by sending "employees" of the education ministry to the Capitolio building armed with pistols and machine guns. By a strange coincidence, the senate lacked a quorum on that day.
40. ANC, Legajo 35, Expediente 1097, 58.
41. ANC, Legajo 35, Expediente 1097, 56.
42. ANC, Legajo 35, Expediente 1097, 37.
43. ANC, Legajo 35, Expediente 1097, 26.
44. Jacinto Torras, "¿Terminarán en 1947 la crisis de abastecimiento y la bolsa negra?," *Bohemia*, January 26, 1947, 29.
45. José Pardo Llada, "La bolsa negra," *Bohemia*, January 19, 1947, 42.
46. ANC, Legajo 35, Expediente 1097, 72–73.
47. ANC, Legajo 35, Expediente 1097, 12–13.
48. ANC, Legajo 35, Expediente 1097, 81.
49. ANC, Legajo 35, Expediente 1097, 50. Entitled "Memorandum para el Sr. Chibás," this document contains minor editorial changes in Eddy's handwriting, suggesting he read it carefully.
50. "En Cuba, Crisis: Un Foco Pestilente," *Bohemia*, April 20, 1947, 45.
51. "En Cuba, Crisis: Un Foco Pestilente," 48. The following week, David produced a cartoon called "Precaution," in which Grau sported a clothespin instead.
52. "En Cuba, Crisis: Casas no asiste al Senado," *Bohemia*, April 27, 1947, 45.

53. "Senadores Auténticos estiman que tiene caracter transitorio el Gabinete recien designado," *Diario de la Marina*, May 3, 1947, 2.
54. "En Cuba, Política: Vamos a Firmar Para Complacer al Presidente," *Bohemia*, May 4, 1947, 43.
55. Miguel de Marcos, "¡Se cansa uno!," *Bohemia*, January 5, 1947, 52.
56. The depth of anger against Casas in particular cannot be overestimated, particularly as shortages and exorbitant prices affected all Cubans. On January 21, 1947, an anti–black market demonstration took place in front of the presidential palace. Grau, who addressed the crowd, was met with whistles, catcalls, and insults when he referred to the government's policy of supplying basic goods.
57. Conte Agüero, *Eduardo Chibás*, 503.
58. Conte Agüero, *Eduardo Chibás*, 503.
59. "Fue Imponente Manifestación de Duelo el Entierro del Alacalde Habanero Dr. Manuel Fernández Supervielle," *Diario de la Marina*, May 6, 1947, 1.
60. "En Cuba, Duelo: Un hombre de honor," 43.
61. Shortly after Supervielle's suicide, Chibás received a letter from someone who had been present at the house of the new mayor, Nicolás Castellanos. According to this account, one of the guests suggested that celebratory drinks were in order. However, Castellanos responded that "this is a time of pain rather than one of joy." Moments later, Carlos Prío, the prime minister, appeared shouting and applauding. He allegedly yelled, "There is no reason for sadness!" and addressing the new mayor's wife, he cried, "Bring some champagne to celebrate as this is a great day for us!" See: ANC, Legajo 35, Expediente 1097, 95.
62. Chibás, who was Grau's chief propagandist at the time, framed opposition to Mayor Menocal's aqueduct in fiercely patriotic terms. During his broadcast of August 27, 1944, Chibás asserted that "Cubans must rid themselves of their colonial mentality, shake themselves free of defeatism, feel proud of their country and march forward with their foreheads raised, toward the conquest of Cuba's economic independence." See Conte Agüero, *Eduardo Chibás*, 322.
63. Charles D. Ameringer, *The Cuban Democratic Experience: The Auténtico Years, 1944–1952* (Gainesville: University of Florida Press, 2000), 33.
64. Conte Agüero, *Eduardo Chibás*, 505
65. Conte Agüero, *Eduardo Chibás*, 505.
66. Conte Agüero, *Eduardo Chibás*, 505.
67. Conte Agüero, *Eduardo Chibás*, 504.
68. Conte Agüero, *Eduardo Chibás*, 506.
69. Far from being a bystander, Natasha Mella was named to the ten-member committee charged with officially forming the new party. She was the youngest member of the group (although three others were in their twenties) and the only woman. However, her surname was among the most recognizable in Cuba and possessed undeniable power. She was also strikingly beautiful, a trait inherited from her father—whose good looks were immortalized in the photos of his lover, the Italian photographer Tina Modotti.
70. Conte Agüero, *Eduardo Chibás*, 508.
71. Conte Agüero, *Eduardo Chibás*, 508.
72. Conte Agüero, *Eduardo Chibás*, 510.

2. "SHOOT ME IN THE HEART—THE ORTODOXOS NEED A MARTYR"

1. ANC, Legajo 34, Expediente 1089, 71.
2. ANC, Legajo 34, Expediente 1089, 52.
3. ANC, Legajo 34, Expediente 1089, 94.
4. Interview with Pastorita Núñez, June 3, 2007.
5. Pedro Prada, *La secretaria de la república* (La Habana: Ciencias Sociales, 2001), 118.

6. Those who "told" Chibás also included more privileged victims of injustice, such as ex–foreign minister Alberto Inocente Álvarez, who met with Chibás in February of 1947. Álvarez revealed that his recent resignation was linked to his unwillingness to support Grau's reelection campaign and accused the current administration of being the "most corrupt in the history of the Republic." Given Álvarez's well-publicized venality during his time as a public servant, this charge was nothing if not ironic. He was also angry with Grau for collecting Álvarez's resignation letter via Cuba's US ambassador Guillermo Belt rather than doing so personally. On Sunday, February 9, Chibás duly revealed these piquant tidbits over the air. See "En Cuba, Doble Duelo," February 16, 1947, 40–41.

7. "Inician mañana trabajos para las adhesiones," *El Crisol*, June 16, 1947, 4. Aside from *El Crisol*, *Alerta* usually published the entire transcript of Eddy's radio transmissions.

8. "Inician mañana trabajos para las adhesiones," *El Crisol*, 4.

9. "El Ultimo 'Survey,'" *Bohemia*, April 25, 1948, 56.

10. ANC, Legajo 34, Expediente 1089, 155.

11. ANC, Legajo 34, Expediente 1090, 66.

12. ANC, Legajo 34, Expediente 1089, 174.

13. Conte Agüero, *Eduardo Chibás*, 512.

14. Jorge Mañach, "Carta a Chibás," *Bohemia*, May 18, 1947, 41.

15. Mañach, "Carta a Chibás," 41.

16. Mañach, "Carta a Chibás," 41.

17. "En Cuba, Un Republicano Menos," *Bohemia*, June 15, 1947, 46.

18. *Diario de la Marina*, July 18, 1944, 4.

19. Miyar served as one of Eddy's seconds during his first duel, in 1937, against Carlos Font—a medical student and member of the Communist-leaning Ala Izquierda. Font had published attacks against Chibás in *Línea*, the organization's mouthpiece. The duel was fought with pistols at a distance of twenty-five paces in a secluded area of Havana's posh Miramar neighborhood. When Chibás, whose poor eyesight was legendary, opened fire, the bullet nearly hit his other second, Justo Carrillo, in the head. Carrillo, the future chief of Cuba's Agricultural and Industrial Development Bank, was understandably unnerved and promptly declared the duel over despite Chibás's objections. See Conte Agüero, *Eduardo Chibás*, 236–240.

20. Among those who backed Chibás on this issue were Manuel Bisbé, Luis Orlando Rodríguez, and Leonardo Fernández Sánchez, along with the party's youth leaders Luis Conte Agüero and Orlando Castro.

21. Luis E. Aguilar, *Cuba 1933: Prologue to Revolution* (Ithaca, NY: Cornell University Press, 1972), 58. In 1926, all of Cuba's political parties decided to work together in support of Machado. This was known as *cooperativismo*. The effect, notes Aguilar, is that "for all practical purposes, Machado had no political opposition."

22. In 1940, Fulgencio Batista won the presidency heading a seven-member coalition even as the Auténticos obtained twenty thousand more votes than any single party. Four years later, the Auténticos were an electoral juggernaut, more than doubling the vote count of their nearest rival. Even so, they would have fallen short without Republican backing.

23. "En Cuba, Política: No me Preocupan las Posiciones," *Bohemia*, March 23, 1947, 47.

24. In 1946, the Mexican daily *Siempre* published a comparison of the senatorial vote two years earlier. Chibás received 126,381 votes, more than any other Auténtico senatorial candidate. However, Pelayo Cuervo Navarro was close behind with 123,905. Both men appeared on the Republican ballot as well, and if these votes are added, Cuervo Navarro actually attracted more votes than Chibás. See Conte Agüero, *Eduardo Chibás*, 415.

25. Unquestionably, Cuervo Navarro's plan also accommodated his personal ambition. Nor was he the only grupo ortodoxo member who was loath to voluntarily pass four years on the sidelines. Even so, he was more immune to accusations of opportunism than any of his pact-friendly peers. Cuervo Navarro began his public career in 1935, at the age of thirty-two, when he served as education minister in the cabinet of President Carlos Mendieta. A lawyer by training and Democrat by affiliation, he ran unsuccessfully for mayor of Havana in 1936 but was elected to Cuba's 1939 constitutional convention on the party slate. The next year, Democratic chief Mario García Menocal struck a deal with Batista before the 1940 polls. In exchange for his support, Menocal would choose the coalition's candidates for vice president, mayor of

Havana, three provincial governorships, and twelve senate seats. After an avalanche of protests by rank-and-file adherents, the party leadership vacillated over whether to accept Batista's terms, to consider a counteroffer from Grau, or to enter the elections solo. Many objected to Batista's embrace of the Communists and his insistence that they remain part of the alliance. Cuervo Navarro was heavily invested in this decision, as the party's municipal assembly had once again nominated him for mayor of Havana. Backing the pact with Batista would all but ensure him the post, and he thus initially endorsed the ex-general. However, he subsequently changed his mind and resigned from the party on March 20, 1940. Another prominent Democrat who bolted over this issue was then-president of the Havana Bar Association, Manuel Fernández Supervielle—who told the press that supporting Batista would betray his principles and political values. In forsaking the Havana mayoralty in 1940, Cuervo Navarro cemented his reputation as a politician of conscience.

26. Interview with Pastorita Núñez, June 3, 2007.
27. "En Cuba, Política: Secta de Jacobinos," *Bohemia*, July 27, 1947, 53.
28. "En Cuba, Pastoral: La Bolsa Negra Excomulgada," *Bohemia*, May 25, 1947, 42.
29. Enrique de la Osa, "El robo del brillante del Capitolio," *Bohemia*, June 8, 1947, reproduced in *Bohemia Digital*, http://www.bohemia.cubasi.cu/2006/mar/03/sumarios/historia/brillante-capitolio.html.
30. José Roseñada, *Diario de la Marina*, June 3, 1947, 4.
31. "Me injurían por dinero, dice Chibás," *Alerta*, June 9, 1947, from ANC, Legajo 6, Expediente 198, 13.
32. "Me injurían por dinero, dice Chibás," ANC, Legajo 6, Expediente 198, 13.
33. "Me injurían por dinero, dice Chibás," ANC, Legajo 6, Expediente 198, 13.
34. "Me injurían por dinero, dice Chibás," ANC, Legajo 6, Expediente 198, 13.
35. "Me injurían por dinero, dice Chibás," ANC, Legajo 6, Expediente 198, 13.
36. "En Cuba, Volvió al Ministerio," *Bohemia*, June 22, 1947, 45. See also: Enrique de la Osa, *En Cuba, primer tiempo, 1947–1948* (La Habana: Ciencias Sociales, 2004), 86.
37. ANC, Legajo 6, Expediente 198, 27.
38. ANC, Legajo 6, Expediente 198, 29.
39. Chibás was acutely aware of the constant financial temptations faced by public officeholders. In 1944, two Chinese Cubans approached his secretary, Conchita Fernández, and told her to let Chibás know he could take $300 per day if he would allow them to set up an illegal gambling den. He was indignant when he learned of the offer but knew such proposals were common. Enrique Perdomo, "Chivás en la Revolución," *Bohemia*, May 16, 1946, 72.
40. Conte Agüero, *Eduardo Chibás*, 515.
41. ANC, Legajo 3, Expediente 99, 148–149.
42. ANC, Legajo 3, Expediente 99, 148.
43. ANC, Legajo 3, Expediente 99, 150.
44. Conte Agüero, *Eduardo Chibás*, 494. Eddy's choice of seconds was telling at this delicate moment in his political career. At a time when he was insisting he was and always would be an Auténtico, Chibás chose the two most prominent leaders of the grupo ortodoxo, Pelayo Cuervo Navarro and Millo Ochoa.
45. Conte Agüero, *Eduardo Chibás*, 491.
46. This required submitting a list of at least fifty thousand members and presenting a suitable emblem. The latter involved some difficulty, as the Superior Electoral Tribunal rejected the PPC's initial insignia, which featured a torch. Acceptance followed only when a palm tree was substituted in its place.
47. "En Cuba, Política: El Mitin del Partido del Pueblo," *Bohemia*, September 14, 1947, 47.
48. "En Cuba, Política: El Mitin del Partido del Pueblo," 47.
49. *El Mundo*, for example, was honored in 1943 with the Maria Moors Cabot Prize for outstanding journalism in Latin America and the Caribbean. This prize, which has been offered since 1938, is the oldest international award in journalism. Within Cuba, *El Mundo*, *Diario de la Marina* (another Cabot prize winner), and *Alerta* were considered the nation's most prestigious newspapers.
50. "Ineludible Rectificación," *El Mundo*, September 19, 1947, reprinted in "Comentando la Actualidad," *Carteles*, September 28, 1947, 55.

51. Enrique de la Osa, "En Cuba, Policía: El drama en el Senado," *Bohemia*, September 21, 1947, reprinted in de la Osa, *En Cuba, primer tiempo*, 176.
52. De la Osa, *En Cuba, primer tiempo*, 176.
53. De la Osa, *En Cuba, primer tiempo*, 176. Ara was hardly an impartial observer given his close ties to UIR.
54. De la Osa, *En Cuba, primer tiempo*, 174.
55. De la Osa, *En Cuba, primer tiempo*, 175.
56. When Grau was inaugurated in October of 1944, Pérez Dámera held the rank of major. During the following six months he was promoted five times. In choosing to elevate a young officer, Grau sought to bypass more established figures with close connections to Batista. Also, he was almost certainly looking for someone whom he could control.
57. Enrique de la Osa, "En Cuba, Un Plácido Retiro Bucólico," *Bohemia*, September 28, 1947, reprinted in de la Osa, *En Cuba, primer tiempo*, 191.
58. ANC, Legajo 9, Expediente 198, 64.
59. ANC, Legajo 9, Expediente 198, 66.
60. The town of Artemisa was of great symbolic value to the revolutionaries as it was the scene of a massacre by Machado's soldiers on May 19, 1930. On that day, members of the opposition Unión Nacional held a meeting there—an act the government considered illegal. An army lieutenant attempting to close down the proceedings was shot, and afterward, troops opened fire on those assembled, killing eight and injuring several dozen.
61. ANC, Legajo 35, Expediente 1092, 19.
62. ANC, Legajo 35, Expediente 1092, 1.
63. ANC, Legajo 35, Expediente 1092, 28.
64. ANC, Legajo 35, Expediente 1092, 164.
65. ANC, Legajo 35, Expediente 1092, 83.
66. "Habló el Senador Chibás Anoche de Distintos Tópicos," *El Crisol*, October 27, 1947, from ANC, Legajo 6, Expediente 198, 105.
67. During 1947, Cuba's senate only managed to celebrate fifteen of thirty-four regular sessions and three of six extraordinary sessions due to a lack of quorum. During this time a total of ten laws were approved. Of these, five eventually landed on the president's desk. Grau, who preferred to rule by decree, vetoed all of them. Cuba's chamber of representatives fared even worse. Seven ordinary sessions and two extraordinary sessions took place out of a proposed thirty-two. The result was six laws passed. Enrique de la Osa noted that Grau, like Batista before him, preferred to keep Cuba's representatives sidelined because they were theoretically in charge of Cuba's budget. See: "En Cuba, Congreso: Una Legislatura Fracasada," *Bohemia*, December 28, 1947, 64.
68. "Habló Anoche por Radio el Senador Eduardo R. Chibás," *El Crisol*, November 10, 1947, from ANC, Legajo 6, Expediente 198, 116.
69. "En Cuba, Política: Independientes, no Aislacionistas," *Bohemia*, November 30, 1947, 55.
70. ANC, Legajo 6, Expediente 198, 140. The final phrase was apparently a last-minute addition as it appears in Chibás's handwriting below the typewritten text.
71. "En Cuba, Política: El Lápiz de Chibás," *Bohemia*, December 14, 1947, 47.
72. "En Cuba, Política: El Lápiz de Chibás," 47.
73. "En Cuba, Política: El Lápiz de Chibás," 47.
74. "En Cuba, Política: El Lápiz de Chibás," 47.
75. "En Cuba, Política: El Copador Copado," *Bohemia*, December 21, 1947, 98.
76. "En Cuba, Política: Es un Especie de Savonarola," *Bohemia*, December 28, 1947, 61.
77. ANC, Legajo 35, Expediente 1093, 174.
78. The widow of Pereda Pulgares, Ofelia Khouray remained a prominent member of the PPC and played a prominent role in the party's Camagüey delegation.
79. "En Cuba, Política: Balas y Votos," *Bohemia*, January 4, 1948, 44.
80. "En Cuba, Política: Balas y Votos," 44.
81. "En Cuba, Política: Balas y Votos," 44.
82. "En Cuba, Política: Balas y Votos," 44.
83. "En Cuba, Política: Balas y Votos," 45.

3. "NO ONE RESPECTS THE CONSTITUTION"

1. Raúl Gutiérrez, "El Pueblo Opina Sobre el Gobierno Actual y los Anteriores de Cuba," *Bohemia*, January 4, 1948, 28–29.
2. Chibás and Quevedo were classmates at Havana's prestigious Colegio de Belén. The Jesuit-run school was considered Cuba's top secondary institution.
3. "En Cuba, Política: Problemas, Más Problemas," *Bohemia*, January 11, 1948, 44–45.
4. "En Cuba, Política: La Gran Tragedia," *Bohemia*, January 25, 1948, 49.
5. Jorge Mañach, "La conciliación ortodoxa," *Bohemia*, January 25, 1948, 42.
6. With his usual penchant for symbolism, Chibás initially hoped to convene the national assembly on January 28, the birthday of Cuba's national martyr and independence hero José Martí. However, the date was moved forward due to objections from those who wanted to resolve the party's business sooner.
7. Conte Agüero, *Eduardo Chibás*, 550.
8. "En Cuba, Política: El Permanente Chibás," *Bohemia*, February 1, 1947, 47.
9. "En Cuba, Política: El Permanente Chibás," 47.
10. The Republicans were a conservative party that extolled tradition, the family, social order, and Christian morality, among other things. Needless to say, they were very much an anti-Communist outfit. When Grau brought the Communists into his government, party president Gustavo Cuervo Rubio resigned, but his successor, Guillermo Alonso Pujol, maintained the alliance. Even so, the Republicans were ambivalent partners throughout Grau's term and many figures, such as Federico Fernández Casas, expressed strong doubts. For the most part, Alonso Pujol tried to quell such discontent by demanding a larger share of government patronage. See: William Stokes, "The 'Cuban Revolution' and the Presidential Elections of 1948," *The Hispanic American Historical Review* 31, no. 1 (Feb., 1951), 45.
11. Auténtico antagonism toward Communism was long-standing and characterized many former members of the Student Directorate, including Carlos Prío and Tony Varona. This hostility was aggravated in 1938, when the Communists struck a deal with Batista to legalize themselves while the Auténticos remained outlawed and persecuted. At the same time, as the Auténticos gained power and popularity, their ranks were swelled by ex-Communists such as Eusebio Mujal and Angel Cofiño.
12. On July 16, 1947, Chibás addressed a letter to *Diario de la Marina* director José Ignacio Rivero to dispel rumors that his party was going to sign a pact with the Communists. However, he also addressed the recent Auténtico takeover of the Confederation of Cuban Workers, writing, "We don't want the Communists to control the CTC but neither do we desire this control to fall into the hands of a group of unscrupulous politicians who are unconditionally loyal to the government and largely unconnected to the working class." See: ANC, Legajo 9, Expediente 285, 5.
13. "En Cuba, Crimen: 'Yo te Dije Que Ibas Vivo o Muerto,'" *Bohemia*, February 1, 1947, 43.
14. An official investigator sent by Grau concluded that Menéndez fired at Casillas before being killed. However, this assertion is dubious given that the train carriage behind Casillas showed no evidence of wayward bullet holes.
15. "Comentando la Actualidad," *Carteles*, February 1, 1948, 20. Pérez Dámera's original statement appeared in the Havana daily *Información*.
16. "Comentando la Actualidad," 20.
17. Conte Agüero, *Eduardo Chibás*, 550–551.
18. The day after Menéndez was killed, the Communist lawmakers Juan Marinello, Blas Roca, and Joaquín Ordoqui visited the presidential palace. Roca asked Grau to dismiss General Pérez Dámera and remove Captain Casillas from his post so he could be tried in a civilian court. Grau repeated the military's argument that Casillas was an exemplary soldier and warmly defended his army chief. Nonetheless, he promised the legislators that justice would be pursued. However, neither Pérez Dámera nor Casillas suffered any consequences during his administration. Casillas would eventually be executed for Menéndez's death in 1959 during the revolutionary government of Fidel Castro.

19. "En Cuba, Ejército," *Bohemia*, January 25, 1948, 44.

20. "Incoherencias y Genovevancias," *El Siglo*, January 28, 1948, reprinted in "Cómo Opina Nuestra Prensa," *Carteles*, February 8, 1948, 40.

21. The Auténtico provincial assembly of Camagüey is a useful primer on the rough-and-tumble nature of Cuban politics during this period. Although the pro-Grau faction narrowly outnumbered that of Suárez Fernández, the latter held his representatives back to avoid a quorum. Needing only one delegate to validate the vote, a Suárez Fernández supporter was persuaded to attend by his *Grauista* brother-in-law. Before being able to do so, he was kidnapped—forcing the assembly to be rescheduled for December 30. For the second session, an official vote would require only a majority of delegates rather than 60 percent. Even with a victory seemingly assured, Grau's adherents, led by Senator Tony Varona, left nothing to chance. The new assembly's location was sent to each representative via special delivery mail. However, only Grau supporters received the correct address. This ensured a unanimous albeit dubious result and led Suárez Fernández to file an appeal with Cuba's Superior Electoral Tribunal.

22. "El Reyecito Criollo," *Bohemia*, January 25, 1948, 44.

23. "En Cuba, Política: Vamos a Firmar Para Complacer el Presidente," *Bohemia*, May 4, 1947, 43.

24. "En Cuba, Política: Crucigrama," *Bohemia*, February 1, 1948, 48.

25. The sobriquet was a favorite of Enrique de la Osa, who also referred to Alemán as "*el cacique de BAGA*" (the chief of BAGA), after the acronym for his ill-gotten political fund, and the "ex-minister of school hunger" in reference to his practice of embezzling funds meant for school breakfasts. While de la Osa was obviously biased, his views agreed with Cuban public opinion. The combination of Alemán's dismal performance as a public servant and Eddy's relentless focus on his corruption greatly damaged his image. For the opinion poll, see Raúl Gutiérrez, "En Camagüey y Las Villas Ganará el Gobierno Según Sea Su Candidato Presidencial," *Bohemia*, January 18, 1948, 53.

26. "En Cuba, Política: 'Eres la Clave de la Situación . . . ,'" *Bohemia*, February 15, 1948, 63.

27. "En Cuba, Política: 'Eres la Clave de la Situación . . . ,'" 52.

28. "En Cuba, Política: 'Eres la Clave de la Situación . . . ,'" 63.

29. Prominent among these were Viriato Gutiérrez, former vice president of Cuba's chamber of representatives; Rafael Guas Inclán, the current governor of Havana province; and Juan Antonio Vázquez Bello, the former Liberal party boss in Santa Clara. All three were millionaires with money they had stolen during Machado's presidency.

30. William S. Stokes, "The 'Cuban Revolution' and the Presidential Elections of 1948," *Hispanic American Historical Review* 31, no. 1 (February 1951): 52.

31. This position was partly rooted in the Liberals' experience in 1944. Before that year's election, President Batista forced them to support his handpicked successor, the Democratic leader Carlos Saladrigas, as head of the Social Democratic Coalition. The Liberals yielded reluctantly as they had registered more adherents than any other party in Cuba. One wing briefly declared the Liberals would renounce the pact unless one of their own headed the ticket. Eventually, they settled for the vice-presidential candidate and an allotment of three senators per province (as opposed to two for the Democrats).

32. This was done via interview with Raoul Alfonso Gonsé, director of the Havana daily *Alerta*.

33. When Alonso Pujol mentioned San Martín, Alemán "jumped as if he had been stung by a wasp." He then dubbed San Martín "the worst candidate" and declared he would leave Cuba if Grau's cousin were elected. See: "En Cuba, Política: Más Barato Te Costaría Un Viaje a Miami," *Bohemia*, February 22, 1948, 51.

34. "En Cuba, Política: Más Barato Te Costaría Un Viaje a Miami," 51.

35. "En Cuba, Política: Más Barato Te Costaría Un Viaje a Miami," 51.

36. "En Cuba, Política: Más Barato Te Costaría Un Viaje a Miami," 51.

37. "En Cuba, Política: Más Barato Te Costaría Un Viaje a Miami," 51.

38. "En Cuba, Política: Más Barato Te Costaría Un Viaje a Miami," 52.

39. This was clearly a ploy orchestrated by Cuervo Navarro, who neither embezzled nor stole but indulged in lawyerly skullduggery when necessary. During the hearing, Joaquín Martínez Sáenz, who was among the truant delegates, claimed he was unaware of when the assembly would meet. The lawyer representing Chibás found this strange given that the date was advertised in the press. Martínez Sáenz averred he "was not reading the papers that much." Reminded that he and Cuervo Navarro often saw each other and the latter would have been likely to remind him about the assembly, Martínez Sáenz said, "during those days, I didn't talk to Pelayo." Confronted with press reports indicating he had appeared in Cuervo Navarro's law office shortly before the assembly, Martínez Sáenz said, "during those meetings we didn't talk about provincial politics." "How strange!" retorted the exasperated lawyer. "Politicians who meet in order to not talk about politics!" See "En Cuba, Política: Pelayo y Joaquín," *Bohemia*, February 22, 1948, 54.

40. "En Cuba, Política: Pelayo y Joaquín," 54.

41. "En Cuba, Política: Pelayo y Joaquín," 54.

42. ANC, Legajo 9, Expediente 285, 18.

43. ANC, Legajo 9, Expediente 285, 18.

44. Henry Wallace (1888–1965) ran for president in 1948 on the Progressive party ticket. He served under President Franklin Delano Roosevelt as vice president (1941–1945) and secretary of agriculture (1933–1940). He was also President Harry Truman's secretary of commerce (1945–1946).

45. ANC, Legajo 9, Expediente 285, 20.

46. ANC, Legajo 9, Expediente 285, 20.

47. ANC, Legajo 9, Expediente 285, 21.

48. ANC, Legajo 9, Expediente 285, 21. The candidate, Leo Isacson, was actually a member of the American Labor Party. He won the seat in New York's Twenty-Fourth District after the incumbent accepted a judgeship. In the snap election of February 17, 1948, Isacson received 22,697 votes, his Democratic opponent obtained 12,598, the Liberal candidate counted 3,800, and the Republican nominee boasted a mere 1,500.

49. Moreover, the "traditional and decrepit" political parties of the United States would be vindicated in November of 1948 when the Democrats recaptured the presidency and won back the Twenty-Fourth Congressional District in New York. Wallace did not win a single electoral vote.

50. Conte Agüero, *Eduardo Chibás*, 555.

51. The phrase (*deber histórico*) appears with regularity in Eddy's letters and radio broadcasts.

52. Castro owed his position as Cuba's national sports director to José Manuel Alemán, the MSR's chief patron. Before that, Castro had been the leading MSR representative at the University of Havana—where he was president of the University Student Federation (Federación Estudiantil Universitario).

53. Enrique de la Osa, "En Cuba, Atentado: 'Nosotros Mismos Somos Culpables . . . ,'" *Bohemia*, February 29, 1948, reprinted in de la Osa, *En Cuba, primer tiempo: 1947–1948*, 365.

54. De la Osa, *En Cuba, primer tiempo: 1947–1948*, 366.

55. "En Cuba, Política: Dos Cosas Iguales a Una Tercera," *Bohemia*, February 29, 1948, 42.

56. "En Cuba, Política: Dos Cosas Iguales a Una Tercera," 42.

57. A *Bohemia* reporter wrote that "during its 65 years of existence—the last 30 devoted to court business—never have such well known figures of Cuban politics congregated within the building's walls." See "En Cuba, Política: La Madre del Cordero," *Bohemia*, March 7, 1948, 49.

58. "En Cuba, Política: La Madre del Cordero," 49.

59. "En Cuba, Política: La Madre del Cordero," 50.

60. Conte Agüero, *Eduardo Chibás*, 556.

61. Conte Agüero, *Eduardo Chibás*, 556. The "third floor" referred to the private quarters of Cuba's presidential palace and was used by politicians of all stripes to refer to Grau.

62. ANC, Legajo 8, Expediente 258.

63. "En Cuba, Política: Como en el Cuento de Poe," *Bohemia*, March 7, 1948, 54.

64. "En Cuba, Política: ¡Este es el País del Relajo!," *Bohemia*, March 14, 1948, 51.

65. Conte Agüero, *Eduardo Chibás*, 557–558.
66. "En Cuba, Política: '¡Esperen Media Hora!,'" *Bohemia*, March 14, 1948, 54.
67. "En Cuba, Política: '¡Esperen Media Hora!,'" 54.
68. "En Cuba, Política: '¡Esperen Media Hora!,'" 54.
69. "En Cuba, Política: 'Como Ciertos Insectos . . . ,'" *Bohemia*, March 21, 1948, 57.
70. Stokes, "The 'Cuban Revolution,'" 55. The presidential palace was situated in Old Havana, about three miles northwest of Auténtico headquarters in Vedado.
71. "En Cuba, Política: 'Como Ciertos Insectos . . . ,'" *Bohemia*, March 21, 1948, 57.
72. "En Cuba, Política: La Fiesta de los Chinos," *Bohemia*, March 21, 1948, 58.
73. "En Cuba, Política: El Peso de las Senadurías," *Bohemia*, March 21, 1948, 59.
74. "En Cuba, Política: Pensando en Griego," *Bohemia*, March 21, 1948, 62.
75. According to José Miguel Tarafa, Martínez Fraga shook hands with him and Senator Miguel de León after the national assembly concluded and pledged not to veto the agreement. See "En Cuba, Política: La Fiesta de los Chinos," 58.
76. "En Cuba, Política: No Podemos Suicidarnos," *Bohemia*, March 21, 1948, 62.
77. These included Havana mayor Nicolás Castellanos, Senator Tony Varona of Camagüey, Congressman Rubén de Leon of Oriente, and Congressman Lomberto Díaz of Pinar del Río.
78. "Editorial: Un Decepcionante Proceso Político," *Bohemia*, March 21, 1947, 53.
79. "Editorial: Un Decepcionante Proceso Político," 53. In fact, the editorial implied Suárez Fernández should follow the bold example of Hernán Cortés, who according to legend burned his ships upon landing on the Caribbean coast of Mexico—thereby eliminating the possibility of escape.
80. "Los Corruptores de la Moral Política," *Carteles*, March 21, 1948, 13.
81. "Los Corruptores de la Moral Política," 13.
82. "En Cuba, Política: Trayectoria del Pensamiento de Miguel Suárez," *Bohemia*, March 21, 1948, 63.
83. "En Cuba, Política: Pensando en Griego," *Bohemia*, March 21, 1948, 62.
84. "En Cuba, Política: Pensando en Griego," 63.
85. Aside from contributing to various publications including *Bohemia* and *Prensa Libre*, Vasconcelos was also editor of *Alerta*.
86. "En Cuba, Política: 'Que Voy a Hacer yo Con 1 Millón de Pesos?,'" *Bohemia*, March 28, 1948, 47.
87. "En Cuba, Política: 'Que Voy a Hacer yo Con 1 Millón de Pesos?,'" 47.
88. Auténtico dread of a lawsuit was deftly satirized in the comic strip "El Reyecito Criollo." The cartoonist portrayed a balloon labeled "appeal" filling up with air, causing panic among Grau and Prío. With trepidation, the two men follow a cord attached and wince when they find Miguelito Suárez Fernández gleefully standing at a pump with Chibás sneering behind him. See "El Reyecito Criollo," *Bohemia*, March 28, 1948, 42.
89. "En Cuba, Política: La Luz Roja," *Bohemia*, March 28, 1948, 46.
90. "En Cuba, Política: La Luz Roja," 46.
91. "En Cuba, Política: La Luz Roja," 46.
92. "En Cuba, Política: La Luz Roja," 46.
93. "En Cuba, Política: La Luz Roja," 47.
94. Conte Agüero, *Eduardo Chibás*, 559. Nor was $341 a meager income by regional standards. Cuba was among the wealthiest nations in Latin America during this time. Another interesting aspect of this broadcast was the fact that Chibás repeated almost verbatim many phrases from the March 21 editorial in *Bohemia*.
95. Conte Agüero, *Eduardo Chibás*, 559.
96. Conte Agüero, *Eduardo Chibás*, 560.
97. "En Cuba, Política: Epitafio del Tercer Frente," *Bohemia*, April 4, 1948, 43.
98. "Declaraciones Exclusivas de 'Eddy' Chibás," *Bohemia*, April 4, 1948, 41.
99. "En Cuba, Política: 'Este es el Fin de la Aventura,'" *Bohemia*, April 11, 1948, 64.
100. "En Cuba, Política: 'Este es el Fin de la Aventura,'" 64. At first, López Dorticós endorsed a pact with the Liberals, asserting they were "not that bad," adding, "the Machado era was a long time ago and we should forget about this page in our history." At a later meeting, he

changed his mind and promoted a pact with the Auténticos, saying, "Prío, even with his errors, represents the revolution."

101. At this time, the PPC provincial chiefs were as follows: Pinar del Río: Dominador Pérez; Havana: Manuel Bisbé; Matanzas: José Manuel Gutiérrez; Las Villas: Agustín Cruz; Camagüey: Aurelio Álvarez; and Oriente: Millo Ochoa.

102. Conte Agüero, *Eduardo Chibás*, 562.

103. "En Cuba, Política: 'Este es el Fin de la Aventura,'" 65.

104. "En Cuba, Política: 'Este es el Fin de la Aventura,'" 65.

105. "En Cuba, Política: 'Este es el Fin de la Aventura,'" 65.

106. "En Cuba, Política: 'Este es el Fin de la Aventura,'" 65.

107. "En Cuba, Política: 'Este es el Fin de la Aventura,'" 65.

108. "En Cuba, Política: 'Este es el Fin de la Aventura,'" 66.

109. "En Cuba, Política: 'Este es el Fin de la Aventura,'" 66.

110. ANC, Legajo 36, Expediente 1103, 10. Genescá y Rovira's parish covered the towns of Cifuentes and Corralillo in Las Villas province. According to the 1943 census, Cifuentes counted 9,830 inhabitants, while Corralillo had 11,781.

111. ANC, Legajo 36, Expediente 1103, 10.

4. "WE ARE ALONE WITH THE PEOPLE"

1. Unlike other Cuban millionaires, Batista claimed to be "special" because of his "preoccupation" with the island's workers. See "En Cuba, Política: Batista y el Nuevo Partido," *Bohemia*, August 1, 1948, 56.

2. *Time* magazine reported that Batista attempted to mollify his ex-wife by giving her valuable real estate, including a twelve-story apartment house and $8 million in cash. See: "Dictator with the People," *Time*, April 21, 1952, http://www.time.com/time/magazine/article/0,9171,889465-4,00.html.

3. "En Cuba, Política: Un Cable de Daytona Beach," *Bohemia*, April 4, 1948, 41.

4. Francisco Ichaso, "Nuestras Sucursales de Miami y de Daytona Beach," *Bohemia*, April 18, 1948, 64.

5. "En Cuba, Poder Judicial: Batista y la Causa Número 30 de 1943," *Bohemia*, April 18, 1948, 54.

6. "En Cuba, Poder Judicial: Batista y la Causa Número 30 de 1943," 54.

7. Besides being Cuba's attorney general, he was also father of one of its most famous revolutionary martyrs—also named Rafael Trejo—who was killed in 1930 during an anti-Machado protest by University of Havana students. After his son's death, Trejo brought a court case against the policemen responsible for shooting his son. As a result, he was jailed for seven months.

8. "En Cuba, Política: El Destino Está en Manos de Genovevo," *Bohemia*, April 11, 1948, 56.

9. Prío was pleased to hear of this journey, telling Suárez Fernández he was "taking a step in the right direction." He urged the senate president to inform Alemán that a united Auténtico party would win the elections. Suárez Fernández was not so sure. While allowing that party unity was imperative, he also believed the Auténticos needed to address high prices spawned by the black market, the scarcity of meat, and lack of electricity in rural areas. Without such "rectifications," he warned, "we won't advance very far." See "En Cuba, Política: ¡Al Fin…!," *Bohemia*, April 18, 1948, 57.

10. Miami had been known as the "Magic City" since the early twentieth century because its rapid growth inspired the impression that it appeared as a fully formed metropolis without ever having been a town.

11. "En Cuba, Política: Falleció sin Testar," *Bohemia*, April 18, 1948, 57.

12. ANC, Legajo 36, Expediente 1103, 1.

13. Among the casualties was Eddy's grand-uncle Eduardo Agramonte, who served as the rebel government's secretary of state and was a colonel in the army of liberation before falling

in battle in 1872 at the age of thirty-one. In terms of how such sacrifices were viewed, it is useful to excerpt a letter from Carlos Manuel de Céspedes, president of the rebel government, to the mother of Ignacio Agramonte. He wrote: "Nothing can console the pain of a mother. That her son is no longer alive is reason for her to weep inconsolably forever. But, madam, you cannot be deprived of the most justifiable pride. . . . For (heroic) men, always persecution and death, for their family an eternal coat of arms, for their *patria* the duty to build for them monuments of gratitude. This is the fate of those whose acts will be recorded in the pages of history." See Louis A. Pérez Jr., *To Die in Cuba: Suicide and Society* (Chapel Hill: University of North Carolina Press, 2005), 101.

14. Conte Agüero, *Eduardo Chibás*, 564–565. Chibás first tried out this line of reasoning during an interview on Unión Radio three days earlier. He had been asked, "What resources are you counting on to win the elections against the millions of BAGA, the syndicate of millionaires and the entrenched interests?"

15. ANC, Legajo 36, Expediente 1103, 31.

16. Fulgencio Batista and José Manuel Alemán were two well-known examples of politicians who doubled as real estate tycoons. However, they were by no means unique. For example, Jaime Mariné, Batista's former minister of sport, purchased a string of hotels in Caracas, Venezuela. Carlos Prío would eventually acquire three fincas in the Cuban countryside, and his older brother Paco bought a sumptuous manse in Havana's exclusive Miramar neighborhood.

17. For a more complete list of contributors to the PPC, see ANC, Legajo 1106, Expediente 1106, 46–48.

18. The Ortodoxo delegation consisted of Millo Ochoa, Manuel Bisbé, Leonardo Fernández Sánchez, and Beto Saumell, the mayor of Bayamo. The participation of Fernández Sánchez is interesting given that he was among the most strident opponents of pacts in the PPC. At the same time, he was also a former Communist.

19. According to Luis Conte Agüero, the traveling Ortodoxo entourage in Oriente featured Eddy's younger brother Raúl, Roberto Agramonte, Manuel Bisbé, Ventura Dellundé, Guillermo de Zéndegui, and the Ortodoxo Women's Wing president María Esther Villoch. They were accompanied by the journalists Tony de la Osa and Juan González Martínez. De la Osa, presumably, was the prime source for his brother Enrique's account of the tour, which appeared in the May 30 issue of *Bohemia*.

20. Conte Agüero, *Eduardo Chibás*, 569.

21. Gloria Cuadras, *Lo que yo vi*, unpublished manuscript, private collection of Olga Portuondo Zuñiga, Santiago de Cuba, 191.

22. Conte Agüero, *Eduardo Chibás*, 568. Eddy was well accustomed to jumping from truck tops into the arms of his admirers, a habit that simultaneously gratified supporters and horrified rivals. Enrique de la Osa noted that "upon getting out of his famous automobile, Chibás would appear in rural towns and mount an open truck from which he would throw himself acrobatically into the multitude as if he wanted to bathe himself in the people of each location. The leaders of the Liberal-Democratic coalition and the (Auténtico-Republican) alliance, habituated only to the cold tactics of money, were scandalized by such demagoguery, as they called it. But Eddy trusted his political instincts in the power of a more emotional contact with the impressionable Cuban voter." See Enrique de la Osa, *En Cuba, primer tiempo: 1947–1948*, 468.

23. De la Osa, *En Cuba, primer tiempo*, 452.

24. De la Osa, *En Cuba, primer tiempo*, 453.

25. "En Cuba, Política: 'Este es el Fin de la Aventura,'" *Bohemia*, April 11, 1948, 65.

26. Conchita Fernández, Eddy's secretary, noted that many men were jealous of Mella because of her extraordinary beauty and her position as an Ortodoxo party delegate. See Pedro Prada, *La secretaria de la república*, 122.

27. "Declaraciones del Dr. Agustín Cruz," *Bohemia*, April 25, 1948, 82.

28. "Declaraciones del Dr. Agustín Cruz," 82.

29. ANC, Legajo 36, Expediente 1103, 137.

30. ANC, Legajo 36, Expediente 1103, 123.

31. ANC, Legajo 36, Expediente 1103, 133.

32. ANC, Legajo 36, Expediente 1104, 34.

33. ANC, Legajo 6, Expediente 200, 9.
34. Chibás alleged the survey cost $150,000, an enormous sum.
35. ANC, Legajo 6, Expediente 200, 6.
36. For the Sinclair Oil Company, Chibás received twenty-five votes, Prío sixteen votes, and Núñez Portuondo nine votes. At the La Corona Cigar Factory, Chibás won thirty-seven votes, while Prío and Núñez Portuondo settled for fifteen apiece. Obviously, these polls were less than scientific. Also, they were in Havana, an Ortodoxo stronghold where the party maintained a strong presence.
37. "¡Vergüenza contra Dinero!," *Diario de la Marina*, May 18, 1948, 15. See also "¡Vergüenza contra Dinero!," *Diario de la Marina*, May 19, 1948, 13. These are but two of many examples.
38. ANC, Legajo 6, Expediente 200, 4.
39. Chibás, of course, had participated in the strikes and received a six-month jail sentence for inciting streetcar operators to join.
40. "En Cuba, Política: La Historia Indiscreta," *Bohemia*, May 2, 1948, 50.
41. "En Cuba, Política: La Historia Indiscreta," 50.
42. Among others, Carreras murdered a brother of Eddy's friend María Teresa Freyre de Andrade. After Machado was overthrown, Cuba's Tribunal of Sanctions condemned Carreras to death for his crimes, but the sentence was never carried out.
43. "En Cuba, Política: La Historia Indiscreta," 50.
44. Carlos Miguel de Céspedes and Rafael Guas Inclán, especially, were very much figures of the present. The former was on the Liberal party's senatorial ticket in Matanzas, and the latter was governor of Havana province. Chibás also accused Emilito Núñez Portuondo, who was running his brother's campaign, of embezzling $40,000 from the Civil Service Retirement Fund.
45. ANC, Legajo 6, Expediente 200, 22. Chibás discreetly neglected to mention that land confiscations had continued unabated after the revolution. Even worse, one of those large landowners with a sketchy history running for a Liberal senate seat was a former Ortodoxo—namely, Federico Fernández Casas. The Auténticos made a great deal of hay out of this fact in their anti-Chibás campaign literature.
46. ANC, Legajo 6, Expediente 200, 15.
47. ANC, Legajo 6, Expediente 200, 12.
48. ANC, Legajo 6, Expediente 200, 13.
49. ANC, Legajo 6, Expediente 200, 27.
50. ANC, Legajo 6, Expediente 200, 50.
51. ANC, Legajo 6, Expediente 200, 52.
52. ANC, Legajo 6, Expediente 200, 1.
53. ANC, Legajo 6, Expediente 200, 1.
54. "En Cuba, Política: Trágica Encrucijada," *Bohemia*, April 11, 1948, 57.
55. ANC, Legajo 6, Expediente 200, 3.
56. ANC, Legajo 6, Expediente 200, 4.
57. ANC, Legajo 6, Expediente 200, 1.
58. Prío had many faults as a politician, but his anti-Communism was both sincere and keenly felt. Like many ex-revolutionaries, Prío resented Communist collaboration with Batista in the late 1930s while the Auténtico party remained illegal and its members endured persecution, death, and exile.
59. ANC, Legajo 6, Expediente 200, 1.
60. With his deft propagandizing touch, Chibás reminded listeners that the march took place on May 17, the same day that Niceto Pérez, a campesino from Oriente province, had been killed by a large landowner and Liberal party member.
61. ANC, Legajo 6, Expediente 200, 21.
62. ANC, Legajo 6, Expediente 200, 2.
63. ANC, Legajo 6, Expediente 200, 3. According to Chibás, his "maximum preoccupation" after winning his senate seat had been addressing the needs of rural Cubans. Believing the Auténticos were ignoring the issue, he spoke to Grau, who told him his first priorities were passing complementary laws for the 1940 constitution and overseeing the budget. See Antonio

Ortega, "'Tengo confianza en el pueblo Cubano,' dice 'Eddy' Chibás," *Bohemia*, May 9, 1948, 53. At one point, Chibás claimed to be so distressed about Grau's inaction regarding the campesinos that he offered to resign from the senate and head a special agency that would oversee improvements in their condition. Grau apparently laughed at this proposal and said, "This is not a job for you." See Arturo Alfonso Roselló, "Explica Chibás la causa y origen de su divorcio del Doctor Grau," *Carteles*, May 23, 1948, 29.

64. A cartoon satirizing this situation appeared in *Bohemia* that same week. It portrayed Carlos Prío serenading a reluctant Chibás with the lyrics, "Come, my love, I'm calling you, come desperately," while Grau looks on hopefully in the background. See "Musica de Lara," *Bohemia*, May 9, 1948, 58.

65. ANC, Legajo 6, Expediente 200, 18.

66. Roselló, "Explica Chibás," 29. Aside from his position at *Carteles*, Roselló also contributed a regular column to *Diario de la Marina* and contributed to *El País*, the pro-Liberal newspaper. His natural sympathies, therefore, were not with Chibás.

67. Gastón Baquero, "Chibás considera necesario restituir al pueblo la fé en los hombres de gobierno para encauzar los destinos de la nación," *Diario de la Marina*, May 9, 1948, 1.

68. In terms of the editorial leanings of these publications, *Bohemia* was slightly left of center but offered a forum for a wide range of viewpoints, from the Communist leader Juan Marinello to the Conservative Francisco Ichaso and everything in between. *Carteles* was rabidly anti-Communist and tilted Conservative. *Diario de la Marina* was Cuba's oldest right-wing daily. The newspaper was pro-Catholic, pro-American, pro-Franco, pro-business, and, of course, an implacable foe of Communism. *El Crisol* was a well-respected Cuban broadsheet of moderate persuasion.

69. Ortega, "'Tengo confianza en el pueblo cubano,'" 53.

70. Ortega, "'Tengo confianza en el pueblo cubano,'" 53.

71. Ortega, "'Tengo confianza en el pueblo cubano,'" 53.

72. Roselló, "Chibás explica," 30.

73. Roselló, "Chibás explica," 30.

74. Roselló, "Chibás explica," 30.

75. Roselló, "Chibás explica," 30.

76. Roselló, "Chibás explica," 30.

77. Roselló, "Chibás explica," 30.

78. The creation of a Tribunal of Accounts was one of the so-called complementary laws of the 1940 constitution whose specifics were supposed to be ironed out by Cuba's legislative branch. However, neither Batista nor Grau was anxious to court oversight of their spending, so the project languished.

79. Roselló, "Chibás explica," 31.

80. Roselló, "Chibás explica," 31.

81. Baquero, "Chibás considera necesario," 23.

82. "Los candidatos presidenciales opinan sobre el grave problema de la electricidad," *Bohemia*, May 23, 1948, 67.

83. "Responde al Dr. Núñez Portuondo al Cuestionario de *Carteles*," *Carteles*, May 30, 1948, 32.

84. The language appeared in an advertisement entitled "Trinomio de Integridad Moral," which appeared on page 69 of the May 23, 1948, issue of *Bohemia*.

85. "Nuestro candidato," *Carteles*, May 23, 1948, 49.

86. Roselló, "Chibás explica," 31.

5. "THE MIRACLE OF CHIBÁS"

1. ANC, Legajo 8, Expediente 241, 1. The song was arranged by Alberto Aloma Echezarreta. The Spanish lyrics are as follows:

Siempre que te pregunto
Que quien es ese hombre
Tú siempre me respondes
CHIBAS, CHIBAS, CHIBAS

Cuando oigas en un radio
Que alguno está gritando
Ya puedes ir pensando
CHIBAS, CHIBAS, CHIBAS

Que digan que está loco
Hablando, hablando
Pero en Junio primero
Arrollando, arrollando

Verás el diez de Octubre
Al pueblo deliriando
Verás gobernando
Está CHIBAS, CHIBAS

2. ANC, Legajo 8, Expediente 241, 1.
3. De la Osa, *En Cuba, primer tiempo*, 470.
4. Whereas Chibás merely lost his bid for Cuba's highest office, others were deprived even more tangibly. For example, the Democrat Carlos Manuel de la Cruz and ex–commerce minister Alberto Inocente Álvarez had bet 100,000 pesos on the election results. Both men had apparently met in the Havana restaurant El Caramelo, whereupon the Democrat boasted to his Auténtico rival that he was willing to bet 1,000 or even 100,000 pesos on the triumph of Ricardo Núñez Portuondo. Initially, Álvarez was uninterested and left the restaurant. He subsequently changed his mind after examining an opinion poll predicting Carlos Prío would win in all six provinces, after which he made a concerted effort to locate de la Cruz in order to seal the terms. See de la Osa, *En Cuba, primer tiempo*, 472.
5. For example, the Auténtico-Republican alliance counted a 36–18 majority in the senate but 11 of those 36 were supporters of Suárez Fernández. See Stokes, "The 'Cuban Revolution,'" 74–75.
6. De la Osa, *En Cuba, primer tiempo*, 474.
7. De la Osa, *En Cuba, primer tiempo*, 472.
8. De la Osa, *En Cuba, primer tiempo*, 473.
9. De la Osa, *En Cuba, primer tiempo*, 473.
10. Stokes, "The 'Cuban Revolution,'" 74.
11. Stokes points out that the Auténtico-Republican alliance received 176,482 fewer votes than it registered, while Chibás increased his total by 156,054. Most of the remaining voters seem to have chosen the Liberal-Democratic coalition, which garnered 48,932 more votes than it registered. See: Stokes, "The 'Cuban Revolution,'" 74.
12. "El Milagro de Chibás," *Bohemia*, June 6, 1948, 95.
13. De la Osa, *En Cuba, primer tiempo*, 481.
14. Sergio Carbó, "Aspectos turbios de la jornada," *Prensa Libre*, June 4, 1948, reprinted in "Cómo opina nuestra prensa," *Carteles*, June 13, 1948, 56.
15. Francisco Ichaso, "Divagación Postcomicial," *Diario de la Marina*, June 3, 1948, 4.
16. "Reconoceré el buen gobierno que haga Prío, dice Chibás," *Diario de la Marina*, June 3, 1948, 14.
17. "Reconoceré el buen gobierno que haga Prío, dice Chibás," 14.
18. "Reconoceré el buen gobierno que haga Prío, dice Chibás," 14.
19. "Reconoceré el buen gobierno que haga Prío, dice Chibás," 14.
20. ANC, Legajo 6, Expediente 200, 59.

21. While the Cuban armed forces generally behaved well, *Bohemia* lamented that the military had announced the final verdict rather than the Superior Electoral Tribunal. The magazine also scolded Grau for celebrating his disciple's victory on the balcony of the presidential palace well before the official results were announced. See: "En Cuba, El Escrutinio del Ejercito," June 13, 1948, 51.
22. For a full description, see: Thomas, *Cuba*, 527.
23. Marinello received 143,033 votes, a mere 7.33 percent of all those cast.
24. "En Cuba, Política: Herencia," *Bohemia*, June 20, 1948, 58.
25. "En Cuba, Política: Herencia," 58.
26. "En Cuba, Política: Herencia," 58.
27. ANC, Legajo 36, Expediente 1105, 116.
28. The case of Millo Ochoa elicited a great deal of comment and speculation in Ortodoxo circles. On June 11, Eddy's friend Ignacio Mendoza wrote, "If [Ochoa] told the [Liberal-Democratic] coalition he would campaign for you and they nominated him anyway, then they are imbeciles but if he didn't tell them he betrayed them and is unworthy of confidence even as he has been loyal to you up till now." At the same time, Mendoza deemed Ochoa a "hero who was sacrificed for you" because his association with the PPC caused many Liberals and Democrats to vote for the Auténtico candidate, who was, in fact, an ex-Liberal. See ANC, Legajo 36, Expediente 1106, 30.
29. ANC, Legajo 36, Expediente 1106, 28.
30. ANC, Legajo 36, Expediente 1103, 109.
31. ANC, Legajo 6, Expediente 200, 138.
32. ANC, Legajo 6, Expediente 200, 138.
33. ANC, Legajo 6, Expediente 200, 138. See also: "En Cuba, Política: Batista y el Nuevo Partido," *Bohemia*, August 1, 1948, 56.
34. ANC, Legajo 6, Expediente 200, 138.
35. ANC, Legajo 36, Expediente 1105, 39.
36. ANC, Legajo 36, Expediente 1105, 39.
37. ANC, Legajo 36, Expediente 1107, 53.
38. ANC, Legajo 36, Expediente 1107.
39. ANC, Legajo 6, Expediente 201, 29.
40. ANC, Legajo 6, Expediente 200, 90.
41. De la Osa, *En Cuba, primer tiempo*, 586.
42. De la Osa, *En Cuba, primer tiempo*, 586.
43. Aside from being a creature of Guillermo Alonso Pujol, or perhaps because of it, Ramón Corona was also a Republican senator from Las Villas province.
44. Satirical sketches involving Primitivo Rodríguez invariably portrayed him holding a hoe, as the term *guataca* in Cuban Spanish refers not only to the farm instrument but also to those who curry favor.
45. ANC, Legajo 6, Expediente 201, 26.
46. ANC, Legajo 6, Expediente 201, 25–26.
47. ANC, Legajo 6, Expediente 201, 27.
48. Before the 1933 revolution, presidents were inaugurated on May 20, the anniversary of Cuba's official independence in 1902. However, this date was tainted by the Platt Amendment's imposition—which guaranteed that the United States could intervene in Cuba's affairs almost at will.
49. "Dictator with the People," *Time*, April 21, 1952,http://www.time.com/time/magazine/article/0,9171,889465-6,00.html.
50. Raoul Alfonso Gonsé, "Los ladrones a la carcel," *Alerta*, October 25, 1948, from ANC, Legajo 36, Expediente 1109, 21.
51. ANC, Legajo 36, Expediente 1109, 21.
52. ANC, Legajo 6, Expediente 201, 77.
53. ANC, Legajo 6, Expediente 201, 66.
54. ANC, Legajo 6, Expediente 201, 72.
55. ANC, Legajo 6, Expediente 201, 74–75.

56. Trinidad threatened to bring charges of libel against Chibás now that he no longer enjoyed parliamentary immunity. However, he refrained from doing so—most likely realizing that a trial would offer Chibás an even broader forum for his accusations.
57. Chibás noted that RHC Cadena Azul had always supported the government in power, having backed Machado, then Batista, then Grau, and now Prío.
58. "Comentando la actualidad," *Carteles*, November 21, 1948, 48.
59. ANC, Legajo 6, Expediente 201, 68.
60. ANC, Legajo 6, Expediente 201, 68.
61. "La semana parlamentaria," *Carteles*, November 14, 1948, 56. As Varona was also a senator from Camagüey, he was the administration's natural advocate in Cuba's upper chamber.
62. ANC, Legajo 6, Expediente 201, 69.
63. "En Cuba, Educación: En Perpetua Polémica," *Bohemia*, October 9, 1949, 109.
64. ANC, Legajo 6, Expediente 201, 79.
65. ANC, Legajo 6, Expediente 201, 79.
66. "La semana parlamentaria," *Carteles*, November 14, 1948, 56.
67. "En Cuba, Destitución: Aliado del Sátrapa Trujillo," *Bohemia*, August 28, 1949, supplement 2. Lavish military budgets were a legacy of Grau's administration, although the logic behind them was fairly sound. After the army enjoyed a privileged place in Cuban politics for ten years, Grau's election in 1944 promised diminished influence. He therefore attempted to buy its loyalty by raising its budget to 20,037,442 pesos by his last year in office. By contrast, during Fulgencio Batista's presidency military spending never rose above 8,500,000 pesos. Of course, generals and other high-ranking officers enriched themselves regardless of who ruled. Pérez Dámera, for example, lined his pockets by raiding the army's retirement fund. Also, in 1946, the pursy general won second prize in the island's lottery—pocketing 50,000 pesos in a process that was widely thought to be rigged.
68. Suárez Fernández controlled the Matanzas and Las Villas provincial assemblies and could have, under Cuba's electoral law, rejected the Auténtico-Republican alliance.
69. ANC, Legajo 6, Expediente 201, 89–90.
70. ANC, Legajo 6, Expediente 201, 90–91.
71. In an attempt to appear evenhanded, Prío also placed two pro-government shows under ban, but their audiences were miniscule. Only the president's most devoted partisans believed he was acting equitably.
72. ANC, Legajo 6, Expediente 201, 94–95.
73. ANC, Legajo 6, Expediente 201, 95.
74. "La semana parlamentaria," *Carteles*, December 12, 1948, 53.
75. ANC, Legajo 6, Expediente 201, 96.
76. ANC, Legajo 6, Expediente 201, 96.
77. ANC, Legajo 6, Expediente 201, 97–98. Chibás also admired the US voting system. During his December 12 radio show, Eddy told listeners he knew Harry Truman would defeat Thomas Dewey even as all the commentators thought otherwise because his rallies were twice as large and "the elections over there are honorable." See: ANC, Legajo 6, Expediente 201, 141.
78. ANC, Legajo 6, Expediente 201, 133.
79. ANC, Legajo 6, Expediente 201, 135.
80. ANC, Legajo 6, Expediente 201, 154.
81. ANC, Legajo 6, Expediente 201, 142.

6. "I WOULD PROUDLY GO TO PRISON TO DEFEND THE CUBAN PEOPLE"

1. "En Cuba, Deceso: Una Vida Fecunda y Combativa," *Bohemia*, January 9, 1949, 53.
2. Both men were also lawyers who had once been partners in the same firm.

3. Carlos Manuel de la Cruz was appointed president of Cuba's State Council in 1934, which placed him next in line for the island's presidency—occupied at that moment by Carlos Mendieta. The State Council was an appointed body of fifty men that advised the cabinet and served as a substitute for the legislative branch until elections were organized in 1936.
4. "En Cuba, Política: Recordando el Pasado," *Bohemia*, January 16, 1949, 55.
5. The exact size of the deficit was a matter of great debate. For example, Treasury Minister Antonio Prío estimated it to be 85 million pesos.
6. Francisco Ichaso, "La Difícil Situación del Gobierno Actual Ante las Malversaciones del Anterior," *Bohemia*, January 31, 1949, 27.
7. Ichaso, "La Difícil Situación," 27.
8. Ichaso, "La Difícil Situación," 27.
9. David, "No es lo mismo," *Bohemia*, January 16, 1949, 54.
10. "Grafoentrevisa exclusiva: Prío," *Bohemia*, January 16, 1949, 60.
11. Conte Agüero, *Eduardo Chibás*, 589.
12. "En Cuba, Política: Diálogo Telefónico," *Bohemia*, January 16, 1949, 55.
13. "En Cuba, Política: Diálogo Telefónico," 55.
14. "Porque hice presidente a Carlos Prío," *Bohemia*, January 31, 1949, 58.
15. "Porque hice presidente a Carlos Prío," 58.
16. "Porque hice presidente a Carlos Prío," 65.
17. "En Cuba, Controversia: 'El más Peligroso de Todos . . . ,'" *Bohemia*, February 6, 1949, 49.
18. "En Cuba, Controversia: 'El más Peligroso de Todos . . . ,'" 49.
19. "En Cuba, Controversia: 'El más Peligroso de Todos . . . ,'" 49.
20. "En Cuba, Controversia: 'El más Peligroso de Todos . . . ,'" 52.
21. "En Cuba, Controversia: 'El más Peligroso de Todos . . . ,'" 52.
22. "En Cuba, Controversia: 'El más Peligroso de Todos . . . ,'" 52.
23. Of the remaining subjects, 13.18 percent replied "I don't know or I don't want to answer," and 16.59 percent said "Neither." See Raúl Gutiérrez, "El Pueblo Opina Sobre Prío y Grau, Chibás y Batista," *Bohemia*, February 6, 1949, 65.
24. "Porque hice presidente a Carlos Prío," 58.
25. "En Cuba, Atentados: 'Apártese todo el mundo,'" *Bohemia*, January 23, 1949, 52. See also: Ameringer, *The Cuban Democratic Experience*, 81.
26. "En Cuba, Atentados: 'Apártese todo el mundo,'" 52.
27. During Prío's presidential campaign, the ARG leader Eufemio Fernández saw to his personal security. After the election, Prío appointed him chief of Cuba's Bureau of Special Investigations.
28. "En Cuba, Atentados: 'Apártese todo el mundo,'" 51.
29. Raúl Gutiérrez, "El Pueblo Opina Sobre Prío y Grau, Chibás y Batista," 65. The poll respondents were from Havana and the nearby municipalities of Marianao, Guanabacoa, and Regla.
30. Francisco Ichaso, "El Grausato en el Aventino," *Bohemia*, February 6, 1949, 42.
31. Later that month, *Bohemia* announced that its most recent issue had sold 190,000 copies. See: "190 Mil Ejemplares," *Bohemia*, February 20, 1949, supplement, 1.
32. "En Cuba, Polémica: Duelo Entre Micrófonos," *Bohemia*, January 31, 1949, 55.
33. "En Cuba, Polémica: Duelo Entre Micrófonos," 55.
34. "En Cuba, Polémica: Duelo Entre Micrófonos," 56.
35. "En Cuba, Poder Judicial: Se Declaró Incompetente," *Bohemia*, February 27, 1949, 63.
36. Electric Bond and Share was actually a holding company created by General Electric in 1905.
37. In the chamber of representatives, Carlos Manuel de la Cruz complained in 1927 that firms such as the Cuban Electric Company had been "bleeding" the population since 1902. See: Aguilar, *Cuba 1933*, 65.
38. J. Isern, "Refutan los Vecinos de La Habana a la Compañía Cubana de Electricidad," *Carteles*, February 1, 1948, 68.
39. "Ante la grave problema de la electricidad," *Bohemia*, May 23, 1948, 66.
40. "En Cuba, Poder Judicial: Se Declaró Incompetente," 62.

41. "Los Candidatos Presidenciales Opinan Sobre el Grave Problema de la Electricidad," *Bohemia*, May 23, 1948, 67, 74.
42. "En Cuba, Poder Judicial: Se Declaró Incompetente," 63.
43. "En Cuba, Poder Judicial: Se Declaró Incompetente," 63.
44. "En Cuba, Poder Judicial: Se Declaró Incompetente," 63.
45. "En Cuba, Poder Judicial: Se Declaró Incompetente," 63.
46. "En Cuba, Poder Judicial: Se Declaró Incompetente," 63.
47. "En Cuba, Poder Judicial: Se Declaró Incompetente," 63–64.
48. Conte Agüero, *Eduardo Chibás*, 591. Chibás was convinced the government meant to take him off the air one way or another. First off, the attempt to shutter his show in November of 1948 was still fresh in his mind. The threat seemed even more concrete after Juan Manuel Márquez, an Ortodoxo city councilman from Marianao, had been banned from the radio in January. Chibás had inveighed against this decision, saying, "Only weak, unpopular and anti-democratic governments who support themselves via fraud, embezzlement and crime fear the free expression of ideas and clear exposition of the truth." See: Conte Agüero, *Eduardo Chibás*, 588.
49. Conte Agüero, *Eduardo Chibás*, 591–592.
50. Eduardo R. Chibás, "Por Defender el Pueblo, Iría a la Cárcel Con Orgullo," *Bohemia*, March 6, 1949, 75.
51. Chibás, "Por Defender el Pueblo," 47.
52. Chibás, "Por Defender el Pueblo," 47.
53. "La FEU se Pronuncia Contra el Fallo del Supremo," *Bohemia*, March 7, 1949, 57.
54. "Dos Documentos de Interés Público: El Comité Coordinador Nacional de Asociaciones Cívicas se Dirige al Presidente de la República," *Bohemia*, March 27, 1949, 63.
55. "El Ejemplo de Oriente," *Bohemia*, March 20, 1949, 71.
56. "En Cuba, Atentado: El Plomo Habla de Nuevo," *Bohemia*, April 10, 1949, 65.
57. "En Cuba, Atentado: El Plomo Habla de Nuevo," 66.
58. "En Cuba, Atentado: El Plomo Habla de Nuevo," 66.
59. "En Cuba, Atentado: El Plomo Habla de Nuevo," 66.
60. "En Cuba, Atentado: El Plomo Habla de Nuevo," 66.
61. The committee members were Lomberto Díaz (Auténtico), Santiago Rey (Republican), Manuel Capestany (Liberal), Rafael Guas Inclán (Liberal), and Antonio Martínez Fraga (Democrat).
62. "En Cuba, Senado: 'Nuestra Posición Quedará en Entredicho,'" *Bohemia*, April 10, 1949, 66–67.
63. "En Cuba, Senado: No quiere asustar a los Inversionistas," *Bohemia*, April 10, 1949, 67.
64. Eduardo R. Chibás, "El Acuerdo Contra el Pueblo," *Bohemia*, April 10, 1949, 60.
65. Eduardo R. Chibás, "¡Otro Empréstito con el Chase!," *Bohemia*, April 10, 1949, 60.
66. Eschewing foreign loans had long been a staple of Cuban presidential campaigns, although such promises were often broken. As a presidential candidate in 1924, Gerardo Machado had offered a ten-point program to the public. The last of his proposals involved paying off Cuba's public debts and avoiding new loans. During the 1948 campaign, Prío had also promised to steer clear of foreign loans.
67. Winthrop Aldrich, a Harvard-educated lawyer, was president of Chase Manhattan Bank between 1930 and 1934. At the time he visited Carlos and Antonio Prío, he was chairman of the board, a position he held during the years 1934–1953. After his banking career, Aldrich served as United States ambassador to Great Britain (1953–1957).
68. Chibás, "¡Otro Empréstito con el Chase!," 87.
69. Eduardo R. Chibás, "Respondiendo al Senador Casanova," *Bohemia*, April 24, 1949, 62.
70. Conte Agüero, *Eduardo Chibás*, 599.
71. Chibás, "Respondiendo al Senador Casanova," 62.
72. Chibás, "Respondiendo al Senador Casanova," 62. Eddy's source for this charge was a formal complaint lodged by Representative Lincoln Rodón, president of Cuba's chamber of representatives.

73. According to Chibás, administration officials with knowledge of the plan included ex–Agriculture Minister Ramón Nodal, current Agruculture Minister Virgilio Pérez, and Teodoro Santiesteban, secretary of the Cuban Tenant Farmers Association.

74. "En Cuba, Palacio: 'Tienen que Meter en un Puño a la Universidad,'" *Bohemia*, April 17, 1949, 59. Pedro Mirassou was also linked to UIR, which doubtless fed his desire to see the MSR triggermen behind bars.

75. "En Cuba, Palacio: 'Tienen que Meter en un Puño a la Universidad,'" 59.

76. "En Cuba, Palacio: 'Tienen que Meter en un Puño a la Universidad,'" 59.

77. "En Cuba, Palacio: 'Tienen que Meter en un Puño a la Universidad,'" 59.

78. "En Cuba, Palacio: 'Tienen que Meter en un Puño a la Universidad,'" 60.

79. "En Cuba, Atentado: 'La Policía Protege a los Asesinos,'" *Bohemia*, April 24, 1949, 71.

80. Conte Agüero, *Eduardo Chibás*, 600. This statement is particularly interesting as Orlando León Lemus had once been a familiar passenger in Chibás's automobile, official or otherwise, while he was an Auténtico senator. During a duel in January of 1945 against the journalist Joaquín López Montes, Chibás, in fact, chose El Colorado as one of his seconds. After his split with the Auténticos, Chibás denounced the party's gangster links. In this sense, his condemnation of Lemus was sincere, but he was entitled to less self-righteousness than his tone assumed.

81. "En Cuba, Poder Judicial: El Deber Inexcusable," *Bohemia*, May 1, 1949, 61.

82. Conte Agüero, *Eduardo Chibás*, 601.

83. "En Cuba, Política: 'Es un Converso,'" *Bohemia*, May 1, 1949, 61.

84. "Condenado Chibás Por Defender al Pueblo Frente al Monopolio Eléctrico," *Bohemia*, May 1, 1949, 68.

85. "Condenado Chibás Por Defender al Pueblo Frente al Monopolio Eléctrico," 68.

86. "En Cuba, Política: Cinco Horas de Debate," *Bohemia*, May 8, 1949, 59.

87. "En Cuba, Política: Cinco Horas de Debate," 59.

88. "En Cuba, Política: Cinco Horas de Debate," 60.

89. "En Cuba, Política: Cinco Horas de Debate," 60.

90. "En Cuba, Política: Cinco Horas de Debate," 59.

91. "En Cuba, Política: Cinco Horas de Debate," 59.

92. "En Cuba, Política: Cinco Horas de Debate," 60–61.

93. "En Cuba, Política: Cinco Horas de Debate," 61.

94. "En Cuba, Política: Cinco Horas de Debate," 62–63.

95. "En Cuba, Política: Cinco Horas de Debate," 61.

96. Mario Kuchilán, "Grafoentrevista Exclusiva: Chibás," *Bohemia*, May 8, 1949, 69. Kuchilán also revealed that being incarcerated was more difficult than Chibás was letting on. According to other inmates, the Ortodoxo chief was having trouble sleeping, and the food damaged his delicate stomach.

97. "En Cuba, Política: 'Es un Error Político,'" *Bohemia*, May 8, 1949, 62.

98. "En Cuba, Política: 'Es un Error Político,'" 63.

99. Eduardo R. Chibás, "Al Pueblo de Cuba," *Prensa Libre*, April 30, 1949, reprinted in Conte Agüero, *Eduardo Chibás*, 605.

100. Conte Agüero, *Eduardo Chibás*, 605.

101. Conte Agüero, *Eduardo Chibás*, 605.

102. Conte Agüero, *Eduardo Chibás*, 605.

103. Machado typically offered freedom to prisoners on the condition that they abandon the country. Batista's offer almost certainly had similar strings attached.

104. Conte Agüero, *Eduardo Chibás*, 606.

105. Conte Agüero, *Eduardo Chibás*, 605.

106. ANC, Legajo 10, Expediente 331.

107. Luis Conte Agüero counted 824 visitors on May 1; 737 on May 8; 827 on May 15; 987 on May 22; and 761 on May 29. See: Conte Agüero, *Eduardo Chibás*, 620.

108. ANC, Legajo 9, Expediente 285, 88.

109. "En Cuba, Política: 'Una Amnistía Votada por el Parlamento,'" *Bohemia*, May 8, 1949, 61. The approval of Ramón Vasconcelos was also important because he had recently been named director of *Alerta*.

110. Raúl Lorenzo was an erstwhile Marxist who subsequently became commerce minister during the presidency of Fulgencio Batista. Aside from his show on Unión Radio, he also published a regular column in *Bohemia*.

111. Raúl Gutiérrez, "El Pueblo Opina Sobre la Condena de Chibás," *Bohemia*, May 8, 1949, 52. Interestingly, a gender gap persisted in this question as well. For instance, 71.77 percent of men were convinced Chibás should have been acquitted whereas the number for women was 82.97 percent.

112. Gutiérrez, "El Pueblo Opina Sobre la Condena de Chibás," 52.

113. Gutiérrez, "El Pueblo Opina Sobre la Condena de Chibás," 52.

114. Gutiérrez, "El Pueblo Opina Sobre la Condena de Chibás," 52.

115. According to Lemus, other Auténtico patrons of the UIR included Diego Vicente Tejera, Interior Minister Rubén de León, and Congressman Guillermo Ara.

116. After the Orfila massacre, for example, El Colorado took refuge in the home of Paco Prío. As a senator, his residence was off-limits to the police.

117. Many, including Chibás, believed this finca was the property of Liberal Representative Manuel Benítez, who had headed the National Police during Batista's presidency and was a former military chief of Pinar del Río province.

118. "En Cuba, La Capital: Marejada Antidemocrática," *Bohemia*, May 15, 1949, supplement, 2.

119. "En Cuba, La Capital: Marejada Antidemocrática," supplement, 2. Once free, Piñango immediately went into hiding, as El Colorado and his cronies assumed he had furnished details of their whereabouts to the police. A *Bohemia* reporter added with foreboding that the gangster's "distrustful" and "determined" friends were already looking for him.

120. "Una foto que parece de otra época," *Bohemia*, May 15, 1949, 64.

121. "En Cuba, Cámara: Inmunidad y Gangsterismo," *Bohemia*, May 15, 1949, supplement, 6.

122. Whereas most gangsters donned sobriquets, Policarpo Soler used a nom de guerre. His real name was Francisco Herrera Alonso.

123. "En Cuba, Cámara: Inmunidad y Gangsterismo," supplement, 6.

124. "En Cuba, Palacio: 'Es Imposible Aguantar Eso,'" *Bohemia*, May 8, 1949, 78.

125. "Una sinuosa maniobra contra la libertad de expresión," *Bohemia*, May 22, 1949, 71.

126. "Una sinuosa maniobra contra la libertad de expresión," 71.

127. A.R., "El Reyecito Criollo," *Bohemia*, May 22, 1949, 59.

128. ANC, Legajo 9, Expediente 285, 100.

129. ANC, Legajo 9, Expediente 285, 101.

130. Conte Agüero, *Eduardo Chibás*, 616.

131. Conte Agüero, *Eduardo Chibás*, 617.

132. The official young person's organization of the PPC was the Sección Juvenil (Youth Section), which counted chapters throughout Cuba. At the same time, there were numerous offshoots. For example, the rally against the Cuban Electric Company in Matanzas was organized in part by the Union Revolucionaria Estudiantil.

133. ANC, Legajo 9, 298. The statement was from Fidel Rocha Alfonso, a Youth Section leader from Esmeralda, but many Ortodoxos used identical language in referring to their party.

134. ANC, Legajo 9, Expediente 300, 1.

135. ANC, Legajo 9, Expediente 300, 1.

136. "En Cuba, Política: 'Ha Sido una Batalla contra Alonso Pujol,'" *Bohemia*, May 22, 1949, 75.

137. "En Cuba, Política: 'Ha Sido una Batalla contra Alonso Pujol,'" 80.

138. Aracelio Iglesias was general secretary of the Union of Laborers and Stevedores.

139. "En Cuba, Amnistía: Un Proceso Encubierto de Inhabilitación," *Bohemia*, May 29, 1949, 57.

140. "En Cuba, Amnistía: Un Proceso Encubierto de Inhabilitación," 57.

141. ANC, Legajo 9, Expediente 285, 101.

142. ANC, Legajo 9, Expediente 285, 102.

143. René Fiallo, "Carta Abierta al Dr. Carlos Prío Socarrás," *Bohemia*, May 29, 1949, 87.

144. "En Cuba, Política: ¡En libertad el penado 981!," *Bohemia*, June 12, 1949, 76.

145. "En Cuba, Política: ¡En libertad el penado 981!," 77.
146. "En Cuba, Política: ¡En libertad el penado 981!," 77.
147. "En Cuba, Política: Batista y el Nuevo Partido," *Bohemia*, August 1, 1948, 56.

7. "THE CAVE OF ALI BABA AND HIS 40,000 THIEVES"

1. Cuban presidents generally showed scant inclination for retirement after serving their terms. For example, the Liberal José Miguel Gómez (1909–1913) subsequently ran for president in 1920 only to be defeated by Alfredo Zayas in an election marred by fraud. The Conservative Mario García Menocal (1913–1921) attempted to regain office in 1925 but was defeated by Gerardo Machado. Meanwhile, Fulgencio Batista (1940–1944) was currently constructing a new party to support another bid for the presidency, and Ramón Grau San Martín (1933, 1944–1948) was impatiently waiting until he could run again. Grau's control of the Auténtico party machinery mirrored that of Gómez, who dominated the Liberals until his death in 1921, and Menocal, who similarly ruled the Conservatives and their successor party, the Democrats, until his demise in 1940.
2. Nearly every notable Cuban politician and military figure owned at least one finca. Prío's favored estate was "La Chata." Miguelito Suárez Fernández owned "La Tranquilidad." Alemán, of course, had purchased "América," the former country refuge of José Miguel Gómez. Grau bucked the trend somewhat by exchanging his comfortable Vedado residence for swankier digs on Miramar's Quinta Avenida.
3. "En Cuba, Política: 'El Lugar no me Importa,'" *Bohemia*, June 19, 1949, 67.
4. "En Cuba, Política: 'El Lugar no me Importa,'" 67.
5. "En Cuba, Política: 'El Lugar no me Importa,'" 67.
6. "En Cuba, Política: 'El Lugar no me Importa,'" 67.
7. "En Cuba, Política: 'El Lugar no me Importa,'" 68.
8. In fact, Casanova would die just over six months after the duel, on December 22, 1949—ten days short of his sixty-sixth birthday.
9. René Fiallo, "Pecadores, Apóstoles y Hombres," *Bohemia*, June 12, 1949, 72.
10. Fiallo, "Pecadores, Apóstoles y Hombres," 93.
11. Eduardo R. Chibás, "Pecadores, Apóstatas y Ladrones," *Bohemia*, June 19, 1949, 81.
12. René Fiallo, "Los Sepulcros Blanqueados," *Bohemia*, July 3, 1949, 81.
13. Fiallo, "Los Sepulcros Blanqueados," 90.
14. Eduardo R. Chibás, "Expulsaremos del templo los mercaderes y ladrones," *Bohemia*, July 10, 1949: reprinted in Conte Agüero, *Eduardo Chibás*, 626.
15. René Fiallo, "El Mal Ladrón," *Bohemia*, July 17, 1949, 79.
16. Fiallo, "El Mal Ladrón," 79. Chibás censuró Fernández Casas on his radio show and also in print. Fiallo here cites an article Chibás wrote for *El Crisol* on April 3, 1946.
17. Fiallo, "El Mal Ladrón," 79.
18. Fiallo, "El Mal Ladrón," 87.
19. Fiallo, "El Mal Ladrón," 87–88.
20. Fiallo, "El Mal Ladrón," 88.
21. Conte Agüero, *Eduardo Chibás*, 642.
22. Conte Agüero, *Eduardo Chibás*, 642.
23. "En Cuba, Polémica: 'Eddy' vs. 'Tony,'" *Bohemia*, October 23, 1949, 73.
24. "En Cuba, Polémica: 'Eddy' vs. 'Tony,'" 73.
25. "En Cuba, Polémica: 'Eddy' vs. 'Tony,'" 73.
26. "En Cuba, Polémica: 'Eddy' vs. 'Tony,'" 73–74.
27. Manuel Antonio de Varona, "Eduardo R. Chibás y yo," *Bohemia*, October 23, 1949, 71.
28. Since Varona could never say he had backed Alemán in 1947 out of political expediency, he responded to the criticism by pointing out that Chibás had praised his initial appointment

as education minister in May of 1946. He asserted that Chibás turned against Alemán only after Grau had declined to support his presidential ambitions.
29. Varona, "Eduardo R. Chibás y yo," 70.
30. Eduardo R. Chibás, "El Primer Ministro y yo," *Bohemia*, October 30, 1949, 73.
31. Chibás, "El Primer Ministro y yo," 73.
32. Chibás, "El Primer Ministro y yo," 72.
33. Chibás, "El Primer Ministro y yo," 72.
34. Chibás, "El Primer Ministro y yo," 72.
35. Chibás, "El Primer Ministro y yo," 72.
36. "En Cuba, Entrevista: Un Verdadero Discípulo de Chibás," *Bohemia*, July 31, 1949, 68. For the most part, gangster bosses were referred to by their nicknames. In this case, El Extraño (the strange one) was the sobriquet of Jesús González Cartas.
37. "En Cuba, Entrevista: Un Verdadero Discípulo de Chibás," 68.
38. Conte Agüero, *Eduardo Chibás*, 629.
39. "En Cuba, Política: 'Eddy' o el Instinto Político," *Bohemia*, July 24, 1949, 67. Asked by a *Bohemia* journalist if he had any comment regarding Ochoa's remarks, Chibás replied that "I don't understand Millo's attitude. The truth is that he was one of the party's most ardent *pactistas* but after seeing our success in the elections, he confessed to me that he had been mistaken. I esteem him very highly and would regret having to confront him over the issue. However, we can't sacrifice one of the party's central tenets for a mayoralty."
40. "En Cuba, Política: 'Eddy' o el Instinto Político," 67.
41. "En Cuba, Política: 'Eddy' o el Instinto Político," 67.
42. "En Cuba, Política: 'Eddy' o el Instinto Político," 67.
43. "En Cuba, Política: 'Eddy' o el Instinto Político," 67.
44. Conte Agüero, *Eduardo Chibás*, 633.
45. Conte Agüero, *Eduardo Chibás*, 636.
46. In Jorge Mañach, the Ortodoxos also boasted the biographer of another Chibás hero—namely, José Martí. As a professor of political economy at the University of Havana, Márquez Sterling added to the party's already formidable roster of professors, including Mañach, Vicentina Antuña, Roberto Agramonte, Rafael García Bárcena, Herminio Portell Vilá, and Manuel Bisbé, among others.
47. "En Cuba, Entrevista: 'La Vergüenza no Pudo Ganar . . . ,'" *Bohemia*, August 7, 1949, 65.
48. "En Cuba, Entrevista: 'La Vergüenza no Pudo Ganar . . . ,'" 65.
49. "En Cuba, Entrevista: 'La Vergüenza no Pudo Ganar . . . ,'" 65.
50. In June of 1949, an expeditionary force of eight hundred Dominican exiles was training in Oriente province and preparing to set sail from the port of Baracoa as part of a multipronged, and ultimately unsuccessful, attack against Trujillo. As part of the same plan, Enrique Henríquez and the gangster Rolando Masferrer were in Haiti devising a land invasion, while Prío's ex-bodyguard and close friend Eufemio Fernández was overseeing preparations for an air assault from Guatemala.
51. "Este Documento Constituyó una de la Causas de la Caída de Genovevo Pérez," *Bohemia*, September 4, 1949, 79.
52. "Este Documento Constituyó una de las Causas de la Caída de Genovevo Pérez," 79. This expedition had been encouraged by Grau, funded by José Manuel Alemán, and squashed by Pérez Dámera after the Orfila shootout. While Cayo Confites had primarily been run by MSR captains such as Rolando Masferrer and Manolo Castro, members of other "action groups" had also participated. Eufemio Fernández, for example, had been a battalion commander. Fidel Castro of UIR was also on hand. Upon returning to Havana, many filibusterers expressed their displeasure with Pérez Dámera. As they marched through the capital to a hero's welcome, a radio reporter asked Masferrer to say a few words. He obliged by cursing the army chief and calling him a traitor. When the journalist admonished Masferrer to watch his language, the temperamental ruffian smashed him with the microphone. See: "Filibuster's End," *Time*, October 13, 1947, http://www.time.com/time/magazine/article/0,9171,933727,00.html.
53. "En Cuba, Destitución: Aliado del Sátrapa Trujillo," *Bohemia*, August 28, 1949, supplement, 3.

54. "En Cuba, Destitución: Aliado del Sátrapa Trujillo," supplement, 3.
55. "En Cuba, Destitución: Aliado del Sátrapa Trujillo," supplement, 3.
56. Pérez Dámera bought "La Larga" in 1945, while still a colonel, and as with many Cuban officers, he used military draftees rather than civilian laborers to work the land. As army chief, Pérez Dámera flew to "La Larga" on a weekly basis using a Cuban air force jet.
57. "En Cuba, Destitución: Aliado del Sátrapa Trujillo," supplement, 1–2. See also: Ameringer, *Cuban Democratic Experience*, 97.
58. "En Cuba, Destitución: 'Están Hablando con el ex Jefe del Ejército.'" *Bohemia*, August 28, supplement, 2. This was not the first time a president had appeared at the Campamento Columbia and rallied the troops against their military commander. In 1941, Fulgencio Batista succeeded in a similar maneuver against Army Chief José Eleuterio Pedraza after the latter objected to a crackdown on corruption (in this case, illegal gambling) within the military. Once Batista won over the soldiers, Pedraza was arrested and placed on a plane to Miami. Of course, Batista had been Cuba's military leader for seven years before being elected as a civilian president in 1940. For Prío, the situation was more daunting even though Pérez Dámera was less threatening than Pedraza—who at one point had driven to the presidential palace accompanied by thirty cars full of machine gun–bearing officers and bodyguards to press his case. For a more detailed account of these events, see: Thomas, *Cuba*, 724–725; and Louis Pérez, *Army Politics in Cuba, 1898–1958* (Pittsburgh: University of Pittsburgh Press, 1976), 119.
59. "En Cuba, Destitución: 'Están Hablando con el ex Jefe del Ejército,'" supplement, 2.
60. Conte Agüero, *Eduardo Chibás*, 636.
61. "En Cuba, Atentado: Sangre y Balas Bajo la Cordialidad," *Bohemia*, September 11, 1949, 65.
62. Wichy Salazar and El Colorado had been founding members of ARG but had fallen out over the latter's decision to profit from the black market. Later on, Salazar joined UIR and El Colorado jumped to MSR. The rivalry between them was thus deepened by the feud between these gangs. As for Policarpo Soler, he had once been a family friend of the Salazars but following an unknown incident vowed to exterminate all of them. This would explain his attempt to snuff out Efigenia. He was also implicated in the murder of Wichy's brother Noel in September of 1948.
63. Conte Agüero, *Eduardo Chibás*, 637.
64. "En Cuba, Atentado: El Alma Máter Afectada," *Bohemia*, September 11, 1949, 66. According to fellow university students who were willing to speak to the press, Buján's use of armed gangsters was meant to win support and intimidate other candidates from challenging him for the FEU presidency. Buján was also seen in the presence of El Colorado and Policarpo Soler, who lent their assistance whenever possible. In one alleged incident, Buján met with the current FEU president, Enrique Ovares, and asked for his adherence, saying, "Look, I am backed by El Colorado. These (armed) men who follow me around belong to him and you will see how he appears here from one moment to the next."
65. "En Cuba, Atentado: En la Quinta de los Molinos," *Bohemia*, September 11, 1949, 66.
66. "En Cuba, Atentado: Invasión Policial," *Bohemia*, September 11, 1949, 67.
67. Conte Agüero, *Eduardo Chibás*, 638.
68. "En Cuba, Policia: ¿Cabriñana o Queensberry?" *Bohemia*, September 25, 1949, 66.
69. Vergara, "Hombre Precavido," *Bohemia*, September 25, 1949, 66.
70. "En Cuba, Atentado: Por Quinta Vez," *Bohemia*, September 25, 1949, 71. University policemen tended to complain that they could not arrest the gangsters in their midst because they were outgunned.
71. "En Cuba, Universidad: 'Ha Sido Muerto por la Espalda . . . ,'" *Bohemia*, September 25, 1949, 65.
72. "En Cuba, Universidad: 'Ha Sido Muerto por la Espalda . . . ,'" 66. Maderne also made much of the fact that González del Valle was brother-in-law to the infamous Mario Salabarría, the assassin of Orfila who was serving a thirty-year jail sentence.
73. "En Cuba, Universidad: 'Ha Sido Muerto por la Espalda . . . ,'" 66.
74. "En Cuba: La Capital: 'En Cuba la Vida Humana no se Respeta . . . ,'" *Bohemia*, October 2, 1949, 65.
75. "En Cuba: La Capital: 'En Cuba la Vida Humana no se Respeta . . . ,'" 66.

76. GRAS officers were known derisively as "green flies" because they cruised around in Oldsmobiles of that color and often harassed Havana residents at random, much like their namesakes in the insect world.
77. "En Cuba: La Capital: Una Mera Cortina de Humo," *Bohemia*, October 2, 1949, 66.
78. "En Cuba: La Capital: Una Brasa de Candela," *Bohemia*, October 2, 1949, 70.
79. "En Cuba: La Capital: Una Brasa de Candela," 70.
80. In his open letter to Carlos Prío from May 8, 1949, while still imprisoned in the Castillo del Príncipe, Chibás wrote that prices for basic goods were falling just about everywhere. For example, in the United States, one hundred pounds of butter had dropped from $20.00 to $11.25. In terms of grains, rye had slipped from $2.50 to $1.26, wheat had gone from $3.05 to $2.18, and flour had descended from $7.65 to $3.70. Other commonly consumed items such as eggs had declined from forty-seven cents per dozen to thirty-one cents per dozen.
81. Raúl Gutiérrez, "Survey Nacional: El Pueblo Enjuicia y Compara el Gobierno del Presidente Prío," *Bohemia*, October 9, 1949, 98.
82. Gutíerrez, "Survey Nacional: El Pueblo Enjuica Y Compara el Gobierno del Presidente Prío," 98.
83. Mario Kuchilán, "Grafoentrevista exclusiva: Antonio Prío," *Bohemia*, June 26, 1949, 21.
84. Foremost among these was the Auténtico congressman from Trinidad, Eduardo López Deustua. However, not everyone blamed Grau's deficit for the layoffs. One of the former president's devotees, Albertico Cruz, attributed the lack of money not to Grau's malfeasance but to the dishonesty of Lincoln Rodón—the Republican president of the chamber of representatives. See "En Cuba, Cámara: 'Este es un Congreso Barato....,'" July 17, 1949, 70.
85. "En Cuba, Cámara: 'Este es un Congreso Barato....,'" 72.
86. "En Cuba, Cámara: 'Este es un Congreso Barato....,'" 72.
87. Francisco Ichaso, "Está ya muy adelantada la tramitación del empréstito," *Bohemia*, July 17, 1949, 104.
88. "Encuestas de *Bohemia:* Sobre la concertación de un empréstito extranjero," 80.
89. Every Cuban president before 1933, with the exception of Mario García Menocal (1913–1921), borrowed money from foreign banks under onerous terms. In 1909, President José Miguel Gómez took out a 16-million-peso loan. Eventually, 21 million in interest was paid. In 1923, President Alfredo Zayas borrowed 50 million pesos upon which the Cuban government paid 34 million in interest.
90. "Encuestas de *Bohemia:* Sobre la concertación de un empréstito extranjero," 81.
91. "Encuestas de *Bohemia:* Sobre la concertación de un empréstito extranjero," 81.
92. Eduardo R. Chibás, "De Eduardo Chibás a Carlos Prío: Contra un Absurdo Empréstito Extranjero," July 31, 1949, 54. Chibás dated Prío's transformation from revolutionary to imperialist servant to April of 1942, when, as chairman of the senate committee of finance and taxes, he supported the so-called Gift Law that canceled 10 million pesos worth of debt incurred by public utilities—four million of which belonged to the Cuban Electric Company.
93. Chibás, "De Eduardo Chibás a Carlos Prío: Contra un Absurdo Empréstito Extranjero," 54.
94. Chibás, "De Eduardo Chibás a Carlos Prío: Contra un Absurdo Empréstito Extranjero," 55.
95. Chibás, "De Eduardo Chibás a Carlos Prío: Contra un Absurdo Empréstito Extranjero," 55.
96. Chibás, "De Eduardo Chibás a Carlos Prío: Contra un Absurdo Empréstito Extranjero," 55.
97. Chibás, "De Eduardo Chibás a Carlos Prío: Contra un Absurdo Empréstito Extranjero," 55.
98. Raúl Gutiérrez, "El Pueblo Opina Sobre el Empréstito," *Bohemia*, July 31, 1949, 64–65.
99. Eduardo R. Chibás, "La Cordialidad en Paños Menores," *Bohemia*, August 28, 1949, 62.
100. Chibás, "La Cordialidad en Paños Menores," 62. Another photo showed a dingy hospital bed in the city of Baracoa, in Oriente province, where money was so short that nurses typically solicited donations in the streets in order to buy coffee and milk for their patients.
101. Chibás, "La Cordialidad en Paños Menores," 63.

102. "En Cuba, Poder Judicial: Aquí También Había Crisis," *Bohemia*, October 16, 1949, 75.
103. Chibás, "La Cordialidad en Paños Menores," 63.
104. Chibás, "La Cordialidad en Paños Menores," 63.
105. "En Cuba, Poder Judicial: Aquí También Había Crisis," 75.
106. Mario Llerena, "¿Qué es la 'Revolución Cubana?,'" *Bohemia*, October 16, 1949, 117.
107. "En Cuba, Palacio: Un Discurso Polémico," *Bohemia*, October 16, 1949, 73.
108. "En Cuba, Palacio: Un Discurso Polémico," 73.
109. "En Cuba, Palacio: Un Discurso Polémico," 73.
110. Eduardo R. Chibás, "Mi Replica al Presidente Prío," *Bohemia*, October 16, 1949, 87.
111. Chibás, "Mi Replica al Presidente Prío," 87.
112. Article 253 of Cuba's constitution mandated that "the state will not arrange loans unless a law of congress is approved by two-thirds of the members of each legislative body and at the same time the necessary permanent revenues to pay the interest and amortization are provided for."
113. Eduardo R. Chibás, "El Empréstito Extranjero (Mi Vida Me Defiende)," *Bohemia*, October 23, 1949, 83.
114. Eduardo R. Chibás, "!El Empréstito en Manos de Alemán!," *Bohemia*, October 30, 1949, 70.
115. Chibás, "!El Empréstito en Manos de Alemán!," 70. On another occasion, Grau told students from the University Committee Against the Loan that Auténticos who supported the measure were "outside the party" and could conceivably be expelled. In other words, his truce with Prío was all but dead. This was clear from his advice to Auténtico legislators who begged him to be silent on the issue. He told them, "Don't think you are going to make money by voting for the loan because later on your political operatives are going to ask for a cut and you will end up without money or the public's trust." See "En Cuba, Empréstito: 'A lo que ha Llegado Esta Gente,'" *Bohemia*, November 6, 1949, 74.
116. "En Cuba, Empréstito: Fué el 31 de Octubre de 1949," *Bohemia*, November 6, 1949, 73.
117. "En Cuba, Empréstito: 'Nos Oponemos al Mensaje No al Empréstito,'" November 6, 1949, 73.
118. A sneering *Bohemia* reporter wrote that Batista stayed away because he "would not dare to put his dubious popularity to the test." See: "En Cuba, Empréstito: 'Contra la Hipoteca del Gobierno,'" *Bohemia*, November 6, 1949, 75.
119. "En Cuba, Senado: La Batalla del Empréstito," *Bohemia*, November 6, 1949, 75. There are a number of possible reasons why Alemán may have opposed the loan. The infusion of cash would allow Prío to rely less on Alemán's largesse and could therefore diminish his influence. Alemán's friendship with Grau may also have been a factor. Finally, Alemán's rivals within the party, particularly the faction led by Miguelito Suárez Fernández, were also sure to benefit from the extra money—a prospect he perhaps hoped to avoid.
120. "En Cuba, Senado: La Batalla del Empréstito," 75.
121. The government had been frantically trying to arrange for Orizondo's return since early November, and for a long time this seemed a less than promising endeavor. Fellow Republican Mario Robau told the press that Orizondo "detests flying" and would only rush back if the administration sent an "airplane filled with money." See "En Cuba, Empréstito: Amenaza y Soborno," *Bohemia*, November 13, 1949, 78. Needless to say, the opposition enjoyed this situation immensely. At one point, the Liberal congressman José Suárez Rivas said, "I hope the president is preparing to build a chimney in the Capitolio because at any moment a stork may appear carrying Señor Orizondo from Paris." See: "En Cuba, Cámara: Una Jornada Sin Gloria," *Bohemia*, November 20, 1949, 76.
122. "En Cuba, Cámara: 'Se Ha Producido Toda Clase de Presiones,'" *Bohemia*, November 20, 1949, 76.
123. "En Cuba, Cámara: 'Se Ha Producido Toda Clase de Presiones,'" 76.
124. "En Cuba, Cámara: 'Se Ha Producido Toda Clase de Presiones,'" 76–77.
125. Raúl Gutiérrez, "Segundo Survey Sobre el Empréstito," *Bohemia*, November 20, 1949, 85. Cubans were asked whether a range of political figures, including Chibás, Ramon Grau San Martín, Fulgencio Batista, and Juan Marinello, would administer the loan more honestly than Carlos Prío. Chibás was easily considered the most honorable of the lot. Head to head, 36.81

percent considered Chibás more honest, while 21.84 percent opted for Prío. A substantial portion, 28.71, also answered "neither."

126. Carlos Prío influenced the process in a twofold manner. First, during the party reorganization of October 1949, he backed candidates for the Auténtico municipal assembly who supported his brother's candidacy. Second, neutral or wavering delegates were lured with financial incentives.

127. "En Cuba, Política: Otro Suceso de Resonancia Nacional," *Bohemia*, November 27, 1949, 73. During his broadcasts of June 4 and June 28, 1949, Chibás had accused Castellanos of stealing funds belonging to the municipality and diverting more than a million pesos earmarked for Havana's aqueduct to create jobs for day laborers who, in their gratitude, would support the Auténticos. These were a few reasons why Chibás believed Castellanos was not fit to be an Ortodoxo.

128. Despite his assurances, Chibás had not officially consulted Ortodoxo leadership regarding Castellanos. His negative response was inspired at least in part by news that Castellanos intended to meet with Carlos Prío, which undoubtedly convinced Chibás the party was being used. Subsequently, however, Castellanos canceled the appointment.

129. "En Cuba, Política: Otro Suceso de Resonancia Nacional," 73.

130. "En Cuba, Política: Otro Suceso de Resonancia Nacional," 73.

131. Castellanos had also told Chibás that if he were nominated as the Ortodoxo candidate, five prominent city councillors (four Auténticos and one Republican) would join him.

132. "En Cuba, Política: 'La Política es el Arte de Organizar la Realidad,'" *Bohemia*, November 27, 1949, 74.

133. "En Cuba, Política: 'La Política es el Arte de Organizar la Realidad,'" 75.

134. Saumell had been mayor of Bayamo, a city in Oriente province with 90,124 residents, according to the 1943 census.

135. "En Cuba, Política: 'La Política es el Arte de Organizar la Realidad,'" 75.

136. Luis Orlando Rodríguez was hardly the only Ortodoxo unhappy with the choice of Manuel Bisbé as the party's mayoral candidate. Carlos Márquez Sterling, for example, claimed the party was isolating itself by choosing someone with no chance of winning. Acción Revolucionaria Ortodoxa (ARO), Fidel Castro's quasi splinter organization, was equally displeased. He published a flyer complaining the "Jesuit" Bisbé had been "imposed" by the party's higher reaches. Curiously, Castro reasoned that Bisbé did not deserve the nomination because he had been a traitor willing to negotiate pacts "even with the Communists." See ANC, Legajo 7, Expediente 212, 4.

137. "En Cuba, Política: 'La Política es el Arte de Organizar la Realidad,'" 75–76. The term jamón (ham) was commonly referred to in Cuban politics as the fruits of office, including money, jobs, perks, etc.

138. Raúl Gutiérrez. "Primer Survey Sobre la Alcaldía de la Habana," *Bohemia*, November 27, 1949, 82–83

139. "En Cuba, Política: 'Un Inconfundible Sello Miguelista . . . ,'" *Bohemia*, November 27, 1949, 77.

140. "En Cuba, Política: Una Tempestad en un Vaso de Agua," *Bohemia*, December 4, 1949, 76. During a meeting of the Ortodoxo executive council on December 1, Eddy's cousin Raúl Primelles accused Dellundé of buying municipal delegates. The congressman Félix Martín, who supported Dellundé, challenged him to provide specific information. When Primelles offered the name of a delegate from the Havana neighborhood of Vives, Dellundé offered a less than convincing denial.

141. "En Cuba, Política: Una Tempestad en un Vaso de Agua," 76.

142. Conte Agüero, *Eduardo Chibás*, 654. This, of course, was when the polls would close during the next presidential election.

8. "I'M NOT ONE OF THOSE GENERALS WHO DIE IN BED"

1. Carlos Vidal, "¿Qué Espera del Nuevo Año?," *Bohemia*, January 1, 1950, 59.
2. Conte Agüero, *Eduardo Chibás*, 657.
3. Conte Agüero, *Eduardo Chibás*, 657.
4. By this time, Nicolás Castellanos had been brought in from the political wilderness by the Republicans, who nominated him as their candidate for Havana's mayoralty. This, of course, was payback courtesy of Guillermo Alonso Pujol for Carlos Prío's pact with the Democrats. Euphoric at finally having a party behind him, Castellanos gleefully excoriated the men who had caused him so many recent difficulties. He deemed Antonio Prío "incompetent," noting that his adversary had spent twenty-two years working for the same bank, earning ninety pesos per month, without a single raise or promotion. "His only ability," said the Havana mayor, "was in amassing a fortune of six million in two years (in the treasury ministry)." Castellanos also referred to the fact that Carlos Prío had offered him a senate seat on the Auténtico ticket for 1950 as a consolation prize, but he replied that Antonio needed that job, if only for the parliamentary immunity given his "embezzlement" from the treasury ministry. See: "En Cuba, Política: '¡Qué no piensen ya en despostularme!,'" *Bohemia*, January 8, 1950, 78–79. Aside from snagging Castellanos, the Republicans also recruited Grau to run for the senate under their banner. While flattered by the gesture, El Viejo did not want people to think he was seeking office in order to secure parliamentary immunity from Lawsuit 82. See "En Cuba, Política: '¡La Dificultad Está en las 174 Millones!,'" *Bohemia*, January 22, 1950, 77.
5. Conte Agüero, *Eduardo Chibás*, 657.
6. "En Cuba, Política: La Proclamación de Antonio," *Bohemia*, January 22, 1950, 73.
7. Primitivo Rodríguez was a lackey par excellence for both Grau and Prío.
8. A *Bohemia* reporter observed that the crowd was short on women and wondered sarcastically whether they preferred the handsome Nicolás Castellanos or the respectable Manuel Bisbé. These virtues were notably absent from Antonio Prío's resume. He lacked his older brother's good looks and was among the most venal and least qualified figures in the cabinet.
9. "En Cuba, Política: Noche de Angustia," *Bohemia*, January 22, 1950, 74.
10. Subsequently, Antonio Prío and his handlers blamed this humiliating episode on the Communists, although there was no evidence they had more of a predilection for raffles than the Cuban population at large. In response, the president's younger brother attempted to bolster his anti-Communist credentials by contributing a red-baiting piece to the island's most right-wing newspaper, *Diario de la Marina*. This was entirely disingenuous, as Antonio Prío spent the day after his debacle at the Palacio de los Deportes negotiating with the Communists for their support.
11. Vergara, "Enfermo de Gravedad," *Bohemia*, January 22, 1950, 75.
12. "En Cuba, Política: Un Reverso Terrible," *Bohemia*, January 22, 1950, 74.
13. "En Cuba, Política: Un Reverso Terrible," 74.
14. "En Cuba, Política: Un Reverso Terrible," 74.
15. "En Cuba, Política: Un Reverso Terrible," 74. While Antonio Prío was undeniably dishonest, he was probably not as corrupt as his predecessor, Isauro Valdés. However, Chibás was fond of superlatives both with regard to himself and his adversaries. Hence, Chibás regularly characterized attacks against him as the most vicious campaigns Cuba had ever seen. By the same token, the venality of this or that government official was often described as the worst in the republic's history.
16. "En Cuba, Política: Márquez Sterling: Huésped de Chibás," *Bohemia*, February 19, 1950, 74.
17. Conte Agüero, *Eduardo Chibás*, 659.
18. "En Cuba, Política: El Infatigable Chibás," March 5, 1950, 75. Chibás also missed the thrill of his Sunday broadcast. In his absence, the show was hosted on February 19 by Pedro Iglesias Betancourt and on February 26 by the lawyer and University of Havana professor Manuel Dorta Duque.

19. Mario Kuchilán, "Grafoentrevista Exclusiva: El Presidente y la Crisis," *Bohemia*, February 5, 1950, 82.

20. Specifically, Chibás mentioned Guillermo Padilla, director general of the Cuban customs service and the lottery, whom he deemed a "contrabandist." See: "En Cuba, Política: El Infatigable Chibás," 75.

21. "En Cuba, Política: El Infatigable Chibás," 74.

22. Conte Agüero, *Eduardo Chibás*, 664.

23. "En Cuba, Deceso: Un Personaje de Leyenda," *Bohemia*, April 2, 1950, 70.

24. Manuel Hernando Torres, "Es Incalculable la Fortuna Que Deja Alemán," *Bohemia*, April 2, 1950, 98.

25. The columnist Francisco Ichaso discounted this excuse, asserting that Grau refused to run because he knew his popularity had diminished significantly and losing a senate election would have been a "mortal blow" to his political career. See: Francisco Ichaso, "Panorama de las Elecciones Parciales," *Bohemia*, April 23, 1950, 51.

26. "En Cuba, Política: 'Ir Contra ese Monstruo de Popularidad Sería un Suicidio,'" *Bohemia*, April 2, 1950, 76.

27. "En Cuba, Política: 'Ir Contra ese Monstruo de Popularidad Sería un Suicidio,'" 76.

28. "En Cuba, Política: 'El Partido me ha Señalado un Puesto de Combate,'" *Bohemia*, April 16, 1950, 78

29. "En Cuba, Política: 'El Partido me ha Señalado un Puesto de Combate,'" 78.

30. "En Cuba, Política: 'El Partido me ha Señalado un Puesto de Combate,'" 78.

31. "En Cuba, Política: 'Ir Contra ese Monstruo de Popularidad Sería un Suicidio,'" 76.

32. Raúl Gutiérrez, "En Un Survey Nacional el Pueblo Opina Sobre el Gobierno, el Nuevo Rumbo, Grau, Batista y Chibás," *Bohemia*, April 2, 1950, 87.

33. Gutiérrez, "En Un Survey Nacional el Pueblo Opina Sobre el Gobierno, el Nuevo Rumbo, Grau, Batista y Chibás," 86.

34. Gutiérrez, "En Un Survey Nacional el Pueblo Opina Sobre el Gobierno, el Nuevo Rumbo, Grau, Batista y Chibás," 88.

35. Francisco Ichaso, "La Opinión Pública Brinda Escaso Apoyo a los Liberes de la 'Coincidencia,'" *Bohemia*, April 9, 1950, 90.

36. Herminio Portell Vilá was one of Cuba's most notable historians but also a candidate for Havana city council on the Ortodoxo ticket. Vicentina Antuña was a Latin professor and officer in the Ortodoxo Women's Wing. Aside from being his cousin's ex-vice-presidential candidate, Roberto Agramonte was head of the Ortodoxo provincial assembly for Havana and a sociology professor.

37. Eduardo Hernández, "24 horas con los candidatos a Alcalde: Manuel Bisbé," *Bohemia*, April 16, 1950, 44, 46.

38. Walfredo Vicente, "El Pardo Llada que Usted no Conoce," *Bohemia*, May 14, 1950, 32.

39. In Cuban Advertising Association surveys tracking radio listeners in Havana and the neighboring municipalities of Marianao, Regla, and Guanabacoa, Pardo Llada's show regularly appeared first in the category of "news shows lasting four minutes or longer." Between February 2 and February 19, 1950, his broadcast drew a 9.52 rating, beating out CMQ's news program, which tallied an 8.50 share. See: "El Ultimo 'Survey,'" *Bohemia*, March 19, 1950, 58.

40. Pardo Llada shared a simple apartment in the La Sierra district of Havana with his wife, María Luisa Alonso, who was a dentist.

41. "En Cuba, Política: 'El Partido me ha Señalado un Puesto de Combate,'" 78.

42. "En Cuba, Política: 'El Partido me ha Señalado un Puesto de Combate,'" 78. Eddy's suggestion that Belt was not really Cuban scored political points but also contained a fair bit of hypocrisy. After all, Eddy's father, Eduardo Justo, was naturalized as a United States citizen in 1891 at a court of Quarter Sessions in Pittsburgh, Pennsylvania, where he had been working as a civil engineer.

43. Chibás wrote the first drafts of his articles and radio speeches in pencil, usually while chain-smoking, after which they were typed by his secretary, Conchita Fernández.

44. Eduardo R. Chibás, "Mensaje al Pueblo Cubano," *Bohemia*, April 23, 1950, 71.

45. Chibás, "Mensaje al Pueblo Cubano," 93. Chibás was far from the only one to poke fun at Belt's American origins. For example, the political satirist Niko published a cartoon in which

two men of obvious American appearance are walking down a Havana street. Off to the side, one Cuban tells the other, "To tell the truth, I don't know whether they are tourists or political sergeants of William Belt." See: Niko, "Confusión," *Bohemia*, April 30, 1950, 77.

46. Chibás, "Mensaje al Pueblo Cubano," 93.
47. Chibás, "Mensaje al Pueblo Cubano," 70.
48. Chibás, "Mensaje al Pueblo Cubano," 70–71.
49. Chibás, "Mensaje al Pueblo Cubano," 71.
50. Of course, Carlos Prío's older brother Paco was already a senator from Pinar del Río, while his brother-in-law Enrique Henríquez occupied a congressional seat from Oriente province.
51. They were Segundo Abreu and Baltasar Arroyo, both of whom abstained from voting out of protest. See: Conte Agüero, *Eduardo Chibás*, 654.
52. Díaz mentioned that the Auténtico party chief in Matanzas, Diego Vicente Tejera, "doesn't content himself with the trust of Carlos (Prío) but rather wants to keep the knife of the veto in his hands for his defense." See "En Cuba, Entrevista: 'La Mayoría Votará por Chibás...,'" *Bohemia*, April 23, 1950, 80.
53. "En Cuba, Entrevista: 'La Mayoría Votará por Chibás...,'" 80. The fact that Díaz and other Auténticos believed Antonio Prío could handily win the mayoralty despite his obvious unpopularity was a testament to their unlimited faith in the party's political machine and the government's resources.
54. "En Cuba, Entrevista: 'La Mayoría Votará por Chibás...,'" 80.
55. "En Cuba, Entrevista: 'La Mayoría Votará por Chibás...,'" 80.
56. "En Cuba, Entrevista: 'La Mayoría Votará por Chibás...,'" 80.
57. "En Cuba, Entrevista: 'La Mayoría Votará por Chibás...,'" 80. Díaz reserved his highest praise for the Ortodoxo leader's campaign skills, saying, "any other candidate would need three months to gain the ground Chibás could cover in 30 days." This may have been hyperbolic but only slightly. Chibás was far and away the best campaigner in Cuba.
58. "¡Ponga su piedra...!," *Bohemia*, April 30, 1950, 25.
59. "La Trinchera del Pueblo Debe Ser...,'" *Bohemia*, May 19, 1950, 81.
60. Antonio Perdomo, "Mi Programa Legislativo Responde a las Necesidades Morales y Políticas del Pueblo Cubano," *Bohemia*, April 30, 1950, 69.
61. On the other hand, Eddy's younger brother Raúl directed the Havana Military Academy—a private high school for boys.
62. Perdomo, "Mi Programa Legislativo Responde a las Necesidades Morales y Políticas del Pueblo Cubano," 69.
63. Conte Agüero, *Eduardo Chibás*, 671.
64. Conte Agüero, *Eduardo Chibás*, 671.
65. "En Cuba: Tribunales: 'Esa Sentencia es Justa...,'" *Bohemia*, May 7, 1950, 73.
66. "En Cuba: Tribunales: 'Esa Sentencia es Justa...,'" 73.
67. "En Cuba: Tribunales: 'Esa Sentencia es Justa...,'" 73.
68. "En Cuba: Tribunales: 'Esa Sentencia es Justa...,'" 73.
69. "En Cuba: Tribunales: 'Esa Sentencia es Justa...,'" 74. The *Bohemia* reporter observing this case was convinced that Judge Merino had been tampered with, noting that he lacked his "habitual composure" while citing his new pro-government line. The journalist added that "those familiar with the judge's habitual eloquence suspect something strange is happening with him." See: "En Cuba: Tribunales: 'Esa Sentencia es Justa...,'" 74.
70. "En Cuba: Tribunales: 'Esa Sentencia es Justa...,'" 75.
71. "En Cuba: Tribunales: 'Esa Sentencia es Justa...,'" 75.
72. Eduardo R. Chibás, "Sangre y Cieno," *Bohemia*, May 14, 1950, 70.
73. Chibás, "Sangre y Cieno," 71. The *porra* was slang for members of President Gerardo Machado's security forces.
74. "En Cuba: Tribunales: 'Esa Sentencia es Justa...,'" *Bohemia*, May 14, 1950, 74.
75. "En Cuba: Tribunales: 'Esa Sentencia es Justa...,'" 74.
76. "En Cuba: Tribunales: 'Esa Sentencia es Justa...,'" 74.
77. "En Cuba: Tribunales: 'Esa Sentencia es Justa...,'" 74.
78. "En Cuba: Tribunales: 'Esa Sentencia es Justa...,'" 75.

79. Victor Muñoz wrote for *El Mundo* and was the first Cuban baseball chronicler to substitute Spanish equivalents for the game's original English terminology. He turned "home run" into *jonrón* and "hit and run" into *corrido y bateo*. As a city councilman, he is best remembered for proposing a law to celebrate Mother's Day—which was approved in 1928, six years after his death.

80. "En Cuba, Política: El Dinero en la Política," *Bohemia*, May 14, 1950, 75.

81. Raúl Gutiérrez, "Tercer Survey Sobre la Alcaldía y Primero Sobre los Senadores," *Bohemia*, May 14, 1950, 84.

82. Gutiérrez, "Tercer Survey Sore la Alcaldía y Primero Sobre los Senadores," 84.

83. Gutiérrez, "Tercer Survey Sore la Alcaldía y Primero Sobre los Senadores," 84.

84. Gutiérrez, "Tercer Survey Sore la Alcaldía y Primero Sobre los Senadores," 84.

85. Gutiérrez, "Tercer Survey Sore la Alcaldía y Primero Sobre los Senadores," 82.

86. Gutiérrez, "Tercer Survey Sore la Alcaldía y Primero Sobre los Senadores," 84.

87. Eduardo R. Chibás, "Virgilio Pérez: Porrista, Homicida y Otras Cosas; William Belt, Machado y Pedraza," *Bohemia*, May 21, 1950, 143.

88. "Poniendo las Cosas en su Lugar: Independencia y Verdad," *Bohemia*, May 28, 1950, supplement, 1.

89. Eduardo R. Chibás, "¿Acaso Virgilio Pérez Representa a la Mujer Cubana?" *Bohemia*, May 28, 1950, supplement, 11.

90. Conte Agüero, *Eduardo Chibás*, 676. Chibás, who devoted obsessive care to his personal appearance, had not worn a guayabera by accident. This was a traditional shirt and quintessential symbol of Cuba. Carlos Prío had incited howls of outrage a few years earlier by banning it from the presidential palace in favor of suits. Conversely, during a visit to Cuba in 1948, President Harry Truman had earned plaudits for donning a guayabera. As for Guillermo Belt, who had spent the previous two months being called "William," he emphasized his Cuban bona fides by wearing one to the voting station.

91. The official vote totals were as follows: Eduardo Chibás: 200,287; Virgilio Pérez: 183,220; Guillermo Belt: 93,143; and Anibal Escalante, 73,359. See: Conte Agüero, *Eduardo Chibás*, 676.

92. "En Cuba, Elecciones: La Lección del Primero de Junio," *Bohemia*, June 11, 1950, 77.

93. "En Cuba, Elecciones: La Lección del Primero de Junio," 77.

94. Each of Havana's mayoral candidates was unhappy with the various polls taken by Raúl Gutiérrez. Castellanos complained they underestimated his popularity, Antonio Prío pretended not to notice them, and Manuel Bisbé whined that surveys reflected the whims of those who paid for them. However, the May 31 questionnaire proved highly accurate. Castellanos was favored by 53.85 percent of respondents and won 53.36 percent in actuality. Antonio Prío was chosen by 34.35 percent and garnered 36.88 percent on election day. Lastly, Manuel Bisbé was named by 11.80 percent and came away with 9.76 percent.

95. Roberto Varona lost despite outspending his opponent, the incumbent Francisco Arredondo, by a 10–1 margin, or 500,000 pesos to 50,000. The prime minister's brother was also given two thousand government jobs to distribute where necessary. See Conchito del Río, "La 2nda Zafra de Cuba: 63 Millones Costaron las Elecciones," *Bohemia*, June 18, 1950, 38.

96. "En Cuba, Elecciones: La Lección del Primero de Junio," *Bohemia*, 76. Then again, José Ramón Fernández, who was a protégé of Education Minister Arturo Sánchez Arango, engaged in similar shenanigans and was defeated.

97. "En Cuba, Elecciones: La Lección del Primero de Junio," 79.

98. ANC, Legajo 38, Expediente 1129, 30.

99. ANC, Legajo 38, Expediente 1129, 50.

100. ANC, Legajo 38, Expediente 1129, 55.

101. Raúl Gutiérrez, "El Pueblo de Cuba, Opina Sobre las Pasadas Elecciones, El Gabinete de Prío y los Posibles Presidentes," *Bohemia*, June 25, 1950, 84.

102. "En Cuba, Survey: Los Presidenciables Opinan," *Bohemia*, July 2, 1950, 75.

103. ANC, Legajo 38, Expediente 1129, 35.

104. "En Cuba, Tribunales: Un Juez y un Magistrado," *Bohemia*, July 30, 1950, 75.

105. "En Cuba, Tribunales: Las Pruebas Definitivas," *Bohemia*, July 2, 1950, 78.

106. "En Cuba, Tribunales: Las Pruebas Definitivas," 79.

107. "En Cuba, Tribunales: Las Pruebas Definitivas," 79.
108. "En Cuba, Asalto: En la Madrugada del 4 del Julio," *Bohemia*, July 9, 1950, 76.
109. "En Cuba, Asalto: En la Madrugada del 4 del Julio," 77.
110. "En Cuba, Asalto: En la Madrugada del 4 del Julio," 77.
111. "En Cuba, Asalto: En la Madrugada del 4 del Julio," 77.
112. "En Cuba, Asalto: En la Madrugada del 4 del Julio," 77.
113. "En Cuba, Denuncia: Chibás Vuelve a Urgencia," *Bohemia*, July 23, 1950, 75.
114. Conte Agüero, *Eduardo Chibás*, 678.
115. Conte Agüero, *Eduardo Chibás*, 678.
116. Noting that Trejo had also tried to suppress Causa 82, a *Bohemia* reporter noted sarcastically that "lack of respect for the current government rather than repeated mockery of the law and justice seems to be, in the opinion of Judge Trejo Loredo, the only offense punishable by his office." See: "El Fiscal Trejo," *Bohemia*, July 23, 1950, 75.
117. "En Cuba, Denuncia: Chibás Vuelve a Urgencia," 75.
118. "En Cuba, Denuncia: Chibás Vuelve a Urgencia," 75.
119. "En Cuba, Denuncia: Chibás Vuelve a Urgencia," 76.
120. Vidal, "El País del Contrasentido," *Bohemia*, July 23, 1950, 79.
121. Eduardo R. Chibás, "¡Yo Acuso!" *Bohemia*, July 30, 1950, 90.
122. Manuel Pérez Galán controlled an estimated 70 percent of Cuba's pineapple production.
123. "En Cuba, Censura: El Decreto-Mordaza," *Bohemia*, August 13, 1950, 75.
124. "En Cuba, Censura: El Decreto-Mordaza," 75.
125. "En Cuba, Censura: El Decreto-Mordaza," 76.
126. "En Cuba, Censura: El Decreto-Mordaza," 76.
127. Goar Mestre, "El Decreto 2.273 es una Franca Invitación a la Usurpación de Funciones," *Bohemia*, August 13, 1950, 71.
128. Carlos Márquez Sterling, "Un Decreto al Estilo Fascista," *Bohemia*, August 13, 1950, 86. In his weekly column, Márquez Sterling deemed the decree's timing "cowardly and cunning" because Chibás, who it was mainly directed against, was in no position to respond. The Ortodoxo leader agreed, saying, "They waited until I checked into the clinic, so I would find it difficult to defend myself or accuse them of what they are plotting in the dark against the Cuban people. Regardless of how much they persecute me," he concluded, "I will very soon appear for my radio show on CMQ to continue fighting the battle of SHAME AGAINST MONEY and SHAME AGAINST INDIGNITY."
129. Eduardo R. Chibás, "Carta Abierta al Presidente Carlos Prío," *Bohemia*, August 20, 1950, 103.
130. Chibás, "Carta Abierta al Presidente Carlos Prío," 103.
131. Chibás, "Carta Abierta al Presidente Carlos Prío," 103.
132. Chibás, "Carta Abierta al Presidente Carlos Prío," 103.
133. Chibás, "Carta Abierta al Presidente Carlos Prío," 103.
134. Chibás, "Carta Abierta al Presidente Carlos Prío," 103.
135. "En Cuba, Clausura: El Periódico 'Hoy' y el Artículo 33," *Bohemia*, September 3, 1950, 78. Senator Eusebio Mujal, who was also head of the Confederation of Cuban Workers, pressed the president for even more drastic action. Rather than merely depriving the Communists of their mouthpiece, he wanted it to be handed over to him and his organization.
136. "En Cuba, Clausura: El Periódico 'Hoy' y el Artículo 33," 78. See also: Ameringer, *The Cuban Democratic Experience*, 114.
137. "En Cuba, Política: 'El Partido Sabrá Luchar Gallardamente . . . ,'" *Bohemia*, September 10, 1950, 75.
138. "En Cuba, Política: 'El Partido Sabrá Luchar Gallardamente . . . ,'" 75. Chibás listed Antonio Prío among the hypocrites, given his attempts to court Communist support while he was running for mayor but who now was at the forefront of those defending *Hoy*'s closure.
139. "En Cuba, Política: 'El Partido Sabrá Luchar Gallardamente . . . ,'" 75. The ultraconservative, pro-Franco *Diario de la Marina* congratulated the government for shutting down *Hoy*. Most of Cuba's print media, however, including *El Mundo*, *Alerta*, and *Bohemia*, strongly disapproved of the measure.
140. "En Cuba, Política: 'El Partido Sabrá Luchar Gallardamente . . . ,'" 76.

141. "En Cuba, Política: 'El Partido Sabrá Luchar Gallardamente...,'" 76.
142. "En Cuba, Política: 'El Partido Sabrá Luchar Gallardamente...,'" 76. Those who backed Chibás on the issue also included Leonardo Fernández Sánchez, Raimundo Lazo, and Mario Alzugaray.
143. "En Cuba, Política: 'Es Tonto Imaginar que Vamos a Entregar el Poder...,'" *Bohemia*, September 10, 1950, 77.
144. "En Cuba, Política: 'Es Tonto Imaginar que Vamos a Entregar el Poder...,'" 77.
145. "En Cuba, Política: 'Es Tonto Imaginar que Vamos a Entregar el Poder...,'" 77.
146. Suárez Fernández charged the government with responsibility for Paniagua's death and resigned his post as senate president in protest. In Cuba's upper house, Suárez Fernández read a public statement claiming he had been warned that he, his family, and his friends had been targeted for assassination. Of course, his long-standing ties to UIR deprived him of any moral high ground. Gang violence, after all, was one of many ways in which Auténticos settled their internal squabbles. During the same session, Pelayo Cuervo Navarro struck while the iron was hot and shared his own gangster story. He related that gunmen had approached Judge Antonio Vignier and offered their services against him and another accuser in the Causa 82 case. When Cuervo Navarro found out, he demanded that Vignier denounce the ruffians to the police, otherwise, he would do so himself before the Supreme Tribunal. Eventually, Cuervo Navarro submitted his evidence to the Bureau of Investigations and no action was taken. He concluded that "since then, I am among those who doubt the efficiency of this Bureau, especially when the government intends to cover up a crime." See: "En Cuba, Senado, 'Mientras el Gangsterismo Siga Protegido por el Gobierno,'" *Bohemia*, October 8, 1950, 75.
147. "Opinan Sobre los 2 Años del Gobierno del Doctor Carlos Prío Socarrás," *Bohemia*, October 15, 1950, 87.
148. "Opinan Sobre los 2 Años del Gobierno del Doctor Carlos Prío Socarrás," 87.
149. "Opinan Sobre los 2 Años del Gobierno del Doctor Carlos Prío Socarrás," 86.
150. Conte Agüero, *Eduardo Chibás*, 692.
151. Conte Agüero, *Eduardo Chibás*, 696.
152. Conte Agüero, *Eduardo Chibás*, 696.
153. The personal popularity of Chibás also acted as a magnet and was not lost on the island's politicians. He claimed that a recent public survey commissioned by Carlos Prío had showed him winning 41 percent of voters. Whether this was the case or not, some political leaders, notably Eduardo Suárez Rivas of the Liberals, sensed that Chibás represented the future and kept their lines of communication open with him.
154. "En Cuba, Política: 'Yo no Transijo Cuando se Trata de Principios,'" *Bohemia*, November 19, 1950, 79.
155. "En Cuba, Política: 'Yo no Transijo Cuando se Trata de Principios,'" 79.
156. Raúl Gutiérrez, "Survey Nacional: Oriente, Camagüey, Las Villas y Toda la Isla, Opinan Sobre el Gobierno y Los Posibles Presidentes," *Bohemia*, December 24, 1950, 74.
157. Gutiérrez, "Survey Nacional: Oriente, Camagüey, Las Villas y Toda la Isla, Opinan Sobre el Gobierno y Los Posibles Presidentes," 77. Nicolás Castellanos, who was already touting his presidential candidacy with full-page ads in newspapers and magazines, finished fourth—with only 2.47 percent.

9. "TIME WILL PROVE ME RIGHT ONCE AGAIN"

1. Néstor Piñango, "Los propagandistas de la oposición," *Bohemia*, January 14, 1951, 52.
2. Virgilio Ferrer Gutiérrez, "Nuestra política es así," *Carteles*, January 21, 1951, 102.
3. "En Cuba, Política," *Bohemia*, January 7, 1951, 64.
4. "Cuban Money Takes Choice N.Y. Realty through Florida Broker Operating Here," *New York Times*, November 12, 1950.

5. Baldomero Álvarez Ríos, "Misteriosas inversiones en propiedades hacen en New York millionarios cubanos," *Bohemia*, January 7, 1951, 32–33, 99.
6. Eduardo R. Chibás, "Respuesta a un reto del gobierno," *Bohemia*, January 14, 1951, 57.
7. Chibás, "Respuesta a un reto del gobierno," 57.
8. "En Cuba, Política," *Bohemia*, January 21, 1951, 59.
9. "En Cuba, Politica," 60.
10. Broadcast television was less than a year old in Cuba and largely confined to affluent homes. However, poorer Cubans who lived in cities and towns often watched in local bars or hotels.
11. In an interview with Aureliano Sánchez Arango, an Auténtico presidential candidate for 1952 and the current minister of education, he referred disparagingly to Batista as "the general of Kuquine" and criticized him in terms reminiscent of Chibás and the Ortodoxos. For example, Sánchez Arango (like the Ortodoxo councilman Herminio Portell Vilá) deemed Batista's senatorial term a "parliamentary farce" and opined that the ghost of Antonio Guiteras kept the ex-dictator from showing his face in public. Perhaps most indicative was the fact that the interviewer noticed Sánchez Arango was "undoubtedly disquieted" by Eddy's popularity in previous questions but showed no similar unease when Batista's name was mentioned. See: "En Cuba, El PRC tiene sus grandezas y Miserias," *Bohemia*, January 14, 1951, 60.
12. The most pressing of these, by Eddy's own admission, was the wretched state of many Cuban peasants. One solution he was investigating involved large-scale cultivation of rice, which could be grown from April to December—during the so-called dead season of the sugar industry. In addition, there already existed a large domestic market for rice in Cuba, most of which was imported from the United States. The above points were underlined in a letter to Chibás from Julio R. Arellano of the Arrocera Oriental, dated January 16, 1951, in response to a missive the Ortodoxo leader had sent on December 8, 1950. The last paragraph of this letter noted that "it has made a very good impression on me to know, through direct experience, that a political party occupies itself with the study of national economic problems instead of dedicating itself exclusively to the conquest of power." ANC, Legajo 38, Expediente 1135,111.
13. "Emplaza el Dr. Prío a los ortodoxos por el bien de la República," *Diario de la Marina*, January 18, 1951, 1, 20.
14. Juan J. Remos, "Deslindes," *Diario de la Marina*, January 20, 1951, 4.
15. Remos, for example, had been minister of education in 1936 under Federico Laredo Bru (1936–1940), Batista's puppet president.
16. "En Cuba, Política: Una gigantesca polémica," *Bohemia*, January 28, 1951, 61.
17. Francisco Ichaso, "Política: Catonismo frenético," *Diario de la Marina*, January 20, 1951, 6.
18. "En Cuba, Política: Una gigantesca polémica," 61.
19. "En Cuba, Política: Una gigantesca polémica," 61.
20. "En Cuba, Política: Una gigantesca polémica," 61.
21. "En Cuba, Política: Una gigantesca polémica," 62.
22. "Editorial: El Tribunal de Garantías Constitucionales y Sociales ha dicho la 'última palabra,'" *Bohemia*, January 28, 1951, 63.
23. Néstor Piñango, "Prío y Grau: Sargentos Políticos de Chibás," *Bohemia*, January 28, 1951, 50. In terms of the loan, the author points out that it was initially intended to finance the construction of a tunnel underneath Havana harbor that would connect the city center to sparsely populated La Cabaña on the other side. The government sought to lure foreign investors by claiming the cheap real estate of La Cabaña, heretofore inaccessible without a tunnel, would be worth millions of pesos once it was a mere five minutes from Havana's Parque Central. Later on, the idea of a tunnel was discarded in favor of a bridge. In any event, the project remained grounded because foreign investors were far less enthusiastic than the administration. Thus, Piñango writes, "There is no tunnel. There is no bridge. But there is a loan."
24. "En Cuba, Política: Una gigantesca polémica," 62.
25. "En Cuba, Política: Una gigantesca polémica," 62.
26. "En Cuba, Política: Una gigantesca polémica," 64.
27. "En Cuba, Política: Una gigantesca polémica," 64.
28. "En Cuba, Política: Una gigantesca polémica," 64.

29. "En Cuba, Política: Una gigantesca polémica," 64. See also: Ameringer, *The Cuban Democratic Experience*, 147.
30. "En Cuba, Política: Una gigantesca polémica," 65.
31. "En Cuba, Política: Un Plan de Pillaje Perfectamente Organizado," *Bohemia*, January 7, 1951, 64.
32. Antonio Prohias, "Insinuación," *Bohemia*, January 21, 1951, 63.
33. Virgilio Ferrer Gutiérrez, "Nuestra política es así," *Carteles*, February 4, 1951, 73.
34. ANC, Legajo 38, Expediente 1137, 25. The last word Chibás underlined was "majority."
35. ANC, Legajo 38, Expediente 1137, 21.
36. "En Cuba, Política: Una gigantesca polémica," 65.
37. The director of the Agricultural and Industrial Development Bank, Justo Carrillo, was a long-standing friend of Chibás and may have declined to partake in the event for this reason.
38. "En Cuba, Política: La Noche del Viernes," *Bohemia*, February 4, 1951, 62.
39. "En Cuba, Política: La Noche del Viernes," 63.
40. "En Cuba, Política: La Noche del Viernes," 63.
41. "Los fanáticos cubanos no quieren managers extranjeros," *Bohemia*, September 20, 1953, 74–75. The article contains a survey in which more than 70 percent of respondents considered themselves baseball fans, including 82 percent of the island's men and nearly 60 percent of its women.
42. Eladio Secades, "Con su gran heroe Adrián Aabala en el montículo, los Rojos derrotaron a los Azules en juego decisivo," *Diario de la Marina*, February 20, 1951, 18.
43. Federico R. Ferrán Ruvero, "Disfrutará de una licencia de 15 días el alcalde Castellanos," *Diario de la Marina*, February 20, 1951, 3.
44. Ferrán Ruvero, "Disfrutará una licencia de 15 días el alcalde Castellanos," 3.
45. José Roseñada, "Realidades," *Diario de la Marina*, February 21, 1951, 4.
46. Conte Agüero, *Eduardo Chibás*, 725.
47. Conte Agüero, *Eduardo Chibás*, 725.
48. Conte Agüero, *Eduardo Chibás*, 725.
49. ANC, Legajo 38, Expediente 1136, 46.
50. ANC, Legajo 38, Expediente 1136, 20.
51. According to Cuba's 1943 census, Guane counted a population of 30,954. The town was notable for being the westernmost terminal on Cuba's railway.
52. ANC, Legajo 38, Expediente 1136, 33.
53. *UN Handbook of National Accounts Statistics* (New York: United Nations, 1962).
54. ANC, Legajo 39, Expediente 1143, 103.
55. Conte Agüero, *Eduardo Chibás*, 728.
56. Conte Agüero, *Eduardo Chibás*, 728.
57. Enrique de la Osa, "Atentado: Parece que fue Ayer," *Bohemia*, January 21, 1951, 57.
58. "En Cuba, Entrevista: Lomberto el Terrible," *Bohemia*, January 7, 1951, 59.
59. "En Cuba, Atendado: Parece que fue Ayer," 57.
60. "En Cuba, Atendado: Parece que fue Ayer," 57.
61. "En Cuba, Atendado: Parece que fue Ayer," 58.
62. "En Cuba, Atendado: Parece que fue Ayer," 58.
63. "En Cuba, Atendado: Parece que fue Ayer," 58.
64. "En Cuba, Atendado: Parece que fue Ayer," 58.
65. "En Cuba, Atendado: Parece que fue Ayer," 58.
66. "En Cuba, Atendado: Parece que fue Ayer," 58.
67. "En Cuba, Atendado: Parece que fue Ayer," 58.
68. "En Cuba, Atendado: Parece que fue Ayer," 58.
69. "En Cuba, Atendado: Parece que fue Ayer," 58.
70. "En Cuba, La Capital: Página Lamentable," *Bohemia*, February 25, 1951, supplement, 1.
71. For an English translation of Articles 33 and 40 of Cuba's 1940 constitution, see http://www.latinamericanstudies.org/constitution/title4.htm.
72. "Niega Chibás al Dr. Masferrer el derecho de réplica por su hora," *Diario de la Marina*, February 14, 1951, 6.

73. "No acepta el PPC que Masferrer se acojoa al derecho de réplica," *Diario de la Marina*, February 15, 1951, 1, 24. See also: "En defensa de la libertad de palabra," *Bohemia*, February 18, 1951, 53.
74. "No acepta el PPC que Masferrer se acoja al derecho de réplica," 24.
75. "En Cuba, La Capital: Página Lamentable," supplement, 2.
76. *Diario de la Marina*, February 16, 1951, 6.
77. "Concede el Gobierno el derecho de réplica al doctor Masferrer," *Diario de la Marina*, February 17, 1951, 1.
78. "Concede el Gobierno el derecho de réplica al doctor Masferrer," 1.
79. "En Cuba, La Capital: Página Lamentable," supplement, 2.
80. "En Cuba, La Capital: Página Lamentable," supplement, 2.
81. "Al Pueblo de Cuba," *Diario de la Marina*, February 17, 1951, 6.
82. On this day, an underground radio broadcast, courtesy of ABC Radical, disseminated the false news that Machado had resigned and called on Cubans to fill the streets. They promptly did so and were fired upon by the police as they marched toward the presidential palace.
83. "En Cuba, La Capital: Página Lamentable," supplement, 2.
84. "En Cuba, La Capital: Página Lamentable," supplement, 2.
85. "En Cuba, La Capital: Página Lamentable," supplement, 2.
86. The Vedado section of Havana is laid out in the form of a grid. Odd-numbered streets (i.e., 1, 3, 5, 7, etc.) running southeast are bisected by avenues denominated by letters (beginning with O and ending with A, after which letters are replaced by even numbers, 2, 4, 6, etc.) running southwest. Some streets are also known by names as well as letters or numbers. For example, Línea, one of the neighborhood's main thoroughfares, runs along Ninth Street in much of Vedado. In a similar vein, Calzada runs along almost the entire length of Seventh Street.
87. "En Cuba, La Capital: Página Lamentable," supplement, 3.
88. "En Cuba, La Capital: Página Lamentable," supplement, 4.
89. "En Cuba, La Capital: Página Lamentable," supplement, 4.
90. "En Cuba, La Capital: Página Lamentable," supplement, 4.
91. "En Cuba, La Capital: Página Lamentable," supplement, 4.
92. "En Cuba, La Capital: Página Lamentable," supplement, 4.
93. "En Cuba, La Capital: Página Lamentable," supplement, 4.
94. "En Cuba, La Capital: Página Lamentable," supplement, 4.
95. Conte Agüero, *Eduardo Chibás*, 737.
96. Nick Machado, "¡Remember Artemisa!," *La Correspondencia*, February 20, 1951. See ANC, Legajo 39, Expediente 1141, 18.
97. "En Cuba, La Capital: Página Lamentable," supplement, 4.
98. Nick Machado, "¡Remember Artemisa!," See: ANC, Legajo 39, Expediente 1141, 18.
99. "En Cuba, La Capital: Página Lamentable," supplement, 4.
100. ANC, Legajo 39, Expediente 1139, 48.
101. ANC, Legajo 39, Expediente 1139, 8.
102. "En Cuba, La Capital: Página Lamentable," supplement, 4.

10. "I AM GOING TO OPEN MY BRIEFCASE"

1. Conte Agüero, *Eduardo Chibás*, 738. This statement was actually the sharpest of double-edged swords. In his will, José Manuel Alemán had designated 5 million pesos for the construction of a hospital to treat children with tuberculosis. This caused a heated debate on the island, as the money had obviously been embezzled and many, including Chibás, believed it should return to the state's coffers. In this sense, even acts of charity by Cuba's nouveau riche politicians were stained by thievery. Conversely, Chibás stressed that his family's coffee plantation had been acquired via "legitimate work" rather than stolen funds.
2. "En Cuba, Política: 'Después de 6 Años ya Nadie Cree en Nosotros . . . ,'" *Bohemia*, March 11, 1951, 59.

3. "En Cuba, Política: 'Después de 6 Años ya Nadie Cree en Nosotros...,'" 59.
4. "En Cuba, Política: 'Después de 6 Años ya Nadie Cree en Nosotros...,'" 59.
5. "En Cuba, Política: 'Después de 6 Años ya Nadie Cree en Nosotros...,'" 59.
6. "En Cuba, Política: Las Impurezas de la Realidad," *Bohemia*, March 11, 1951, 60.
7. Eduardo R. Chibás, "Pacto de Renegados," *Bohemia*, March 11, 1951, 54.
8. Chibás," "Pacto de Renegados," 54.
9. Chibás, "Pacto de Renegados," 54.
10. Chibás, "Pacto de Renegados," 54.
11. Raúl Gutiérrez, "El Pueblo Opina Sobre La Guerra en Correa y el Pacto Liberal," *Bohemia*, March 18, 1952, 24.
12. Gutiérrez, "El Pueblo Opina Sobre La Guerra en Correa y el Pacto Liberal," 23.
13. "En Cuba, Política: 'Una Sociedad Anónima para Lucrar...,'" *Bohemia*, April 1, 1951, 58.
14. Emilio Núñez Blanco would later support Fulgencio Batista after his coup in March of 1952. He subsequently became notable for marrying Mirta Díaz-Balart, the ex-wife of Fidel Castro.
15. ANC, Legajo 39, Expediente 1144, 54.
16. Eduardo R. Chibás, "Pacto de Renegados," *Bohemia*, March 11, 1951, 54.
17. Eduardo R. Chibás, "El Pacto de la Desvergüenza," *Bohemia*, March 18, 1951, 20.
18. Eduardo R. Chibás, "Pacto de Renegados," 55.
19. "En Cuba, Política: Las Impurezas de la Realidad," 61.
20. "En Cuba, Tribunales: 'Lo Consentía Todo...,'" *Bohemia*, March 25, 1951, 78.
21. A *Bohemia* reporter wryly observed that Grau's trial under Machado was political in nature while his prospective one promised to be "common" and was not "inspired by the government." See: "En Cuba, Tribunales: 'Lo Consentía Todo....'"
22. "En Cuba, Tribunales: 'Lo Consentía Todo...,'" 78.
23. "En Cuba, Tribunales: 'Lo Consentía Todo...,'" 78.
24. "En Cuba, Tribunales: 'Lo Consentía Todo...,'" 78.
25. "En Cuba, Tribunales: 'Lo Consentía Todo...,'" 79.
26. "En Cuba, Tribunales: 'Lo Consentía Todo...,'" 79–80.
27. "En Cuba, Tribunales: 'Lo Consentía Todo...,'" 80.
28. "En Cuba, Tribunales: 'Lo Consentía Todo...,'" 80.
29. "En Cuba, Tribunales: 'Lo Consentía Todo...,'" 80.
30. Fernán Villalva, "El Procesamiento del Ex Presidente Grau," *Carteles*, March 25, 1951, 74.
31. After Grau's antigovernment harangue on Saturday, Carlos Prío dispatched Félix Lancís to negotiate a truce between both sides. In exchange for official support, Grau dispensed with his criticism of the Auténtico-Liberal pact and agreed to assist the administration in its war of words against the Ortodoxos.
32. "En Cuba, Tribunales: 'Ni Acuso ni me Defiendo; soy un Juez,'" *Bohemia*, March 25, 1951, 80.
33. "En Cuba, Tribunales: 'Ni Acuso ni me Defiendo; soy un Juez,'" 80.
34. "En Cuba, Tribunales: 'Ni Acuso ni me Defiendo; soy un Juez,'" 80.
35. "En Cuba, Tribunales: 'Ni Acuso ni me Defiendo; soy un Juez,'" 80.
36. "En Cuba, Tribunales: 'Ni Acuso ni me Defiendo; soy un Juez,'" 80.
37. Article 154 of the constitution states: "The president of the republic shall preside over the council of ministers. When the president does not attend sessions of the council, the prime minister shall preside. The prime minister represents the general politics of the government, and shall represent the latter before congress."
38. "En Cuba, Política: Grau San Martín Ante la Prensa," *Bohemia*, April 1, 1951, 60.
39. "En Cuba, Política: Grau San Martín Ante la Prensa," 60.
40. "En Cuba, Política: Grau San Martín Ante la Prensa," 60.
41. "Opinan Sobre el Procesamiento del Dr. Ramón Grau San Martín," *Bohemia*, April 1, 1951, 72.
42. "Opinan Sobre el Procesamiento del Dr. Ramón Grau San Martín," 72.
43. "Opinan Sobre el Procesamiento del Dr. Ramón Grau San Martín," 71.

44. "Opinan Sobre el Procesamiento del Dr. Ramón Grau San Martín," 71.
45. "Un Documento Trascendental," *Bohemia*, April 1, 1951, 51.
46. Eduardo R. Chibás, "¡A La Carcel Los Ladrones!," *Bohemia*, April 1, 1951, 55.
47. "En Cuba, Abogados: 'La Viva Estampa de la Inercia,'" *Bohemia*, April 22, 1951, 57.
48. "En Cuba, Abogados: 'La Viva Estampa de la Inercia,'" 57.
49. "En Cuba, Abogados: 'La Viva Estampa de la Inercia,'" 57.
50. "En Cuba, Abogados: 'La Viva Estampa de la Inercia,'" 58.
51. "En Cuba, Poder Judicial: La Tercera Recusación," *Bohemia*, May 13, 1951, 62.
52. "En Cuba, Poder Judicial: La Tercera Recusación," 62.
53. "En Cuba, Poder Judicial: La Tercera Recusación," 62.
54. "En Cuba, Poder Judicial: La Tercera Recusación," 62.
55. "En Cuba, Poder Judicial: La Tercera Recusación," 62.
56. "Estoy Orgulloso de mi Conducta y no Tengo de que Arrepentirme," *Bohemia*, May 13, 1951, 69.
57. Niko, "Frase Comercial," *Bohemia*, May 13, 1951, 64.
58. Antonio, "Anuncios Clasificados," *Bohemia*, May 13, 1951, 61.
59. "En Cuba, Tribunales: 'Es un Digno Sucesor de Justiniani . . . ,'" *Bohemia*, May 27, 1951, 70.
60. "En Cuba, Tribunales: 'Es un Digno Sucesor de Justiniani . . . ,'" 70.
61. "En Cuba, Tribunales: 'Es un Digno Sucesor de Justiniani . . . ,'" 70.
62. "En Cuba, Tribunales: 'Es un Digno Sucesor de Justiniani . . . ,'" 70.
63. "En Cuba, Tribunales: 'Es un Digno Sucesor de Justiniani . . . ,'" 70.
64. "En Cuba, Survey: La Voz del Pueblo," *Bohemia*, May 27, 1951, 68.
65. "En Cuba, Survey: La Voz del Pueblo," 68.
66. Raúl Gutiérrez, "El Pueblo de Cuba Opina Sobre el Gobierno Actual y los Posibles Presidentes," *Bohemia*, May 20, 1951, supplement, 8.
67. President Prío was popular in areas where public works were carried out, but regions lacking them rued their absence. For this reason, construction projects were listed in the poll as Prío's greatest achievement and his second-largest failure. See: Gutiérrez, "El Pueblo de Cuba Opina Sobre el Gobierno Actual y los Posibles Presidentes," supplement, 9–10.
68. Gutiérrez, "El Pueblo de Cuba Opina Sobre el Gobierno Actual y los Posibles Presidentes," supplement, 10.
69. Gutiérrez, "El Pueblo de Cuba Opina Sobre el Gobierno Actual y los Posibles Presidentes," supplement, 11.
70. "En Cuba, Survey: La Voz del Pueblo," 67.
71. "En Cuba, Survey: La Voz del Pueblo," 67.
72. "En Cuba, Survey: La Voz del Pueblo," 67.
73. "En Cuba, Survey: La Voz del Pueblo," 68.
74. Eduardo R. Chibás, "Respuesta al Presidente de la Republica," *Bohemia*, June 3, 1951, 64. As was often the case, Chibás fashioned the transcript of his May 27 broadcast into a *Bohemia* article that ran the following week.
75. Chibás, "Respuesta al Presidente de la Republica," 64.
76. Chibás, "Respuesta al Presidente de la Republica," 64. According to the advocacy group Veterans of Independence, the government had paid only 43 percent of back pensions to soldiers from the liberation struggle. Many Cubans assumed that a portion of the public loans would be used to rectify the situation, but this was not the case. Personal appeals were made to politicians of all stripes, including Chibás, who was deeply moved, and Carlos Prío, who responded with soothing words but nothing substantive. With elections on the horizon, he almost certainly preferred to use the money on his party's presidential campaign.
77. Chibás, "Respuesta al Presidente de la Republica," 64.
78. Chibás, "Respuesta al Presidente de la Republica," 64.
79. Chibás, "Respuesta al Presidente de la Republica," 65.
80. Fernando Villaverde, "Como me lo contaron," *Carteles*, May 27, 1951, 73.
81. "En Cuba, Poder Judicial: La Recusación de Justiniani," *Bohemia*, June 3, 1951, supplement, 4.
82. ANC, Legajo 39, Expediente 1144, 15.

83. This flare-up merely reprised a long-standing hatred between the two men. During the years 1934–1939, Sánchez Arango belonged to the Auténtico party's armed wing—which was devoted to toppling the Batista-backed government by force. Meanwhile, Benítez was a military officer who persecuted the outlawed Auténticos along with other violent anti-Batista revolutionaries. Along with other Batista intimates, he enriched himself during this period as well. Later on, he became associated with Cuba's gambling industry. During their back and forth, Sánchez Arango alluded to this, calling his adversary a "racketeer" who had gained great wealth "from the sweat of our people." See "En Cuba, Poder Judicial: La Recusación de Justiniani," supplement, 4.

84. Under Sánchez Arango's stewardship, such exalted entertainment was commonplace. A few weeks earlier, for example, the education ministry had sponsored a production of *Les Sylphides* by the Ballet Alicia Alonso in the very same square.

85. "En Cuba, Polémica: Dos Profesores en Discordia," *Bohemia*, June 10, 1951, supplement, 7.

86. "En Cuba, Polémica: Dos Profesores en Discordia," supplement, 7.

87. "En Cuba, Polémica: La Carta Delatora," *Bohemia*, June 24, 1951, 66.

88. The text of the letter was as follows: "Dear José Manuel: I have tried to communicate with you by telephone but have been unable to reach you. Just now, Ricardo Núñez has told me that I have been designated as a representative in the negotiations with the Republican party and I am now leaving immediately for Miami. You must act quickly to avoid this, otherwise Ricardo will be president and this is convenient for neither of us. Yours, Eduardo." See: "En Cuba, Polémica: La Carta Delatora," 66.

89. "En Cuba, Polémica: La Carta Delatora," 66.

90. The congressional correspondent for *Carteles* lamented that Suárez Rivas and Chibás, with the connivance of senate president Tony Varona, had wasted the final meeting before September on political theater rather than matters of substance. See El Duende del Capitolio, "Retablo Parlamentario," *Carteles*, July 1, 1951, 28.

91. "En Cuba, Polémica: La Carta Delatora," 72.

92. Conte Agüero, *Eduardo Chibás*, 759.

93. Lela Sánchez Echeverría, *La polémica infinita: Aureliano vs. Chibás y viceversa* (Colombia: Quebecor World Bogotá, 2004), 93. Sánchez Arango's suggested candidates for the tribunal of honor were Fernando Ortiz, Miguel Ángel Quevedo, and Alejandro Herrera Arango, who headed the National Industrial Association. Ortiz declined the invitation, citing his absence from politics since 1926 and the advice of his doctors to refrain from "polemical activities." He added that the increasing incidence of polemics was proof of the "disorganization and ineffectiveness of the republic's basic institutions." For his part, Quevedo passed due to an excess of work, ownership of an "impartial" magazine, and his "longtime friendship" with both men. See: Sánchez Echeverría, *La polémica infinita*, 95.

94. Eduardo R. Chibás, "Los Presupuestos Nacionales, La Cuota Azucarera de Cuba, Los Pesqueros Cubanos," *Bohemia*, July 1, 1951, 62.

95. Chibás, "Los Presupuestos Nacionales, La Cuota Azucarera de Cuba, Los Pesqueros Cubanos," 62.

96. Chibás, "Los Presupuestos Nacionales, La Cuota Azucarera de Cuba, Los Pesqueros Cubanos," 62.

97. Sánchez Echeverría, *La polémica infinita*, 97.

98. Sánchez Echeverría, *La polémica infinita*, 98.

99. Sánchez Echeverría, *La polémica infinita*, 98.

100. ANC, Legajo 9, Expediente 285, 182.

101. ANC, Legajo 9, Expediente 285, 181.

102. ANC, Legajo 9, Expediente 285, 181.

103. ANC, Legajo 9, Expediente 285, 184–185.

104. "En Cuba, Azucar: Los Derechos de Cuba," *Bohemia*, July 15, 1951, 79.

105. "En Cuba, Azucar: Los Derechos de Cuba," 79.

106. The Mexican government was responsible for excluding Cuban fishermen from the Gulf.

107. "En Cuba, Azucar: Los Derechos de Cuba," 80.

108. "En Cuba, Azucar: Los Derechos de Cuba," 80.
109. "En Cuba, Azucar: Los Derechos de Cuba," 80.
110. "En Cuba, Azucar: Los Derechos de Cuba," 80.
111. Chibás had at least two good reasons to avoid being judged by the *Ante la Prensa* hosts. First, one of them was Miguel de Marcos, who had already called him a "defamer." Second, he almost certainly feared the government would offer all manner of inducements to the others. After all, this was how the administration behaved when dealing with the judicial branch. Given the stakes here, he had no reason to doubt the cards would be stacked against him—even though another *Ante la Prensa* panelist, Rafael Estenger, often defended him.
112. Conte Agüero, *Eduardo Chibás*, 767–768.
113. Conte Agüero, *Eduardo Chibás*, 768.
114. Conte Agüero, *Eduardo Chibás*, 770. Earlier in the week, the *Diario de la Marina* editor-in-chief Gastón Baquero published an open letter to Sánchez Arango warning, "This polemic is total craziness. You are an honest man and Chibás knows it. During the debate, his speech on Guatemala will be notable for its lack of proof. But Eduardo Chibás not you or the government will, once again, have Cuba's attention and curiosity at his disposal." See Sánchez Echeverría, *La polémica infinita*, 112.
115. Sánchez Echeverría, *La polémica infinita*, 112.
116. "La Polémica Chibás-Sánchez Arango," *Carteles*, July 29, 1951, 57.
117. Sánchez Echeverría, *La polémica infinita*, 115.
118. Conte Agüero, *Eduardo Chibás*, 772.
119. Sánchez Echeverría, *La polémica infinita*, 123.
120. Conte Agüero, *Eduardo Chibás*, 773. In Spanish, the song goes: "¿Dónde están las pruebas, dónde están? / Cuando abren la maleta ya verán."
121. ANC, Legajo 39, Expediente 1147, 60.
122. ANC, Legajo 39, Expediente 1147, 97.
123. ANC, Legajo 39, Expediente 1147, 146.
124. ANC, Legajo 39, Expediente 1147, 115.
125. Sánchez Echeverría, *La polémica infinita*, 124.
126. Prada, *La secretaria de la república*, 135.
127. Sánchez Echeverría, *La polémica infinita*, app.
128. Many years later, Conchita Fernández confessed, "I swear I will die convinced that if the party leaders and all the Ortodoxos would have closed ranks around him, with no breaches, and without being afraid to fight for him, he would not have feared the people were losing confidence in him and would not have committed suicide." See: Prada, *La secretaria de la república*, 135–136.
129. "En Cuba, Polémica: ¡La Tercera Semana!," *Bohemia*, August 5, 1951, 75.
130. "En Cuba, Polémica: ¡La Tercera Semana!," 75.
131. "En Cuba, Polémica: ¡La Tercera Semana!," 75.
132. Addressing this point, Enrique de la Osa wrote that Sánchez Arango "had nothing to lose . . . and much to gain" by confronting the Ortodoxo leader. By the same token, he chastised Chibás for the "error" of engaging in a polemic against an opponent who was his political inferior in every respect. See: "En Cuba, Polémica: ¡La Tercera Semana!," 75.
133. "En Cuba, Polémica: ¡La Tercera Semana!," 76.
134. "En Cuba, Polémica: ¡La Tercera Semana!," 76.
135. Sánchez Echeverría, *La polémica infinita*, app.
136. Eduardo R. Chibás, "¡Yo Acuso!," *Carteles*, August 12, 1951, 73. In a further jibe, Chibás held that Sánchez Arango did not invest in the United States because his past ties with Communists rendered him unwelcome there.
137. Chibás, "¡Yo Acuso!," 73.
138. "En Cuba, La Capital: 'A Chibás Le Duele Cuba,'" *Bohemia*, August 12, 1951, 71.
139. "En Cuba, La Capital: 'A Chibás Le Duele Cuba,'" 67. See also Conte Agüero, *Eduardo Chibás*, 782–783.
140. "En Cuba, La Capital: 'A Chibás Le Duele Cuba,'" 67.
141. "Testamento Político de Chibás," *Bohemia*, August 26, 1951, 96.
142. "Testamento Político de Chibás," 96.

143. "Testamento Político de Chibás," 96.
144. "Testamento Político de Chibás," 96.
145. "Testamento Político de Chibás," 96.
146. "Testamento Político de Chibás," 96.
147. "En Cuba, La Capital: El Ultimo Aldabonazo," *Bohemia*, August 12, 1951, 67.
148. "En Cuba, La Capital: El Ultimo Aldabonazo," 67.
149. "En Cuba, La Capital: El Ultimo Aldabonazo," 67.
150. The Auténticos who appeared that evening included Grau's erstwhile education minister Luis Pérez Espinós, along with the congressmen Francisco Cairol and Gilberto Leyva.
151. "En Cuba, La Capital: El Ultimo Aldabonazo," 68.
152. "En Cuba, La Capital: El Ultimo Aldabonazo," 68.
153. "En Cuba, La Capital: El Ultimo Aldabonazo," 68.
154. "En Cuba, La Capital: 'A Chibás le Duele Cuba,'" 71.
155. "En Cuba, La Capital: 'A Chibás le Duele Cuba,'" 71.
156. "En Cuba, La Capital: 'A Chibás le Duele Cuba,'" 71.
157. "En Cuba, La Capital: 'A Chibás le Duele Cuba,'" 71.
158. "En Cuba, Duelo Nacional: Ha Fallecido una Gran Esperanza," *Bohemia*, August 19, 1951, reprinted in Enrique de la Osa, *En Cuba, segundo tiempo: 1948–1952* (La Habana: Ciencias Sociales, 2005), 369.
159. José Chelala, "Mis Últimas Entrevistas con Chibás," *Bohemia*, August 26, 1951, 57.
160. De la Osa, *En Cuba, segundo tiempo*, 369.

EPILOGUE

1. "En Cuba, Funerales: El Pueblo ha Sabido Escuchar el Último Adabonazo," *Bohemia*, August 26, 1951, 73.
2. Rodolfo Rodríguez Zaldívar, "Pasarán Mil Años Antes de Que Haya Otro Sepelio Como Este de Chibás," *Bohemia*, August 26, 1951, 81.
3. "En Cuba, Fué el Festival de su Victoria," *Bohemia*, August 26, 1951, 74.
4. ANC, Legajo 36, Expediente 3615, 23.
5. ANC, Legajo 36, Expediente 3615, 23.
6. ANC, Legajo 36, Expediente 3615, 1. Specifically, Pardo Llada viewed Chibás as the newest addition to a glorious timeline that began in 1868 with Carlos Manuel de Céspedes and Ignacio Agramonte, continued in 1895 with José Martí and Antonio Maceo, and carried on during the early years of the republic with the soldier-statesmen Manuel Sanguily and Bartolomé Masó.
7. "En Cuba, Fue el Festival de su Victoria," 74.
8. "En Cuba, Fue el Festival de su Victoria," 75.
9. Luis Rolando Cabrera and Paco Altuna, "El Aldabonazo de Chibás Resuena en la Conciencia Popular," *Bohemia*, September 2, 1951, 25.
10. Cabrera and Altuna, "El Aldabonazo de Chibás Resuena en la Conciencia Popular," 26.
11. Rafael Coello, "2,920 Días Junto a la Tumba de Eduardo Chibás," *Carteles*, August 16, 1959, 47.
12. ANC, Legajo 36, Expediente 3615, 9.
13. Cabrera and Altuna, "El Aldabonazo de Chibás Resuena en la Concienca Popular," 25.
14. Cabrera and Altuna, "El Aldabonazo de Chibás Resuena en la Concienca Popular," 24.
15. Cabrera and Altuna, "El Aldabonazo de Chibás Resuena en la Concienca Popular," 25.
16. Cabrera and Altuna, "El Aldabonazo de Chibás Resuena en la Concienca Popular," 25.
17. Louis Pérez, *Army Politics in Cuba, 1898–1958* (Pittsburgh: University of Pittsburgh Press, 1976), 124.
18. All three men had been appointed to their posts as Auténticos during Grau's presidency.
19. According to a poll from December of 1951, the Auténtico candidate Carlos Hevia led with 33.8 percent of those surveyed, while Roberto Agramonte trailed slightly behind with 30 percent. Batista was well back in third place with a mere 14.2 percent. See: Jorge I.

Domínguez, *Cuba: Order and Revolution* (Cambridge, MA: Harvard University Press, 1978), 113.

20. Thomas, *Cuba*, 779. Besides Landeira, other soldiers behaved honorably as well—although they were clearly among the minority. Notable among these was Colonel Eduardo Martín Elena, the army chief of Matanzas province. Asked to join the revolt in progress, he indignantly replied that "I will not stain my reputation by supporting an uprising against the republic. You may as well imprison me. I will never lend my assistance to this sort of thing or violate the constitution." See: De la Osa, *En Cuba, segundo tiempo*, 498.

21. De la Osa, *En Cuba, segundo tiempo*, 494.

22. De la Osa, *En Cuba, segundo tiempo*, 494.

23. De la Osa, *En Cuba, segundo tiempo*, 494–495.

24. De la Osa, *En Cuba, segundo tiempo*, 495.

25. The elections, which were tightly scripted, did not in fact take place until November 1, 1954.

26. Although Santovenia harbored ambivalent feelings regarding the coup, the erstwhile ABC man who had briefly been an Ortodoxo ultimately accepted a position as head of Cuba's Agricultural and Industrial Development Bank.

27. Andrés Rivero Agüero had been a prominent member of Batista's political party, PAU, before the coup and also served as agriculture minister during Batista's term as elected president (1940–1944). Their personal affinity can be traced in part to the fact that both grew up poor in Oriente province and improved themselves via education. Rivero Agüero, in fact, taught himself how to read at the age of sixteen and eventually obtained a law degree from the University of Havana.

28. Born of Spanish parents, Miguel Ángel Campa attended Havana's most prestigious high school, the Jesuit-run Colegio de Belén, which also counted Chibás as an alumnus. Batista confirmed his absolute faith in Campa by naming him ambassador to the United States between 1955 and 1958.

29. During this period, military men and police officers routinely appeared without warning at the residences of recalcitrant legislators or other assorted critics—sometimes with gruesome results but always to instill a healthy sense of fear. For example, in 1937, Carlos Márquez Sterling, who was then a Liberal lawmaker in Cuba's chamber of representatives, made the mistake of criticizing Batista during a debate in the Capitolio. The following day, he received a visit from the dreaded Captain Belisario Hernández—who was one of Batista's more imposing enforcers. In the end, Márquez Sterling escaped harm only because his wife called a number of fellow legislators, some of whom showed up at the house. Their presence caused Hernández to retire, but the overall message was clear. See: Frank Argote-Freyre, *Fulgencio Batista: Volume 1, From Revolutionary to Strongman* (Piscataway, NJ: Rutgers University Press, 2006), 244–245.

30. Between 1952 and 1954, Sánchez Arango conducted a legendary cat-and-mouse game with Batista's security forces. His dashing, often nerve-racking escapes, usually with the police on the verge of trapping him, became the source of a new word in the Cuban vocabulary—the *aurelianada*, which was used to describe unlikely getaways. By June of 1954, Sánchez stopped pressing his luck and sought asylum in the Uruguayan embassy. See: "Cuba: Hairbreadth Escape," *Time*, June 7, 1954, http://www.time.com/time/magazine/article/0,9171,806865,00.html.

31. García Bárcena renounced his position at the War College following Batista's coup.

32. Tad Szulc, *Fidel: A Critical Portrait* (New York: William Morrow, 1986), 256.

33. Szulc, *Fidel*, 252.

34. Szulc, *Fidel*, 252.

35. Naty Revulta also was instructed to deliver copies to Ortodoxo party leaders, including Raúl Chibás and Roberto Agramonte.

36. The army casualties included nineteen dead and twenty-seven wounded.

37. Fidel Castro, *History Will Absolve Me* (La Habana: Editorial de Ciencias Sociales), http://www.marxists.org/history/cuba/archive/castro/1953/10/16.htm.

38. Castro, *History Will Absolve Me*.

39. Castro, *History Will Absolve Me*.

40. Antonio Rafael de la Cova, *The Moncada Attack, Birth of the Cuban Revolution* (Columbia: University of South Carolina Press, 2007), 28–29.

41. Hugh Thomas notes that "had it not been for the repression, the Moncada attack would doubtless have been dismissed as one more wild and semi-gangster incident in the life of Fidel Castro. The repression and the trial made Castro appear henceforth as something of a hero. Professional, Catholic, liberal or middle class opinion was outraged. . . . Professional people in Santiago, people who had either seen or had met someone who had seen something of what happened, turned almost without exception away from Batista." See: Thomas, *Cuba*, 843–844.

42. Agramonte's refusal begat a war of words with Auténtico president Tony Varona, who had led the effort to cultivate Ortodoxo support. Among other things, Varona claimed Agramonte was playing into Batista's hands by dividing Cuba's political opposition. Quite disingenuously, he also charged that Agramonte's harsh words for the Auténticos were the "same poison" that had provided Batista with an excuse for his golpe de estado. See: Charles Ameringer, "The Auténtico Party and the Political Opposition in Cuba, 1952–1957," *Hispanic American Historical Review* 65, no. 2 (1985): 332.

43. The quarrel between Agramonte and Ochoa actually dated to the period immediately after Eddy's death. Apparently, Ochoa felt he should have been the Ortodoxo presidential candidate in 1952 but claimed Agramonte stole the nomination by means of "an internal coup" within the party. See: Raúl Chibás, *Memorias de la Revolución Cubana* (Stanford: Hoover Institution on War, Revolution and Peace, n.d.), 7.

44. Guillermo Alonso Pujol joined the Auténticos in April of 1953, thereby abandoning the Cuban National Party—his personal political outfit. Also present at the negotiations was Eduardo Suárez Rivas, who resigned as president of the Liberals in October of 1952 and thereafter became an Auténtico. Súarez Rivas bolted because he believed too many Liberals, including his brother José, were cozying up to Batista.

45. Thomas, *Cuba*, 795. To burnish his sleaze-busting credentials, Batista announced he would revive Causa 82 against Grau.

46. Ameringer, "The Auténtico Party," 338.

47. Thomas, *Cuba*, 860.

48. Only 52.6 percent of registered Cubans voted in 1954. In 1948, during the previous presidential election, turnout was a more robust 79.5 percent. Obviously, many Cubans felt no need to participate in a race whose outcome seemed a foregone conclusion. Others, no doubt, abstained because they were accustomed to selling their votes and in this instance there were few if any takers. See: Domínguez, *Cuba*, 124.

49. Chibás, *Memorias*, 2.

50. Chibás, *Memorias*, 7.

51. The amnesty law was approved by Batista in April of 1955 and covered both political prisoners and exiles. Hence, Fidel Castro was freed from the Isle of Pines on May 15, and on August 11, Carlos Prío returned home from abroad.

52. Dina Martínez Díaz, "Crisis política en Cuba en la década del 50: disintegración de la Ortodoxia," *Revista de la Universidad de Oriente*, no. 88 (1999): 189.

53. Chibás, *Memorias*, 7.

54. Chibás, *Memorias*, 79. During a meeting in Manuel Bisbé's house, with Francisco Carone and Roberto Agramonte present as well, Raúl Chibás recounted that Cuervo Navarro had expressed his preference for assassinating Batista. He repeated this opinion to Raúl after they left the house. He did not take Cuervo Navarro's comments seriously at the time, believing that assassination "was not the best way of resolving our national problem."

55. Chibás, *Memorias*, 82.

56. "Despatch from the Embassy in Cuba to the Department of State." See:http://www.latinamericanstudies.org/cable/cable-10-3-57a.htm. While Batista had promised to vacate the presidency, he suggested a return to his old role of army chief might be in order. Leaving the doggedly loyal Rivero Agüero in place would thus allow him to rule from behind the scenes as he had during the years 1934–1940.

57. Ruby Hart Phillips, *Cuba: Island of Paradox* (New York: McDowell, Obolensky, 1959), 381.

58. Louis Pérez maintains that "the arms embargo and the subsequent protest over the use of army units trained and equipped by the United States contributed powerfully to the final collapse of morale within the Cuban armed services. Throughout the 1950s army *esprit de corps* had been reinforced by American military decorations awarded to senior Cuban officers. . . . North American military personnel frequently participated in official army functions as invited guests of honor. Several hundred Cuban officers had received training in the United States. The military establishment had been created, trained, provisioned, and armed by the United States: its highest military honor emanated from Washington, and for almost half a century it had been invested with North American support. Thus the arms embargo could crush at once the army's self-confidence and its faith in the constituted government." See: Louis A. Pérez Jr., *Army Politics in Cuba, 1898–1958* (Pittsburgh: University of Pittsburgh Press, 1976), 160–161.

59. Pérez, *Army Politics in Cuba*, 155.

60. Argote-Freyre, *Fulgencio Batista*, 1.

61. "Castro Speaks at Chibás Tomb," http://lanic.utexas.edu/project/castro/db/1959/19590117.html.

62. "Castro Speaks at Chibás Tomb."

63. "Castro Speaks at Chibás Tomb."

64. "Castro Speaks at Chibás Tomb."

65. "Castro Speaks at Chibás Tomb."

66. Eddy based some of his campaign pledges, notably the prohibition of latifundia and restrictions on land ownership, on Article 90 of Cuba's 1940 constitution.

67. "At Ringside when Cuba Clobbered Democracy," *Life*, July 27, 1959, 27.

68. Thomas, *Cuba*, 1231.

69. "What Ails Castro? Fidel Sickens and Defectors Flee," *Life*, August 15, 1960, 35.

70. Thomas, *Cuba*, 1320.

71. Armando Hart Dávalos, "Eduardo Chibás," *Granma*, August 24, 2007, http://www.rimed.cu/index.php?option=com_content&view=article&id=3938:eduardo-chibas&catid=52&Itemid=79.

72. Eliades Acosta Matos, "El aldabonazo aún resuena," *Juventud Rebelde*, August 26, 2007, 9.

Bibliography

ARCHIVAL SOURCES

Havana, Cuba

Archivo Nacional de Cuba (abbreviated in the Notes as "ANC")
  Fondo Eduardo R. Chibás
Biblioteca de la Universidad de la Habana
  Sección de Libros Raros

College Park, MD

National Archives and Records Administration
  State Department Records

NEWSPAPERS AND MAGAZINES

Acción
Alerta
Avance
Bohemia
Carteles
Diario de Cuba
Diario de la Marina
El Crisol
El Mundo
El País
Granma

Havana Herald
Havana Post
Heraldo de Cuba
Información
La Campaña
La Correspondencia
La Última Hora
Life
Luz
New York Daily News
New York Times
Noticias de Hoy
PM
Principios
Pueblo
Saint Petersburg Times
Siempre
Tiempo en Cuba
Time

INTERVIEWS

Pastorita Núñez, June 3, 2007, Havana, Cuba
Marissa Chibás Preston, May 15, 2007, New York, NY

BOOKS, ARTICLES, AND MANUSCRIPTS

Aguilar, Luis E. *Cuba 1933: Prologue to Revolution*. Ithaca, NY: Cornell University Press, 1972.
Alavez Martín, Elena. *Eduardo Chibás en la hora de ortodoxia*. La Habana: Editorial de Ciencias Sociales, 1994.
———. *Ortodoxia en el ideario americano*. La Habana: Editorial de Ciencias Sociales, 2002.
Alexander, Robert J. *Latin American Political Parties*. New York: Praeger Publishers, 1973.
Allahar, Anton, ed. *Caribbean Charisma: Reflections on Leadership, Legitimacy and Populist Politics*. Boulder, CO: Lynne Rienner, 2001.
Almond, Gabriel A., and Sidney Verba. *The Civic Culture*. Princeton, NJ: Princeton University Press, 1963.
Ameringer, Charles D. "The Auténtico Party and the Political Opposition in Cuba, 1952–1957." *Hispanic American Historical Review* 65, no. 2 (1985): 332.
———. *The Cuban Democratic Experience: The Auténtico Years, 1944–1952*. Gainesville: University of Florida Press, 2000.
Arenas, Reinaldo. *Antes que anochezca*. Barcelona: Tusquets, 1996.
Argote-Freyre, Frank. *Fulgencio Batista: Volume 1, From Revolutionary to Strongman*. Piscataway, NJ: Rutgers University Press, 2006.
———. "The Political Afterlife of Eduardo Chibás: The Evolution of a Symbol, 1951–1991." *Cuban Studies* 32 (2001): 74–97.

Armas, Ramón de, Francisco López Segrera, and Germán Sánchez. *Los Partidos políticos burgueses en Cuba neocolonial, 1909–1952*. La Habana: Editorial de Ciencias Sociales, 1985.
Azcuy y Cruz, Aracelio. *El autenticismo en la Habana*. La Habana: Editorial Lex, 1951.
Báez, Vicente, ed. *La Enciclopedia de Cuba*. Vol 9. *Gobiernos Republicanos*. Madrid: Playor, S.A., 1975.
Baeza Flores, Alberto. *Las cadenas vienen de lejos: Cuba, América Latina y la libertad*. Mexico: Editorial Letras, 1960.
Balfour, Sebastian. *Castro: Profiles in Power*. New York: Longman, 1995.
Bonachea, Rolando E., and Nelson P. Valdés, eds. *Revolutionary Struggle, 1947–1958*. Vol. 1 of *Selected Works of Fidel Castro*. Cambridge, MA: MIT Press, 1972.
Boswell, James. *Life of Samuel Johnson*. London: Oxford University Press, 1927.
Braden, Spruille. *Diplomats and Demagogues: The Memoirs of Spruille Braden*. New Rochelle, NY: Arlington House, 1971.
Cabrera Infante, Guillermo. *Mea Cuba*. New York: Farrar, Straus and Giroux, 1994.
Cairo, Ana, ed. *Mella: 100 años*, Vol. 1–2. La Habana: Editorial Oriente, 2003.
———. *Eduardo Chibás: Imaginarios*. Santiago de Cuba: Editorial Oriente, 2010.
Carone, Francisco. *Mi defensa de Chibás*. La Habana: Editorial Lex, 1949.
Carrillo, Justo. *Cuba 1933: Students, Yankees and Soldiers*. Coral Gables, FL: University of Miami North-South Center, 1994.
Castro, Fidel. *History Will Absolve Me*. La Habana: Editorial de Ciencias Sociales. http://www.marxists.org/history/cuba/archive/castro/1953/10/16.htm.
Chapman, Charles E. *A History of the Cuban Republic: A Study in Hispanic American Politics*. New York: Macmillan, 1927.
Chibás, Raúl. *Memorias de la Revolución Cubana*. Unpublished memoirs. Hoover Institution on War, Revolution and Peace, Stanford University.
Cirules, Enrique. *The Mafia in Havana: A Caribbean Mob Story*. New York: Ocean Press, 2004.
Colburn, Forrest D. *Latin America at the End of Politics*. Princeton, NJ: Princeton University Press, 2002.
Conniff, Michael L., ed. *Latin American Populism in Comparative Perspective*. Albuquerque: University of New Mexico Press, 1982.
———. *Populism in Latin America*. Tuscaloosa: University of Alabama Press, 1999.
Conte Agüero, Luis. *Eduardo Chibás, el Adalid de Cuba*. México: Editorial Jus, 1955.
Costa, Octavio R. *Luis J. Botifill: An Exemplary Cuban*. Coral Gables, FL: University of Miami, North-South Center, 1992.
Cuadras, Gloria. *Lo que yo vi*. Unpublished memoir.
De la Cova, Antonio Rafael. *The Moncada Attack: Birth of the Cuban Revolution*. Columbia: University of South Carolina Press, 2007.
De la Osa, Enrique. *En Cuba, primer tiempo: 1947–1948*. La Habana: Ciencias Sociales, 2004.
———. *En Cuba, segundo tiempo: 1948–1952*. La Habana: Ciencias Sociales, 2005.
De la Torre, Carlos. "The Ambiguous Meanings of Latin American Populisms." *Social Research* 59, no. 2 (Summer 1992): 385–414.
———. *Populist Seduction in Latin America: The Ecuadorian Experience*. Athens: Ohio University Center for International Studies, 2000.
Del Pilar, Díaz Castañón, ed. *Editos Ineditos: Documentos olvidados de la historia de Cuba*. La Habana: Ciencias Sociales, 2005.
Díaz Acosta, Norma. *Universidad del aire (conferencias y concursos)*. La Habana: Ciencias Sociales, 2001.
Díaz Roque, José, and Doris Era González. *Eduardo Chibás: El gran cívico*. Cienfuegos: Ediciones Mecenas, 2005.
Di Tella, Torcuato S. *Latin American Politics: A Theoretical Approach*. Austin: University of Texas Press, 2001.
———. "Populismo y reforma en America Latina." *Desarrollo economico* 4, no. 16 (1965): 391–425.

Domínguez, Jorge I. *Cuba: Order and Revolution*. Cambridge, MA: Harvard University Press, 1978.
Dornbusch, Rudiger, and Sebastian Edwards. *The Macroeconomics of Populism in Latin America*. Chicago: University of Chicago Press, 1991.
Dunkerley, James. *Political Suicide in Latin America and Other Essays*. New York: Verso, 1992.
Farber, Samuel. *The Origins of the Cuban Revolution Reconsidered*. Chapel Hill: University of North Carolina Press, 2006.
———. *Revolution and Reaction in Cuba: From Machado to Castro, 1933–1960*. Middletown, CT: Wesleyan University Press, 1976.
Ferrer, Ada. *Insurgent Cuba: Race, Nation and Revolution, 1868–1898*. Chapel Hill: University of North Carolina Press, 1999.
Font, Mauricio, and Alfonso W. Quiroz. *The Cuban Republic and José Martí: Reception and Use of a National Symbol*. Lanham, MD: Lexington Books, 2006.
Germani, Gino. *The Sociology of Modernization: Studies on Its Historical and Theoretical Aspects with Special Regard to the Latin American Case*. New Brunswick, NJ: Transaction Books, 1981.
———. *Authoritarianism, Fascism, and National Populism*. New Brunswick, NJ: Transaction Books, 1978.
Germani, Gino, Torcuato S. Di Tella and Octavio Ianni. *Populismo y contradicciones de clase en Latinoamerica*. México: Editorial Era, 1973.
Gerth, H. H., and C. Wright Mills, eds. and trans. *From Max Weber: Essays in Sociology*. New York: Oxford University Press, 1946.
Goldenberg, Boris. *The Cuban Revolution and Latin America*. New York: Praeger, 1965.
Helg, Aline. *Our Rightful Share: The Afro-Cuban Struggle for Equality, 1886–1912*. Chapel Hill: University of North Carolina Press, 1995.
Hernández, José M. *Cuba and the United States: Intervention and Militarism, 1868–1933*. Austin: University of Texas Press, 1993.
Hispanic American Report. Stanford University Press.
Howard, Philip A. *Changing History: Afro-Cuban Cabildos and Societies of Color in the Nineteenth Century*. Baton Rouge: Louisiana State University Press, 1998.
Iglesias Utset, Marial. *Las metáforas del cambio en la via cotidiana: Cuba 1898–1902*. La Habana: Ediciones Unión, 2003.
Illán, José M. *Cuba: Datos sobre una economía en ruinas*. Miami: s.p., 1964.
International Bank for Reconstruction and Development (IBRD). *Report on Cuba*. Baltimore: Johns Hopkins University Press, 1951.
Jensen, Larry R. *Children of Colonial Despotism: Press, Politics and Culture in Cuba, 1790–1840*. Tampa: University of South Florida Press, 1988.
Jiménez, Guillermo. *Los Propietarios de Cuba 1958*. La Habana: Ciencias Sociales, 2008.
Kirk, John M. "From 'Inadaptado Sublime' to 'Líder Revolucionario': Some Further Thoughts on the Presentation of José Martí." *Latin American Research Review* 15, no. 3 (1980): 127–47.
Knight, Alan. "Populism and Neo-Populism in Latin America, Especially Mexico." *Journal of Latin American Studies* 30, Part 2 (May 1998): 223–48.
Langley, Lester. *The Cuban Policy of the United States: A Brief History*. New York: John Wiley and Sons, 1968.
Levine, Robert M. *Father of the Poor? Vargas and His Era*. New York: Cambridge University Press, 1998.
———. *The Vargas Regime: The Critical Years, 1934–1938*. New York: Columbia University Press, 1970.
López-Civeira, Francisca. *La crisis de los partidos políticos burgueses en Cuba, 1925–1958*. La Habana: Ministerio de Educación Superior, 1990.
López Vilaboy, José. *Motivos y culpables de la destrucción de Cuba*. San Juan, PR: ELPRIN, 1973.
Lowry, Nelson. *Rural Cuba*. Minneapolis: University of Minnesota Press, 1950.

Machover, Jacobo, ed. *La Habana 1952–1961: El final de un mundo, el principio de una ilusión.* Madrid: Alianza Editorial, 1995.
Malloy, James, and Mitchell Selligson, eds. *Authoritarians and Democrats: Regime Transition in Latin America.* Pittsburgh: University of Pittsburgh Press, 1987.
Mainwaring, Scott, and Matthew Soberg Shugart, eds. *Presidentialism and Democracy in Latin America.* New York: Cambridge University Press, 1997.
Mañach, Jorge. *Indagación del choteo.* La Habana: La Veronica, 1940.
———. *Martí el Apóstol.* Madrid: Espasa-Calpe, 1933.
———. *Teoría de la frontera.* Río Piedras: Editorial Universitaria, Universidad de Puerto Rico, 1970.
Martínez Díaz, Dina. "Crisis política en Cuba en la década del 50: Disintegración de la Ortodoxia." *Revista de la Universidad de Oriente* no. 88 (1999): 189.
Massie, Robert K. *Peter the Great: His Life and World.* New York: Alfred A. Knopf, 1981.
McGillivray, Gillian. *Blazing Cane: Sugar Communities, Class and State Formation in Cuba, 1868–1959.* Durham, NC: Duke University Press, 2009.
O'Donnell, Guillermo, Philippe C. Schmitter, and Laurence Whitehead, eds. *Transitions from Authoritarian Rule: Latin America.* Baltimore: Johns Hopkins University Press, 1986.
Ortiz, Fernando. *Las responsabilidades de los Estados Unidos en los males de Cuba.* Washington, DC: Cuban Information Bureau, 1932.
———. *Orbita de Fernando Ortíz.* La Habana: UNEAC, 1973.
Padula, Alfred. "The Fall of the Bourgeoisie: Cuba 1959–1961." PhD diss., University of New Mexico, 1974.
Page, Charles Albert. "The Development of Organized Labor in Cuba." PhD diss., University of California, 1952.
Pappademos, Melina. *Black Political Activism and the Cuban Republic.* Chapel Hill: University of North Carolina Press, 2011.
Parker, David S. "Law, Honor and Impunity in Spanish America: The Debate over Dueling, 1870–1920." *Law and History Review* 19, no. 2 (Summer 2001): 311–41.
Pérez Jr., Louis A. *Army Politics in Cuba, 1898–1958.* Pittsburgh: University of Pittsburgh Press, 1976.
———. *Cuba and the United States: Ties of Singular Intimacy.* Athens: University of Georgia Press, 1990.
———. *Essays on Cuban History: Historiography and Research.* Gainesville: University Presses of Florida, 1995.
———. *Intervention, Revolution and Politics in Cuba, 1913–1921.* Pittsburgh: University of Pittsburgh Press, 1978.
———. *On Becoming Cuban: Identity, Nationality and Culture.* Chapel Hill: University of North Carolina Press, 1999.
———. *To Die in Cuba: Suicide and Society.* Chapel Hill: University of North Carolina Press, 2005.
Pérez-Stable, Marifeli. *The Cuban Revolution: Origins, Course and Legacy.* New York: Oxford University Press, 1993.
Phillips, Ruby Hart. *Cuba: Island of Paradox.* New York: McDowell, Obolensky, 1959.
Portell Vilá, Herminio. *Nueva historia de la República de Cuba, 1898–1979.* Miami: La Moderna Poesía, 1986.
Prada, Pedro. *La secretaria de la república.* La Habana: Ciencias Sociales, 2001.
Quiroz, Alfonso W. "Implicit Costs of Empire: Bureaucratic Corruption in Nineteenth-Century Cuba." *Journal of Latin American Studies*, no. 35 (Cambridge: Cambridge University Press, 2003): 473–511.
Read, Gerald. "Politics and Education: The Cuban Merry-Go-Round." *History of Education Journal* 4, no. 3 (Spring 1953): 104–10.
Riera Hernández, Mario. *Un presidente cordial: Carlos Prío Socarrás, 1927–1964.* Miami: n.p., 1966.
Roberts, W. Adolphe. *Havana: The Portrait of a City.* New York: Coward-McCann, 1953.
Rodríguez Salgado, Ramón. *Ortodoxia chibasista: Nacimento, liderazgo y acción de un movimiento político.* La Habana: Editora Historia, 1998.

———. *Vergüenza contra dinero*. La Habana: Editora Política, 2007.
Roig de Leuchsenring, Emilio. *Males y vicios de Cuba republicana: Sus causas y sus remedios*. La Habana: n.p., 1959.
Sagrado Baeza, Rafael. "Suicidio como política." *Patrimonio Cultural* 35 (Fall 2005): 26–28.
Salwen, Michael Brian. *Radio and Televisión in Cuba: The Pre-Castro Era*. Ames: Iowa State University Press, 1994.
Sánchez Arango, Aureliano. *Trincheras de ideas . . . y piedras*. San Juan, PR: Editorial San Juan, 1972.
Sánchez Echeverría, Lela. *La polémica infinita: Aureliano vs. Chibás y viceversa*. Bogotá: Quebecor World Bogotá, 2004.
Scarpaci, Joseph L., Roberto Segre, and Mario Coyula. *Havana: Two Faces of the Antillean Metropolis*. Chapel Hill: University of North Carolina Press, 1997.
Schiff, Stacy. *A Great Improvisation: Franklin, France and the Birth of America*. New York: Henry Holt, 2005.
Skierka, Volker. *Fidel Castro: A Biography*. Translated by Patrick Camiller. Malden, MA: Polity Press, 2004.
Soto, Lionel. *La Revolución del 33*, 3 Vols. La Habana: Editorial Pueblo y Educación, 1985.
Stokes, William S. "The Cuban Parliamentary System in Action, 1940–1947." *The Journal of Politics* 11, no. 2 (May 1949): 335–64.
———. "The 'Cuban Revolution' and the Presidential Elections of 1948." *Hispanic American Historical Review* 31, no. 1 (February 1951): 37–79.
Suárez Rivas, Eduardo. *Los días iguales*. Miami: s.n., 1974.
Suchlicki, Jaime. *University Students and Revolution in Cuba, 1920–1968*. Coral Gables, FL: University of Miami Press, 1969.
Sweig, Julia. *Inside the Cuban Revolution: Fidel Castro and the Urban Underground*. Cambridge, MA: Harvard University Press, 2002.
Szulc, Tad. *Fidel: A Critical Portrait*. New York: William Morrow, 1986.
Taibo, Paco Ignacio. *Tony Guiteras: Un hombre Guapo*. La Habana: Ciencias Sociales, 2009.
Thomas, Hugh. *Cuba: The Pursuit of Freedom*. New York: Harper & Row, 1971.
UN Handbook of National Accounts Statistics. New York: United Nations, 1962.
Vargas Llosa, Alvaro. "Populism in Latin America." Address to Hudson Institute Center for Latin American Studies. November 16, 2005.
Vázquez García, Humberto. *El Gobierno de la Kubanidad*. Santiago de Cuba: Editorial Oriente, 2005.
Venturi, Franco. *Roots of Revolution: A History of the Populist and Socialist Movements in Nineteenth-Century Russia*. New York: Universal Library, 1966.
Weiss Fagen, Patricia. "Antonio Maceo: Heroes, History and Historiography." *Latin American Research Review* 11, no. 3 (1976): 69–93.
Whitney, Robert. *State and Revolution in Cuba: Mass Mobilization and Political Change, 1920–1940*. Chapel Hill: University of North Carolina Press, 2001.
Wright, Steven J. *Cuba, Sugar and the United States*. Ann Arbor, MI: University Microfilms International, 1983.

Index

Acosta Casares, Salvador, 53
Agramonte, Ignacio, 59, 60, 63, 129, 237, 242, 266n13, 296n6
Agramonte, Eduardo, 266n13
Agramonte, Luisa, 59
Agramonte, Roberto, 5, 27, 59, 73, 108, 112, 128, 148, 149, 154, 161, 163, 177, 191, 192, 197, 199, 200, 204, 232, 234, 238, 239, 246, 248, 249, 267n19, 278n46, 284n36, 296n19, 297n35, 298n42, 298n43, 298n54; dismissed as foreign minister, 252; exile in Puerto Rico, 253; foreign minister for Fidel Castro, 251
Agüero, Eric, 104, 123
Aguiar, Juan de, 251
Aguirre, Francisco, 199
Ainciart, Antonio, 201
Aldrich, Winthrop, 103, 274n67
Alfonso, Manuel, 219
Alemán, José Braulio, 156
Alemán, José Manuel, 3, 4, 11, 12, 14, 18, 24, 26, 28, 30, 41, 42, 43–44, 49, 58, 67, 68, 74, 80, 85, 86, 107, 119, 120–122, 125, 133, 141, 143, 144, 152, 160, 162, 164, 167, 182, 187, 188, 193, 210, 211, 212, 213, 217, 221, 222, 223, 232, 257n37, 263n25, 263n33, 264n52, 267n16, 277n2, 277n28, 278n52, 281n119, 294n88; death, 156; estimates of his fortune, 157; leaves 5 million pesos in his will for construction of tuberculosis hospital, 291n1; rise within the education ministry, 156; robbery of national treasury, 82–83
Algaze, Israel, 216
Alliegro, Anselmo, 12, 111, 157, 188, 193
Alonso, Alicia, 294n84
Alonso Pujol, Guillermo, 15, 42, 43–44, 52, 58, 80, 81, 106–107, 115, 119, 148, 151, 152, 156, 158, 160, 171, 182, 192, 193, 212, 222, 223, 230, 233, 246, 262n10, 263n33, 271n43, 283n4, 298n44; vice presidential candidacy, 67
Alsina, Paulina, 12, 28, 46
Álvarez, Alberto Inocente, 3, 11, 26, 68, 159, 162, 212, 259n6, 270n4
Álvarez de la Vega, Aurelio, 27, 35, 62, 266n101; death, 93, 94
Álvarez del Real, Evelio, 52
Álvarez Maruri, Aurelio, 166
Álvarez Ríos, Baldomero, 187
Alzugaray, Mario, 288n142
Amador, Juan, 110, 133
Anaya Murillo, Leonardo, 156
Andreu, José, 81, 137, 179
Antuña, Vicentina, 161, 278n46, 284n36
Ara, Guillermo, 30, 167, 276n115
Arana, Javier, 130
Arango Fumagalli, 216
Arazoza, Carlos de, 49, 144, 212
Arenas, Reinaldo, 1

308   *Index*

Arévalo, Juan, 229
Arteaga, Cardinal Manuel, 24
Ávila, Raúl, 28

Bandera, Carmelina, 100
Banet, Vicente, 154
Baquero, Gastón, 68, 70, 116, 295n114
Barreras, Antonio, 177
Batista, Fulgencio, 5, 37, 52, 63, 74, 75, 93–94, 95, 97, 106, 110, 111–113, 117, 128, 137, 139, 144, 156, 158, 160, 172, 177, 181, 184, 188, 189, 193, 203, 212, 214, 215, 219, 229, 232, 246, 247, 263n31, 266n1, 266n2, 267n16, 269n78, 272n57, 272n67, 275n103, 276n110, 276n117, 277n1, 279n58, 281n118, 281n125, 294n83, 296n19, 297n29, 298n42, 298n45, 298n54, 298n56; 1940 presidency, 12; 1940 election victory, 259n22, 259n25; 1952 coup, 239, 240, 241, 242; 1954 elections, 247; 1958 elections, 250; approves amnesty law of 1955, 298n51; corruption, 66; creation of PAU, 78; exile, 250; preference for ruling by decree, 261n67; recruited for Liberal senate seat, 57–58; return to Cuba in 1948, 89–90
Batista, Mirta, 125, 126
Batista, Panchín, 147, 149, 167
Bauer, John, 98
Bayer, Antonio, 197, 199
Becerra, Humberto, 144, 174
Belt, Guillermo, 158, 162, 168, 225, 284n42, 284n45, 286n91
Benítez, Manuel, 221, 276n117, 294n83
Bisbé, Manuel, 11, 23, 44, 49, 54, 75, 88, 90, 104, 107, 108, 114, 128, 136, 146, 147, 148, 149, 154, 158, 160, 161, 169, 170, 171, 180, 200, 259n20, 266n101, 267n18, 267n19, 278n46, 282n136, 283n8, 286n94, 298n54; U.N. ambassador for Fidel Castro, 251
Blanco Calás, Francisco, 104
Bosch, Orlando, 104
Bosch, Pepin, 152, 154
Bringuier, José Enrique, 35, 51, 89
Buján, José, 133, 279n64
Buttari, Edgardo, 82, 167

Caballero Rojo, Jorge, 234
Cabezas, José, 107, 110
Cabrera, Ruperto, 28, 131, 240
Caíñas Milanés, Armando, 109, 136
Caìñas Milanés, Luis, 67
Cairol, Francisco, 123, 296n150
Campa, Miguel Ángel, 241, 297n28
Cantero, Pedro, 102, 106
Capestany, Manuel, 102
Caramés Monteagudo, José Manuel, 96, 102, 113, 131, 161; fistfight with José Pardo Llada, 134–135; resignation as Havana police chief, 136
Carbó, Sergio, 41, 44, 80, 111
Carbonell, Néstor, 123
Carone, Francisco, 107, 109, 298n54
Carrera Jústiz, Pablo, 62, 241
Carrillo, Justo, 259n19, 290n37
Casals, Rafael, 201
Casanova, José Manuel, 26, 104, 120, 144, 158, 277n8
Casas, César, 11, 13, 14, 15, 18, 25, 58, 67, 68, 212, 258n56
Casero, Luis, 171
Casillas Dupuy, Joaquín, 39, 40, 262n18
Castellanos, Nicolás, 147–149, 152, 160, 162, 167, 169, 171, 183, 192, 194, 208, 212, 223, 233, 241, 258n61, 282n127, 282n128, 282n131, 283n4, 283n8, 286n94, 288n157
Castro, Fidel, 1, 5, 18, 46, 60, 61, 101, 248, 262n18, 278n52, 282n136, 292n14; declaration of Cuba as socialist state, 253; feud with Masferrer, 245; freed from prison by 1955 amnesty law, 254; influential father, 245; Moncada attack, 243, 244, 246; National Literacy Campaign, 252; public criticism of President Urrutia, 253; raises statue to Chibás, 252; in Sierra Maestra, 249; speech at tomb of Eduardo Chibás, 251, 252; trial, 244, 245
Castro, Manolo, 46, 96, 114, 264n52, 278n52
Castro, Orlando, 117, 147, 148, 202, 232, 233, 259n20
Céspedes, Carlos Manuel de, 82, 266n13, 296n6

Céspedes, Carlos Miguel de, 65, 71, 93–94, 158
Chaves Milanés, Francisco, 142
Chelala Aguilera, José, 110, 180, 184, 195, 235
Chibás, Eduardo Justo, 284n42
Chibás, Eduardo René ("Eddy"): 1948 election "miracle," 73–75; accusations of fraud during 1948 elections, 76; accuses Carlos Prío of purchasing Manhattan skyscrapers, 187, 188, 189; accuses Carlos Prío of robbing Causa 82 documents, 175; accuses Supreme Tribunal judges of corruption, 106; belief that Grau was planning a coup in 1948, 42; campaign for senate in 1950, 162–166; concern for campesinos, 268n63; criticism of Anti-Gangster Law, 84; criticism of Auténticos over Orfila massacre, 30; criticism of Batista's return, 89, 90; criticism of Carlos Prío's "first semester," 103; criticism of Cuban Electric Company, 98–100; cultivation of the poor, 19, 20; defends legal strategy from prison, 116; denounces $25 million public loan, 187; denounces the "gag decree" as unconstitutional, 200; difficulties in prison in 1948, 275n96; duel with Carlos Font in 1937, 259n19; duel with Joaquín López Montes in 1945, 275n80; duel with José Manuel Casanova, 120; duel with Santiago Rey, 256n23; duels with Carlos and Paco Prío, 26; early career, 2–3; explains his break with Grau, 24–25; falling out with Pelayo Cuervo Navarro, 34; final political instructions, 235; grupo ortodoxo, 11, 12; idea for shame vs. money slogan, 59–60; influence in contemporary Cuba, 5; investigates rice cultivation to help poor peasants, 289n12; is thrown by Caporal, 195; the "last loud knock," 232; launches Ortodoxo party, 17, 18; lead in opinion polls of 1949, 97; leads June 25, 1950 presidential poll, 172; leads May 1951 presidential poll, 219; leads opinion polls for senate in 1950, 168; leads presidential poll of December 1950, 184; opportunities for corruption, 260n39; opposes 1944 plan for Havana aqueduct 1n62; opposition to government loan, 138–146; ortodoxo platform for 1948, 68–71; polemic with Aureliano Sánchez Arango, 223–231, 295n114, 295n128, 295n132, 295n136; polemic with Eduardo Suárez Rivas, 222–223, 294n88, 294n90; polemic with Masferrer, 197–204; polemic with René Fiallo, 120–123; polemic with Tony Varona, 123–126; proclaimed Auténtico presidential nominee by Oriente assembly, 257n30; prowess as a campaigner, 285n59; ratings of radio show, 20; "romantic" election campaign of 1948, 55–56; sentenced to prison for defamation, 107; submits brief against embezzlement of Sugar Workers' Retirement Fund, 173; third front, 47, 48; vacation in New York after successful surgery, 182–183; warns of possible military coup, 90; wins 1950 senate election, 170
Chibás, Raúl, 177, 242, 267n19, 285n61, 297n35, 298n54; exile in United States, 253; Ortodoxo president, 248, 249; Western Railways director, 251
Clark, Sergio, 177
Clemenceau, Georges, 80
Cofiño, Ángel, 84, 262n11
Coll, Jesús, 141, 175
Collier, Bert, 157
Conte Agüero, Luis, 17, 231–232, 232, 234, 242, 245, 249, 259n20
Corona, Ramón, 81, 271n43
Cossío del Pino, Alejo, 30, 38, 52, 146, 147, 178
Coyula, Miguel, 37, 80
Crespo, Manuel, 65
Cruz, Agustín, 22, 23, 33, 54, 55, 63, 184, 266n101
Cruz, Alberto ("Albertico"), 211, 280n84
Cuadras, Gloria, 61, 115
Cuervo Navarro, Pelayo, 11, 22, 23, 27, 30, 33–34, 44, 45, 46, 54, 62, 86, 102, 108, 145, 160, 184, 191, 192, 202, 214, 219, 225, 232, 242, 247, 251, 259n24,

259n25, 260n44, 264n39, 288n146, 298n54; Causa 82 (Lawsuit 82), 94, 95, 105, 141, 173–175, 176, 212, 216, 217; criticism of Chibás for polemic with Sánchez Arango, 228; death, 249; Ortodoxo president, 249
Cuervo Rubio, Gustavo, 71, 93, 262n10
Curti, Segundo, 16, 95, 108, 109, 121, 131

Da'Lama, Armando, 167
De la Cruz, Carlos Manuel, 93–94, 141, 175, 176, 270n4, 273n3
De la Fé, Ernesto, 102
De la Osa, Enrique, 61, 74, 75, 132, 136, 156, 178, 195, 197, 229, 261n67, 263n25, 267n22, 295n132
De la Osa, Tony, 195, 267n19
De la Paz Fonseca, María, 238
De la Suarée, Octavio, 227
Del Busto, Rafael, 113, 145
Del Porto, Heriberto, 158
Dellundé, Ventura, 98–100, 106, 149, 242, 267n19, 282n140
Díaz Balart, Mirta, 292n14
Díaz Biart, Sigfredo, 197
Díaz Duque, Luis, 198, 199
Díaz Ortega, Eduardo, 63
Díaz, Lomberto, 86, 99, 109, 116, 163, 197, 200, 202, 203, 204, 285n52, 285n53, 285n57
Dorta Duque, Manuel, 202, 219, 283n18

Escalante, Aníbal, 108, 146, 162, 168
Escribiano, Joaquín, 55
Estévez, Carlos, 216
Estrada Palma, Tomás, 37, 139
Estenger, Rafael, 167, 188, 213, 219, 295n111

Febles, Manuel, 152
Fernández, Conchita, 19, 110, 116, 154, 177, 182, 233, 235, 260n39, 267n26, 284n43, 295n128; hired by Fidel Castro, 252
Fernández, Eufemio, 84, 130, 278n50, 278n52
Fernández Casas, Federico, 22, 32, 64, 102, 122, 184, 245, 247, 248, 249, 262n10, 268n45

Fernández Cristóbal, Francisco, 133
Fernández Jorva, Armando, 135
Fernández Sánchez, Leonardo, 21, 23, 33, 51, 158, 207, 237, 259n20, 267n18, 288n142
Fernández Supervielle, Alfredo, 60
Fernández Supervielle, Manuel, 7–9, 16, 17, 138, 153, 171, 230, 255n3, 256n5, 256n10, 256n17, 258n61, 259n25
Ferrer Gutiérrez, Virgilio, 187
Fiallo, René, 116, 159; polemic with Chibás, 120–123
Figueras, Ernesto, 176
Figueroa, Isidro, 127, 148, 246
Figueroa, Polo, 53
Freyre de Andrade, María Teresa, 51, 54
Fuentes, Justo, 46, 101–102, 104
Fuentes, Tino, 163, 171

Galano, Adriano, 51
Galle, Charles de, 80
Gallegos, Rómulo, 90
Gans, Oscar, 175, 176, 201, 203; devises "gag decree," 178, 179
García Agüero, Salvador, 20, 88, 182
García Bárcena, Rafael, 33, 51, 239, 248, 278n46, 297n31; Movimiento Nacional Revolucionario, 243
García Ibáñez, Roberto, 107, 108, 128, 148, 149
García Inclán, Guido, 107, 110, 178, 214
García Menocal, Mario, 76, 259n25, 277n1, 280n90
García Menocal, Raúl, 16, 42, 49, 54, 74, 159, 247, 256n5, 258n62
García Ramos, Salvador, 57, 65
García Montes, Jorge, 53
Godoy, Gastón, 215
Gómez, Abelardo, 90
Gómez, Máximo, 93, 183, 237
Gómez, Miguel Mariano, 111, 159
Gómez, José Miguel, 237, 257n36, 277n1, 277n2, 280n89
Gómez García, Raúl, 244
Gonsé, Raoul Alfonso, 83, 228
González, Eugenio, 177
González, Rubén Darío, 96
González Cartas, Jesús ("El Extraño), 127, 130, 199, 278n36

González Cháves, Camilo, 130
González del Valle, Modesto, 135
González Martínez, Juan, 267n19
Govantes, Evelio, 57
Goyburu, José Bernardo, 147
Grau San Martín, Ramón, 3, 4, 7, 10, 15, 16, 17, 24–25, 28, 37, 39, 41, 41–42, 67, 77, 80–81, 84, 86, 87, 90, 93, 103, 117, 119–120, 121, 125, 126, 129, 137, 138, 139, 141, 142, 143–144, 148, 152, 156, 158, 160, 168, 171, 173, 174, 175, 203, 204, 232, 256n5, 256n17, 256n23, 259n25, 262n10, 263n21, 265n88, 269n78, 271n21, 272n57, 272n67, 277n2, 277n28, 278n52, 280n84, 281n115, 281n125, 284n25, 292n31, 298n45; 1933 provisional presidency, 2; 1954 elections, 247; 1958 elections, 250; criticism for Orfila massacre, 29; handpicks Carlos Prío as 1948 Auténtico presidential nominee, 49; indictment for corruption, 210–217; interpellation of Alemán and Casas, 14, 15; opposition to 1944 plan for Havana aqueduct, 258n62; preference for ruling by decree, 261n68; regrets about Carlos Prío, 95; tampers with Supreme Electoral Tribunal judges, 52; thwarts Supervielle's plans for aqueduct, 8
Grau Alsina, Francisco ("Pancho"), 81, 82, 144, 167, 217
Guerra, Ramiro, 110
Guas Inclán, Rafael, 65, 89, 192, 263n29, 268n44
Guevara, Ernesto ("Che"), 252
Guiteras, Antonio, 107, 289n11
Gutiérrez, José Manuel, 37, 54, 55, 62, 128, 129, 184, 192, 246, 266n101
Gutiérrez, Viriato, 263n29
Gutiérrez Santana, Julio, 174
Gutiérrez Serrano, Raúl, 64, 140, 146, 149, 160, 168, 169, 170, 184, 218, 219, 231, 286n94

Hart Dávalos, Armando, 243, 253
Henríquez, Enrique, 88, 130, 278n50, 285n52
Hernández, Belisario, 297n29
Hernández, Eduardo ("Guayo"), 28

Hernández, Pepillo, 128
Hernández Nardo, Enrique, 15, 46
Hernández Garriga, Salvador, 198, 199
Herrera Arango, Alejandro, 294n93
Herrero, Gustavo, 219
Hevia, Arturo, 173
Hevia, Carlos, 5, 46, 80, 81, 152, 159, 163, 219, 225, 296n19
Hill, Edwin C., 2, 255n5
Hitler, Adolf, 129
Hornedo, Alfredo, 52, 144
Huguet Domínguez, Humberto, 197

Ichaso, Francisco, 75, 94, 117, 138, 160, 167, 170, 171, 189, 224, 227, 269n68, 284n25
Iglesias, Aracelio, 116
Iglesias Betancourt, Pedro, 20, 154, 155, 158, 164, 235, 283n18

Jinjaume, José de Jesús, 136
Justiniani, Federico, 173–175, 175, 177, 210, 211, 212, 214–215, 216, 217, 221

Khouray, Ofelia, 78, 261n78
Khrushchev, Nikita, 253
Kuchián, Mario, 138, 242

Lamar, Mario, 215
Lancís, Félix, 208, 212, 219, 234, 292n31
Lara García, Wilfredo, 133
Laredo Brú, Francisco, 52, 241
Lazo, Raimundo, 221, 288n142
Lechuga, Carlos, 124, 167, 169, 224, 225
León, Rubén de, 82, 136, 144, 152, 202, 203, 276n115
León Lemus, Orlando ("El Colorado"), 101, 102, 104, 105, 112, 113, 136, 275n80, 276n119, 279n62, 279n64; death, 247
Lesnik, Max, 144
Leyva, Gilberto, 231, 296n150
Llaca Argudín, Francisco, 52
Llerena, Mario, 142
Lobo, Jacobo, 60
López Deustua, Eduardo, 280n84
López Dorticós, 54, 265n100
López Montes, Joaquín, 166, 180, 275n80
Lorenzo, Raúl, 111, 276n110

312 *Index*

Loynaz del Castillo, Enrique, 144, 161, 233
Luciano, Lucky, 26

Maceo, Antonio, 122, 143, 242, 296n6
Maceo, Eusebio, 122
Machado, Nick, 204
Machado y Morales, Gerardo, 2, 37, 48, 65, 93, 98, 102, 103, 110, 135, 138, 154, 156, 159, 162, 167, 171, 209, 211, 232, 247, 249, 261n60, 265n100, 272n57, 274n66, 275n103, 277n1, 291n82
Maderne, Feliciano, 135
Mañach, Jorge, 21–22, 37, 120, 162, 182, 191, 192, 221, 243, 248, 278n46
Mañalich, Ovidio, 215
Marcos, Miguel de, 188, 224, 295n111
Mariné, Jaime, 95, 193, 267n16
Marinello, Juan, 77, 90, 144, 262n18, 269n68, 281n125
Maristany, Carlos, 113
Márquez, Juan Manuel, 251, 274n48
Márquez Sterling, Carlos, 129, 154, 162, 176, 179, 191–192, 202, 204, 243, 248, 249, 278n46, 282n136, 287n128, 297n29; presidential candidacy, 250
Martí, José, 65, 143, 152, 183, 184, 193, 237, 239, 244, 296n6
Martín, Félix, 115, 282n140
Martín Elena, Eduardo, 297n20
Martínez, Agustín, 116
Martínez Fraga, Antonio, 47, 49, 53, 88, 102, 108
Martínez Sáenz, Joaquín, 23, 34, 46, 54, 55, 62, 151, 241, 264n39
Masferrer, Kiki, 163
Masferrer, Rolando, 96, 101, 102, 108, 113, 135, 163, 241, 278n50, 278n52; invokes "gag decree," 199; polemic with Chibás, 197–204
Masó, Bartolomé, 296n6
Massó, Gustavo, 96
Maza, Emilio, 142
Medrano, Humberto, 134, 179
Megías, Sergio, 181, 199, 200, 202, 214
Mejía Maderne, Gustavo, 135
Mella, Julio Antonio, 18

Mella, Natasha, 18, 62, 117, 258n69, 267n26
Menció, Carlos, 217
Mendieta, Carlos, 259n25, 273n3
Mendoza, Ignacio, 31, 60, 271n28
Menéndez, Jesús, 8, 39–40, 61, 87, 170, 256n10, 262n18
Merino, Eloy, 166, 285n69
Mestre, Abel, 199, 233
Mestre, Goar, 113, 178, 179, 199, 233
Mir, Hugo, 64
Mirassou, Pedro, 104
Miró Cardona, José, 217
Miyar, Ramón ("Mongo"), 23, 259n19
Morell Romero, José, 8, 180
Morín Dopico, Antonio, 28, 29
Mosquera, Gilberto, 216–218
Mujal, Eusebio, 199, 214, 234, 241, 262n11, 287n135
Muñoz, Victor, 168, 286n79
Mussolini, Benito, 129

Nazario Sargent, Aurelio, 171, 202
Nodal, Ramón, 275n73
Núñez, Froilán, 216
Núñez, Pastorita, 19, 24, 51, 253
Núñez Blanco, Emilio, 209, 215, 222, 228, 292n14
Núñez Portuondo, Emilio ("Emilito"), 52, 65, 68, 233, 268n44
Núñez Portuondo, Ricardo, 39, 42, 46, 48, 49, 52, 57, 64, 65, 66, 71, 77, 209, 222, 270n4; defeat in 1948 presidential election, 74

Ochoa, Emilio ("Millo'), 18, 22, 23, 33, 37, 38, 46, 47, 48, 50, 54, 55, 60, 78, 128, 129, 147, 149, 158, 171, 184, 202, 207, 231, 232, 235, 238, 245, 248, 248–250, 257n30, 257n39, 260n44, 266n101, 267n18, 271n28, 278n39, 298n43; Montreal Pact, 246
Ochoa, Eduardo ("Guarro"), 23, 78, 128
Ordoqui, Joaquín, 146, 262n18
Orizondo, Manuel, 146, 281n121
Ortega, Antonio, 69
Ortega, Luis, 100
Ortiz, Arsenio, 65
Ortiz, Fernando, 21, 90, 161, 294n93

Ortiz Fáez, Gustavo, 46, 114
Orizondo, Manuel, 146
Orúe, Francisco, 170
Osegueda, Raúl, 229
Otero Ben, José, 201, 203, 204
Ovares, Enrique, 279n64

Padilla, Guillermo, 284n20
País, Frank, 243
Paniagua Recalt, Tulio, 182
Pardo Llada, José, 4, 106, 107, 110, 111, 113, 117, 147, 158, 161, 162, 171, 174, 178, 179, 190, 202, 221, 227, 230, 232, 237, 245, 246, 247, 248, 249, 250, 284n39, 284n40, 296n6; fistfight with José Manuel Caramés, 134–135
Pazos, Felipe, 249
Pedraza, José Eleuterio, 110, 162, 279n58
Pelleyá, José Luis, 232
Peña, Lázaro, 67, 136
Peraza, Regla, 51, 54
Pérez, Dominador, 54, 266n101
Pérez, Gerardo, 163, 167
Pérez, Virgilio, 95, 139, 159, 162, 162–166, 167–170, 171, 172, 178, 212, 275n73
Pérez Dámera, Genovevo, 30, 31, 39, 40–41, 42, 58, 62, 73, 113, 115, 119, 183, 261n56, 262n18, 272n67, 278n52, 279n56, 279n58; contempt for civilian authority, 87–88, 90; dismissal as chief-of-staff, 130–132
Pérez Espinós, Luis, 16, 234, 296n150
Pérez Galán, Manuel, 177
Perón, Juan, 83, 84, 90, 98, 204, 229
Phillips, Ruby Hart, 250
Pichardo, Gabriel, 106
Piñango, Nestor, 96, 112, 187, 191, 276n119, 289n23
Pinelli, Germán, 28
Portell Vilá, Herminio, 161, 180, 191, 239, 243, 248, 278n46, 284n36, 289n11
Primelles, Raúl, 282n140
Prío Socarrás, Antonio, 86, 95, 100, 103, 112, 126, 133, 138, 139, 146, 147, 149, 152–154, 160, 162, 163, 167, 169, 171, 175, 176, 179, 191, 208, 212, 217, 219, 229, 283n4, 283n8, 283n10, 283n15, 285n53, 286n94, 287n138

Prío Socarrás, Carlos, 4, 15, 26, 41, 42, 43, 46, 50, 52, 58, 64, 66, 76, 80, 83, 85, 86, 88, 93, 94–97, 100, 103–104, 107, 108, 109, 110, 111–112, 113, 114, 115–116, 116, 117, 119–120, 121, 122, 126, 133–134, 135, 136, 137, 138, 139, 140, 140–142, 143, 145, 146, 151, 152, 154, 157, 159, 160, 162, 163, 165, 167, 171, 173, 174, 175, 176, 178, 179, 181, 182, 184, 187–188, 189, 190, 191, 193, 199, 203, 204, 210, 211, 212, 213, 215, 216, 217, 218, 219, 221, 225, 227, 229, 232, 234, 240, 241, 246, 247, 248, 258n61, 262n11, 265n88, 265n100, 266n9, 267n16, 270n4, 272n57, 272n71, 274n66, 274n67, 277n2, 279n58, 280n93, 281n115, 281n119, 282n128, 283n4, 285n50, 285n52, 288n153, 292n31, 293n67, 293n76, 298n51; anti-communism, 268n58; Anti-Gangster Law, 84; backing of Directorio Revolucionario, 249; bans guayaberas from the presidential palace, 286n90; chosen as Auténtico presidential nominee for 1948, 49; creates GRAS to fight gangsters, 113; deficiencies as presidential candidate, 67–68; dismissal of Genovevo Pérez Dámera as chief-of-staff, 130–132; duel with Chibás, 26; finalizes pact with Liberals in 1951, 208; first cabinet, 80–82; manipulates Auténtico municipal assembly to nominate his brother Antonio as mayor of Havana, 282n126; National Bank, 85; Organic Budgetary Law, 85; shuts down radio shows of Chibás and Salvador García Agüero, 88; tampers with Cuban judges, 142, 177; unleashes GRAS on Cuban gangsters, 136; wins 1948 presidential election, 73–74
Prío Socarrás, Francisco ("Paco"), 85, 95, 102, 103, 126, 162, 190, 191, 208, 217, 267n16, 285n50; duel with Chibás, 26
Prío Socárras, Mireya, 163, 191
Prohías, Antonio, 192
Pubillones, Ángel, 188
Puente, Orlando, 190

Quesada, Manuel, 39
Quevedo, Miguel Ángel, 37, 107, 111, 113, 143, 162, 169, 195, 233, 252, 294n93
Quilez, Alfredo, 231

Ramírez Corría, Carlos, 121
Ramírez, Rigoberto, 165
Regalado, Rogelio, 99
Regueiro, Juan, 96
Remos, Juan, 189
Revuelta, Naty, 244, 297n35
Rey, Santiago, 86, 99, 102, 204, 223, 247, 256n23
Riaño, Ricardo, 124
Rivero, José Ignacio ("Pepín"), 262n12
Rivero Agüero, Andrés, 241, 297n27, 298n56; presidential candidacy, 250
Roa, Raúl, 121, 123, 135
Roca, Blas, 38, 262n18
Rodón, Lincoln, 119, 146, 274n72, 280n84
Rodríguez, Luis Orlando, 10, 23, 33, 147, 149, 179, 180, 190, 191, 192, 202, 227, 233, 242, 259n20, 282n136; ambassador to Venezuela for Fidel Castro, 253; dismissed as interior minister, 252; elected to chamber of representatives in 1950, 171; interior minister for Fidel Castro, 251
Rodríguez, Primitivo, 81, 108, 152, 271n44
Rodríguez Díaz, Antonio, 179, 233, 235
Roosevelt, Franklin Delano, 264n44
Rosales, Paquito, 39
Roselló, Arturo Alfonso, 68, 70
Roseñada, José, 194
Rousseau, Enrique, 74
Rubiera, Vicente, 84
Rubio, Humberto, 120
Ruisánchez, Ramón, 125
Ruiz, Fabio 1n38

Salabarría, Mario, 28–29, 31, 101, 257n38
Saladrigas, Carlos, 263n31
Salas Amaro, Alberto, 250
Salazar, Eduardo, 98
Salazar Callicó, Efigenia, 133, 279n62
Salazar Callicó, Luis Felipe ("Wichy"), 105, 133, 135, 279n62
Sánchez Alfonso, Eduardo, 210

Sánchez Arango, Aureliano, 81, 85, 95, 136, 152, 159, 191, 219, 221, 242, 243, 289n11, 294n83, 294n84, 294n93, 295n114, 295n136, 297n30; interpellation, 86; polemic with Chibás, 223–231, 233
Sanguily, Julio, 60
Sanguily, Manuel, 296n6
San Martín, José ("Pepe"), 41, 42, 43, 158, 181, 219, 233, 263n33
Santiesteban, Teodoro, 275n74
Santos, Daniel, 135
Santovenia, Emeterio, 37, 241, 297n26
Sardiñas, Eligio (Kid Chocolate), 21
Saumell, Alberto ("Beto"), 107, 123, 148, 149, 180, 207, 267n18
Secades, Eladio, 194
Soler, Aurora, 133
Soler, Policarpo, 105, 113, 133, 134, 136, 276n122, 279n62, 279n64
Solórzano, Julián de, 142
Sorí Marín, Humberto, 215
Soto Carmenatti, Eustaquio, 104, 105
Stalin, Joseph, 160
Stokes, William, 75
Suárez Fernández, Miguel ("Miguelito"), 14, 32, 41, 42, 43–44, 46, 49–50, 53, 54, 58, 74, 81, 86, 87, 95, 105, 108–109, 112, 116, 119, 136, 138, 139, 159, 163, 169, 172, 179, 182, 200, 208, 212, 219, 234, 263n21, 265n88, 266n9, 272n68, 277n2, 281n119, 288n146; arranges pact with Democrats, 115; third front, 47–48
Suárez Rivas, Eduardo, 1, 16, 30, 37, 57, 84, 85, 86, 89, 109, 116, 119, 144, 145, 151, 192, 208, 210, 214, 288n153, 294n90, 298n44; letter to José Manuel Alemán urging him to scuttle pact between Liberals and Republicans in 1948, 294n88; polemic with Chibás, 222–223
Suárez Rivas, José, 108, 146, 281n121
Surí Castillo, Emilio, 39, 113, 136

Tarafa, José Miguel, 48
Tejada Setién, Teodoro, 138
Tejera, Diego Vicente, 46, 81, 95, 105, 163, 181, 204, 208, 211, 276n115,

285n52
Tejera, Titi, 163
Torres, Manuel Hernando,, 157
Torres Sánchez, Pastor, 63
Torres Tomás, Francisco, 98, 106
Trinidad, Amado, 83–84, 98, 272n56
Trejo, Rafael, 176, 266n7
Trejo Loredo, Rafael, 57, 141, 176, 266n7, 287n116
Tro, Emilio, 28–29, 30, 31
Trujillo, Rafael, 30, 130, 156, 278n50
Truman, Harry, 139, 264n44, 272n78, 286n90

Uría, Quirino, 200, 202
Urrutia, Manuel, 253

Valdés, Isauro, 81, 173, 283n15
Varona, Enrique José, 143
Varona, Manuel Antonio ("Tony"), 85, 97, 102, 115, 119, 131, 143, 146, 163, 165, 171, 180, 182, 191, 202, 204, 208, 212, 215, 217, 219, 234, 246, 247, 262n11, 263n21, 277n28, 286n95, 294n90, 298n42; polemic with Chibás, 123–126
Varona, Roberto, 163, 171, 286n95
Vasconcelos, Ramón, 52, 111, 159, 180, 204, 214, 216, 219, 233, 247, 275n109
Vázquez Bello, Juan Antonio, 65, 263n29
Vázquez Contreras, Rolando, 97
Vázquez, Gerardo, 171, 180
Vega, Pablo, 128
Vega Ceballos, Victor, 145
Vidal, Carlos, 151, 176
Vidal, Fidel, 177
Vignier, Antonio, 141, 153, 173, 288n146
Vincente, Walfredo, 161

Wallace, Henry, 45, 264n44, 264n49

Yrigoyen, Hipólito, 128

Zayas, Alfredo, 216, 280n89
Zayas, Francisco, 107
Zayas Bazán, Eduardo, 144
Zaydín, Ramón, 85
Zéndegui, Guillermo de, 234, 267n19
Zola, Emile, 124

www.ingramcontent.com/pod-product-compliance
Lightning Source LLC
Chambersburg PA
CBHW071801300426
44116CB00009B/1163